British Abolitionism
and the Question of Moral Progress in History

British Abolitionism

and the Question of Moral Progress in History

Edited by Donald A. Yerxa

The University of South Carolina Press

© 2012 University of South Carolina

Published by the University of South Carolina Press
Columbia, South Carolina 29208

www.sc.edu/uscpress

Manufactured in the United States of America

21 20 19 18 17 16 15 14 13 12   10 9 8 7 6 5 4 3 2 1

Library of Congress Cataloging-in-Publication Data

British abolitionism and the question of moral progress in history / edited
by Donald A. Yerxa.
    p. cm.
  Includes bibliographical references and index.
  ISBN 978-1-61117-015-3 (cloth : alk. paper)
  1. Antislavery movements—Moral and ethical aspects—Great Britain.
 2. Progress—Moral and ethical aspects. 3. Moral conditions. 4. Ethics—History.
 I. Yerxa, Donald A., 1950–
  HT1162.B72 2012
  326'.80941—dc23

                                                            2011048944

This book was printed on a recycled paper with 30 percent postconsumer waste content.

Contents

Acknowledgments

I wish to thank the following officers of the John Templeton Foundation for their support and encouragement: John M. Templeton Jr. (chairman and president); Charles L. Harper Jr. (formerly executive director and senior vice president); Kimon H. Sargeant (vice president, human sciences); and Pamela Thompson (formerly vice president, communications). Indeed it was Chuck Harper and Kimon Sargeant who first approached me about using the two hundredth anniversary of the abolition of the British slave trade as a springboard for discussing whether the study of such episodes in the past might provide insights leading to human betterment in the future. I would also like to thank Bill Nichols for all his work.

It has been a privilege to work with the distinguished scholars who appear in this volume, all of whom are leaders in their respective fields. Not only have they graced this volume with their specialized historical knowledge, but collectively they also reflect how historians approach "big questions" that are situated near or at the limits of history. Special thanks go to David Brion Davis for his superb public lecture at Central Hall Westminster (reprinted in this volume) and to David Hempton and Jeremy Black for their responses. I am grateful to two scholars whose work does not appear in this volume, Eamon Duffy and Thomas L. Haskell, for their comments on some of the chapters. They were extremely helpful in furthering our discussions. I also thank the anonymous reviewers along with Jonathan Haupt, Linda Fogle, and especially Bill Adams of the University of South Carolina Press for their many helpful editorial suggestions.

I should also note that I have shared the last forty years of my life with a remarkable partner and friend, my wife, Lois. I cannot thank her enough for her love, encouragement, support, and enormous patience.

Donald A. Yerxa

Introduction

Historians, Moral Progress, and the Limits of History

DONALD A. YERXA

Asking "big questions" is basic to humanity. While they surely will not go away, questions about such things as the origin of the cosmos or the meaning of life are approached in different ways. Religion, obviously, represents the most common and persistent way humankind has addressed such questions, with seemingly endless variations. The academy offers other avenues of exploration using methodologies that feature critical examination of evidence and that rule out such things as divine wild cards and special revelations. And then, of course, there are the arts.

Currently there is much talk in and at the periphery of the academy about the necessity of tackling big questions in the light, for example, of contemporary scientific understanding or the current state of our educational systems. Few argue against this, though predictably there is no unanimity on what the short list of truly big questions is, let alone the appropriate venue(s) for raising them. One person's big question may well be a fairly pedestrian matter for another. And in the face of some big questions, academics often prefer to remain silent rather than speak about that which their methods give them little or no warrant for tackling. Still, appeals are made for educators to confront students with the big questions and offer them guidance in constructing "meaningful philosophies of life." Others emphasize the importance of exploring foundational questions such as whether the universe has a purpose or whether the laws of nature in fact constitute ultimate reality.

Historians by and large avoid the really big questions, save to chronicle humanity's attempts to grapple with them. Of course, there are exceptions. The recent appearance of the aspiring field of "big history"—an amalgam of cosmology, evolutionary biology, and world history—is perhaps the best example.[1] But historians qua historians prefer to address more manageable topics better suited to their method and practice—a commonsensical approach of interrogating reliable evidence and constructing narratives that make the best inferences to explanation. This is certainly not to suggest that historians are mere antiquarians or that they lack the capacity to comment on significant, broad questions. A recently published anthology demonstrates that prominent U.K. historians can be coaxed to shed their inhibitions and speak to expansive questions, such as why wars, revolutions, or intellectual movements happen; why empires rise and fall; and what the impacts of geography and climate are on history.[2] These are important questions indeed, but ones historians can address with some measure of evidentiary and disciplinary warrant.

What about another level of big questions, such as whether the past reveals shape, purpose, or meaning(s)? Generally speaking, historians are content to leave such speculative matters to others—philosophers, theologians, and pundits. Historians prefer "specified particulars—this time, that place, these events."[3] For good reason they are instinctively skittish about trespassing beyond the limits of history. Though the disciplinary borders may not always be clearly marked, historians usually know when they have left them behind. The present volume, however, explores one big question—is there moral progress in history?—and a corollary—can the study of those occasions in the past when societies seemed to make moral strides yield clues for human betterment in today's world?

The idea of progress dates from antiquity and ranks, according to Robert Nisbet, among the most important ideas produced by Western civilization.[4] Similarly, one of the leading philosophers and intellectual historians of our time, Leszek Kolakowski, considers progress and its relation to morality to be one of humanity's most intriguing and significant questions.[5] Yet while there have been some notable scholarly explorations of the idea of progress in recent decades,[6] contemporary historians tend to avoid the subject. The reason for this is no mystery. Moral progress smacks of Whiggishness and the kind of teleological approach that is anathema to academic historians. We have the distinguished Cambridge University historian Herbert Butterfield in part to thank for this. This is not the place for an extended discussion of Butterfield's critique of Whiggish history, especially since Wilfred McClay skillfully examines Butterfield's thinking later in this volume. Suffice it to say here that although he was not entirely consistent in his critique, Butterfield objected to the study of the past for the sake of the present. He warned of the distortions that result whenever historians engage in "self-congratulatory presentism" that views "the values or institutions of their day as the end-point of historical progress."[7] This sensibility has become a touchstone of scholarly historical inquiry and is evidenced by historians' near-universal affirmation of contingency (history is unpredictable and by no means determined) and agency (history is the result of the actions of autonomous human agents), as well as their deep concern for historical context (temporal and spatial particulars are of utmost importance). The upshot is that historians routinely stigmatize Whiggish and teleologically oriented history.[8]

The fact that contingency, agency, and context drive the engines of historical inquiry today is not something to mourn. However, it may have spawned an overly cautious approach to the past that one historian has dubbed "the prig interpretation of history."[9] Though not a historian, the political philosopher John Gray captures well this skittishness as it relates to moral progress. Echoing the great historian of science George Sarton,[10] Gray proclaims that only in the area of science—and presumably medicine and technology—has there been genuine progress. In ethics or politics, he claims, progress is an illusion. Of course, there have been "gains" over time, but these are not cumulative. Improvement, Gray argues, can never be cumulative: "What has been gained can also be lost, and over time surely will be."[11]

Historians, moreover, routinely invoke a sad litany of the horrific violence of the past century to mock naive notions of moral progress.[12] How can one argue for moral progress after the carnage of two world wars, the Holocaust, and other depressing episodes of ethnic or ideological cleansing? Beyond all this, what (or whose) yardstick will historians use to measure moral progress? Case closed.

Well, maybe not. Some economists, such as the Nobel laureates Robert W. Fogel and Robert E. Lucas Jr. and in this volume Gary Walton, caution historians against constructing flawed narratives of modern history that effectively dismiss empirical evidence of dramatic improvement in the aggregate of human well-being, especially in the last century. These economists point to such long-term economic and demographic trends as population growth, infant mortality, body heights and weights, and per capita income—and say, in effect, not so fast![13]

A few historians have also broken ranks to advance nuanced versions of moral progress. The Pulitzer Prize–winning historian David Hackett Fischer, for example, recently concluded that the growth of liberty and freedom is "the central theme of American history." His examination of the evidence convinces him that over the past four centuries, "every American generation without exception has become more free and has enlarged the meaning of liberty and freedom in one way or another." Making the case for directionality in history, as Fischer does, is not the same thing as arguing for determinism and teleology. But he is clearly embracing a version of moral progress compatible with contingency.[14] In this volume Wilfred McClay provocatively asserts that belief in progress is so "thoroughly inscribed in our cultural makeup," it may well be inescapable. What we must do, he contends, is to stop distancing ourselves from the notion of progress with our "sneer quote" mentality and "find better ways of talking about it and thinking about it, ways of chastening it, restraining it, and protecting it against its excesses." In addition John Gray, while staunchly arguing that moral progress is an illusion and a "mechanism of self-deception," observes that it can have positive consequences. For example, it probably did inspire social advances such as the abolition of slavery.[15]

Like moral progress, the notion of a usable past has a long pedigree, though the phrase itself dates back only to 1918, or perhaps a few years earlier, when the cultural-literary critic Van Wyck Brooks apparently coined it.[16] The phrase gained added currency in the 1960s with the historian Henry Steele Commager's widely read volume of essays and again in the 1980s with Richard E. Neustadt and Ernest R. May's influential case studies on the uses of history for decision makers.[17] Recently Margaret MacMillan and John Tosh have published book-length essays encouraging academic historians to participate more actively in public policy debates.[18] However, unlike moral progress, the concept of a usable past is not something historians can as easily avoid. Historians are constantly asked to justify the utility of the study of history to students in introductory courses and in the turf wars waged in general education curriculum committees. That said, a robust notion of a usable past has tended to suffer death by endless qualification. Once again we brush up against the prevailing anti-Whig sentiments residing in today's academy. Context matters a great deal. Recognizing their inability to do so perfectly, historians—save for a distinct minority enamored with poststructuralist theory—nevertheless do their best to approach the past on its own terms prior to any attempt to render it usable for the present. After all, the godfather of anti-Whiggery, Herbert Butterfield, famously observed that the historian's primary task is to attempt "to see life with the eyes of another century than our own."[19]

Margaret MacMillan rightly chastises the historical profession for "turning inward." The work of academic historians is overly concerned, she argues, with self-referential matters.[20] Academic historians are too quick to abandon to others approaches to the past that they feel tarnish scholarly integrity.[21] So it is no surprise that the question of moral progress and even the notion of a usable past may not be at, or even near, the top of the list of most academic historians' concerns. Academic historians need to be reminded, though, that as significant as their contributions have been to our understanding of the past, they do not own history. These are indeed the sort of big questions about the past that ordinary people pose—legitimately so, I maintain.

Celebration of the two hundredth anniversary of the abolition of the British slave trade has provided the backdrop for the following essays. The historians assembled here were asked, without presuming any outcomes in advance, to consider whether in fact abolitionism provides a clear example of moral progress in history that could offer clues to human betterment in the twenty-first century.

After receiving hundreds of antislavery petitions and debating the issue for years, the British Parliament passed the Abolition of the Slave Trade Act in March 1807. Starting on May 1, 1807, no slaver could legally sail from a British port. Following the Napoleonic Wars, British abolitionist sentiment increased, and substantial public pressure was brought to bear on Parliament to emancipate all British slaves gradually. In August 1833 Parliament passed the Great Emancipation Act, which made provision for the gradual emancipation of slaves throughout the British Empire. Abolitionists on both sides of the Atlantic hailed it as one of the great humanitarian achievements in history. Indeed the Irish historian W. E. H. Lecky famously concluded in 1869 that "the unwearied, unostentatious, and inglorious crusade of England against slavery very may probably be regarded as among the three or four perfectly virtuous acts recorded in the history of nations."[22] As David Brion Davis observes, however, in his brilliant synthesis of slavery in the New World, British abolitionism is "controversial, complex, and even baffling."[23] It has occasioned a significant historiographical debate lasting over sixty years. The key issue has been how to account for abolition-ists' motives and the groundswell of public support for the antislavery cause. Davis suggests that historians find it difficult to accept that something as economically significant as the slave trade could be abolished on essentially religious and humanitar-ian grounds. After all, by 1805 "the colonial plantation economy," he informs us, "accounted for about one-fifth of Britain's total trade."[24] Prominent abolitionists such as William Wilberforce, Thomas Clarkson, and Thomas Fowell Buxton used Chris-tian arguments to combat "inhuman bondage," but surely other, material factors were in play. A great deal of ink has been spilled assessing the relationship of antislavery to capitalism and free market ideology. The upshot of this research is the conclusion that the antislavery impulse went against British economic interests, both real and per-ceived. So how do we explain the successes of a humanitarian movement advocating reforms that could have precipitated economic disaster? Davis argues that while it is important to appreciate the complex interplay of economic, political, and ideologi-cal factors, we must recognize the significance of a moral vision that "could tran-scend narrow self-interest and achieve genuine reform."[25]

The bicentennial commemoration of the abolition of the British slave trade afforded an appropriate occasion to evaluate the significance of this humanitarian movement in the light of the larger question of moral progress. In the first section of this volume David Brion Davis, Jeremy Black, David Hempton, Lamin Sanneh, Eric Arnesen, and C. Behan McCullagh do this. Of special concern is the question of assessing the relative importance of religious and humanitarian impulses in a complex economic and political context. Abolitionism flirted with what Seymour Drescher has called "econocide" or economic suicide,[26] and yet the movement generated con-siderable public pressure on politicians. How do historians account for this? Was there a clear connection in this case study between religious belief and social transfor-mation? What material and cultural structures were needed to translate altruism into successful political movements? Davis, Black, Hempton, and Sanneh speak to these questions, while Arnesen assesses the recent literature on British abolitionism, draw-ing attention to the tensions between popular and academic history writing.[27] McCullagh concludes the first section and provides transition into the other sections of this volume by demonstrating how the abolition of the slave trade might offer some encouragement for the possibility of moral progress.

The second section looks at the question of moral progress in two specific histori-cal contexts. Peter Harrison focuses on the late seventeenth century, a transitional period when the progress in science shifted from moral improvement to understand-ing and mastery of the natural world. Using some of Immanuel Kant's essays as a springboard, Allan Megill reflects on ambiguities in meaning of "moral progress in history."

The third section addresses more directly the fundamental question of this vol-ume: is it even possible to talk about moral progress in history? Gary Walton makes a case for human betterment in recent history, as measured by a variety of demo-graphic and economic indexes. Bruce Kuklick challenges naive notions of moral progress in the past and takes particular aim at religiously informed historical inquiry. Wilfred McClay explores key works of three influential thinkers of the mid–twenti-eth century—Herbert Butterfield, Christopher Dawson, and Reinhold Niebuhr—all of whom were "centrally concerned with discovering the reasons why the idea of progress in history had become so problematic." McClay argues that progress "is a big idea that we cannot do without, and . . . can ill afford to hold in disdain."

The final section examines the notion of moral progress in two different Chris-tian traditions. Jon Roberts provides a descriptive analysis of how American liberal Protestant leaders and theologians understood the concept of moral progress in the latter decades of the nineteenth century and the early decades of the twentieth. George Marsden, who has written about the place of Christian scholarship in the academy,[28] looks at more theologically conservative Christianity. In this normatively oriented essay, he questions "whether more traditional forms of Christian faith have typically contributed to moral progress in the modern world."

Felipe Fernández-Armesto closes the volume with the claim that a better case can be made for moral stagnation in history than moral progress. He believes that cul-tural change and its acceleration is the "biggest" question for historians, one that is likely to be more productive to examine than moral progress, given the present state of our knowledge.

The explorations of moral progress and a usable past in this volume raise many ques-tions. Fernández-Armesto is absolutely right to ask how we account for change in his-tory. What are the engines of change? Is change the result of deep evolutionary forces? Cross-cultural contacts? Responses to environmental and climatological challenges? How do we account for periods of tremendous innovation and transformation, whether measured materially, culturally, or even morally? What is the nature of the interplay between human agency and larger forces and structures?

These questions point to even more expansive—some would say speculative—metahistorical questions. Does the past have overarching meaning, shape, or coher-ence? Is the only meaning, shape, or coherence we derive from the past limited to whatever historians read into it? Do historians discover patterns, or do they invent them? Are big questions such as these automatically ruled off-limits because of methodological constraints? If so, does methodology dictate ontology? More impor-tantly, to what extent do humans have a profound need to make sense out of the past?

Much of the meaning we derive from the past is not, of course, at the lofty level of making sense of it all—"big meaning," if you will.[29] In addition no single motive can account for the entirety of historical inquiry. But at some level William Green is right to contend that "historians continue to encounter the past with a driving will to reduce it to manageable order, to harness its spirit, and to reconstruct relationships—in effect, to wrench order from chaos and afford meaning to the human experience."[30]

It would be an interesting and, I suspect, illuminating exercise to poll academic historians to ascertain what they consider to be the big questions in history and then compare the results with a similar polling of the educated public outside of the profession. A case could be made that historians' big questions are relatively tame compared to those that people such as the evolutionary biologist Jared Diamond and the public intellectual Robert Wright, for example, pose. In *Guns, Germs, and Steel,* Diamond attempts to explain how geographical and environmental factors have affected the fates of human societies and the trajectory of history.[31] In *Nonzero* Wright combines Darwinian perspectives with game theory to offer a case for directionality in history that is suggestive of purpose.[32] Indeed historians may be open to the criticism that they assiduously avoid dealing with the truly big questions, content to provide important contextual support for others not bound so tightly by the guild's constraints. Humans do seem to have an instinctual need to make sense of the world they inhabit, and they use various conceptual and metaphysical lenses to look to the past for insight and meaning. Given this, should historians play a more active role in exploring "the grander scheme of things"? Do they have any responsibility to show how the past might help us to make sense of it all?

None of these questions and reflections is meant to diminish the importance of what historians normally do. Nor am I suggesting in any way that they should abandon the practices of their profession and cavalierly ignore the limits of history. There is great value in historians' characteristic epistemological modesty. Thorough examination of reliable evidence and the creative interplay of the empirical, interpretive, conceptual, and narrative dimensions of the historians' craft have yielded utterly impressive results. Although it reaches no consensus on the matter of moral progress in history—indeed it was not expected to—this volume demonstrates the value of carefully focused historical research as well as the sensibilities of those whose historical consciousness has been shaped by decades of study and reflection.

Historical inquiry, however, unfolds simultaneously and fruitfully at multiple levels—from microhistories that illuminate the particular to grand metanarratives such as "big history." We have an astonishing range of historical analyses because we interrogate the past at so many different levels in so many different ways, as this volume illustrates. Some questions we ask of the past take us beyond the warrant of historical method and practice, though not beyond the boundaries of human curiosity and interest. Butterfield once observed that the really big questions do not go away merely by ruling them off-limits.[33]

In response to the human longing for "big meaning," there is, then, merit in encouraging historians to explore such notions as moral progress in history. But any hypothesizing on such grand themes must be tutored and informed—perhaps even checked—by the judicious approach of historical scholarship. A creative tension may well exist between the impulse to soar and the need to be grounded—a tension that could lead to greater understanding of the past.

NOTES

1. See David Christian, *Maps of Time: An Introduction to Big History* (Berkeley: University of California Press, 2004).

2. Harriet Swain, ed., *Big Questions in History* (London: Vintage Books, 2006).

3. John Demos, "Response to Adam Hochschild," *Historically Speaking* 9, no. 4 (March/April 2008): 7.

4. Robert Nisbet, *History of the Idea of Progress* (New York: Basic Books, 1980), 4. Although Nisbet concludes that the notion of moral progress has been a strand in the long history of progress, Allan Megill later in this volume dates its modern genesis to Immanuel Kant in the late eighteenth century. Like Nisbet, Charles Van Doren, who defines progress as "irreversible meliorative change," traces the idea of progress to antiquity. But he argues that only since the early modern period has it been "a leading (if not the leading) idea in the West." A major bone of contention for modern thinkers is whether moral progress entails a change in human nature or is essentially a function of better behavior. Those arguing the former almost always deny that moral progress has occurred. See Charles Van Doren, *The Idea of Progress* (New York: Frederick A. Praeger, 1967), esp. 3–17 and 418–51.

5. Leszek Kolakowski, *Why Is There Something Rather than Nothing?* (New York: Basic Books, 2007), esp. 172–73.

6. Nisbet, *History of the Idea of Progress;* Christopher Lasch, *The True and Only Heaven: Progress and Its Critics* (New York: W. W. Norton, 1991).

7. Herbert Butterfield, *The Whig Interpretation of History* (1931; repr., New York: W. W. Norton, 1965). Two excellent recent studies explore Butterfield's thinking about the Whig distortion in historiography: C. T. McIntyre, *Herbert Butterfield: Historian as Dissenter* (New Haven, Conn.: Yale University Press, 2004), esp. 56–77, 95–97, and 117–22; and Keith C. Sewell, *Herbert Butterfield and the Interpretation of History* (New York: Palgrave Macmillan, 2005), esp. 30–47. The cited phrases are from Daniel Ritschel, review of C. T. McIntyre's *Herbert Butterfield: Historian as Dissenter* (H-Albion, H-Net Reviews, December 2005: www.h-net.org/reviews/showrev.php?id=11043 [accessed August 24, 2011]).

8. For example, in his highly acclaimed volume on early medieval history, Chris Wickham assures his readers: "Above all, I have tried to avoid teleology." He goes on to offer a succinct, one-sentence anti-Whig manifesto: "Only an attempt to look squarely at each past in terms of its own social reality can get us out of this [teleological] trap." See Chris Wickham, *The Inheritance of Rome: Illuminating the Dark Ages, 400–1000* (New York: Viking, 2009), 11–12.

9. Steven G. Brush, "Scientists as Historians," *Osiris,* 2nd ser., 10 (1995): 215–32.

10. See the essays by Peter Harrison and Wilfred McClay in this volume.

11. John Gray, *Heresies: Against Progress and Other Illusions* (London: Granta, 2004), 2–4. For a challenging discussion of the notion of scientific progress and the case for noncumulative, "problem-solving scientific progressiveness," see Larry Laudan, *Progress and Its Problems: Toward a Theory of Scientific Growth* (Berkeley: University of California Press, 1977), esp. 1–8, 147–50, and 223–25. I suspect that in addition to science, technology, and medicine, about

the only other area of human activity that historians would almost universally recognize as progressive is their own methodology. Historians are unabashedly Whiggish about historical method and practice even while vigorously decrying the "noble dream" of historical objectivity. For discussions of progress in historical inquiry, see Raymond Martin, "Progress in Historical Studies," *History and Theory* 37, no. 1 (February 1998): 14–39; and John Vincent, *An Intelligent Person's Guide to History,* rev. ed. (London: Duckworth Overlook, 2005), 111.

12. For a chilling essay on the carnage of the twentieth century seen in the light of technological, medical, and other advances, see Niall Ferguson, *The War of the World: History in an Age of Hatred* (London: Allen Lane, 2006), esp. xxxiii–xli.

13. For a perspective that acknowledges these indexes of progress but interprets intensified periods of transformation in the light of the "spiritual struggles" they generate, see Robert W. Fogel, *The Fourth Great Awakening and the Future of Egalitarianism* (Chicago: University of Chicago Press, 2000), esp. 236–42. See also Robert E. Lucas Jr., "Progress in History," *Historically Speaking* 7, no. 5 (May/June 2006): 28–29.

14. David Hackett Fischer, *Liberty and Freedom: A Visual History of America's Founding Ideas* (New York: Oxford University Press, 2005), 721–22. See also Donald A. Yerxa, "David Hackett Fischer's *Liberty and Freedom* in Historiographical Perspective," *Historically Speaking* 7 (September/October 2005): 16–17.

15. Gray, *Heresies,* 4–5.

16. Van Wyck Brooks, "On Creating a Usable Past," *Dial* 64 (April 11, 1918): 337–41.

17. Henry Steele Commager, *The Search for a Usable Past: And Other Essays in Historiography* (New York: Knopf, 1967); Richard E. Neustadt and Ernest R. May, *Thinking in Time: The Uses of History for Decision Makers* (New York: Free Press, 1986).

18. Margaret MacMillan, *Dangerous Games: The Uses and Abuses of History* (New York: Modern Library, 2009); John Tosh, *Why History Matters* (New York: Palgrave Macmillan, 2008).

19. Butterfield, *Whig Interpretation,* 16. For a very different view—one shaped by postmodern sensibilities—see David Harlan, *The Degradation of American History* (Chicago: University of Chicago Press, 1997). Harlan argues, "Content is more important than context. Understanding what Lincoln's Second Inaugural Address says to us [now] . . . is more important than understanding what it said to Americans living in the middle of the nineteenth century. Else why should we bother with it? Why should we read Abraham Lincoln if we think he has nothing important to tell us about what *we* should value, how *we* should live?" (p. 187).

20. MacMillan, *Dangerous Games,* 35.

21. See Tosh, *Why History Matters,* viii.

22. Lecky is quoted in David Brion Davis, *Inhuman Bondage: The Rise and Fall of Slavery in the New World* (New York: Oxford University Press, 2006), 234. This paragraph relies heavily on Davis's chapter "Explanations of British Abolitionism," 231–49, as well as on Hugh Thomas, *The Slave Trade: The Story of the Atlantic Slave Trade, 1440–1870* (New York: Simon & Schuster, 1997), 537–57.

23. Davis, *Inhuman Bondage,* 231.

24. Ibid., 245.

25. Ibid., 249.

26. Seymour Drescher, *Econocide: British Slavery in the Era of Abolition* (Pittsburgh: University of Pittsburgh Press, 1977).

27. A much-shortened version of Arnesen's chapter was published in *Historically Speaking* 8, no. 6 (July/August 2007): 22–24. It led to an exchange between Adam Hochschild, author of *Bury the Chains: Prophets and Rebels in the Fight to Free an Empire's Slaves* (Boston: Houghton Mifflin, 2005), and Arnesen (*Historically Speaking* 9, no. 2 [November/December 2007]: 43), which in turn led to a major forum involving nearly twenty academic historians, writers, and editors (*Historically Speaking* 9, no. 4 [March/April 2008]: 2–23; repr. in Donald A. Yerxa, ed., *Recent Themes on Historians and the Public* [Columbia: University of South Carolina Press, 2009], 68–132).

28. George M. Marsden, *The Outrageous Idea of Christian Scholarship* (New York: Oxford University Press, 1997). He has also suggested that historians tend to "ignore, marginalize, or caricature" exclusivist religion despite its significant impact on American history. See Marsden, "Can Jonathan Edwards (and His Heirs) Be Integrated into the American History Narrative?," *Historically Speaking* 5, no. 6 (July/August 2004): 13–15.

29. The phrase is Wilfred McClay's. I am indebted to Bill McClay and Jon Roberts, two good friends and wonderful colleagues, for their comments and suggestions of an earlier version of this introduction. Their thoughts helped to refine this concluding argument, though they are not responsible, of course, for what I have written.

30. William A. Green, *History, Historians, and the Dynamics of Change* (Westport, Conn.: Praeger, 1993).

31. Jared Diamond, *Guns, Germs, and Steel: The Fates of Human Societies* (New York: W. W. Norton, 1997).

32. Robert Wright, *Nonzero: The Logic of Human Destiny* (New York: Pantheon, 2000).

33. Herbert Butterfield, *Man on His Past* [the Wiles Lectures at Queen's University, Belfast, 1954] (Cambridge: Cambridge University Press, 1955), 141.

I

British Abolitionism

Slavery, Emancipation, and Progress

David Brion Davis

For those of us who still think of history as a kind of moral philosophy teaching by example, it is precisely the multiple character of truth—the varied angles of vision that are also the subject of imaginative literature—that one must seek to capture.[1] If such inquiry has any therapeutic value, it arises from the discovery that the most comforting and reassuring conclusions are not the only dimensions of historical experience. Despite the beliefs of many contemporary Americans, there is no hidden force with respect to the future that enables all good things, such as democracy, moral behavior, justice, and economic and technological progress, to go together. That said, while there is little evidence that human nature has changed for the better over the past two millennia, a few historical events, such as Britain's abolition of its extremely profitable slave trade, suggest that human history has also been something more than an endless contest of greed and power.

The idea of progress implies that a particular course of change leads toward that which is beneficial and desirable for humanity as a whole. As early as the 1760s colonial slavery seemed incompatible with this standard in the eyes of many progressive-minded readers of newspapers, pamphlets, novels, and poetry in Paris, Edinburgh, Birmingham, Philadelphia, Boston, London, and even parts of Virginia. It may therefore seem somewhat startling for me to devote much of this essay to an argument that echoes some of the proslavery writings of nineteenth-century southerners—namely that from the time of the ancient Greeks onward, for well over two thousand years, chattel slavery became linked with various forms of economic and social progress; and that the first major acts of slave emancipation led to various kinds of failure, contrary to the emancipators' expectations. Of course, I believe that slavery is the very epitome of social evil, but I do not agree with the theories of historical progress that present it as an anachronism or as a barrier to economic growth and an impediment to free people's incentive and desire for innovation and self-improvement. I hope that the approach I take will enable us to see the abolitionists' achievement as an even *more* improbable and praiseworthy "mighty experiment," as Britain's colonial secretary Edward Stanley had described the emancipation bill in 1833 to the House of Commons.[2]

We need to recognize that the fifteenth-century spread of black slavery from the Mediterranean to such sugar-producing islands as Madeira and São Tomé and finally to the West Indies and Brazil was closely tied to the expansion of European trade, technology, and religion, and hence with Christian Europe's gradual strategic gains over the rival Islamic world. Plantation slavery, far from being an aberration invented by lawless buccaneers and lazy New World adventurers, as nineteenth-century liberals often charged, was a creation of the most progressive peoples and forces in Europe—Italian merchants; Iberian explorers; Jewish inventors, traders, and cartographers; Dutch, German, and British investors and bankers. From the colonization of the Atlantic sugar islands off the coast of West Africa to the westward extension of the American South's so-called cotton kingdom, black slavery was an intrinsic part of the rise of the West.

Of course, I recognize the fact that chattel slavery has long appeared in societies, such as those in sub-Saharan Africa, which never approached Western concepts of progress. But unlike serfdom, which we associate with the nonprogressive early Middle Ages, chattel slavery became an institution of central importance in Athens, the world's first democracy and the seat of all kinds of cultural achievement, as well as in other vibrant Greek urban centers. Slave labor was no less essential in Rome and in much of the Roman Empire. Various kinds of chattel slavery appeared in some of the more advanced early Islamic states and then in the late medieval and Renaissance Mediterranean, extending finally to Portugal and the sugar-producing Atlantic Islands, prior to the discovery of America.

While some ancient writers equated slavery with progress—and the historians Ludwig Edelstein, Robert Nisbet, Eric R. Dodds, and F. J. Teggart have shown that the idea of progress is an ancient, not a modern, invention—I will be mostly concerned with the way the linkage between slavery and progress, and then antislavery and progress, has appeared in more modern times. Still, it is often forgotten that Aristotle's famous defense of slavery is embedded within his discussion of human "progress" from the patriarchal village, where "the ox is the poor man's slave," to the fully developed polis, where advances in the arts, sciences, and law support that perfect exercise of virtue that is the goal of the city-state. Barbarians, according to Aristotle, made no distinction between slaves and women, for the barbarians were, in effect, a "community of slaves" who lacked a natural leader. But while nature had obligingly designed barbarians to be slaves, such natural, animate "tools" were also indispensable for the well-being of the household and the polis.

From the Ur-Nammu tablet, one of the oldest surviving records of human law, to the eighteenth-century B.C.E. Hammurabi Code and fragments of early Egyptian judicial decisions, it is clear that the world's first "advanced" societies, in the eyes of the later Western world, shared a generalized concept of slavery that Greek philosophers and Roman jurists later systematized and refined. Slavery had different meanings in ancient Mesopotamia, fourth-century Greece, and the Roman Empire. Nevertheless, despite the historical changes in polity, religion, technology, and modes of production, one is struck by the antiquity and almost universal acceptance of the *concept* of the slave as a human being who is legally owned, used, sold, or otherwise disposed of as if he or she were a domestic animal. This parallel persisted in the similarity of naming, branding, and even pricing of slaves according to their equivalent in cows, horses, camels, and pigs. Moreover the same premodern societies considered the slave sufficiently responsible to be punished for escape or other crimes and to be rewarded by positions of trust and prestige, manumission, or eventual assimilation to his owner's family and society.

In a sense slaves were the world's first "modern" people. The archetypical slave was a foreigner, an outsider torn from her or his protective family matrix by capture, treacherous sale, greed, debt, the threat of famine, or punishment for a crime. While some slaves were eventually absorbed into the enslaving society, the "modernity" of most slaves lay in their continuing marginality and vulnerability. As a replaceable and interchangeable outsider faced with the unpredictable need of adjusting to a wholly alien culture, the slave was the prototype for the migratory labor and confused identity that we associate with the industrial and postindustrial eras.

In an age attuned to classical models and precedents, nineteenth-century educated southerners found their own way of life mirrored by passages from Aristotle, Plutarch, Polybius, Livy, Tacitus, Cato, and Pliny. They therefore invoked the examples of ancient Greece and Rome to show that slavery could provide the necessary foundation or "mudsill" for the highest achievements of freedom and civilization. According to the southern proslavery theorist William Harper, the great republics of antiquity demonstrated that "slavery is compatible with the freedom, stability, and long duration of civil government, with denseness of population, great power, and the highest civilization." Another proslavery writer, George Frederick Holmes, pointed out that Roman slaveholders "conquered the world, legislated for all succeeding ages, and laid the broad foundations of modern civilization and modern institutions." Harper added that "slavery anticipates the benefits of civilization" by exempting a significant section of society from the necessity of physical labor and thereby freeing them for intellectual and artistic pursuits that benefited society as a whole. No less important, he stressed, slavery retards the evils of civilization by requiring masters to provide for all the slaves' needs, in contrast to the employers of the isolated and desperately poor working class in industrial Britain. An eminent modern scholar, Keith Hopkins, agrees that "democracy in Athens and plebian privileges in Rome were made possible by the combination of imperial conquest and slavery."[3]

Imperial conquest and slavery were also the prerequisites for the Arabs' great advances in science, mathematics, and standard of living, even though the Arab economies were truly dependent on slave labor only in a few mining and agricultural regions. In approximately one hundred years, beginning with the Arab conquests of Iraq, Syria, and Egypt in the 630s and 640s c.e., the Arabs and their Muslim converts conquered an area that reached from the Pyrenees to the Indus River and that included Spain, North Africa, Armenia, Caucasia, Iran, and much of modern Pakistan. These triumphs produced an immense flow of slaves for employment as servants, soldiers, members of harems, eunuch chaperons, and bureaucrats. Whether the slave was degraded to the status of chattel property, as was the case with thousands of sub-Saharan African slaves, or elevated as a top bureaucrat, he could be thought of as an extension of his owner's will. Such a relationship, unmediated by family restrictions or by the normal stages of generational succession, gave masters the illusion of omnipotence, of escaping the bonds of kin. It was not accidental that Muslims extended slavery to concubines, who complemented the legal allotment of wives, or to eunuchs, whose seeds could not pollute the lines of legitimate kinship descent. In many societies even the most privileged slave could be quickly killed or sold as a result of a sudden change in his master's will or desires.

If proslavery southerners had known what we know today about the booming white slave trade from the Black Sea, from the thirteenth century to the late fifteenth century, as well as the "progress" or progression of sugar cultivation from India to Sicily and other Mediterranean islands and then to Madeira and São Tomé, and if they had known about the Italian slave-trading entrepreneurs and German bankers and investors in a slave system in the age of the Italian Renaissance, they could have built an even stronger case. As M. I. Finley, a great historian of the ancient world, wrote in 1976, historically it was "free labor," not slavery, that "was the peculiar institution."[4]

Following the Western capture of Constantinople in the Fourth Crusade (1204), Italian merchants participated in a booming long-distance seaborne trade that transported tens of thousands of "white" Armenian, Bulgarian, Circassian, Mingrelian, and Georgian slaves from regions around the Black Sea to Mediterranean markets extending from Muslim Egypt and Syria to Christian Crete, Cyprus, Sicily, and eastern Spain. They were used for the production of sugar as well as for numerous other services. Between 1414 and 1423 no fewer than ten thousand bondsmen (mostly bondswomen, to meet the demand for household servants) were sold in Florence alone. In the early 1400s this white slave trade from the Black Sea foreshadowed almost every aspect of the African slave trade, which was about to begin—from complex organization to permanent posts or forts for trade and long-distance shipment by sea to multinational markets. With respect to cultural progress, this means that slave trading undergirded the Italian Renaissance of Ficino and the Platonic Academy, to say nothing of Michelangelo, Botticelli, Leonardo da Vinci, and appropriately Machiavelli.[5]

In 1453 the Ottoman Turks captured Constantinople and thus the entrance from the Mediterranean into the Black Sea. The Turks gradually diverted the flow of Black Sea and Balkan captives solely to Islamic markets, thus cutting off the Christian Mediterranean from its major source of slaves. Aside from captured Muslims, the

only alternative to Crimea and the steppes of western Asia, given the understood prohibition against enslaving Western Europeans, was sub-Saharan Africa. For a time
this new demand actually stimulated the Arab caravan slave trade across the Sahara.
Hence a few black slaves taken to the shores of Libya and Tunisia were dispersed to
Sicily, Naples, Majorca, southern France, and Mediterranean Spain; in Sicily a notary
writing in Latin referred to *sclavi negri,* literally "black Slavs," who outnumbered
white slaves by the 1490s. It is significant that the Western European words for
"slave" were all derived from the ethnic name "Slav."[6]

At the same time Genoese capital and technology had strengthened Portuguese sea
power. Portugal's harbors had proven to be ideal for the small ships, mostly owned by
Italian merchants, that carried commodities from the Near East to England and
Western Europe. Some of the same Italian merchant and banking families long
involved in the Black Sea slave trade now sent agents to Seville and Lisbon, where
they became pioneers in developing the African slave trade. For example, Bartolomeo
Marchionni, who represented one such family, moved from Florence to Lisbon in
1470 (when Leonardo da Vinci was eighteen years old). He soon owned sugar plantations in Madeira, a wealthy sugar colony dependent on the labor of black African
slaves, and the king of Portugal granted him a monopoly for slave trading on the
Guinea coast. Marchionni even sent some black slaves back to Florence. There could
hardly be a clearer example of the continuity between the late medieval Black
Sea–Mediterranean slave networks and the emerging Atlantic slave system, both ener-
gized by the expansion and westward movement of sugar cultivation.[7]

Here I can point only to some of the links between the later Atlantic slave system
and various aspects of progress. There is now a broad consensus among historians
that plantation slavery, far from being archaic, not only was highly productive but
also anticipated much of the efficiency, organization, and global interconnectedness
of modern capitalism. Beginning in the mid-1600s the Atlantic slave trade evoked
increasing competition as England, Holland, France, and even Denmark and Sweden
invaded the African turf long dominated by Portugal. Thus we find African slave
trading, slave colonies, and sugar refining lurking behind the Holland of Peter Paul
Rubens, Jan Vermeer, Rembrandt, and the highly learned Hugo Grotius, who struggled to prove that slavery was an integral part of a system of authority and discipline
that gave expression to the world's rational order.[8]

In retrospect it appears that the entire New World enterprise depended on the
enormous and expandable flow of slave labor from Africa. By 1820 over 9 million
slaves had departed from Africa for the New World, as opposed to only 2.6 million
whites, many of them convicts or indentured servants, who had left Europe. Thus by
1820 African slaves constituted about 77 percent of the enormous population that
had sailed toward the Americas. From 1660 to 1820 this emigrating flow included
over five African slaves for every European. From 1820 to 1880 the African slave
trade, most of it now illegal, continued to ship off from Africa nearly 2.3 million

more slaves, mainly to Brazil and Cuba. In other words, there can be no doubt that black slave labor was essential in creating and developing the "original" New World that began by the 1840s to attract so many millions of European immigrants. For our purposes the really crucial point is the fact that from 1660 to 1807 Britain was by far the major carrier of these African slaves, which means that the world's most prosperous and powerful nation—the model at that time of cultural and industrial progress—could not have been more deeply involved with slave trading and wealthy slave colonies.[9]

By the early 1700s most English merchants and political leaders agreed with the eminent economist Malachy Postlethwayt, who wrote, "The Negroe-Trade and the natural Consequences resulting from it, may be justly esteemed an inexhaustible Fund of Wealth and Naval Power to this Nation."[10] For Josiah Child, Charles Davenant, and other influential political economists who thought in terms of global strategy and the development of a self-sufficient, mercantilist, and imperial economy, the African trade had those characteristics of a divinely contrived system, the kind of system that greatly appealed to the eighteenth-century mind, in France as well as in England.[11]

As for the antebellum United States, far from being a marginal misfortune, African American slavery pulsated at the heart of the national economy and thus at the core of American political culture. It was no accident that the United States had southern slaveholder presidents for fifty of the seventy-two years between the inaugurations of Washington and Lincoln, or that most of the northern presidents strongly supported the interests of the slaveholding South. If by the 1850s the North seemed well launched on an alternative road of industrial capitalism, the two sections were closely linked in terms of trade, finance, insurance, family bonds, and even the slave-grown cotton, rice, hemp, tobacco, and sugar that northerners consumed in exchange for all the products they sold in the South. In addition by the 1850s, following the annexation of Texas and California, the high confidence of some slaveholding southerners emerged in dreams of annexing and expanding a tropical empire ranging from Cuba to Nicaragua. Meanwhile in 1820 Secretary of State John Quincy Adams, who had spent much of his youth in Europe, expressed surprise and shock when fellow cabinet member John C. Calhoun confided to him that one of the major benefits of racial slavery was its effect on lower-class whites, who could now take pride in their skin color and feel equal to the wealthiest and most powerful whites. Thus slavery, in Calhoun's eyes, defused class conflict, a judgment that clearly conveyed much truth. Precisely because slavery was the most extreme instance of inequality, it helped to make other relationships seem relatively equal.[12]

The large planters soon ranked among America's richest men. Indeed by 1860 two-thirds of the wealthiest Americans lived in the South—a fact that became difficult to believe after the devastation of the Civil War and the full industrialization of the North.[13] As late as 1863, even after Lincoln's Emancipation Proclamation, the president of a North Carolina railroad could assure his stockholders that although slave prices were very high then, they were probably only one-half the worth they would have at the end of the war![14] This is only one of many examples of the strength and confidence of the slaveholding South, which did have a realistic hope of winning independence, even with European support.

In 1860 the slaves' value came to an estimated $3.5 billion in 1860 dollars. That would be about $68.4 billion in 2003 dollars. But a more revealing figure is the fact that the nation's Gross National Product in 1860 was only about 20 percent above the value of slaves, which means that as a share of today's Gross National Product, the slaves' value would come to an estimated $9.75 trillion.[15]

As investment capital, the value of the nation's slaves in 1860 had far exceeded (by perhaps a billion dollars) the cash value of all the farms in the South, including the border states of Delaware, Maryland, Kentucky, and Missouri. In 1860 the southern slaves were also worth three times the cost of constructing all the nation's railroads or three times the combined capital invested nationally in business and industrial property.

By 1840 the South grew more than 60 percent of the world's cotton and supplied not only Britain and New England but also the rising industries of continental Europe, including Russia. Throughout the antebellum period, cotton accounted for over half the value of all American exports, and thus paid for the major share of the nation's imports and foreign investment. A stimulant to northern industry, cotton also contributed to the growth of New York City as a distributing and exporting center that drew income from commissions, freight charges, interest, insurance, and other services connected with the marketing of America's number one commodity.

The later impoverishment of the South nourished the myth that the slave economy had always been historically "backward," stagnating, and unproductive. We now know that investment in slaves brought a considerable profit and that the southern economy grew rapidly throughout the pre–Civil War decades. It is true, however, that the system depended largely on the international demand for cotton as the world entered the age of industrialization, led by the British textile industry. At times the South's production of cotton exceeded international demand, and cotton prices fell sharply in the economic recessions that followed the panics of 1819 and 1837. But until the Civil War, the world market for cotton textiles grew at such a phenomenal rate that both southern planters and British manufacturers thought only of infinite expansion. While the region made some progress in the 1850s in the construction of industries and railroads, it lagged with respect to immigration, urbanization, and a diversified economy. Nevertheless the North's economic and urban development was quite recent, and the slaveholding states were more prosperous than most of the countries of Western Europe.

Even for objective observers who favored the abolition of slavery, the record of actual emancipations was not encouraging. The first mass emancipation in world history, what is termed the Haitian Revolution, also marked the first time that slaves had in effect freed themselves. In 1790 French Saint Domingue, the western third of the island of Hispaniola, produced more wealth than any colony in the New World, thanks to the cruel oppression of a half-million slaves, most of them fairly recent arrivals from Africa. Then, following a huge uprising of thousands of slaves in 1791, Toussaint Louverture led black armies in the defeat of the governing French forces, in the repulsion of Spanish and English invasions, and finally in checking a large expeditionary army sent by Napoleon. Despite Toussaint's hopes for reestablishing a plantation regime based on free labor, his capture and death were followed by geno- cidal warfare on the part of the French, who were defeated and evicted in 1803 by Jean-Jacques Dessalines. In 1804 Dessalines declared the independence of Haiti, made himself emperor, and ordered the slaughter of most of the remaining whites. As a result of twelve years of destructive war, followed by an American embargo and payment in 1825 of enormous reparations to France, to say nothing of Haiti's inter- nal conflicts and poor leadership, the wealthiest colony in the New World became known as a sinkhole of poverty and oppression. Abolitionists could only fall back on the argument that only well-managed emancipation could prevent such destructive slave rebellions—or do their best to ignore Haiti altogether.

The second major chapter in the history of slave abolition, the gradual emancipa- tion acts in the northern United States, also brought failed expectations. The slow freeing of slaves evoked a dramatic rise in antiblack racism, and the liberated blacks were mostly cut off from formal education, decent jobs, and the elemental rights of citizenship. From the start even Quaker abolitionists were reluctant to give their brethren in England requested information on the status of freed blacks, who were seen to be overrepresented in prisons and institutions for the helpless poor. The sig- nificance of northern slave emancipation was largely concealed by the inpouring of European immigrants, who continued to provide a large supply of cheap labor. It is highly revealing that, in striking contrast to the British, American abolitionists from the 1830s on gave virtually no attention to their predecessors who had fought for emancipation in the legislatures of the North.

The most crucial example for antebellum Americans was of course Britain's deci- sion in the 1830s to free some eight hundred thousand slaves, mainly in the Carib- bean. The historian Steven Heath Mitton has identified an important turning point in August 1843, when the British minister Edward Fox met secretly in Washington with the proslavery secretary of state Abel P. Upshur. Fox conveyed the conservative Peel ministry's startling proposal to pay the transportation costs for American free blacks to migrate to the British West Indies, where they would become free workers under contract. Fox admitted that the British colonies were "suffering severely in their productive industry from a dearth of agricultural laborers." Mitton argues that up to this point Upshur and even Calhoun, who following Upshur's death in February 1844 would succeed him as secretary of state, believed that British emancipation had been an economic success—as supposedly proved in 1840 by the testimony of the respected British Quaker abolitionist Joseph John Gurney.[16]

As one would expect, Upshur rejected Fox's proposal on grounds of states' rights and also because he could not imagine allowing a British-directed recruiting effort moving through the South, especially at a time when British policy "had already given rise to the Underground Railroad to Canada." Far more important, this striking evidence of the failure of British West Indian emancipation greatly alarmed Upshur and Calhoun with respect to Britain's future economic motives for undermining such competing slave societies as Cuba, Brazil, and the United States. Upshur ordered the U.S. minister in Jamaica, Robert Monroe Harrison, to present a comprehensive report on the results of emancipation in that colony. In 1843 Upshur's State Department publicized Harrison's statistics, claiming that the price of freeholds in Jamaica had declined by half, that coffee and sugar production had declined by as much as 50 percent, and that some large plantations were worth less than 10 percent of their preemancipation value. Harrison predicted that Jamaica "will therefore be ultimately abandoned, and become like San Domingo [Haiti]," and he also warned that England would now seek to reduce other competitive slave societies to a similar state.[17]

As the historian Seymour Drescher has recently shown, even British faith in their own quasi-scientific experiment of emancipation began to melt fairly soon after the abolition of so-called apprenticeship, in 1838, enabled thousands of blacks in the larger colonies, such as Jamaica, Trinidad, and British Guiana, to leave the plantations and find farmland of their own. Drescher vividly chronicles this decline as West Indian planters faced invincible competition not only from Cuban and Brazilian slave-grown sugar but also from European sugar beets. According to Benjamin Disraeli, the great Tory leader, the experiment was "the greatest blunder in the history of the English people, [and it] had simultaneously ruined the British colonies, encouraged the African slave trade, and revealed 'the quackery of economic science!'" By 1857 many knowledgeable Britons agreed with the *London Times*: "Confessedly . . . the process was a failure; it destroyed an immense property, ruined thousands of good families, degraded the negroes still lower then they were, and, after all, increased the mass of Slavery in less scrupulous hands [that is, Cuba, Brazil, and the United States]." Even the antislavery *Economist* agreed that "with the example of West Indian emancipation before them, it could not be expected that Southern statesmen [in the United States] would ever risk the liberation of their slaves on such conditions."[18] In 1855, less than eight years before Lincoln's Emancipation Proclamation, one of Britain's most venerable political economists predicted that "we do not venture to hope that we or our sons or our grandsons, will see American slavery extirpated from the earth."[19]

Ironically, while American abolitionists continued to win much support by celebrating the August first day of Britain's experiment of 1833, it would require Abraham

Lincoln's wholly unexpected emancipation of American slaves in the Civil War to make British emancipation look like a courageous, pioneering effort that led the world toward the freeing of all slaves. But in 1858, when Lincoln was debating Stephen Douglass and was acutely conscious of Britain's emancipation of slaves and more recent efforts to import tens of thousands of East Indian contract laborers to do the work former slaves refused to do, he predicted that any peaceful emancipation in America would take at least one hundred years—that is, until what we think of as the "civil rights" era of the 1960s. Much earlier, in 1807, the British abolitionist leader William Wilberforce had estimated that the lag between outlawing the slave trade in 1808 and freeing the slaves would be over two hundred years, "and that only if no new lands were added to the British islands."[20] As it turned out, Lincoln and Wilberforce, who both played crucial roles leading to the outcome, could not have been more wrong. From 1784 to 1788, when the first small antislavery societies were organized in Philadelphia, New York, London, Manchester, and Paris, slavery was legal in every part of the Western Hemisphere except Vermont and Massachusetts. One hundred years later, in 1888, when Brazil finally emancipated its slaves, the institution had been outlawed throughout the hemisphere, serfdom had been abolished in Russia and eastern Europe, and Britain was leading other nations in a broad effort to eliminate bondage in the Islamic world and in Asia and Africa more generally. Given our review of the millennia during which slavery had been associated with various kinds of progress, this century-long global move toward individual liberty is all the more astonishing. Of course, the twentieth century witnessed different kinds of enslavement in Soviet gulags and in Nazi factories and concentration camps, and even today we read of millions of sex slaves, coerced labor of various kinds, and even some surviving chattel bondage in the so-called developing world. But this modernization and globalization of slavelike workers make the abolitionist achievement still more remarkable since it proves that slavery was not doomed to end by some implacable force of historical progress. Here I give most credit to the abolitionists, since without them I think that during the century from the 1780s to the 1880s very little would have been done.

When we briefly turn to the ways in which writers of the abolitionist period dealt with the positive connections we have surveyed between slavery and human progress, the first point concerns ancient Greece and Rome. Here we find most authors taking the approach represented by the historians William Blair and Henri Wallon, who held that "slavery decimated nations rather than saved them, corrupted morals rather than refined them, ruined rather than benefited the family and the state. . . . The bad points were the direct results of slavery, the good ones of freedom."[21] Opposing that view of slavery's universal evil, John Millar and Auguste Comte, writing in 1771 and 1840 respectively, stood for the position that slavery had served a useful function at an early stage of human history, replacing cannibalism and human sacrifice, but had then been rendered a "monstrous aberration" by the ascending stages of history. Millar presented the increasingly popular argument that no revolution in history had advanced human happiness as much as the abolition of slavery in medieval Europe. This meant that modern defenders of the institution were pitting themselves against the stream of history. With respect to streams, Thomas Clarkson's two-volume *History of the Rise, Progress and Accomplishment of the Abolition of the African Slave-Trade by the British Parliament,* published in 1808, presents a river map in which streams of numerous critics of the slave trade, beginning in the 1500s, unite to form two great torrents, one for each side of the Atlantic, connected first by the Quakers. The "streams" of benevolent influence that finally converged in the abolition movement proved, according to Clarkson, that "to Christianity alone are we indebted for the new and sublime spectacle of seeing men going beyond the bounds of individual usefulness to each other—of seeing them carry their charity, as a united Brotherhood, into distant lands."[22]

At the risk of oversimplification, one may think of a "scientific" tradition concerning slavery that extends from the writings of Benjamin Franklin, Adam Smith, and John Millar to such later figures as Auguste Comte and Karl Marx. Despite their profound differences in other respects, these writers viewed slavery as an institution that could be understood only in terms of its social and economic utility and its relation to the laws of historical progress. Beginning with Franklin and Smith, such theorists took it for granted that slave labor was less efficient and normally more expensive than free labor, and that slave societies inhibited the growth of population and thus of industry and national wealth. Accordingly slave societies could arise only under special circumstances: a primitive stage of social organization and property accumulation; or where the supply of free labor was inadequate to exploit the resources of extensive new land, as in the American tropics; or where artificial protections and monopolies allowed the lust for power to supersede economic self-interest. Modern slavery, from this viewpoint, was a senseless anachronism, but without outside intervention it might persist as long as special circumstances required it.

The dominant Christian view was also ambiguous on the lessons to be learned from antiquity. Most abolitionists, supported by such historians of antiquity as Henri Wallon, Edouard Biot, and Paul Allard, presupposed an irreconcilable conflict between slavery and the Christian message that all men were created in the image of God and were equal before God. According to the prevailing nineteenth-century dogma, it was Christianity that had first softened the harsh laws and manners of the Roman world and had then improved the condition of slaves until, gently and almost imperceptibly, they had been elevated to a state of freedom. This was the grand theme of Wallon and Biot, who both won prizes in a competition sponsored by the Académie des Sciences Morales et Politiques for the best explanation of the abolition of ancient slavery. What such Christian apologists shared with Comte and Marx—who represented opposing ideological positions—was the belief that the abolition of ancient slavery had depended on the unfolding of an immanent historical design. In the words of Augustin Cochin, who popularized the Christian historiography, "All of this work of transformation is due much less to the external changes of governments, institutions, and laws than to an internal change in souls."[23] This faith in the indirect benefits of Christianization—like the faith in the indirect benefits of political and economic freedom—gave way only slowly and incompletely to the belief in a new or second dispensation, distinguished by conscious decision, collective effort, and mobilization of public opinion. As described in 1823 by the new Liverpool Society for the Abolition of Slavery, the great discovery that made "the present age . . . remarkable beyond any that has preceded it, for the rapid and surprising improvement which has taken place in the moral character and disposition of mankind," was "the practice of combining society itself in intellectual masses, for the purpose of obtaining some certain, defined, and acknowledged good, which is generally allowed to be essential to the well-being of the whole."[24] This discovery of a new kind of progress owed much to the eighteenth-century voluntary associations for civic improvement, and even more to the liberating precedents of the American and French Revolutions. The description of the Liverpool abolitionists could be applied to a great variety of reform movements. Whatever the goal, the "intellectual masses" were emboldened by the promise of rational planning, coordinated effort, and division of labor, to say nothing of the increasing availability of cheaper and more efficient methods of printing and distributing propaganda to an increasingly literate public.

British and American abolitionists created a collage in which they repeatedly juxtaposed images of peaceful and orderly evolution with apocalyptic rhetoric demanding the death of a satanic institution. Although their conceptions of progress included elements of continuity, it was more centrally attuned to a moment of collective rebirth and transfiguration, which was the way many Britons celebrated the passage of the 1807 bill for slave-trade abolition. As in medieval times, slave emancipation would ultimately depend on divine Providence as manifested in the Christian spirit. But now the efficacy of Christianity could be proved, in the face of competing worldly pressures, only by a dramatic worldly act. Providence could reveal itself only through a new human ability—that of an enlightened and righteous public to control the course of events.

NOTES

1. I wish to thank Oxford University Press for permission to use some material that first appeared in my books *Slavery and Human Progress* (New York: Oxford University Press, 1984) and *Inhuman Bondage: The Rise and Fall of Slavery in the New World* (New York: Oxford University Press, 2006).

2. See Seymour Drescher, *The Mighty Experiment: Free Labor versus Slavery in British Emancipation* (New York: Oxford University Press, 2002), prologue.

3. Keith Hopkins, *Conquerors and Slaves: Sociological Studies in Roman History* (Cambridge: Cambridge University Press, 1978), 114.

4. Stanley L. Engerman, *Slavery, Emancipation, & Freedom: Comparative Perspectives* (Baton Rouge: Louisiana State University Press, 2007), 2.

5. Davis, *Slavery and Human Progress,* 52–57; William D. Phillips Jr., *Slavery from Roman Times to the Early Transatlantic Trade* (Minneapolis: University of Minnesota Press, 1985), passim; Charles Verlinden, *The Beginnings of Modern Colonization: Eleven Essays with an Introduction,* trans. Yvonne Freccero (Ithaca, N.Y.: Cornell University Press, 1970), 35–40, 79–97.

6. Charles Verlinden, "L'esclavage en sicile au bas moyen âge," *Institut historique belge de Rome* 35 (1963): 42–43, 68–79, 90–93; Verlinden, "L'esclavage noir en France méridionale et courants de traite en Afrique," *Annales du Midi* 78 (1966): 335–43; Verlinden, *L'esclavage dans l'Europe médiévale,* 2: *Italie—Colonies italiennes du Levant—Levant latin—Empire byzantin* (Gent: Rijksuniversiteit te Gent, 1977), 208–20, 233–38, 329–30, 353–54.

7. Verlinden, *L'esclavage dans l'Europe médiévale,* 235, 377; Hugh Thomas, *The Slave Trade* (New York: Simon & Schuster, 1997), 10–11, 13–14, 84–86.

8. David Brion Davis, *The Problem of Slavery in Western Culture* (New York: Oxford University Press, 1999), 114–16.

9. David Eltis, "Free and Coerced Migrations from the Old World to the New," in *Coerced and Free Migration: Global Perspectives,* edited by Eltis (Stanford, Calif.: Stanford University Press, 2002), 33–74. As a result of high slave mortality and negative population growth rates (outside mainland North America, north of the Rio Grande), by 1825 blacks constituted only 18 to 19 percent of the New World population, some 18 percent of which was mixed (including mixture with Indians), 24 percent Native American, and 40 percent white. I am much indebted to Professors David Eltis and Stanley L. Engerman for providing me with these updated estimates, including the volume of the African slave trade.

10. [Malachy Postlethwayt], *The Natural and Private Advantages of the African Trade Considered: Being an Enquiry How Far It Concerns the Trading Interest of Great Britain, Effectually to Support and Maintain the Forts and Settlements in Africa; Belonging to the Royal African Company of England . . .* (London: J & P Knapton, 1746), 1–2. Later angered by Parliament's abandonment of the Royal African Company, Postlethwayt changed his mind regarding the benefits of the slave trade and argued that Britain's economic future did not lie in sugar and slaves but in beating France to the interior of Africa (Davis, *Problem of Slavery in Western Culture,* 160–61).

11. Davis, *Problem of Slavery in Western Culture,* 151–53.

12. Charles Francis Adams, ed., *Memoirs of John Quincy Adams* (Philadelphia: J. B. Lippincott & Co., 1874–77), vol. 5 (March 3, 1820), 10–11.

13. Lee Soltow, *Men of Wealth in the United States, 1850–1870* (New Haven, Conn.: Yale University Press, 1975), 65–66; Robert W. Fogel and Stanley L. Engerman, eds., *Without Consent or Contract: The Rise and Fall of American Slavery; Technical Papers,* 2 vols. (New York: W. W. Norton, 1992), 1:84.

14. See *Proceedings of the Fourteenth Annual Meeting of the Stockholders of the North Carolina Rail Road Company* (Raleigh: North Carolina Railroad Company, July 1863).

15. I am much indebted to Professor Stanley L. Engerman for verifying these numbers in personal correspondence. I should stress that the structure and meaning of the gross national product were very different in 1860; the comparison is simply one way of viewing the relative importance of slave property before the Civil War destroyed such immoral gains.

16. Steven Heath Mitton, "The Free World Confronted: The Problem of Slavery and Progress in American Foreign Relations, 1833–1844" (Ph.D. diss., Louisiana State University, 2005), 133–45. Edward B. Rugemer has strongly questioned Mitton's view that Upshur and Calhoun had accepted Gurney's verdict on the economic success of British emancipation; see Rugemer, "Robert Monroe Harrison, British Abolition, Southern Anglophobia and Texas Annexation," *Slavery and Abolition* 28, no. 2 (August 2007): 169–91.

17. Robert Monroe Harrison to Abel P. Upshur, October 11, 1843, quoted in Mitton, "The Free World Confronted," 161.

18. *London Times,* July 18, 1857, quoted in Drescher, *Mighty Experiment,* 201–3. It should be stressed that a few smaller British colonies, such as Barbados and Antigua, had no unsettled land to which the freed people could move, and they did maintain a plantation system and actually increased output (Engerman, *Slavery, Emancipation, & Freedom,* 53–54).

19. Drescher, *Mighty Experiment,* 183, 200–201.

20. Engerman, *Slavery, Emancipation, & Freedom,* 32–33.

21. William Blair, *An Inquiry into the State of Slavery amongst the Romans: From the Earliest Period, till the Establishment of the Lombards in Italy* (Edinburgh: T. Clark, 1833), 197–98; Henri Wallon, *Histoire de l'esclavage dans l'antiquité* (Paris: Imprimerie royale, 1847), 2:438. For a more detailed discussion of Wallon and Auguste Comte, see Davis, *Problem of Slavery in Western Culture,* 17–21.

22. Thomas Clarkson, *The History of the Rise, Progress and Accomplishment of the Abolition of the African Slave-Trade by the British Parliament,* 2 vols. (London: Longman, Hurst, Rees, and Orme, 1808), 1:8, 179–80.

23. Augustin Cochin, *The Results of Slavery* (Boston: Walker, Wise, and Co., 1863), 345.

24. *Declaration of the Objects of the Liverpool Society for Promoting the Abolition of Slavery, 25th March, 1823* (Liverpool: Liverpool Society for the Abolition of Slavery, Printed by James Smith, 1823), 3.

Suppressing the Slave Trade

JEREMY BLACK

> As this island now appertains to His Britannic Majesty by right of con-
> quest, and for the moment must of course be governed by the laws of Great
> Britain (which know not of slavery) I do not conceive it to be within my
> power *forcibly* to send back any individuals of the description mentioned by
> your Excellency.
>
> *Admiral Cockburn, Royal Navy (Cumberland Island),*
> *February 15, 1815, in response to a request for the return of escaped slaves*

T he last stages of the slave trade and slavery invite two separate narratives. On
the one hand, there is the abolitionist narrative, the how and why both ended.[1]
On the other, there is room for emphasis on the continuation of both the slave trade
and slavery prior to, or even after, abolition. Indeed the slave trade and slavery each
remained important in the nineteenth century, even though it was, more significantly, the age of abolitionism. In truth both continuation and abolition need to be
included in the same narrative because they cannot be understood apart. This analytical synergy reflects the extent to which the economic, ideological, and moral
underpinnings of these separate narratives not only took on meaning with reference
to the other but also were shaped in a dynamic fashion by their relationship.

This essay offers a summary of the global suppression of oceanic slave trading
together with emancipations of slaves. The emphasis is on cultural and ideological
factors, especially religion, in abolition as opposed to economic determinism. At the
same time, despite the great achievements that are discussed, there were many limitations and unforeseen consequences, ranging from the persistence of slave trading
and new forms of coerced labor to the often cynical merger of antislavery with imperialism.

It would be easy to approach this essay from an anti-Western perspective, which
indeed is standard as far as the subject is concerned. But this is a simplistic stance that
reveals more about present than past. Moreover the crude anti-Western account of
slavery needs to take note of the disillusionment many Africanist historians experienced as optimism about independence gave way to a more pessimistic account based

on a grimmer reality. Moving to the present, recent and current developments in Sudan and Zimbabwe, including their relationship with their prime foreign sponsor, China, provide a way, however ahistorical, to understand the African basis of the slave trade, a basis that included widespread slavery in Africa itself.

The abolition of the slave trade was a distinctive feature of the nineteenth-century West. In contrast, other societies unwilling to abolish the trade had to be coerced into line. An emphasis on the role of slavery in other cultures and periods underlines the extent to which it was not simply a pathogen of the rise of Western capitalism, an approach taken in a public debate, although not in the scholarly literature. Despite the attraction for some from particular political persuasions, the abolition of slavery and the slave trade cannot be seen simply as a consequence of a particular stage in the Western economy, not least a shifting of the factors of production and profitability. Instead it is necessary to look to a different genesis for abolitionism, namely a cultural-ideological one, while at the same time accepting that this had materialist roots. An emphasis on cultural-ideological factors in abolitionism is in accord with the general thrust of much historical work in recent years, indeed decades, one away from materialist determinism and instead toward more multiple and indeterminate analysis.

Abolitionism offers lessons for today that are suggestive. They outline the possibility of advancing what can be considered progressive moral vistas for government policy. That these vistas were focused on and by the leading world power, Britain, however, ensures a major difference between the nineteenth century and the present age. In the former there was no approximation of world government or forum for cooperation comparable to the United Nations and the other institutions and treaties created under American auspices to further a new world order after World War II. As a result moral suasion at the international level was, in diplomatic terms, essentially bilateral rather than multilateral, but more generally it did not have an institutional component. Attempts at a multilateral level to persuade other powers to participate in more than declamatory diplomacy against the slave trade achieved very little.[2]

In contrast to the situation in the nineteenth century, not least the centrality of bilateral relations, the modern, far more insistent nature of international moral suasion creates many problems for the leading world power, the United States.[3] These problems are accentuated by the decline in American "soft power" both in the 1960s and more recently.[4] Furthermore the weak purchase of internationalism in American popular politics leads to difficulties for any attempt to anchor American moral suasion in international structures. Since direct comparisons between the two international systems are problematic, it is more useful to look for particular characteristics, not least in order to consider their applicability in different contexts. That is the background for this essay on suppressing the slave trade and ending slavery.

Taking up the nonmaterialist perspective, it is appropriate to note the weight of the key abolitionist currents provided by religious pressure and secular idealism. The first was particularly important in the Protestant world, although there had always also been a significant current of Catholic uneasiness about, and sometimes hostility to, slavery. This can be seen in particular among Spanish thinkers in the sixteenth century. Slavery and slave trading were illegal in most of Europe and had been for some time, despite some ambiguity about the status of enslaved persons entering Europe. The absence of slavery in Europe was striking in comparison with other parts of the world, and it contributed to a situation in which it lacked normative value for public opinion.

In Europe the slave trade was abolished first by Denmark in 1792, although the law did not come into force until 1803, and meanwhile the slave population in the Danish West Indies (the American Virgin Islands from 1917) was built up from about twenty-five thousand to approximately thirty-five thousand. A variety of factors were at play, and that point is worth underlining because it should subvert any tendency to seek simple explanations and then to generalize them at the scale of the West. Indeed a major theme of this essay is the extraordinary number of international relationships and contingent factors that went into ending the slave trade. The emphasis on complicating specificity is deliberate and in part provides the analytical dimension to this narrative.

In Denmark the role of government was central, and unlike in Britain, there was no abolitionist campaign. In part Danish abolition prefigured the situation with most powers over the following century in that it reflected an awareness of the international context. This was particularly the issue for powers other than the foremost in the system, which, again, is often (though not invariably) the situation for modern states with regard to ideological issues. It was believed in Denmark that Britain and France would soon abolish the trade and would then seek to prevent other powers from participating, which proved to be an erroneous expectation in the short term but an accurate one thereafter.

The Slave Trade Commission in Denmark also argued that slave conditions on the islands would improve if imports were banned, as it would be necessary to look after the slaves in order to encourage them to reproduce. In short, slavery would become less reprehensible, a view also taken by British abolitionists.[5] In addition in the Protestant world criticism of the slave trade and slavery developed in the Netherlands.[6]

Changes in Britain were more important because of her position as the leading European imperial and naval power. Furthermore her key role in the slave trade and in the Caribbean slave economy ensured the importance of British attitudes and influence on other states. This was a dimension that contrasted with the earlier competition in the slave trade, although that competition continued as an aspect of abolitionist pressure. Britain's influence on other states rose greatly as a result of her major, and eventually successful, role in resistance to revolutionary and Napoleonic France from 1793 to 1815. Britain emerged from its wars with France as the preeminent global power.

There was, of course, an ideological dimension to British abolitionism. Christian assumptions about the inherent unity of mankind, and concerning the need to gather Africans to Christ, influenced British opinion significantly. Methodist leader John Wesley strongly attacked both slavery and the slave trade in his *Thoughts upon Slavery* (1774). In 1791 he sent William Wilberforce a dying message urging him to maintain the abolitionist cause. In British polite society by the early 1770s both slavery and the slave trade were increasingly seen as morally unacceptable.[7]

Commercial benefits from the abolition of the slave trade were predicted by some commentators. Malachy Postlethwayt, for example, argued in his *Universal Dictionary of Trade and Commerce* that the trade stirred up conflict among African rulers and thus obstructed both British trade and "the civilising of these people."[8] Belief in such benefits became far stronger in the early nineteenth century, not least as British merchants looked for new export markets, particularly in the face, first, of the Continental System—the Napoleonic attempt to weaken Britain by banning her trade with Europe—and after the defeat of Napoleon in 1815 of continental protectionism—for example, the German *Zollverein* (Customs Union) established in 1834. Competition from American producers was an additional problem. Furthermore the massive expansion of British industry meant that there were more goods for sale, as well as a desire for raw materials. Thus a very different basis for trade with Africa was proposed.

William, Lord Mansfield's ruling in the case of James Somersett (sometimes Somerset) in 1771–72 that West Indian slave owners could not forcibly take their slaves from England, made slavery unenforceable there and was matched by reluctance among Londoners to help return runaway slaves. Abolitionist sentiment directed against the slave trade became more overt from the 1780s and was an aspect of the powerful reform pressure and religious revivalism of the period. Quakers played a prominent role, but they and others were effective in part because of a more widespread shift in opinion, a situation more generally true of campaigning movements in Britain and elsewhere.

The strength of associational practices presented ready possibilities for organization. In 1787 the Society for the Abolition of the Slave Trade was established as a national lobbying group. Provincial liaison committees, also established that year, mobilized extensive support. Exeter's list of supporters in 1788, for example, contained over 250 names. If many came from outside the city, they nevertheless showed the range of support, including sixty women among the subscribers. The last was indicative of the prominent role of women in British abolitionism.[9]

Pressure from the Society for the Abolition of the Slave Trade helped lead to the Dolben Act of 1788, by which conditions on British slave ships were regulated. The responsiveness of the slave trade to the change in circumstances was speedily demonstrated. Profitability had to be brought into line with legislation. Restrictions on the number of slaves that British ships could carry led to an increase in the costs to the slave trader and encouraged the use of larger ships. In 1789 a less rigorous but similar act was passed by the Dutch, and in 1799 British restrictions were strengthened.

Abolitionist sentiment also affected the arts, leading to the production of visual and literary images of the horrors of slavery, such as the medallion of the Society for the Abolition of the Slave Trade designed by William Hackwood and manufactured at Josiah Wedgwood's factory. Antislavery became a fashionable cause, joining the powerful sentimental, romantic, and evangelical currents in the British culture of the period. Furthermore there was a mass of pamphlet literature and discussion of the issue in humanitarian novels, and also extensive comments on the abolitionist fight. Abolitionists sought information on the slave trade and the colonies, leading to Thomas Clarkson's *The Substance of Evidence on Sundry Persons in the Slave Trade* (1788).

Pressure to abolish the trade, however, was hindered by the importance of the West Indies to the British economy, as well as by the opposition of King George III and much of the House of Lords. Dolben's Bill, for example, was bitterly opposed in the House of Lords by the lord chancellor, Lord Thurlow, a favorite of the king, while other ministers such as Lord Hawkesbury, the president of the Board of Trade, another royal favorite, who was greatly concerned about the prosperity of the West Indies, and Viscount Sydney, the home secretary, offered more muted opposition.

The votes indicated the strength of opposition. In 1791 Wilberforce's motion to bring in a bill for the abolition of the trade was defeated in the House of Commons by 163 to 88. The following year his motion for abolition in 1796 was passed by 151 to 132, but the Lords postponed the matter by resolving to hear evidence. In 1793 Wilberforce's motion to hasten the actions of the Lords was rejected, as was that to abolish the supply of slaves to foreign powers. In 1794 the latter motion passed the House of Commons but was rejected in the House of Lords. In 1795 the Commons refused leave to bring in a bill for abolition, and in 1796 the bill was rejected on a third reading. In 1804 the measure passed the Commons but was defeated in the Lords, while in 1805 it failed the second reading in the Commons.

There was also a populist tone to opposition to abolition, one that is too often overlooked in the stress on a benign shift toward a more evangelical zeitgeist in Britain. In William Dent's caricature "Abolition of the Slave Trade, or the Man the Master," published in London on May 26, 1789, produce is shown waiting for a purchaser because its price has gone up.[10] Part of the opposition to abolitionism derived from the continued conviction that slavery was compatible with Christianity, and also that it was sanctioned by its existence in the Old Testament. This argument was not widespread, although the Dutch Reformed Church, the established church in Cape Colony, argued that slaves were not entitled to enter the church and that conversion to Christianity would not make slaves akin to Europeans because they had been born to slavery as part of a divine plan. The Dutch settlers opposed missionary activity among their slaves, as did many plantation owners in the West Indies.[11] By

1800 there were nearly seventeen thousand slaves in Cape Colony, brought by sea from the Indian Ocean.

The authority of the classical world also contributed to the acceptability of slavery. To supporters of slavery, an acceptance of blacks as fully human did not preclude slavery. Instead blacks were presented as degraded by their social and environmental backgrounds.

In part opposition to abolition more specifically reflected the conservative response in Britain to reform agitation after the French Revolution, which broke out in 1789. The revolution indeed had been linked to a secular idealism that had embraced abolitionism as one of its themes. In February 1788 La Société des Amis des Noirs had been founded, with help from British abolitionists. Although the French were far less active than their British counterparts, the society pressed for the abolition of the slave trade and, eventually and without compensation, of slavery. One of its founders, Jacques-Pierre Brissot, argued that with education blacks had the same capacities as whites.[12]

In the utopian idealism of the French Revolution, the liberties affirmed by the revolutionaries were believed to be inherent in humanity and thus globally applicable. In January 1792 the attention of the National Assembly was directed by its Colonial Committee toward Madagascar. Instead of a French territorial expansion to be achieved by conquest and for the people to be reduced to slavery, there was a call for an alliance.[13]

Initially, however, the slave trade was not banned by France; indeed it reached its peak during the years 1789–91. This reflected the importance of the West Indies to the French economy, especially during the boom that followed the American Revolution and the dominance of the colonies by the white colonists. It was argued that slaves were not French and therefore that slavery and the freedoms of revolution were compatible. The major slave rising in France's leading Caribbean colony, Saint Domingue, in 1791 altered the situation and also helped competing sugar-producing areas: the British colonies and especially Portuguese-ruled Brazil. This rising led to a complex conflict in Saint Domingue. The slave rebels liberated themselves from slavery, and to win their support for the French cause, in August 1793 the civil commissioner Léger Sonthonax freed the slaves in the Northern Province. The following February the National Convention abolished slavery in all French colonies, a step that was unwelcome to most of the white settlers.[14]

This idealism, however, did not protect the French position in Saint Domingue, which instead after a bitter war became the independent black state of Haiti. There were important African echoes in the rising and the subsequent warfare, but the rising also drew on European practices and on the ideology of revolutionary France.[15] Fighting in Haiti demonstrated what was also seen with the British West Indies regiments, that blacks were far better than Europeans as warriors in the West Indies, especially because their resistance to malarial diseases was higher.[16] The conflict also displayed brutal racist, antisocietal violence on both sides.[17] Prefiguring their very different later role in subsequently ending the slave trade, the British played an important part in ensuring the success of the Haitian revolution, with a crucial blockade of Saint Domingue's ports in 1803 when war between the two powers resumed after the peace negotiated in 1802. Alongside the resumption of large-scale rebellion in October 1803, this wrecked the French attempt to recapture the colony and thus Napoleon's western strategy, a failure also seen in the sale of Louisiana to the United States that year.

There were also slave revolts elsewhere in the Caribbean world in the 1790s, including, in the British colonies, Fedon's rebellion on Grenada in 1795–96 and risings or conspiracies in Dominica and St. Vincent, followed by a conspiracy on Tobago in 1802.[18] All were unsuccessful, as was the Pointee Coupee slave rebellion in Louisiana in 1795 and smaller-scale slave violence. The success of the Haitian revolution, however, led to a marked increase in the always-present climate of fear in white society. This fear was accentuated by the killing of settlers on Grenada in 1795. The Maroons of Dominica, who were already a serious problem in 1785, were suppressed only in 1814, in part as a result of defections and in part due to the burning of their cultivated patches.

French revolutionary idealism also fell victim to the reaction and consolidation associated with Napoleon: slavery was restored in Guadeloupe (after the bloody repression of opposition by black troops) and Cayenne (French Guiana) in 1802; and the entry to France of West Indian blacks and mixed-race people was prohibited. The slave trade was also restored.[19] Moreover slave rebels were less successful in Latin America than in Saint Domingue. The small-scale 1798 "Revolt of the Tailors" in Salvador, Brazil, which included slaves as well as mulattos and whites, called for the abolition of slavery, but it was suppressed in the context of white fear.[20] The extent and impact of slave revolts, both on the slave ships and in the colonies, are important issues as they relate to the question of African agency in reducing the profitability and appeal of the slave trade and slavery, and thus of encouraging abolitionism. The evidence for this thesis is limited, however, not least as far as the slave trade is concerned.

The British situation differed from that in France. Abolitionism declined in the 1790s for both economic and ideological reasons. The boom in sugar exports from the British West Indies caused by the chaos in rival Saint Domingue was important, as was the widespread opposition to populist reform that stemmed from hostility to the French Revolution. Thereafter, however, there was, in contrast to the situation in France, an upsurge in abolitionism in the 1800s. This led to the formal end of the British slave trade.[21] The end of both this slave trade and of slavery itself has been ascribed by some commentators to a lack of profitability caused by economic development, rather than to humanitarianism.[22] This view, however, underplays the multiplicity of factors that contributed to it. Some studies attribute much to economic problems in the plantation economy of the West Indies. These problems stemmed from the impact of the American Revolution and, crucially, of subsequent British protectionism on the trade between North America and the West Indies. This trade was very important to the supplies for and markets of the latter.[23] There are, on the contrary, also indications that slave plantations in the West Indies remained profitable.[24] In part this reflected the ability of plantation owners to innovate. An aspect of this innovation included better care for the slaves, although Jamaica, Trinidad, and British Guiana were still not approaching demographic self-sufficiency by the 1820s. As a result, unlike Barbados and the United States, where self-sufficiency had been early achieved in the Chesapeake region, they would have greatly profited from continuing slave imports. Instead the cost of acquiring and sustaining the workforce rose, in part because of moves against the slave trade and in part as a result of market forces. By the time of emancipation, the material consumption levels of the slaves were similar to those of manual workers in Britain.[25] Aside from its continued profitability, the West Indies' plantation economy remained an important asset base. Furthermore the limited convertibility of assets did not encourage disinvestments from slavery: too much money was tied up in mortgages and annuities that were difficult to liquidate in a hurry. Moreover, however reprehensible in modern terms, the planters had a good pragmatic case for the generous compensation they pressed for and received, rather than the loan originally proposed.

Instead of problems within the slave economy of the British West Indies, it is more appropriate to look at the outside pressures toward abolition. These led indeed rather swiftly to a situation in which it became the general assumption of the "official mind" that action against the trade was a proper aspect of British policy.[26] These pressures included and contributed to a marginalization of groups, especially West Indian planters, that had encouraged and profited from British, and indeed European, demand for tropical goods.

Instead the reforming, liberal, middle-class British culture that was growing in importance and helping to define both civility and Britishness regarded the slave trade and slavery as abhorrent, anachronistic, and associated with everything it deplored. Abolitionists indeed were encouraged and assisted by a confidence in public support. This greatly influenced the debate amid the elite, forcing the defenders of slavery onto the defensive and thus further ensuring that slavery seemed out-of-date.

Abolitionism, moreover, offered a country weary of the seemingly intractable war with Napoleon the opportunity to sense itself as playing a key role in the advance of true liberty. Abolitionist medals show how self-conscious this was.[27] This was particularly valuable in 1806–7 as Britain's allies Austria and Prussia succumbed after sweeping French victories at Austerlitz (1805) and Jena (1806) respectively. Moreover all sorts of reform impulses in Britain converged on abolitionism, including concern over the treatment of animals.[28] In 1805 the ministry of William Pitt the Younger, a statesman who saw himself as progressive and who profited from his appeal to Britain's reforming middle-class constituency, issued Orders in Council that banned the import of slaves into newly captured territories after 1807 and, in the meantime, limited the introduction of slaves to 30 percent of the number already there. The proclamation was taken much further by the next government, the more reformist Ministry of All the Talents, which took power after Pitt's death in early 1806. In 1806 the new ministry supported the Foreign Slave Trade Act, ending the supply of slaves to conquered territories and foreign colonies. This was presented on pruden-tial grounds, as a way to limit the economic strength of these territories when some were returned as part of the peace settlement at the end of the war as they would be: Cuba, Guadeloupe, and Martinique had been returned by Britain in 1763, and the last two were to be returned anew after the Napoleonic War.

The high point of the abolitionist process occurred when the Abolition Act of 1807 banned slave trading by British subjects and the import of slaves into the other colonies. The act came into force on May 1, 1807, and on March 1, 1808, for those slave ships already at sea. Subsequently in 1811 participation in the slave trade was made a felony.

Britain also used its international strength and influence to put pressure on other states to abolish or limit the slave trade, for not only did the trade now seem morally wrong, but once abolished for British colonies, it was also correctly seen as giving an advantage to rival plantation economies and thus to their general economies. George Canning, the foreign secretary from 1807 to 1809, ordered British diplomats to begin negotiations aimed at securing treaties that would end the trade. Naval power, amphibious capability, and transoceanic power projection ensured that the British were in a dominant position and well placed to advance their views.

Once war resumed with Napoleon in 1803—a war that lasted until 1814 and was briefly and successfully resumed in 1815—the British seized Saint Lucia, Tobago, Demerara and Essequibo (now both in Guyana), and Surinam in 1803–4, following with the Danish West Islands: Saint Croix, Saint Thomas, and Saint John's in 1807; Martinique and Cayenne in 1809; and Guadeloupe, Saint Eustatius, and Saint Martin in 1810. Fort Louis, the last French base in West Africa, fell in 1809. Robert, Viscount Castlereagh, the foreign secretary after Canning, was pressed in 1812 to support the capture of Dutch and Danish settlements on the West African coast as this would lead to "the more effectual abolishing the Slave Trade, which, during my residence on the coast, was carried on to a great extent with the said Dutch and Dan-ish settlements by Spanish and Portuguese vessels and Americans under Spanish colours."[29] Although their pressure was widely resented by others, both during the Napoleonic War and thereafter, as self-interested interference and undesirable moralizing, the British were in a position to make demands. In 1810 pressure was exerted on Portugal, then very much a dependent ally protected from Napoleon by British troops, to restrict the slave trade to its territories in preparation for abolition. Because Brazil, the leading slave economy, and Angola, its prime source of slaves, were Portuguese colonies, the Portuguese position was important. Indeed in Angola the Portuguese controlled the largest colony in Africa.[30] In 1815 Napoleon, on his return from Elba, abolished the French slave trade, possibly as a way to appeal to progressive British opinion. Subsequently, after Napoleon's defeat at Waterloo, the returned Bourbon regime of Louis XVIII, like Portugal very much a dependent ally of Britain, was persuaded by the latter to ban the slave trade. This was of great concern to British abolitionists, as the French slave trade, if it continued, was seen as an opportunity for British investment. Under British pressure the Congress of Vienna issued a declaration against the trade. Indeed the congress led, albeit only temporarily, to the institutionalization of suppression in the form of the short-lived but multilateral diplomatic committee established in London to monitor the trade.

This was not the end of the process of incessant British pressure. In January 1815 an Anglo-Portuguese treaty limited the slave trade in Brazil to south of the equator, ending the supply of slaves from the Guinea coast in West Africa. Then in September 1817 an Anglo-Spanish treaty contained similar provisions; Spain, in contrast, had rejected such pressure in 1814. In 1814, with effect from 1818, the Dutch slave trade was abolished. Again this reflected British influence, as the Netherlands was also a dependent ally.

In 1807, with effect from January 1, 1808, the slave trade was banished by the United States, but there was scant attempt to enforce the ban. Orders in council, however, issued on November 11, 1807, were used by the British to justify seizing American slavers. The Court of Appeals of 1810 accepted the argument of the barrister James Stephen, Wilberforce's brother-in-law and a member of the Clapham Sect who had become convinced of the horrors of slavery by his time in the West Indies. Stephen argued that slave trading was a violation of the law of nations, the laws of humanity, and Anglo-American law, and that therefore neutral slave ships could be legitimately seized.[31] During the War of 1812 British willingness to receive and arm escaped slaves aroused American anger. British commentators suggested, moreover, that encouraging slave resistance was a way to weaken the United States. In 1814 Henry, Viscount Sidmouth, the home secretary, received a proposal suggesting that the British change the politics of America by turning to the slaves: they were to be emancipated in Virginia and Maryland, which was to be supported as a separate country.[32] In the closing stages of the war, the British military devoted particular attention to this option.

The Atlantic slave trade continued, however, not least because slavery had not been abolished. At the international conference at Aix-la-Chapelle in 1818, a British attempt to establish an agreement of all maritime states supported by an international police force on the coast of Africa was rejected, with the French playing the key role.[33] In fact even British participation in the trade persisted, both legally and illegally, directly and indirectly. This included the purchase of slaves, both for British colonies and for British-owned operations elsewhere, such as mining for gold in Brazil and for copper in Cuba, as well as the provision of goods, credit, insurance, and ships to foreign slave traders, and direct roles in slavery. Delays in emancipation enabled British investors and others to continue to invest in other slave systems and helped maintain the profitability of the slave trade. They also encouraged purchases of slaves designed to preempt the end of legal imports, while the slave trade between British colonies remained legal for a time.

Britain played a major role investing in an undercapitalized Atlantic world, and the provision of capital was particularly valuable to slave societies. For example, British finance helped support rail construction in plantation economies such as Brazil, Cuba, and the United States. The British were not alone in this process. American manufactured goods supplied to Africa played a significant role in the slave trade from the 1840s.[34] Although demand for new labor in the plantation economies was in large part met from the children of existing slaves, the continuation of slavery ensured that even where the slave trade had been abolished smuggling persisted, although it was not extensive to the British West Indies. An illicit slave trade continued in the French Atlantic world, especially to Cayenne (French Guiana) but also to the French Caribbean. The French had at least 193 slaving voyages between 1814 and 1820, although few after 1831. Deception extended to the shipping of slaves, termed *libertos* by the Portuguese and *engagés à temps* by the French. The French financed their trade with the export of goods to Africa, but this was a small flow compared to that from Britain. The French and Dutch also sold slaves to Puerto Rico, circumventing treaties banning their import direct from Africa by moving them via their Caribbean ports and reclassifying them.[35] In response to action against the trade, there was a need, however, to search for new sources of slaves, and this led to the development of slaving from South-East Africa. This was a distant source, where the slaves were in part purchased in return for textiles shipped from Bombay. However, distance hit profitability, and as a result most slaves shipped from Africa via the Portuguese ports of Mozambique and Quelimane went to nearby Mauritius and Réunion in the Indian Ocean, and not to Brazil: proximity took precedence over the political link.

The impact of European slaving activity in Mozambique on African society has been a source of controversy. Some historians contend that it, rather than Zulu expansion, was in part responsible for the conflict in the interior known as the *mfecane*,[36] although other scholars reject this notion.[37] A more appropriate approach is one that avoids mono-causal interpretations, emphasizes the role of dynamic internal forces in generating change in African societies, and presents European pressures and opportunities in this context.[38] Demand, one that reflected labor needs, kept the trade alive. In particular the slave trade to the leading and increasingly important market of Brazil was not effectively ended until 1850, and that to the second market, Cuba, until 1867 (the relevant Spanish legislation was passed the previous year). Cuba, which until occupied by the United States in 1898 was a Spanish possession, imported an annual average of 10,700 slaves in 1836–60. The profitable nature of the Brazilian and Cuban sugar economies, the commitment to the lifestyle and ethos of slaveholding, and a lack of relevant European immigrant labor all kept the trade successful. The decline of the slave economies of nearby Haiti and Jamaica also encouraged an increase of slavery in Cuba.

Demand for slaves encouraged supply as well as shifts in the supply system. For example, the number of slaves shipped through Portuguese-controlled ports in the Cabinda region to the north of the River Congo rose in the 1820s. In part this was due to the decline of the French and Dutch trade from this region, but the expansion of the Atlantic slave trade further east into the African interior was also significant.[39] American slavers greatly profited from demand in Brazil and Cuba.

Until the late 1830s the Bight of Benin and until the 1850s the Angolan coast north to Cabinda remained important sources of slaves. The export of slaves to Brazil helped keep the trade buoyant, and the British role in the Bight of Benin had been replaced by Brazilian, Dutch, Portuguese, and Spanish traders. Furthermore the raiding warfare that provided large numbers of slaves remained important across Africa and responded to shifts in the Atlantic transit system. For example, Opubu the Great, ruler of the important port of Bonny on the Bight of Biafra (1792–1830), responded to British moves against the slave trade by selling palm oil to Britain while at the same time developing his slave interests with Portugal.[40] The slave trade helped Asante expansion, although this expansion was also financed from other sources.[41] Dahomey also played a prominent role,[42] as did Madagascar.[43] In the interior Islamic jihads were linked to slaving.[44] At the same time the remarkably rapid African shift to palm oil and other "legitimate" exports also had a huge impact on Africans.

The flow of slaves to Brazil was principally financed by the shipping to Angola, in return, of textiles along with cheap brandy and firearms. Britain and Brazil were the leading sources of the textiles, and Britain's role was important to Anglo-Brazilian trade. This helped complicate the attitudes of the British government to the continuation of the slave trade, for there was pressure on behalf of British manufacturing interests. The textile trade also helped spur Brazilian production. As a result of the continued flow of new slaves, Brazil and Cuba remained more African in the nineteenth century than did the British West Indies or the southern United States. This had important long-term consequences in terms of their societies and cultures, and these consequences continue to this day.

In the United States the initial acceptance of slavery was a product of the federal character of the new state and of the fundamental role of slaveholding, not only in the economies of the southern states but also to their sense of identity and distinctiveness. It is a common mistake to say that the framers of the American Constitution agreed that the American slave trade would be abolished in twenty years. In fact the Constitution prohibited the government from interfering with the slave trade for twenty years, and this provision was not amendable. South Carolina and Georgia both expected a future need for slave imports.

From 1808, however, the slave trade to the United States was no longer legal. However, there was still an important slave trade within the United States; indeed it became more important in the nineteenth century, particularly from the Old to the New South. This was similar to the situation in Brazil, where the sugar planters of the northeast sold slaves to the coffee planters further south. Using the railway to create new links and opportunities, they were expanding westward into the province of São Paulo.[45] Similarly delays in emancipation provided a market for slave trade within the Caribbean, particularly once direct trade with Africa was limited. Caribbean slave supplies, for example, became more important to the Spanish colony of Puerto Rico from 1847.[46] Aside from slave sales, the prevalence of slave hiring in the American South further ensured considerable geographical mobility among slaves. This helped keep slavery responsive to the market, and thus part of a dynamic economic system. Without a trade in slaves, there would have been less room for such entrepreneurship and for the interaction with capital that purchase and hiring offered.[47]

The major expansion of cotton cultivation transformed the slave economy in the United States. This owed much to Eli Whitney's invention in 1793 of the cotton gin, a hand-operated machine that made it possible to separate the cotton seeds from the fiber. This process encouraged the planting of "upland" cotton. It was hardy and therefore widely cultivable across the South. Upland cotton, however, was difficult to deseed by hand, unlike the Sea Island cotton hitherto grown, which had been largely restricted to the Atlantic coastlands. As a result of the cotton gin annual cotton output in the United States rose from three thousand bales in 1793 to over three million in the 1850s.[48] The profitability of the cotton economy was important to the continued appeal of slavery in the South, and as tobacco became less well capitalized, slaves from the tobacco country were sold for work on cotton plantations. This ensured that slaves became less important in the Chesapeake states, where in contrast to the situation further south, there had been a natural growth in the slave population from the 1720s. The success of the cotton economy and the ability to boost the birthrate of American slaves were such that southern apologists did not regard the slave system as anachronistic. Furthermore there was an interest in spreading slavery, an interest linked to the southern commitment to expansionism both within the United States and with the expansion of the nation. While Texas was under Mexican rule (1821–35), the attempt by the Mexican government to prevent importation of slaves aroused much anger among the American colonists.

Britain meanwhile expended much diplomatic capital on moves against the slave trade. Notably, diplomatic recognition of the states that arose from the collapse of Spain's empire in Latin America depended on their abolition of the slave trade. British support was important to abolitionism in formerly Spanish America, but so also were the example and process of rebellion against Spain that had led to independence. These rebellions challenged existing patterns of authority but also saw a breakdown of order far greater than that in the American Revolution, one that many slaves exploited in order to escape or rebel. Slavery itself was abolished in Chile in 1823, in Mexico in 1829, in Bolivia in 1831, and in Paraguay and Uruguay in 1842. In Argentina (1853), Colombia (1851), Peru (1855), and Venezuela (1854) abolition took longer.[49] British pressure was not restricted to Latin America. In addition British recognition of the then-independent Republic of Texas was granted in 1840 on the same basis of abolition of the slave trade. Indeed in 1844 the American secretary of state John C. Calhoun told the British envoy that Britain had promoted the abolition of slavery in Texas in order to undermine it in the United States.

Britain also exerted pressure on other states, including France and the United States, to implement their own bans on the trade. British demands and the practice of searching ships generated considerable anger. Indeed British pressure was in part countered by the continuation of slavery in the United States, and American influence, in particular, helped in the continued slave trade to Cuba. So also did the lack of a Spanish abolitionist movement.

In 1839 the Palmerston Act authorized British warships to seize slave ships registered in Portugal and sailing under the Portuguese flag, a measure in part intended to hit the use of the flag by Brazilian slave dealers. It was vigorously implemented. Some traders then switched to the French flag. New treaties to enforce the end of the trade were signed with Portugal in 1842 and with France in 1845.[50] The former crucially extended the mutual right to search.

This issue caused particular problems in Anglo-Brazilian relations. In 1826 Brazil, concerned about the possibility of Portuguese reconquest, accepted a treaty with Britain, ratified in 1827, promising to make the trade illegal within three years. Furthermore in 1831 the Brazilian General Assembly passed a law ordering the liberation of all slaves entering Brazil. In anticipation of the abolition of the slave trade, the treaty led to a marked rise in demand for slaves, and also in their price. In addition there was also renewed interest in the recruitment of native Indian labor.

Demand for slaves and prices fell in 1830–33 before both, however, rose anew. This reflected the pathetic nature of Brazilian enforcement, which reflected a strong sense that slavery and the slave trade were essential, as well as anger about British interference and Brazilian measures to enforce the law. In the late 1830s political pressure grew for the end of restrictions on the trade, and the slave trade was openly conducted with the Brazilian navy doing little to interfere. The low price of slaves in Africa indeed encouraged the revival in the transatlantic trade. The inflow of slaves to Brazil greatly increased to an annual rate of over fifty thousand in the late 1840s (the annual average in 1826–50 was thirty-eight thousand), so that by 1850 there were over two million slaves in Brazil.[51] It is important to keep in mind the variety of slave societies. The Brazilian situation was very different from that in the United States, the leading slave society, as the latter was no longer linked into the international slave trade.

Many slaves worked in Brazil in the booming coffee industry, which benefited greatly from increased demand from the growing population of Europe. This was an aspect of the linkage between globalization and involuntary labor movements, whether of slaves or of other forms of coerced labor. More generally plantation agriculture did well in Brazil.

In 1847, however, an Anglo-Portuguese treaty abolishing the trade was signed. This affected both Angolan and Portuguese slavers; the latter had already been the target of British legislation in 1839. In 1845, moreover, the British Parliament passed a Slave Trade Act authorizing the British navy to treat suspected slave ships as if pirates. In doing so Parliament was seeking to enforce unilaterally the provision of the Anglo-Brazilian treaty of 1826, which deemed the Brazilian slave trade piratical. The 1845 act was a piece of legislation that testified to a strong sense of national power as well as mission, but it also reflected long-standing tension with other powers over British rights over their nationals and property. The act led to the pursuit of ships into Brazilian ports in 1850, much to the anger of the Brazilians, who were not in a position to resist Britain either politically or economically. Britain could obtain coffee and sugar from elsewhere, and Brazil greatly needed British capital.

Stronger British pressure within Brazil was exerted from 1850 when the slave trade was formally abolished by Brazil in the Eusébio de Queiroz law, a measure that in turn owed much to British action. Indeed the British subsidized Brazilian abolitionism. The last cargo of slaves was unloaded in 1856. More generally, by helping push up the price of slaves, which rose greatly in the 1850s and even higher thereafter, British pressure ensured that slave owning was too expensive for many Brazilians. This reduced the role of slave owning.[52] Coercion thus helped make it economically redundant and politically weaker.

Pressure was also exerted on Cuba, sufficiently so for David Turnbull, the British consul, to be accused of incitement to slave risings.[53] The situation in Brazil and Cuba underlined the extent to which slavery came to an end in slave societies as a result of external pressures. The varied role of such pressures was an instance of a more general characteristic of slavery.

Public abolitionist sentiment remained strong in Britain, with an instructive Irish dimension,[54] and encouraged government action. This sentiment was directed against both foreign activity and British participation in, for example, the Brazilian mining industry. Britain's role in the suppression of the slave trade affected British institutions, not least the Foreign Office. The large Slave Trade Department was one of the first functional departments of the Foreign Office, and its emergence and evolution illustrates the bureaucratization of diplomacy. It provided the Foreign Office with a degree of expertise, particularly on African matters, that it might otherwise not have had. This was also the case with the Royal Navy, especially the enthusiasm displayed by younger naval officers of the West African Squadron in their campaign against the trade.

In the context of the suppression of the slave trade, the Royal Navy became a global force for change, challenging not only slavers but also established maritime law. The sense of moral purpose behind British policy rested on the state's unchallenged naval power[55] and was given a powerful naval dimension by the antislavery patrols off Africa and Brazil and in the West Indies. Indeed in 1807, when Britain was at war with France and naval resources were stretched blockading its ports, two warships were sent to African waters to begin the campaign against the slave trade. Abolitionists pressed for the retention of bases in West Africa in order to increase the effectiveness of naval action against the trade.

The use of naval pressure against the Barbary States of North Africa, which seized Europeans as slaves, acted as a bridge to make such pressure against Western traders elsewhere seem more acceptable. This was a long-standing theme, but it is indicative that the biggest deployment of this type occurred in 1816. Admiral Lord Exmouth and a fleet of twenty-one British warships, with the support of a squadron of Dutch frigates, demanded the end of Christian slavery in Algiers. When no answer was returned, they opened fire. A massive bombardment of forty thousand roundshot and shells destroyed the Algerine ships and much of the city. Umar, the dey (ruler), yielded, and over sixteen hundred slaves, mostly from Spain and the Italian principalities, were freed. This was heralded as a great triumph.[56] The British presented themselves as acting on behalf of the civilized world and as assuming a responsibility formerly undertaken by the Bourbon powers. In 1819 a British squadron returned to Algiers, while in 1824 the threat of bombardment led the dey, now Husain III, to capitulate again to British demands. That year also the bey of Tunis was made to stop the sale of Christian slaves.

The most important British antislavery naval force in the first half of the century was based in West Africa (until 1840 part of the Cape Command). The navy expanded this force from the 1820s to the 1840s, and in the late 1830s British naval action helped greatly to reduce the flow of slaves from the Bight of Biafra.[57] Warships based in Cape Town, a Dutch naval base that was a British possession from 1806, also played an important role, and antislavery patrols were extended south of the equator in 1839, enabling Britain to enforce the outlawing of the slave trade to Brazil. In 1839 unilateral action was taken against Portuguese slavers after negotiations had failed. The major West African major slaving port of Lagos was attacked in 1851. Its slaving facilities were destroyed, and local rulers were made to sign treaties with Britain ending the slave trade.

Antislaving activities were not restricted to the Atlantic but rather were also important in the Indian Ocean and in East Asian waters. The former was an aspect of the African slave trade, although the latter arose from a very different geography of slaving. There were also operations against piracy, which was often focused on slave raiding, for example off Sarawak in northern Borneo. In 1843–49 HMS

Dido and other warships joined James Brooke in stamping out pirates who resisted his influence there.

The advent of steam power added a new dimension to the naval struggle. It increased the maneuverability of ships, making it easier to sound inshore and hazardous waters and to attack ships in anchorages. This made a major difference in the struggle against the slave trade, as slavers were fast, maneuverable, difficult to capture, and could take shelter in inshore waters. It was also necessary for the British navy, from the 1840s, to respond to the use of steamships by slavers keen to outpace the patrols.

Alongside coercion there was a more benign attempt to link steam power with abolitionism. In the 1830s Macgregor Laird, founder of the African Steamship Company, sought with the use of steamships to make the River Niger in West Africa a commercial thoroughfare for British trade, which he hoped would undermine the slave trade. This was also a theme of Sir Thomas Buxton's *The African Slave Trade and Its Remedy* (1839) and of the Society for the Extinction of the Slave Trade and the Civilisation of Africa.

The role of the British navy ensured that opposition to the slave trade would not be just a matter of diplomatic pressure. It also meant that there was a constant flow of news to help keep abolitionism at the forefront of attention in Britain. The role of the navy also demonstrated the extent to which exogenous (external) pressures were crucial to the ending as well as the end of the slave trade.

Although with only limited energy, the American navy also took part in the struggle against slavery, sometimes in cooperation with the British. This overlapped with the protection of American and international trade against privateering and piracy, and looked toward modern concepts of a benign role for American power. The combined goals led to a major American naval commitment to the Caribbean from the 1820s, with operations offshore and ashore in Cuba, Puerto Rico, Santo Domingo, and the Yucatán. In 1822 American naval activity ranged further afield, with the Webster-Ashburton Treaty of 1842 with Britain leading to a more active stance in the shape of the creation of an Africa squadron. In 1843 sailors and marines from four American warships landed on the Ivory Coast in West Africa to discourage the slave trade and to act against those who had attacked American shipping. American naval activity was handicapped by limited resources,[58] but other navies did not take a comparable role against the slave trade.

Aside from action against the trade itself, British pressure was brought to bear on African rulers to end the slave trade and instead to agree to legitimate trade.[59] This was an aspect of a more general interest in deriving benefit from inland Africa. For example, in 1812 Major General Charles Stevenson sent Robert, 2nd Earl of Liverpool, secretary for war and the colonies, a memorandum urging control of Timbuktu on the Niger River in order to dominate trade and recruit soldiers.[60] As with the continuing slave trade, pressure, however, was exerted in Africa within a context in which due allowance had to be made for the strength of its rulers and their ability to chart their own path. This was brought home in 1821 when the five-thousand-strong British Royal African Colonial Corps under Colonel Sir Charles MacCarthy, governor of Sierra Leone, was destroyed by a larger, more enthusiastic, and well-equipped Asante army. The governor's head became a war trophy and was used as a ceremonial drinking cup, a particularly lurid instance of Western failure. Mac-Carthy's replacement, Major General Charles Turner, recommended total withdrawal from the Gold Coast. Instead the British withdrew to hold only Cape Coast Castle, which had been their key position in the slave trade, and Accra.[61] Indeed in the 1810s and 1820s Egyptian expansionism in North-East Africa was more successful than its European counterpart in West Africa. Egyptian expansionism continued to be important into the 1870s, with Darfur, Equatoria, and Harrar all acquired that decade. Slave raiding and trading were important aspects of this spreading Islamic control.[62] The relatively greater success for non-Western powers repeated a long-standing pattern in Africa, one that is neglected in much of the literature. It was only, in fact, from the 1840s that European power really became more insistent on the West African coast. French imperialism was extended, with colonies established in Gabon (1842) and Ivory Coast (1843), while Spain established another, Rio Muni, the basis of the modern state of Equatorial Guinea, in 1843.

Paradoxically the slave trade was ended as the ability of Western states to project power into the African interior became stronger, prefiguring the later, very different case that Western colonialism receded after World War II, at a time when absolute Western military power reached a hitherto unprecedented level. Slavery came to an end when attitudes of racial superiority and social Darwinism were becoming more clearly articulated, which underlines the complexities of linkage and causation.

The French, for example, expanded their strength in the valley of the River Senegal from 1854, developing an effective chain of riverine forts linked by steamboats.[63] Having had their 1864 expedition wrecked by disease, the British in 1873–74 launched a successful punitive expedition against the Asante. Benefiting from superior weapons—Gatling guns, 7-pounder artillery, and breech-loading rifles, as opposed to Asante muskets—they defeated the Asante at Amoafu (1874) and burned down the Asante capital, Kumasi. The assistance of other African peoples, especially the Fante, was also important in this campaign.[64] Victory over the Asante led to the emancipation of slaves in the Gold Coast. At the same time enslavement continued elsewhere in Africa as an aspect of warfare. For example, in what is now Botswana, the expanding Ngwato kingdom conquered and enslaved the Sarwa.[65] It is easy to move from the abolition of the Western slave trade to that of slavery, but as with the demise of European imperial control in 1945–75, it is important to note that these were not simultaneous and that there were crosscurrents. In pressing for the abolition of the slave trade in 1792 and 1807, Wilberforce indeed had denied that he supported immediate emancipation. He did not believe that the slaves were yet ready, an argument prefiguring that later made by supporters of decolonization in particular colonies with reference to others. Abolitionists had hoped that the end of the slave trade would lead to greater care of the remaining slaves by their owners and to the withering of slavery.

In contrast there is a sense that the slave world was being strengthened in some respects at the same time that the slave trade was being ended. This was true not only of Mauritius in the Indian Ocean but also of the colonies of Demerara-Essequibo and Berbice on the Guiana coast of South America, seized by the British from the Dutch in 1803. Plantation agriculture, the large-scale importation of African slaves, and a switch from cotton and coffee to sugar all followed British conquest there,[66] as they did on Trinidad, seized from Spain by Britain in 1797. Thus these colonies were more like those of the late seventeenth-century West Indies than the more mature slave societies of the West Indies of the period, where a lower percentage of the slaves were African-born and where the work regime was less cruel.[67] The continued strength of slavery helped generate fresh abolitionist pressure in Britain from the mid-1820s, although it is necessary to note that this was less important politically than was successful pressure for the end of civil disabilities on Catholics and on Protestant Nonconformists. In 1823 the House of Commons passed a resolution for the gradual abolition of slavery, although it had been modified to take more note of the planters' interests. In addition the Anti-Slavery Society was founded that year. This pressure was mirrored in the West Indies by slaves keen to gain their freedom; some believed that their owners were withholding concessions granted by the Crown.

Slave owners, in turn, showed no desire to end slavery. Indeed in the early 1830s there was talk in Jamaica of secession from British rule in response to abolitionist pressure in Britain and legislation aimed at the owners' powers of discipline over their slaves. Racism remained strong in the Caribbean world. It was brutally displayed in the harsh suppression of slave rebellions, as on Barbados in 1816 (Bussa's rebellion), in Demerara in 1823, and on Jamaica in 1831–32, the Baptist War, the last in part a rebellion in response to proslavery agitation among part of the white population. This was the largest slave rising in the British West Indies.[68] There was opposition elsewhere as well. In the French colony of Martinique, there was a major rising in 1831. There were slave risings in Virginia in 1800 and 1831, Louisiana in 1811, Cuba in 1812,[69] and in South Carolina in 1822—the Denmark Vesey conspiracy, which included a plan for the seizure or destruction of Charleston. American determination to end slave flight from Georgia to Florida lay behind the Seminole Wars (1817–18, 1835–42, 1855–58), as the Seminole Indians in Florida provided refuge for escaped slaves.[70] Indeed in the second war an armistice came to an end, and Seminole resistance revived in 1837 when the Americans allowed slavers to enter Florida and seize Seminoles and blacks. In contrast, an important success for the Americans was obtained in 1838 when Major General Thomas Jesup announced that blacks who abandoned the Seminoles and joined the Americans would become free. This cost the Seminoles four hundred black fighters.

Religious zeal played an important role in slave risings in this period, for example on Jamaica and around Bahia in Brazil between 1808 and 1835: the 1835 Bahia revolt was of Muslim slaves and freedmen.[71] Opposition to slavery was also expressed in murders, flight, and suicide. Each was frequent. In part they reflected harsh conditions. In Brazil, especially but not only in the northeastern part, conditions remained hard and often violent, particularly on the sugar and coffee plantations. Food and clothing for the slaves were inadequate, and the work was remorseless, hard, and long. Death rates among slaves were high, in part due to epidemic diseases but in part due to the work regime. In addition there was a gender dimension. The conditions of work for pregnant women led to many stillbirths, while mothers lacked sufficient milk. However, underlining the variety of slave life, the 1872 census showed that 30 percent of slaves worked in towns, and conditions were better there. A more humane treatment of rural slaves began only in about 1870 when their price rose.[72] In Cuba, which like Brazil was a low-cost producer, slavery remained important to the sugar mono-culture of much of the economy, especially in western Cuba. The sugar economy depended on American investment, markets, and technology, while the British embrace of free trade helped Cuban production by ending the preferential measures that had ensured markets for sugar from Britain's colonies. Some British plantation owners indeed immigrated to Cuba.

In Britain abolitionist tactics reprised those earlier directed against the slave trade, with press agitation, public meetings, and pressure on Parliament. Concern about the plight of Christian slaves made the issue more potent, as did decreased confidence that the end of the slave trade would lead to the end of slavery. Instead of gradual improvement, pressure grew for immediate emancipation. Reports of the slave rising in Jamaica in 1831–32 and of the brutality of its suppression helped make slavery appear undesirable and redundant. The colonists clearly could not keep order.

The Whig ministry that pushed through the Great Reform Act of 1832 revising the electoral franchise to the benefit of the middle class also passed the Emancipation Act of 1833, emancipating slaves on August 1, 1834, Emancipation Day, and financially compensating slave owners. Many Whig candidates had included an antislavery platform in their electoral addresses, and Whig victories in the general elections of the early 1830s were crucial. The bill received the royal assent on August 28, 1833. Charles, 2nd Earl Grey, the prime minister, had been, as Lord Howick, foreign secretary and leader of the House of Commons when the slave trade had been abolished in 1807, and he had opened the key debate in the House of Commons on February 23, 1807. Thus emancipation was an aspect of the more general process by which the Whigs, returned to power, replayed their earlier aspirations.

Initially, as a transition, all slaves over six years old were to become apprenticed laborers, obliged to work for their former masters for forty-five hours a week: field workers for six years, and others for four. A clause, however, forbade the punishment of former slaves. In the end this interim system, which led to protests from many former slaves, was ended in August 1838. This system reflected uncertainty about the practicality of emancipation, an uncertainty seen also in the preferential tariff granted sugar imported from the British West Indies.

This was far from the end of the story as far as Britain was concerned. The already-strong opposition to the slave trade elsewhere was joined by action directed against slavery in other countries. Antislavery agitation continued after the Emancipation Act, with the British and Foreign Anti-Slavery Society founded in 1839 being particularly influential. World antislavery conventions were held in London in 1840 and 1843. In contrast the French government banned a world conference planned for Paris in 1842. For France, as for other slave societies, the economic problems that affected the British West Indies appeared to demonstrate the continued value of coerced labor. So also did the British acceptance of indentured Indians into the region. Indeed emancipation was an uneconomic risk.[73] Antislavery, moreover, was less important and popular in most of continental Europe, whether in Catholic France or the Protestant Netherlands,[74] than in Britain. In part this was due to the lack of a public politics comparable in form or content to Britain. In France the Société de la Morale Chrétienne, founded in 1821, was small, and a disproportionately high percentage of its members were Protestants, a marginal group politically. However, in the more liberal July monarchy that followed the 1830 revolution, laws were passed in 1833 ending the branding and mutilation of slaves and giving free blacks political and civil rights. Effective action against the French slave trade was taken in part also because the new government was more ready to ignore popular complaints about British pressure.

The end of slavery in the French colonies followed in 1848. This included French Africa, principally Algeria and Senegal. The British example was important in weakening French slavery, not least because it provided French slaves with new opportunities for escape to British colonies where there was no slavery. The intermixing of French and British colonies in the West Indies was significant here. The increased influence of reforming middle-class circles was important in France, but the decisive pressure came from a small group of writers and politicians, especially Victor Schoekher, who argued for immediate emancipation.

There have been efforts to ascribe abolition to slave unrest in the French colonies. This is contentious; it detracts attention from the crucial metropolitan context of decision making, not least the establishment of the Second Republic in 1848. However, major uprisings in Martinique and Guadeloupe in 1848 certainly speeded the application of emancipation. In addition the argument that revolt was a possibility had been pushed hard by French abolitionists.[75] As in Britain and Denmark, there was compensation for the slave owners.

In 1848 slavery in the Danish West Indian islands was abolished when the threat of rebellion among the slave population forced the Danish governor-general to free the slaves. Sweden had done so the previous year for its West Indian colony of St. Barthélemy, while much of formerly Spanish America abolished slavery between 1842 and 1855. Portugal followed in 1861, the Dutch (notably with their colony of Surinam) in 1863, the United States in 1865 (with the Thirteenth Amendment to the Constitution), Spain in its colonies, Puerto Rico in 1873, Cuba in 1886 (emancipation gradually began in 1870), and most importantly Brazil in 1888.

The American Civil War was crucially significant to the fate of slavery throughout the New World. The outcome of the war and the resulting fate of over four million American slaves were by no means foregone conclusions. Had the Confederacy won independence, slavery might not only have been preserved but also have expanded or been sustained both in the West Indies and in areas contiguous with the Confederacy, principally parts of Mexico. By the autumn of 1862, when Robert E. Lee launched his first invasion of the North, Napoleon III and William Gladstone were pressing Lord Palmerston to intervene and recognize the Confederacy. Especially given General George McClellan's previous performance, the Union victory at Antietam on September 17, 1862, was fortuitous and depended in part on the accidental Union discovery, just before the battle, of a copy of Lee's general orders.

Antietam led to Lincoln's Preliminary Emancipation Proclamation, which was part of the hardening of Union war goals in 1862–63 as victory over the Confederacy came to seem more distant, and conciliation was abandoned. Even then the importance of the loyal border states (Delaware, Maryland, Kentucky, and Missouri) was such that when on January 1, 1863, President Abraham Lincoln declared that Union victory in the Civil War would lead to the end of slavery, this related only to the Confederacy and not to these border states. Lincoln's proclamation had a major impact on British opinion and indirectly on slavery in Cuba and Brazil. Moreover the end of slavery in the New World made the earlier British emancipation of eight hundred thousand slaves appear brave and prescient.[76] Had it instead continued in the Confederacy, then this emancipation would have had a different significance.

Emancipation in the United States left Brazil as the leading slave society. Prior to 1888 the majority of blacks in Brazil were already free, in part because of increased manumission under the Law of the Free Womb or Rio Branco Law of 1871, which stated that all future children born to slave mothers would become free from the age of twenty-one (a clause that led to false registrations by owners), while in addition slaves were allowed to purchase their freedom. Slavery was regarded in influential circles, especially in the expanding cities, as a cause of unrest (which indeed increased in the 1880s) and a source of national embarrassment and relative backwardness. The Brasilian Society against Slavery was founded in 1880.

As part of the process by which New World settler societies were culturally dependent on the Old World, the elite looked to Europe to validate their sense of progress and were affected by the extent to which slavery was increasingly presented as an uncivilized characteristic of barbaric societies and as incompatible with civil liberty.

The British role was important here. The combination of the end of the slave trade with economic expansion meant that slavery was no longer able to supply Brazil's labor needs, including those in the traditional center of slavery, the northeastern section, and this helped make it seem anachronistic. Not only quantity but also type of labor were issues, as a growing need for artisans could not be met from the traditional Brazilian slave economy.

This was an aspect of the degree to which modernization led to the demise of slavery, not only culturally and ideologically but also for economic reasons. At the same time Western economic growth had helped provide the demand, finance, and technological innovation that kept slavery a major option. This is a reminder of the ambivalent relationship between modernization and slavery. As the role of slavery in the Brazilian economy declined, so it seemed anachronistic. As a result slave owners became increasingly isolated, with free labor becoming more important even in some plantation areas, such as São Paulo. The end of the slave trade had led to higher slave prices and a concentration of ownership,[77] and this reduced political support, a similar process to that in the American South.

In 1884 two Brazilian provinces emancipated slaves, creating free labor zones, and in 1885 all slaves over the age of sixty were freed. Furthermore increased numbers of slaves fled, many to the cities such as Rio de Janeiro, so that by 1887 there were fewer than one million slaves, only about 5 percent of the Brazilian population. There was far more support for slave flight than in the United States, with much of the populace as well as the bulk of the authorities unwilling to support the owners. This contrasted markedly with the situation in the United States, a contrast that was very important to the subsequent history of the two countries. In Brazil the slave owners were without a mass domestic constituency, and their eventual isolation was more similar to that of counterparts in the Caribbean than those in the American South.

In Brazil the military was not keen on hunting escaped slaves, while conversely, unlike in the United States, there was no serious southern separatism based on slavery. This was a key aspect of the largely nonviolent nature of Brazilian abolitionism. There was no equivalent to the situation in Cuba, where the Ten Years War of 1868–78, an unsuccessful independence struggle against Spanish rule that had seen partial abolition in rebel areas, encouraged the move for gradual abolition on the island as a whole.

Whereas in the American South there was stress on regarding white society as the people, a stress that was to encourage racial exclusion as a form and focus of southern cultural identity, in Brazil the emphasis was on a multicultural society. In Brazil the 1888 Golden Law, passed by an overwhelming majority in parliament, freed the remaining slaves, about three-quarters of a million in total, without compensation. This law helped legalize the situation caused by large-scale flight and has also been seen as an attempt to retain workers on the land.[78] The end of slavery in the Western world, however, did not completely transform labor relations, whether in Britain's colonies or in other former slave societies such as Brazil.[79] Control over labor continued. In the British colonies, as elsewhere, many former slaves were pressed into continuing to work in sugar production.[80] Legal systems were employed to limit the mobility and freedom of former slaves, for example by restricting emigration and also what was presented as vagrancy. Rents were also used to control laborers and to reduce labor costs. Resistance included strikes as well as leaving the plantations. The difficult situation for workers in the British colonies after 1838 undercuts any simple attempt to create a contrast between slavery and freedom.[81] Yet the conditions of labor for slaves and ex-slaves reflected far more than the legal situation.[82] Across the world most former slaves did not experience sweeping change in their lives, and many remained dependent in some form or other on their ex-masters or on new masters and often were treated brutally by the government and military, as in Cuba.

Furthermore, despite the abolition of the slave trade and slavery, labor continued to flow to the colonies. Former slaves tended to take up small-scale independent farming rather than work on plantations, and this helped lead to demands for fresh labor in the colonies. Meanwhile the very flexibility of economic service and subjugation ensured the continuation of systems of labor control and these encompassed labor flows. The same was true of Russia, where in 1861 Tsar Alexander II emancipated the serfs.

In place of slaves the British West Indies, especially Trinidad, British Guiana, and other colonies, received plentiful cheap Indian indentured labor.[83] Critics claimed that the indentured labor systems, which were also employed in Mauritius, Surinam, Cuba, and the French Caribbean, represented the continuation of the slave trade in its latter stages, not least due to the coercive character of these systems. In the Pacific the kidnap of islanders for slave labor involved brutality and killing, leading in 1872 to the Pacific Islanders' Protection (Kidnapping) Act.[84] In the United States in 1865 the Thirteenth Amendment to the Constitution led to the freeing of about four million slaves, but the Reconstruction Acts of 1867, which dissolved the southern state governments and reintroduced federal control, were not sustained. Federal troops were withdrawn from the South in 1877; the black militias recruited by Radical Republican state governments lost control or were disbanded; and the blacks in the South were very much left as second-class citizens, a situation that persisted until the 1950s and 1960s.

The end of the transatlantic slave trade also led to the development of plantation economies in parts of Atlantic Africa, particularly Angola. This represented a response to labor availability in Africa but also a shift in the terms of Western trade with Africa away from a willingness to pay for labor in the shape of slaves and toward paying for it in the form of products. There continued indeed to be multiple overlaps between servitude and trade in the Atlantic African economy.

In West Africa the end of the slave trade hit those kingdoms that had derived wealth from it, although the slave trade increased in East Africa, seriously affecting much of the interior of the continent. Indeed the Mahdi's support in Sudan owed much to backing from slave traders opposed to measures seeking to combat the trade, notably those by Charles Gordon, governor of Equatoria (1873–76) and governor-general of the Sudan (1876–80).[85] The Arab penetration of sub-Saharan Africa increased. For example, links with the kingdom of Buganda in modern Uganda developed from 1844, and it became a major exporter of slaves, a process eased by the importance of slavery for internal purposes, including public works.

The increase in the slave trade in East Africa reflected the slave-based plantation systems that developed on Africa's Indian Ocean coast, producing, for example, cloves, the export of which boomed in the 1810s–40s. Furthermore the export of slaves to the Islamic world, for example, Arabia, continued. Kilwa was the leading port in East Africa with a major trade from there to the Persian Gulf, much of it handled by Omani merchants. Their profits helped finance economic activity, which in turn produced needs for slave labor. Slaves to Arabia, in contrast, were moved relatively short distances, particularly from the Red Sea ports of Suakin and Massawa, which were fed by slave trading into Sudan and Ethiopia.

Slave labor in East Africa was largely, as in the New World, plantation labor, but the situation was different in Arabia and the Persian Gulf region. This serves as a reminder of the complexities and variations of the economics of slavery as well as the variety of slave conditions and therefore of the slave experience. Slaves in Arabia and the Persian Gulf were used for many activities, but there was no dominance by large-scale institutions of the plantation type, although slaves were used for date plantations for Oman. Instead slaves were a mobile-labor force appropriate to different needs.

As slaving was largely brought to an end in the Atlantic in the 1860s, so the British struggle against it in East African waters became more prominent, with the Cape Squadron being assigned to the task and merging in 1864 with the East Indies Squadron. The struggle with Arab slavers was presented in a heroic light and fully covered in British newspapers and other publications. Slaves of Indian traders in East Africa were confiscated by the British consul in 1860 as the traders were British subjects. Empire thus served as a way to enforce British norms.

Opposition to slavery was not restricted to the oceans but also encouraged moral activism toward Africa, especially hostility to the slave trade in Central and East Africa. This had a number of consequences, including the development of a British presence in Zanzibar[86] and a strengthening of the determination to blaze the trail for Christian grace and morality, seen for example in the actions of and response to David Livingstone, who helped secure British pressure to persuade the sultan of Zanzibar to outlaw the slave trade in 1873. HMS *London,* an old ship of the line, was sent to Zanzibar to enforce this, and the acquisition of Zanzibar as a protectorate from Germany in 1890, in exchange for the island of Heligoland in the North Sea, led to the end of the trade. Similarly French conquest of Madagascar was followed by the abolition of slavery there in 1896.

In Africa the treatment of slaves held within native society became more problematic as the Europeans became colonial rulers across most of the Continent. The Europeans were committed to abolition as part of the civilizing mission used to justify imperialism as progressive. This was underlined by the Congress of Berlin in 1885 and by the antislavery conference at Brussels in 1889. This mission, however, risked offending local vested interests that were seen as crucial to the stability of imperial control, for example that of the British in northern Nigeria, where they established a protectorate in 1900. There were also concerns about the economic impact of abolition. Nevertheless slavery was largely ended, by colonial policy and thanks to the slaves' attempts to seek advantage from their changing environment. The continuation of slave raiding was in 1902 a pretext for war with the Sokoto caliphate in northern Nigeria. Slave survivals continued and are a subject of current concern, notably about the situation in Sudan, but the scale of the problem has been transformed.

The central theme in this essay has been Western activism. Other narratives and analyses are certainly possible, notably black resistance. But the focus here is on Western action, and that opens up debates about intentionality. The stress here is on an ideological approach. Moreover this contrasts with the different attitude within the Islamic world of the nineteenth century. That may not be a conclusion that suits modern ideological suppositions and commitments, but that is not the purpose of this essay.

NOTES

1. I have benefited greatly from the comments of David Brion Davis, Keith Hamilton, David Northrup, Thomas Otte, and three anonymous readers on an earlier draft. I also profited from the opportunity to speak on the subject at Burgh House (Hampstead Museum) in October 2007.

2. It should be noted, however, that although the mixed commission courts, which were responsible for adjudicating on the fate of captured slave ships, were established on the basis of bilateral agreements, they were undoubtedly institutional. Moreover insofar as British appointees could serve conterminously on several such courts—for example in Freetown, Sierra Leone—the courts might also be said to have had a multilateral element. Some American legal historians now regard the mixed commission courts as the first human rights courts. While the courts were concerned with ships rather than individuals, thousands of people were liberated.

3. John Fonte, "Liberal Democracy vs. Transnational Progressivism: The Ideological War within the West," *Orbis* 46 (Summer 2002): 449–67.

4. Joshua Kurlantzick, *Charm Offensive: How China's Soft Power Is Transforming the World* (New Haven, Conn.: Yale University Press, 2007).

5. Erik Gøbel, "The Danish Edict of 16th March 1792 to Abolish the Slave Trade," in *Orbis et orbem: Liber amicorum Jan Everaert,* edited by Jan Parmentier and Sander Spanoghe (Ghent: Academia Press, 2001), 251–63. More generally see David Eltis and James Walvin, eds., *The Abolition of the Atlantic Slave Trade: Origins and Effects in Europe, Africa, and the Americas* (Madison: University of Wisconsin Press, 1981).

6. Angelie Sens, "Dutch Debates on Overseas Man and His World, 1770–1820," in *Colonial Empires Compared: Britain and the Netherlands, 1750–1850,* edited by Bob Moore and Henk van Nierop (Hampshire, U.K.: Ashgate, 2003), 86–87.

7. P. J. Marshall, *The Making and Unmaking of Empires: Britain, India, and America, c. 1750–1783* (Oxford: Oxford University Press, 2005), 195.

8. Malachy Postlethwayt, *Universal Dictionary,* 4th ed., 2 vols. (London: W. Strahan et al., 1774), 1:n.p., entry for Africa.

9. Todd Gray, *Devon and the Slave Trade: Documents on African Enslavement, Abolition and Emancipation from 1562 to 1867* (Exeter, U.K.: Mint Press, 2007), 166–68. For the situation in Scotland, see Iain Whyte, *Scotland and the Abolition of Black Slavery, 1756–1838* (Edinburgh: Edinburgh University Press, 2006).

10. Library of Congress, Washington, D.C., British Caricature Collection, 2–575.

11. R. E. Close, "Toleration and Its Limits in the Late Hanoverian Empire: The Cape Colony 1795–1828," in *Hanoverian Britain and Empire,* edited by Stephen Taylor, Richard Connors, and Clyve Jones (Rochester, N.Y.: Boydell, 1998), 303.

12. Marcel Dorigny and Bernard Gainot, *La Société des Amis des Noirs, 1788–1799: Contributions à l'histoire de l'abolition de l'esclavage* (Paris: UNESCO, 1998).

13. *Archives parlementaires de 1787 à 1860: Recueil complet des débats législatifs et politiques des chambers françaises,* 127 vols. (Paris: Dupont, 1879–1913), 37:152.

14. David Geggus, "Racial Equality, Slavery and Colonial Secession during the Constituent Assembly," *American Historical Review* 94 (December 1989): 1290–1308; Jennifer J. Pierce, "The Struggle for Black Liberty: Revolution and Emancipation in Saint Domingue," in *Selected Papers of the Consortium on Revolutionary Europe, 1997,* 168–79.

15. Carolyn E. Fink, *The Making of Haiti: The Saint Domingue Revolution from Below* (Knoxville: University of Tennessee Press, 1990).

16. Roger Norman Buckley, *Slaves in Red Coats: The British West India Regiments, 1795–1815* (New Haven, Conn.: Yale University Press, 1979).

17. Philippe R. Girard, "Liberté, Égalité, Esclavage: French Revolutionary Ideals and the Failure of the Leclerc Expedition to Saint-Domingue," *French Colonial History* 6 (2005): 67–68.

18. Bernard Marshall, "Slave Resistance and White Reaction in the British Windward Islands, 1763–1833," *Caribbean Quarterly* 28, no. 3 (1982): 39–40.

19. Jacques Adélaïde-Merlande, René Bélénus, and Frédéric Régent, *La Rébellion de la Guadeloupe, 1801–1802* (Gourbeyre: Société d'Histoire de la Guadeloupe, 2002).

20. Kenneth R. Maxwell, *Conflicts and Conspiracies: Brazil and Portugal, 1750–1808* (Cambridge: Cambridge University Press, 1973), 222.

21. Adam Hochschild, *Bury the Chains: Prophets and Rebels in the Fight to Free an Empire's Slaves* (Boston: Houghton Mifflin, 2005).

22. Eric Williams, *Capitalism and Slavery* (Chapel Hill: University of North Carolina Press, 1944).

23. Selwyn H. H. Carrington, *The Sugar Industry and the Abolition of the Slave Trade, 1775–1810* (Gainesville: University of Florida Press, 2002).

24. Seymour Drescher, *Econocide: British Slavery in the Era of Abolition* (Pittsburgh: University of Pittsburgh Press, 1977).

25. John R. Ward, *British West Indian Slavery, 1750–1834: The Process of Amelioration* (Oxford: Clarendon Press, 1988).

26. Roger Anstey, "Capitalism and Slavery: A Critique," *Economic History Review,* 2nd ser., 21, no. 2 (1968): 320.

27. Seymour Drescher, "Whose Abolition? Popular Pressure and the Ending of the British Slave Trade," *Past and Present* 143 (May 1994): 136–66, esp. 165–66.

28. Karl Jacoby, "Slaves by Nature? Domestic Animals and Human Slaves," *Slavery and Abolition* 15 (April 1994): 96–97.

29. William Hutton to Robert, Viscount Castlereagh, September 11, 1812. This letter survives in the papers of Henry, 3rd Earl Bathurst, Secretary of State for War and the Colonies, British Library, Department of Manuscripts, Loan 57, vol. 21, no. 100.

30. Stephen Farrell, Melanie Unwin, and James Walvin, eds., *The British Slave Trade: Abolition, Parliament and People,* special issue of *Parliamentary History* (Edinburgh: Edinburgh University Press, 2007).

31. Ann M. Burton, "British Evangelicals, Economic Warfare and the Abolition of the Atlantic Slave Trade, 1794–1810," *Anglican and Episcopal History* 65 (1996): 197–225, esp. 223.

32. C. J. Bartlett and Gene A. Smith, "A 'Species of Milito-Nautico-Guerrilla-Plundering Warfare': Admiral Alexander Cochrane's Naval Campaign against the United States, 1814–1815," in *Britain and America Go to War: The Impact of War and Warfare in Anglo-America, 1754–1815,* edited by Julie Flavell and Stephen Conway (Gainesville: University of Florida Press, 2004), 187–90; John Harriott to Henry, Viscount Sidmouth, May 7, 1814, Exeter, Devon Record Office, Sidmouth papers, 152M/C1814/OF13. See also 152M/C1813/OF3 and London, National Archives, War Office papers 1/141, pp. 63–67.

33. Foreign and Commonwealth Office Historians, History Note number 17, *Slavery in Diplomacy: The Foreign Office and the Suppression of the Transatlantic Slave Trade* (London: Foreign and Commonwealth Office, 2007), 11.

34. David Eltis, "The British Contribution to the Nineteenth-Century Transatlantic Slave Trade," *Economic History Review,* 2nd ser., 32, no. 2 (1979): 211–27.

35. Lawrence C. Jennings, "French Policy towards Trading with African and Brazilian Slave Merchants," *Journal of African History* 17, no. 4 (1976): 515–28; Joseph C. Dorsey, *Slave Traffic in the Age of Abolition: Puerto Rico, West Africa, and the Non-Hispanic Caribbean, 1815–1859* (Gainesville: University of Florida Press, 2003).

36. Julian Cobbing, "The Mfecane as Alibi: Thoughts on Dithakong and Mbolompo," *Journal of African History* 29, no. 3 (1998): 487–519.

37. For example, see J. D. Omer-Cooper, "Has the Mfecane a Future? A Response to the Cobbing Critique," *Journal of Southern African Studies* 19, no. 2 (June 1993): 273–94.

38. Elizabeth A. Eldredge, "Sources of Conflict in Southern Africa, *c.* 1800–1830: The 'Mfecane' Reconsidered," *Journal of African History* 33, no. 1 (1992): 1–35, esp. 34–35.

39. Herbert S. Klein and Stanley L. Engerman, "Shipping Patterns and Mortality in the African Slave Trade to Rio de Janeiro, 1825–1830," *Cahiers d'études africaines* 15, no. 59 (1975): 385–87.

40. Kenneth Onwuka Dike, *Trade and Politics in the Niger Delta, 1830–1885: An Introduction to the Economic and Political History of Nigeria* (Oxford: Clarendon Press, 1956), 68–69.

41. Kwame Arhin, "The Structure of Greater Ashanti (1700–1824)," *Journal of African History* 8, no. 1 (1967): 65–85; Kwame Arhin, "The Financing of Ashanti Expansion, 1700–1820," *Africa* 37, no. 3 (1967): 283–91.

42. David Ross, "Mid–Nineteenth Century Dahomey: Recent Views vs. Contemporary Evidence," *History in Africa* 12 (1985): 307–23.

43. Gwyn Campbell, "Madagascar and the Slave Trade, 1810–1895," *Journal of African History* 22, no. 2 (1981): 203–27; Gwyn Campbell, "The East African Slave Trade, 1861–1895: The 'Southern Complex,'" *International Journal of African Historical Studies* 22, no. 1 (1989): 1–26.

44. M. Mason, 'The *Jihad* in the South: An Outline of the Nineteenth-Century Nupe Hegemony in North-Eastern Yorubaland and Afenmai," *Journal of the Historical Society of Nigeria* 5, no. 2 (1970): 193–209; Rex S. O'Fahey, "Slavery and the Slave Trade in Darfur," *Journal of African History* 14, no. 1 (1973): 29–43.

45. C. A. Bayly, *The Birth of the Modern World 1780–1914: Global Connections and Comparisons* (Oxford: Blackwell, 2004), 404–5.

46. Dorsey, *Slave Traffic in the Age of Abolition.*

47. Michael Tadman, *Speculators and Slaves: Masters, Traders, and Slaves in the Old South* (Madison: University of Wisconsin Press, 1996); Walter Johnson, *Soul by Soul: Life inside the Antebellum Slave Market* (Cambridge, Mass.: Harvard University Press, 1999); Jonathan D. Martin, *Divided Mastery: Slave Hiring in the American South* (Cambridge, Mass.: Harvard University Press, 2004).

48. Charles O. Paullin, *Atlas of the Historical Geography of the United States* (Washington, D.C.: Carnegie Institution, 1932); Donald B. Dodd, *Historical Atlas of Alabama* (Tuscaloosa: University of Alabama Press, 1974); Raymond D. Gastil, *Culture Regions of the United States* (Seattle: University of Washington Press, 1975).

49. Marcel Dorigny and Bernard Gainot, *Atlas des Esclavages: Traites, sociétés coloniales, abolitions de l'Antiquité à nos jours* (Paris: Éditions Autrement, 2006), 64–65.

50. William Law Mathieson, *Great Britain and the Slave Trade, 1839–65* (London: Longmans, 1929).

51. Robert Edgar Conrad, *World of Sorrow: The African Slave Trade to Brazil* (Baton Rouge: Louisiana State University Press, 1986).

52. Leslie Bethell, *The Abolition of the Brazilian Slave Trade* (Cambridge: Cambridge University Press, 1970).

53. Arthur F. Corwin, *Spain and the Abolition of Slavery in Cuba, 1817–1886* (Austin: University of Texas Press, 1967); David R. Murray, *Odious Commerce: Britain, Spain and the Abolition of the Cuban Slave Trade* (Cambridge: Cambridge University Press, 1980).

54. Christine Kinealy, "The Liberator: Daniel O'Connell and Anti-Slavery," *History Today* 57, no. 12 (December 2007): 51–57.

55. Paul Michael Kielstra, *The Politics of Slave Trade Suppression in Britain and France, 1814–48: Diplomacy, Morality and Economics* (New York: Palgrave, 2000).

56. C. Northcote Parkinson, *Edward Pellew, Viscount Exmouth, Admiral of the Red* (London: Methuen, 1934), 419–72.

57. David Northrup, "The Compatibility of the Slave and Palm Oil Trades in the Bight of Biafra," *Journal of African History* 17, no. 3 (1976): 357.

58. Donald L. Canney, *Africa Squadron: The U.S. Navy and the Slave Trade, 1842–1861* (Dulles, Va.: Potomac Books, 2006); C. Herbert Gilliland, *Voyage to a Thousand Cares: Master's Mate Lawrence with the African Squadron, 1844–1846* (Annapolis, Md.: Naval Institute Press, 2004).

59. A. Adu Boahen, *Britain, the Sahara and the Western Sudan, 1788–1861* (Oxford: Oxford University Press, 1964).

60. Maj. Gen. Charles Stevenson to Robert, 2nd Earl of Liverpool, February 1, 1812, Exeter, Devon County Record Office, 152H/C1812/OF27.

61. Neville Thompson, *Earl Bathurst and the British Empire* (Barnsley: Leo Cooper, 1999), 167–68.

62. Janet J. Ewald, *Soldiers, Traders and Slaves: State Formation and Economic Transformation in the Greater Nile Valley, 1700–1885* (Madison: University of Wisconsin Press, 1990).

63. David W. Robinson, *The Holy War of Umar Tal: The Western Sudan in the Mid–Nineteenth Century* (Oxford: Clarendon Press, 1985), 330.

64. Ivor Wilks, *Asante in the Nineteenth Century* (Cambridge: Cambridge University Press, 1975).

65. Michael Crowder and Suzanne Miers, "The Politics of Slavery in Bechuanaland: Power Struggles and the Plight of the Basarwa in the Bamangwato Reserve, 1926–1940," in *The End of Slavery in Africa,* edited by Suzanne Miers and Richard Roberts (Madison: University of Wisconsin Press, 1988), 175–76.

66. John Lean and Trevor Burnard, "Hearing Slave Voices: The Fiscal's Reports of Berbice and Demerara-Essequebo," *Archives* 27, no. 106 (2002): 122.

67. Anthony J. Barker, *Slavery and Antislavery in Mauritius, 1810–33: The Conflict between Economic Expansion and Humanitarian Reform under British Rule* (London: St. Martin's Press, 1996); B. W. Higman, *Slave Populations of the British Caribbean, 1807–1834* (Baltimore: Johns Hopkins University Press, 1984).

68. Mary Turner, *Slaves and Missionaries: The Disintegration of Jamaican Slave Society, 1787–1834* (Urbana: University of Illinois Press, 1982); Emilia Viotti daCosta, *Crowns of Glory, Tears of Blood:. The Demerara Slave Rebellion of 1823* (New York: Oxford University Press, 1994).

69. Matt D. Childs, *The 1812 Aponte Rebellion in Cuba and the Struggle against Atlantic Slavery* (Chapel Hill: University of North Carolina Press, 2006).

70. John D. Milligan, "Slave Rebelliousness and the Florida Maroon," *Prologue* 6, no. 1 (Spring 1974): 4–18.

71. João José Reis, *Slave Rebellion in Brazil: The Muslim Uprising of 1835 in Bahia* (Baltimore: Johns Hopkins University Press, 1993).

72. Mary C. Karasch, *Slave Life in Rio de Janeiro, 1808–1850* (Princeton, N.J.: Princeton University Press, 1987); Bert J. Barickman, *A Bahian Counterpoint: Sugar, Tobacco, Cassava, and Slavery in the Recôncavo, 1780–1860* (Stanford, Calif.: Stanford University Press, 1998).

73. Seymour Drescher, *The Mighty Experiment: Free Labor versus Slavery in British Emancipation* (New York: Oxford University Press, 2002).

74. Seymour Drescher, *From Slavery to Freedom: Comparative Studies in the Rise and Fall of Atlantic Slavery* (New York: New York University Press, 1999).

75. Laurent Dubois, "The Road to 1848: Interpreting French Anti-Slavery," *Slavery and Abolition* 22, no. 3 (2001): 150–57.

76. David Brion Davis, "Slavery, Emancipation, and Progress," *Historically Speaking* 8 (July/August 2007): 14.

77. Seymour Drescher, "Brazilian Abolition in Comparative Perspective," *Hispanic American Historical Review* 68 (August 1988): 433.

78. Robert Brent Toplin, *The Abolition of Slavery in Brazil* (New York: McClelland and Stewart, 1972); Robert Edgar Conrad, *The Destruction of Brazilian Slavery, 1850–1888* (Berkeley: University of California Press, 1972); Philip A. Howard, *Changing History: Afro-Cuban Cabildos and Societies of Color in the Nineteenth Century* (Baton Rouge: Louisiana State University Press, 1998).

79. Suzanne Miers, *Slavery in the Twentieth Century: The Evolution of a Global Problem* (Walnut Creek, Calif.: AltaMira Press, 2003).

80. O. Nigel Bolland, "Systems of Domination after Slavery: The Control of Land and Labor in the British West Indies after 1838," *Comparative Studies in Society and History* 23, no. 4 (1981): 591–619, esp. 612–17.

81. Willemina Kloosterboer, *Involuntary Labour since the Abolition of Slavery* (Leiden: E. J. Brill, 1960); David Eltis, ed., *Coerced and Free Migration: Global Perspectives* (Stanford, Calif.: Stanford University Press, 2002).

82. Philip D. Morgan, "Work and Culture: The Task System and the World of Low-Country Blacks, 1700 to 1880," *William and Mary Quarterly*, 3rd ser., 39 (1982): 563–99.

83. Madhavi Kale, *Fragments of Empire: Capital, Slavery and Indian Indentured Labor Migration in the British Caribbean* (Philadelphia: University of Pennsylvania Press, 1998).

84. Jennifer M. T. Carter, *Painting the Islands Vermilion: Archibald Watson and the Brig Carl* (Melbourne: Melbourne University Press, 1999).

85. Abdul Sheriff, *Slaves, Spices and Ivory in Zanzibar* (London: James Currey, 1987); Thomas Ricks, "Slaves and Slave Traders in the Persian Gulf, 18th and 19th Centuries: An Assessment," in *The Economics of the Indian Ocean Slave Trade in the Nineteenth Century*, edited by William Gervase Clarence-Smith (London: Frank Cass, 1989), 60–70; Alice Moore-Harell, "Economic and Political Aspects of the Slave Trade in Ethiopia and the Sudan in the Second Half of the Nineteenth Century," *International Journal of African Historical Studies* 32, no. 2/3 (1999): 407–21.

86. Reginald Coupland, *The Exploitation of East Africa, 1856–90: The Slave Trade and the Scramble* (London: Faber and Faber, 1939).

Popular Evangelicalism and the Shaping of British Moral Sensibilities, 1770–1840

David Hempton

H istorians, unlike scientists in a laboratory, cannot easily isolate variables or test hypotheses in a perfectly controlled environment. The past, even what we can know of it, is messy, eclectic, and replete with unintended consequences. The problem with historians, however much we may deny it, is that we enter the past through the wardrobe of the predetermined questions we wish to answer. Nowhere is this more obvious than when we attempt to map changes of sensibility—the most difficult historical mapping of all—such as those associated with the rise of antislavery and abolitionist sentiment. Even when the problem is reduced to one national tradition in a defined period, the range of possible explanations, as the luxuriant historiography on slavery attests, is extensive. Over the course of writing on British abolitionism historians have variously emphasized the role of heroic individuals (often motivated by serious religious convictions), changes in economic conditions and perceptions, the political calculations of the governing classes, the unanticipated coalescence of unlikely circumstances, and subtle shifts in cultural sensibilities.[1] Those changes in cultural sensibilities have in turn been explored through the additional lenses of gender, race, religion, identity, and economic theory. However subtle and well informed these approaches may be, the primary question at issue, namely how to explain both the extent and the limits of antislavery sentiment, forces an unavoidable narrowing of one's gaze to the issue of slavery itself.

However, to begin to understand the emergence of antislavery activity, a birdlike peripheral vision, beyond the single issue of slavery itself, is not only desirable but also essential. In the British Isles between 1770 and 1840 a large number of interlocking changes were taking place, of which the rise of antislavery sentiment is only one. Ultimately there is no easy solution to the problem posed by our predisposition toward singularity of vision, but one approach, and the one chosen here, is to look at the political *ecology* of one of the most important antislavery constituencies, namely popular evangelicalism. Within that broad constituency there is general agreement among historians that by the early 1830s the Methodists played a particularly significant role. According to recent calculations, during the high water mark of petitioning against slavery in 1832–33, Methodists accounted for about 80 percent of all Nonconformist signatures and over 95 percent of all Wesleyan Methodists signed petitions. This proportion was the highest by far of any English religious denomination.[2] How then can one account for the superficially startling fact that a small religious society that started within the old High Church wing of the Established Church, and whose founder and leader largely eschewed political activism, became by the 1830s such a significant backbone of the popular antislavery movement?[3]

The approach pursued in this essay is analogous to that adopted by systems biologists who seek to understand the remarkably complex behavior of individual cells as they interact with the even more complex systems of cells within which they are located. To use less scientific language, my intent is to try to account for the rise of Methodist antislavery sentiment within the broader context of Methodist organizational development and stance toward the wider world, while paying attention to what was happening in that wider world.[4] More particularly the essay will try to show the complex way in which theological work done by one person, John Wesley, ended up having large-scale historical impact over time through the reproduction of ideas in the lives of religious organizations and their adherents. The approach taken here, however, is anything but a version of theological or ideological determinism that assumes, sometimes consciously and sometimes unconsciously, that there is an unrefracted ray passing from the theology to the praxis of religious organizations. As historians know only too well, social contexts change and complexify individual and organizational behavior. A second aim of this essay is to show that a better understanding of how the singular Methodist antislavery cell functions in the antislavery movement sheds light on how the whole ecological system worked in the crucial years from 1770 to 1840 when both Methodist membership *and* antislavery sentiment grew exponentially, often in the same locations. Perhaps the best place to start is in the decade of the 1770s with the writings on public affairs of the Methodist founder, John Wesley.

In the 1770s John Wesley, who mostly urged his followers to avoid political issues, published a range of opinions on controversial issues that helped chart the political course for his followers over the next half century and beyond. In 1772 he published *Thoughts upon Liberty,* in which he criticized John Wilkes and metropolitan radicalism; in 1773 he published *Thoughts on the Scarcity of Provisions,* a vigorous attack on the greed and waste of the rich; in 1774 he published *Thoughts upon Slavery,* an attack on slavery based heavily on the work of the Quaker abolitionist Anthony Benezet; in 1775 he published his *Thoughts on the American Colonies,* which was largely plagiarized from Samuel Johnson and therefore shared his view about the inappropriateness of the American cause; and in 1780 he wrote *A Letter to the Printer of the 'Public Advertiser' Occasioned by the Late Act Passed in Favour of Popery,* in which he defended a publication of Lord George Gordon's Protestant Association against Savile's Relief Act of 1778.[5] Throughout the decade Wesley, as an elderly man who suffered bouts of serious illness, was also preoccupied about securing the future of Methodism by protecting its distinctive connectional structure and itinerant ministry. In a nutshell, Wesley set the Methodist political compass to point to antiradicalism, antimaterialism, antislavery, anti-Catholicism, anticorruption, and anti-Socinianism, all laced with a strong emphasis on Methodism's need to establish itself as a religious movement independent of outside coercion from church and state. He wanted more toleration for his own movement and less political freedoms for others, especially Roman Catholics; he enjoined obedience to the established order but hated the theatrical materialism of the rich at the top of English society; and he opposed slavery but spoke against the wider political mobilization of his movement lest it become deflected from its religious mission. Above all he wanted to spread scriptural holiness across the land—and to other lands for that matter—without the restrictions of governments, churches, or officials. With that background in mind it is time to turn to Methodist antislavery sentiment as part of a wider ecology of popular evangelical political sensibilities in the late eighteenth and early nineteenth centuries.

Methodism's antislavery trajectory, while relatively easy to chart, is more difficult to interpret.[6] The story probably begins with the visit of the Wesley brothers to Georgia and parts of South Carolina in the 1730s as agents of the Anglican Society for Propagating the Gospel. In their respective journals of the period, Charles is more generally forthcoming about the inhumanities of slavery than John, who, though not disengaged from the sufferings of the slaves, is usually more concerned about their education and spiritual condition than their privations as slaves. By contrast Charles's journal entry for August 2, 1736, when both brothers visited Charleston, is a litany of eyewitness accounts of grim abuses: "It was endless to recount all the shocking instances of diabolical cruelty which these men (as they call themselves) daily practice upon their fellow-creatures; and that on the most trivial of occasions." He recorded one instance of a woman beaten unconscious, revived, and then beaten again before having hot candle wax poured on her skin, all for the great offense of overfilling a teacup.[7] As is well known, the Wesley brothers returned from Georgia in some disarray, and the issue of slavery, though not entirely absent from the Wesleyan corpus, especially when related to Methodist expansion in the Caribbean Islands, makes only episodic appearances over the course of the next thirty-six years.

That changed in 1772, however, when John Wesley came under the influence of the antislavery activists Granville Sharp and Anthony Benezet. Perhaps stimulated by the publicity surrounding Somersett's Case[8] and Sharp's own writings against slavery, Wesley received from Sharp a tract written by Benezet (probably *Some Historical Account of Guinea,* published in 1771). A triangular correspondence then ensued between Sharp, Benezet, and Wesley and resulted in Wesley's own antislavery tract, *Thoughts upon Slavery,* published early in 1774.[9] As was typical of Wesley, he borrowed shamelessly from Benezet's work, but less typical were the grounds upon which

Wesley repudiated slavery. Although he wrote against the conventional economic arguments for slavery, the crux of his case was that slavery was indefensibly cruel and barbaric and was therefore quite apart from any religious argument, a moral offense against natural rights, natural justice, and natural law. After outlining the iniquities of the slave trade and the cruelties of plantation agriculture Wesley got to the center of his argument:

> IV. 1. This is the plain, unaggravated matter of fact. Such is the manner wherein our African slaves are procured; such the manner wherein they are removed from their native land, and wherein they are treated in our plantations. I would now inquire, whether these things can be defended, on the principles of even heathen honesty; whether they can be reconciled (setting the Bible out of the question) with any degree of either justice or mercy.
>
> 2. The grand plea is, "They are authorized by law." But can law, human law, change the nature of things? Can it turn darkness into light, or evil into good? By no means. Notwithstanding ten thousand laws, right is right, and wrong is wrong still. There must still remain an essential difference between justice and injustice, cruelty and mercy. So that I still ask, Who can reconcile this treatment of the Negroes, first and last, with either mercy or justice?
>
> Where is the justice of inflicting the severest evils on those that have done us no wrong? of depriving those that never injured us in word or deed, of every comfort of life? of tearing them from their native country, and depriving them of liberty itself, to which an Angolan has the same natural right as an Englishman, and on which he sets as high a value? Yea, where is the justice of taking away the lives of innocent, inoffensive men; murdering thousands of them in their own land, by the hands of their own countrymen; many thousands, year after year, on shipboard, and then casting them like dung into the sea; and tens of thousands in that cruel slavery to which they are so unjustly reduced?
>
> 3. But waving, for the present, all other considerations, I strike at the root of this complicated villany; I absolutely deny all slave-holding to be consistent with any degree of natural justice. If, therefore, you have any regard to justice, (to say nothing of mercy, nor the revealed law of God,) render unto all their due. Give liberty to whom liberty is due, that is, to every child of man, to every partaker of human nature. Let none serve you but by his own act and deed, by his own voluntary choice. Away with all whips, all chains, all compulsion! Be gentle toward all men; and see that you invariably do unto every one as you would he should do unto you.[10]

Wesley's repudiation of slavery on grounds of natural rights contrasts with his rejection of such arguments as applied to the claims for greater political representation by English radicals. The reason for Wesley's differential advocacy of natural rights, of course, lay in his belief that the freeborn Englishman was already free and not subject to the whims of masters, while African slaves were patently not. Wesley's pamphlet went to at least four editions in the British Isles within a year and was circulated to every Methodist society in the country. There were also at least thirteen American editions. As was the way in Wesleyan Methodism, the master had spoken. Antislavery was now the official default position of the Methodist movement throughout the British Isles, the Caribbean Islands, and North America.

Having declared his hand, Wesley did not let up on his criticism of slavery. In 1775 he published his *Calm Address to Our American Colonies,* accusing the Americans of hypocrisy in their squeals for liberty while they oppressed black slaves; in 1776 he published *A Seasonable Address to the More Serious Part of the Inhabitants of Great Britain,* in which he called the slave trade "a trade of blood, and has stained our land with blood"; and in 1778 he published a *Serious Address to the People of England, with Regard to the State of the Nation,* in which he described the slave trade as the greatest reproach in England's history. Wesley's antislavery views were also embraced by the first generation of preachers sent to North America, including Thomas Rankin, Francis Asbury, and Thomas Coke.[11]

In the same decade when Wesley was waxing eloquently on behalf of slaves, he was also waxing equally eloquently against the political claims of English radicals and Roman Catholics. He was not alone among English evangelicals to take these views. Hannah More, whose influential poem on slavery was reprinted in the *Arminian* magazine, authored the anti-Catholic squib *Bishop Bonner's Ghost,* in which she brought together the freedoms enunciated by the Protestant Reformation and the abolition of the slave trade. The poem is an inverted satire cast in the voice of Bishop Bonner's ghost and is signed "A Good Old Papist, Ann. Dom. 1900." Bonner's ghost laments the moral light, the spread of knowledge, and the empowerment of the laity ushered in by the dangerous heresies of the Reformation. The imaginary words are spoken to the evangelical bishop Beilby Porteus, the bishop of London (1787–1809) and one of Anglicanism's few outspoken abolitionists. The theme is Porteus's concern for physical and spiritual liberty against the enforced bondage of Roman Catholics and slave traders. Here are the last four stanzas of the poem in which Hannah More casts herself as a prophetic ventriloquist putting words into the mouth of Bonner's ghost, c. 1900:

> But tortur'd memory vainly speaks
> The projects we design'd;
> While this apostate Bishop [Porteus] seeks
> The freedom of mankind
>
> O, born in ev'ry thing to shake
> The systems planned by me!

So heterodox, that he would make
Both soul and body free

Nor clime, nor colour stays his hand;
With charity deprav'd,
He would from Thames' to Gambia's Strand,
Have all be free and sav'd.

And who shall change his wayward heart,
His wilful spirit turn?
For those his labours can't convert
His weakness will not burn.[12]

In keeping with the sardonic tone of the poem, More attached a short explanatory paragraph, still speaking through the mouthpiece of Bonner's ghost: "By the lapse of time the three last stanzas are become unintelligible. Old Chronicles say, that towards the latter end of the 18th century, a bill was brought into the British Parliament by an active young Reformer, for the Abolition of a *pretended* Traffic of the Human Species. But this only shows how little faith is to be given to the exaggerations of History; for as no vestige of this incredible Trade now remains, we look upon the whole story to have been one of those fictions, not uncommon among Authors, to blacken the memory of former ages."

Bishop Bonner's Ghost is in effect an inverted English progress narrative written in popular poetic form and celebrating the Protestant Reformation, the dissemination of print, the end of the Roman Catholic system of thraldom and financial exactions, the demise of priestly celibacy, and the abolition of the slave trade and slavery itself. The common refrains are freedom of body, mind, and spirit and the salvation of the soul. In this way More embraced the rhetorically affluent, if logically absurd, position of portraying slavery as a species of Roman Catholicism. An indication of how seriously Hannah More applied the anti-Catholic side of her narrative of English historical development can be seen in the charitable donations she made in her will. She gave five hundred pounds to the Anti-Slavery Society and more than twice that amount to an array of societies designed to convert Roman Catholic Ireland to Evangelical Protestantism.[13] Even though Hannah More's circle of high-born evangelicals could sometimes pour scorn on Methodist enthusiasm and sought to distance themselves from so-called Methodist Jacobinism, she and Wesley were one in their espousal of an English chauvinist version of freedom against the spiritual slavery of Roman Catholicism and the physical slavery of human servitude promoted by English slave traders.[14] How widely then were these views disseminated, how influential were they, and how did the ecology of popular evangelical attitudes reinforce or undermine one another as political events unfolded?

In terms of dissemination of antislavery ideas not much was achieved within Methodism between 1774 and 1787. At first it looked as if Wesley's pronounced anti-slavery views would determine the future policy not only of the British but also of the American branch of Methodism, but the decade of the 1780s witnessed a slow retreat in North America from an absolutist position to one that took pragmatic account of evangelistic exigencies and southern sensibilities.[15] In Britain the *Arminian* magazine, a widely disseminated Methodist periodical, was largely silent on the issue of slavery, but the formation of the Society for the Abolition of the Slave Trade in May 1787 led to another gear shift in Methodist mobilization. Given Wesley's traditional hostility to "pressure from without," it was no small step for him when he wrote to Granville Sharp supporting the new society, and he quickly reissued his *Thoughts upon Slavery*. In 1788 the volume of antislavery materials in the *Arminian* increased. In April and May the resolutions of the Society for the Abolition of the Slave Trade were published; in July and August Wesley printed "A Summary View of the Slave Trade"; and in October and November Hannah More's poem on slavery was reproduced. Her poem may have been particularly influential. Written by a woman and published in the periodical of a movement comprised of a majority of women, the poem unashamedly appeals to the feelings of women and mothers:

> Whe'er to Afric's shores I turn my eyes,
> Horrors of deepest, deadliest guilt arise;
> I see, by more than Fancy's mirror shown,
> The burning village, and the blazing town;
> See the dire victim torn from social life,
> The shrieking babe, the agonizing wife!
> She, wretch forlorn! Is dragged by hostile hands;
> To distant tyrants sold, in distant lands!
> Transmitted miseries, and successive chains,
> The sole sad heritage her child obtains!
> Even this last wretched boon their foes deny,
> To weep together, or together die!
> By felon hands, by one relentless stroke,
> See the fond links of feeling Nature broke!
> The fibres twisting round a parent's heart,
> Torn from their grasp, and bleeding as they part.[16]

What could be more horrific for any woman to contemplate than to be forcefully abducted from country and kin only to be brutally separated from her last consolation, her own child?

More's poem in the *Arminian* was soon followed by other contributions, including a poem written by Charles Wesley, the lyricist of the Methodist movement. In addition to the conventional arguments against the inhumanities of slavery, Charles

Wesley dared to suggest that the power and providence of God and the laws of nature were arraigned against slavery:

> Hark, he answers—wild tornados,
> Strewing yonder sea with wrecks,
> Wasting town, plantations, meadows,
> Is the voice with which he speaks.
> He foreseeing what vexations
> Afric's sons would undergo,
> Fix'd their tyrants habitations
> Where his whirlwinds answer "no!"[17]

Only days before he died, John Wesley in a letter charged with emotion and with the gravity of age gave his paternal blessing to a youthful Wilberforce's campaign against "that execrable villany, which is the scandal of religion, of England, and of human nature," hoping even that "American slavery (the vilest that ever saw the sun)" would vanish in due course.[18]

With the Wesley brothers gone but with the Methodist movement now the fastest growing religious tradition in the transatlantic world, the obvious question was, what would happen to the Methodist commitment against slavery? At first sight it seemed that it would be business as usual. The year after Wesley died, one of his closest preachers, Samuel Bradburn, published *An Address to the People Called Methodists; Concerning the Wickedness of Encouraging Slavery.*[19] Bradburn was a volatile figure whom Wesley alternately praised for great abilities and scolded for weak judgment. Born in Gibraltar the son of a soldier, Bradburn grew up in the north of England, where he was apprenticed to a shoemaker. He was a self-taught artisan who read ancient languages and established a reputation as a fiery preacher. In his address to the Methodists many of the old Wesleyan themes are in evidence, including graphic accounts of the sheer barbarity of slavery; the idea that Christ, "the intentional Savior of the negroes," died for all humankind; and the fact that the Bible, both Old and New Testaments, explicitly condemns slavery.[20] What makes Bradburn's pamphlet so characteristically Methodist, however, is his appeal to Methodist discipline in avoiding luxury drugs such as sugar and rum as a weapon to subvert the economics of the slave trade and his appeal to the numerical power of the Methodist movement to "persuade" the legislature to take a moral stand against slavery. Although his pamphlet speaks confidently of the Providence of God, it speaks even more clearly of the responsibility of humans. "While we thus as Christians, take God into account," he writes, "we must use every rational and scriptural mean, that may conduce to the end we have in view, otherwise we shall be (what those who knew us not have often called us) ignorant, wild enthusiasts."[21] In other words, through the exercise of hard-won discipline Methodists could eschew luxury, win self-respect, build a good reputation, and end the slave trade all at the same time. Here in a nutshell is the Methodist gospel of earnest self-discipline as a means and a way of achieving freedom for oneself and for others. In writing thus, Bradburn placed himself in the plain Methodist tradition, but there is something else that shows up in his pamphlet.

Bradburn, who was part of a new generation of English artisans radicalized by the American and French Revolutions, penned some lines that the Wesley brothers would not have endorsed. Not only is the tone of Bradburn's tract politically hostile to Parliament and "old corruption," but also he explicitly called Methodists to direct political action by petitioning Parliament (not just as British citizens but also as self-identified Methodists), mobilizing the Methodist preachers, canvassing members of Parliament, and supporting a boycott of rum and sugar. Bradburn did not stop there. In ringing phrases he declared that "there is no moral obligation that binds mankind to obey any laws, but such as are designed upon the whole, to promote *the good of the governed*" and that the customary Methodist injunction not to "meddle with politics" was not meant to protect the unwarranted extension of unconstitutional power such as he considered was at stake in the legislature's perpetuation of slavery. In words that John Wesley could never have written, Bradburn identified the antislavery cause with the French revolutionaries who stormed the Bastille, adding that "the revolution in France has in some measure, affected all Europe. The spirit of Philanthropy accompanies the spirit of Liberty."

Bradburn's pamphlet, revealingly published in Manchester—the great early center of artisan antislavery activity—not in London, had two principal effects.[22] By urging a sugar boycott it helped mobilize Methodist women who were the custodians of domestic supplies, and it helped align Methodist antislavery sentiment with the rising tide of artisan radicalism in the industrializing districts of England in the early 1790s.[23] But this was dangerous territory for the Methodists. Not only was Methodism experiencing bitter internal disputes about how quickly and how completely it should move away from the shelter of the Anglican Established Church now that its founder was dead, but also the itinerant preaching privileges of Methodists could not be guaranteed in a period of life-or-death warfare against not just France but also the principles of the French Revolution. Bradburn's hot rhetoric would never have passed Wesley's strict censorship of connectional publications, but the king was dead and new forces had been unleashed. Bradburn and some others now displayed their newfound independence by boldly conducting Methodist services during church hours, something Wesley had never permitted, and he laced his sermons with calls to *Vox populi* and "*unbounded liberty,* founded upon the *Rights of Man.*"[24] It was not long, however, before Wesley's ghost visited his bold young successor. Not only was Methodist enthusiasm for the French Revolution tempered by the Parisian descent into chaos, patriotic war fever, and the ubiquitous "Church-and-King" mobs in English towns and cities, but also Methodism itself seemed to be on the brink of tearing itself apart.

On the one hand, William Pitt's government was making dark noises about demanding pledges of loyalty from Methodist leaders with the alternative of their facing penal legislation against itinerant preaching, and on the other hand, radical Methodists were coalescing under the aegis of Alexander Kilham, who led the first significant secession from the parent movement. In the decade after the French Revolution, Methodism was being confronted with incompatible elite and popular expectations. Bradburn's ground had been cut from under him, and he knew it. Faced with the unwelcome consequences of his indiscreet rhetoric, he switched horses in 1795 and supported a pledge of loyalty to the government, effectively abandoning the Methodist radicalism he had once fomented. Referring to Kilham and the Methodist radicals he once supported, he told a fellow preacher, "I mean to act as I have done, so far as I can; but never to give countenance to raw desperadoes, who proceed in a manner that tends to anarchy and ruin. As to the cries about the *poor*, the *war*, etc., a great deal of this is for want of information and attention. The distress of 9 in 10 of the poor is *entirely their own fault*, and unconnected with the war . . . and as to the war itself . . . I think it is easy to prove it has done more good than hurt to the nation." W. R. Ward's appropriate conclusion was, "To such comments on a famine of European dimensions was the erstwhile champion of the Rights of Man reduced by the necessities of connectional politics."[25]

As Methodism settled into a lengthy battle to secure its own right to exist in a period of national warfare, culminating in a Methodist-inspired new Toleration Act passed in 1812, the antislavery momentum within the connection that had built up in the years 1787–92 went into apparent decline. In that sense the fate of Bradburn was but a symbol for the whole antislavery cause. But appearances can be deceptive. Beneath the surface of print, preaching, and politics were at least five slow-burning fuses that had the capacity to ignite a subsequent mobilization against slavery: the slow politicization of women who had taken a lead in the sugar boycott; the rapid growth of interdenominational and Methodist Sunday schools, which spread literacy among the English working classes; the de facto separation of Methodism from the Church of England in 1795, which further eroded Methodism's filial debt to the established order; the continued expansion of Methodist missions, especially in the Caribbean Islands; and despite official resistance, the participation of Methodists in many of the radical causes of the early nineteenth century. Space and the state of current research do not permit a full exploration of all of these trends, especially the spread of literacy (including biblical literacy and its impact on antislavery sentiment), but from the point of view of our ecology model more needs to be said about some of them, including the contribution made by women and the relationship between popular radicalism and antislavery agitation within the Methodist movement.

Women were important in the early antislavery cause in manifold ways. They were often the stirrers of a more humane sensibility in some of the elite homes of early antislavery activists.[26] They were authors of a distinctive genre of poems and imaginative literature. They supported the sugar boycott and subscribed financially to the Abolition Society.[27] Quaker women in particular were to the fore in antislavery circles on both sides of the Atlantic. Although the charting of antislavery sentiment and activity among Methodist women before the great petitioning campaigns of the period 1823–33 still awaits its historian, some of the evidence is suggestive. One of the more remarkable surviving narratives is that of Dorothy Ripley, a Methodist who was also influenced by the Quakers. Born in Whitby, Yorkshire, in 1769, Ripley left England for America in 1801 to plead the cause of African slaves in the New World, and she soon secured a private interview with President Thomas Jefferson. She wanted Jefferson's personal approbation, as a slaveholder, for her to continue her work on behalf of "distressed Africans" in America. Jefferson was courteous, but he repeated his opinions expressed in *Notes on the State of Virginia* that the mental powers of Africans were not equal even to those of the Indians. Ripley replied that

> God had made all nations of one blood and that ancient Britons were degraded very much once in their powers of reason and this people being neglected many centuries, their power of reason was dimmed from long abuse of the same. I was inclined to think, if the present generation of children were separated from their parents and educated by virtuous persons, who would teach them habits of industry and economy, they might then prove a blessing to the country. To train them up with the view that they were not the same race would prove only a curse to the land, especially the females, whom I felt myself concerned for the most on account of their exposed situations to the vile passions of men.[28]

Ripley was bold enough to ask Jefferson how many slaves he owned (three hundred at one time but diminishing, was the answer) and was surprised both by the number and by the fact that Jefferson, an indisputably cultivated man, could buy, sell, and own human flesh. The interview, although polite, was not comfortable for either of them, but it seems clear that a female Methodist prophetess from the north of England had a stronger moral compass than did a prince of the Enlightenment and the president of the United States. Ripley had an unusual access to the seat of power, but she was not unusual as a Methodist woman offended by slavery. When the antislavery movement emerged again in the 1820s from the doldrums of the war and the postwar depression, women were once again to the forefront, this time as organizers of antislavery associations and signers of the ubiquitous petitions.[29]

Extensive research on the mobilization of public opinion against slavery in the 1820s has confirmed the importance of popular evangelicalism of all stripes to the antislavery agitation, but it has also shown that evangelicalism itself did not create mass mobilization; rather abolitionism proliferated in the same ideological and political context that was also favorable to Evangelical Nonconformity. Abolitionism not only attracted the support of the evangelical middle classes who had economic as well as religious interests in abolition, but it also appealed to the urban artisans as part of a wider political protest against paternalism, dependency, and corruption in the early industrial revolution. Both political radicalism and popular evangelicalism thrived in the kinds of urban communities that emerged in the early stages of industrial growth, and they shared some similar characteristics. Both were attacked, correctly as it turned out, for undermining traditional authority in church and state in the era of the French Revolution; both were based on voluntary associations and made extensive use of touring lecturers or itinerant preachers and popular print; both led to enlarged spheres of action for women and sometimes children; and both were capable of appealing to different social strata and of creating communities in which moral/religious values were treated seriously.

However, evangelicalism had also something distinctive to bring to the antislavery movement. The dramatic expansion of overseas missions in the first third of the nineteenth century helped narrow the geographical and psychological gap between social realities in Britain and the colonies, which some have argued was an essential precondition of a genuinely popular mobilization against slavery. Hindrances to mission, including the ignorance of slaves and the preaching restrictions imposed by planters, began to occupy more space in religious periodicals in the 1820s. Tales of imprisoned missionaries and of persecuted slave converts added emotional intensity to the annual meetings of the missionary societies. Richard Watson told the anniversary meeting of the Methodist Missionary Society in 1830 that overseas missions had increased "our sympathies with the oppressed and miserable of all lands. It is impossible for men to care for the souls of others without caring for their bodies also. . . . We cannot care for the salvation of the negro without caring for his emancipation from bondage."[30]

If Methodism's increasing commitment to global mission, especially in one of its early strongholds, the Caribbean Islands, was bringing the issue of slavery back to the surface, the political realities of the post–Napoleonic War period were working in the opposite direction. In particular, Methodist leaders under the increasingly powerful arch conservative Jabez Bunting were fighting hard during the Peterloo years against the rise of urban radicalism that had "infected" Methodist societies throughout the north of England. A second issue arose from Methodism's vigorous mission to a largely Roman Catholic Ireland. Methodists and popular evangelicals of all stripes in the early nineteenth century engaged in a vigorous attempt to convert Ireland to Evangelical Protestantism.[31] During what is sometimes known as the Second Reformation movement, London-based evangelical societies committed unprecedented resources to the Irish mission. At the same time Irish Catholics under the leadership of Daniel O'Connell were beginning to use their sheer numerical power as a battering ram to break down the doors of Britain's Protestant constitution and admit Roman Catholics to Parliament. The Methodists liked neither O'Connell's objectives nor his tactics. Throughout the later 1820s the exigencies of Methodism's Irish mission took precedence over the exigencies of its Caribbean mission. Anti-Catholicism trumped antislavery, and that was reflected both in Methodist discourse and in the great bulk of Methodist and evangelical petitioning. Moreover the great surge in "pressure from without" from Irish Catholics, English Dissenters, and urban radicals in post–Napoleonic War Britain alarmed Methodist leaders as much as it alarmed sections of the political establishment. Fomenting popular political excitement, even against things it did not like, was not what the evangelical leadership wanted, and the antislavery campaign became a collateral casualty of those who feared for the political stability of the nation.[32]

There were yet more layers of complexity facing the Methodists over slavery, especially arising from the success of Methodist missions in the Caribbean. Supervising the Methodist missions was a Methodist missionary committee, and supervising the committee was the enormous personal presence of Jabez Bunting, who in the early 1820s was president of the conference, the connectional editor, the senior secretary of the Missionary Society, and the most recognized metropolitan voice for the Methodist movement. As senior secretary to the Missionary Society, Bunting revised and modified the *Instructions to Missionaries,* which effectively contained the Methodist official policy on missions. The instructions had Bunting's characteristically cautious footprints all over them. "Some of these instructions were specially addressed to West Indian missionaries 'placed in stations of considerable delicacy' and requiring 'peculiar circumspection and prudence.' 'Their only business' was 'to promote the moral and religious improvement of the slaves' to whom 'they might have access, without in the least degree, in public or private, interfering with their civil condition.'"[33]

Although he was committed to antislavery, Bunting's careful discretion was forced into the open in 1823 when he was invited by Zachary Macaulay to join and help launch the "London Society for Mitigating and Gradually Abolishing the State of Slavery throughout the British Dominions." In a crisis of conscience over competing responsibilities, Bunting honorably resigned his secretaryship of the Methodist Missionary Society, but in the complicated debates that followed, the antislavery Methodists gained the ascendancy and the whole movement came more fully on board with the antislavery cause. Even so, Bunting never fully relinquished his caution about the consequences of such a move. In 1832 he refused to vote for an abolitionist candidate in the Liverpool election because he was a Unitarian and a radical, and in 1833 he expressed unease about Methodists coming so obviously to the fore in the petitioning movement. He (along with many others) was particularly frightened of the giant meetings organized by Daniel O'Connell in Ireland, which were designed to coerce the British Parliament into passing Roman Catholic emancipation and the repeal of the union. "Our duty, and our policy too, require us to be the 'quiet in the land,' as far and as long as we innocently can. I decidedly think that the holy cause of Anti-Slavery has already been disgraced and prejudiced in some quarters by the system of 'agitation,' after the fashion of Irish Papists and Repealers, which have been employed to promote it. The wrath of man worketh not the righteousness of God. . . . Whether we ought, *as a Missionary Society,* to meddle with the *merely civil* or *political* part of the subject, I very much doubt."[34]

However, Bunting's appeal to the old Wesleyan principle of "no politics" as a way of quieting the Methodist societies was beginning to run out of steam by the late 1820s. Circumstances changed in 1829 after the repeal of the Test and Corporation Acts and the passage of the Roman Catholic Emancipation Act. Methodists who were no longer fearful for their religious liberties and who were still resentful of their persecution in the West Indies were both chastened and emboldened by the success of pressure from without in Ireland. The annual Wesleyan Conference of 1830 not only endorsed individual Methodists petitioning against slavery but also gave its blessing to confessional petitioning (Methodists petitioning as Methodists, not as subjects) and to securing pledges from parliamentary candidates. These were positions that were regarded as overtly radical when Samuel Bradburn first proposed them back in 1792. Once unleashed, the power of the Methodist connectional organization and the strength of its moral outrage against slavery resulted in a remarkable surge in petitioning against slavery in the early 1830s.

Seymour Drescher has shown that there is a strong correlation between the rapid growth of popular evangelicalism as a proportion of the English population and the scale of antislavery petitioning. The numbers are striking. Of the 297,672 signatures on antislavery petitions from nonconformist denominations in 1832–33, Methodists supplied 236, 592, or 79.5 percent of the total.[35] Another factor in drawing Methodists out into the open by the early 1830s was the way in which British abolitionists were increasingly able to suggest, to the religious public at any rate, that the Caribbean slave revolts (Barbados in 1816, Demerara in 1823, and Jamaica in 1831–32) were to some extent relatively restrained and legitimate forms of protest against intolerable evils. Their arguments were not always internally consistent, but they helped assuage religious fears of uncontrollable black mobs wreaking havoc on persons and property by arguing that the Christianity of the Baptist and Methodist missionaries had stimulated legitimate aspirations for freedom, moderated violence, and exposed ever more clearly the repressive violence of planters and masters. In this way the deeply ingrained Methodist fear of violence and social instability was partly dissolved; if the Caribbean Islands were indeed on the verge of slave insurrection, the cause was not the Christianity of the missionaries but the repressive brutality of the planters.[36]

The purpose of detailing the high proportion of Methodists, both male and female, in the petitioning against slavery in 1832–33 is not to reenter the well-worn debates about the role of extraparliamentary pressure in shifting the political climate toward antislavery in these crucial years, or even to weigh in the balance with other factors the importance of extraparliamentary protest in the campaign against slavery, but rather to ask the question, why were popular evangelicals in Britain enthusiastic supporters of the antislavery cause in the first place?

One obvious place to start is with the moral authority of John Wesley and the influence of his *Thoughts upon Slavery* (1774) on the subsequent history of Methodism. Few religious movements in history have had their opinions molded and their circulating print controlled with such relentless rigor as Methodism has. Once declared, Wesley's uncompromising hostility to human slavery was hard for Methodists to resist. But why was Wesley, unlike some other leaders of the evangelical movement such as John Newton and George Whitefield, so unequivocal in his opposition to slavery root and branch and not just the slave trade?[37] Irv Brendlinger has shown how Wesley's views on human depravity, prevenient grace, universal atonement, freedom of the will, Christian perfection, unconditional love, and stewardship of the earth's resources all had profound implications for the way he approached the issue of slavery.[38] Wesley did not believe in polygenesis, or the separate creation of the races; he did not believe in differential human depravity (that blacks were more depraved than whites); he did not believe in predetermined states or predetermined elections; and he did not believe that perfect love and scriptural holiness could coexist with the self-evident cruelty and enforced bondage of slavery. In short, Wesley's opposition to slavery was not a random opinion expressed in 1774 as part of a wider set of speculative ideas on social matters but rather the irresistible conclusion of every major theological idea he held dear.

Wesley was, of course, not unique among British Protestants to find slavery an affront against God's love and purposes for humankind. Evangelical Anglicans and Quakers have already been mentioned, but there were many others. The eminent Baptist theologian Abraham Booth denounced slavery in a pamphlet published in 1792;[39] Joseph Priestley, the Unitarian intellectual, published a sermon against slavery in 1788—the symbolic hundredth anniversary of Britain's Glorious Revolution when British religious and political freedoms were allegedly secured against Roman Catholic absolutists;[40] and William Paley wrote against slavery as an offence against God's governing laws and benevolence.[41] But if Wesley was far from unique among British Protestants, he was the first religious leader of major significance in England to publish his opinions, and there was in his Arminian theological convictions a deeper sense of "responsible grace" as a motivation for Methodists actively to fight evil and realize God's perfect love in hearts and communities.[42] Wesley drew attention to human responsibility in cooperating with God's grace not only in the process of salvation but also in the working out of scriptural holiness in a corrupt world. David Brion Davis has shown that although Wesley shared many ideas in common with his evangelical contemporaries, his foundational belief that every human being (not just the elect) could live a sanctified life (not merely be justified) marked him out, especially from the Calvinist Evangelicals.[43]

In the light of this discussion what is perhaps surprising is not so much the vehemence of Wesley's opposition to slavery but rather his apparent reluctance to mobilize the Methodist movement against it. That reluctance was not so much owing to the lack of passion in Wesley's antislavery stance as it had to do with his profound resistance to anything that would politicize his movement and deflect it from its primary spiritual function. Wesley's fears on this count were far from groundless. Methodism's history is littered with the stories of working-class radicals, often educated in Methodist Sunday schools, who embraced radical causes, including antislavery, and then abandoned their faith altogether. Some were ruthlessly expelled from Methodist societies for their radicalism, and others simply traveled the road from fidelity to infidelity, becoming more politicized in the process. For example, Joseph Barker, who was raised in a Methodist home of hand-loom weavers, attended a Methodist Sunday school, became active in the antislavery cause in the 1820s, embraced Garrisonian abolitionism in the 1840s, and became one of the foremost leaders of the secularist movement in Britain and America.[44] As was the case with many of the secularist leaders, Barker returned to orthodox Christianity later, but the trajectory of his life is but one of many examples of how Methodism could educate infidels as well as soldiers of Christ.[45] It is hard to understand Methodism's reluctance to embrace political causes with unrestrained enthusiasm without a realistic appreciation of the perceived spiritual dangers of such a policy.

Wesley's opposition to slavery is a necessary but insufficient explanation for the growth of the large antislavery constituency within Methodism. Another way into this problem is to look at the two most powerful genres of the Methodist wing of the evangelical revival: conversion narratives and hymns. In an important recent study Bruce Hindmarsh has shown how conversion narratives both reflected and partly instituted a modern sense of the individual.[46] In a sense they were religious and psychological markers on the way to the modern self-defined by personal choice and self-fashioning. This development had both individual and communitarian dimensions. Individuals had their lives reconstituted, but so too did the voluntary communities of the faithful to which they owed corporate allegiance. Hindmarsh skillfully positions conversion narratives on "the trailing edge of Christendom and the leading edge of modernity" in the construction of new views about the self. As with conversion narratives, so with hymns, which were the great transmission agents of Methodist theology to quite humble people.[47] Consider, for example, the following stanzas from some of Charles Wesley's most popular and enduring hymns:

> Long my imprisoned spirit lay,
> fast bound in sin and nature's night;
> thine eye diffused a quickening ray;
> I woke, the dungeon flamed with light;
> My chains fell off, my heart was free,
> I rose, went forth, and followed thee.

He breaks the power of cancelled sin,
he sets the prisoner free;
his blood can make the foulest clean;
his blood availed for me

He speaks, and listening to his voice,
new life the dead receive,
the mournful, broken hearts rejoice,
the humble poor believe.

I want a principle within of watchful, Godly fear,
a sensibility of sin, a pain to feel it near.
I want the first approach to feel of pride or wrong desire
To catch the wandering of my will, and quench the kindling fire.[48]

These hymns and many others like them speak of enslavement to sin, the universal offer of salvation, the capacity for new life, and the empowerment of individual selves expressed in countless personal pronouns. In other words, for all the allegations made against populist evangelicalism as the last hurrah of the dark ages of enthusiasm and superstition, its most distinctive religious expressions, namely conversion narratives and hymns, could be read as modernist expressions of personal freedom and self-actualization.

This aspect of Methodism has been taken to a new level of sophistication by Phyllis Mack.[49] The heart of her argument is that eighteenth-century Methodists, both men and women, worked so hard at the disciplines of self-mastery and holy living that they laid the foundations for freedom and empowerment. Although much of this was directed internally in the period up to Wesley's death, it was given an outward turn by Methodism's maturity as a movement, its growing concern for the wider world, and its ability to absorb insights from both Enlightenment and Christian traditions. Methodists were able to "fuse self-transcendence and agency" and by so doing were able to participate in the activist agendas of the nineteenth century. All this was facilitated by formidable connectional machinery, a huge publishing operation, and new information about the rest of the world brought to them by their growing army of missionaries. The "Missionary Intelligence" section of the *Methodist* magazine, which was instituted in 1803, brought Methodist self-actualization onto the world stage and demanded a response from its readership. It is easy to see how all this tumbled into antislavery sentiment. It was almost the perfect issue to propel Methodists out into the public square without appearing to capitulate to partisan politicization. Their founder had spoken against it; it was self-evidently a moral issue; it got in the way of world mission; it offended important components of their theological DNA; it had originated and come of age under premodern conditions; it particularly offended female sensibilities; and it was sustained by political, commercial, and ideological interests that were standing in their way. But how did the Methodist mobilization against slavery fit into the movement's wider political consciousness? How did its political ecology work?

Antislavery was not the first political issue to tease the Methodists out of the "no politics" bunker that Wesley had dug for them. The first and most important issue was the survival of their own religious system under pressure from the traditional defenders of church and king in the era of the Atlantic revolutions. Methodists first learned the tools of political mobilization in a life-and-death struggle to protect itinerant preaching from the coercive powers of Anglican bishops and nervous politicians who could not afford to have uncontrolled orators traveling the country during the war against the French Revolution. The Methodist victory in that struggle developed organizational muscle, bred confidence, and produced a new self-reliance. The next issue arose out of Methodism's anti-Catholicism, which was based on a fusion of its inheritance of a Protestant narrative of England's past and its missionary endeavors in Ireland. However, on this occasion Methodist muscle could not stop Roman Catholic emancipation, nor could it convert large numbers of Irish Catholics. Nothing showed the limits of Methodism's reach in the British Isles more than its failure to build an Irish branch of the movement with anything like the numbers it had briefly promised in the aftermath of the Rebellion of the United Irishmen in 1798.[50] The third great issue, antislavery, is the one most remembered by historians, especially Methodist historians, because it places Methodism at the center of movements for human equality rather than self-interest or intolerance.

How then is one to interpret the Methodists' enthusiasm for increased religious toleration for themselves but less for Roman Catholics, their growing commitment to the antislavery cause but not necessarily to antislavery agitation, their enthusiasm for sacred liberty but not for the liberties envisioned by political radicals, and their desire to empower people but not to lift them out of their station? I have suggested that this apparently peculiar ecology of values has its roots in the theology, worldviews, and sensibilities of the populist evangelicals and their interaction with changes in late eighteenth- and early nineteenth-century British culture.

But how does all this relate to one of the chief themes of this volume, namely the idea of progress in human history? The answer, of course, depends on what one means by progress. If one means the slow erosion of the kind of religion that was based on the coercive powers of medieval established churches, then Methodism as a voluntary organization of free individuals could be regarded as a progressive movement. The expanded Toleration Act of 1812 is both a real and a symbolic example of that interpretation of progress. Methodism could also fit some other definitions of progress, including its emphasis on human agency, its commitment to the education of the masses through Sunday and elementary schools, and its insatiable desire to become a global religious movement. Good, if more contested, cases could be made for its contributions to female empowerment, its repudiation of cruel sports involving animals, its modern attitude to time and work discipline, its embrace of free markets, and its nurturing of family love.

On the other side of the ledger, if Methodists had had their way, there would have been limited religious toleration afforded to Roman Catholics and non-Trinitarian Protestants; there would have been no popular mobilization for the extension of the suffrage and the reform of Parliament; and there would have been no rapprochement of any kind with the non-Christian religions of the world. Moreover when one compares the passage of Roman Catholic emancipation in 1829 with the abolition of colonial slavery in 1833, it is clear that the former was passed by an undemocratic parliament *against* the wishes of the great majority of the English population, while the latter was passed by a reformed, if far from democratic, parliament as an *expression* of the wishes of the majority of the English population.[51]

Ironically it was well for the Catholic cause that modernist democratic ideas were not in the ascendancy in 1829. Progress makes its gains in strange and paradoxical ways. Modernity, economic improvement, democracy, antislavery, and religious toleration are often regarded as the cellular components of the historical animal we call progress, but the operation of the Methodist cell of this system shows how complex and contradictory the mechanisms could be.

Progress is therefore not only an elusive concept but also is of necessity based on somewhat subjective determinants. What the Methodist campaign against the slave trade and British colonial slavery shows is that a fusion of evangelical humanitarian zeal (including its missionary aspirations) and enlightenment notions of natural rights produced a powerful popular mobilization of men and women against an evil of unimaginable proportions. From John Wesley's first encounters with slavery in Georgia and South Carolina in the 1730s to the full-blown Methodist petitioning campaign against slavery in British dominions in the 1830s, there was a century of erratic mobilization and unexpected contingencies before Methodism's moral capital and earnest discipline were cashed out into relatively effective political action. The public square was a place early Methodists never expected or even desired to reach. It was the good fortune of the antislavery cause that they did.

NOTES

1. Some of the most important trajectories of interpretation may be found in the following books: Roger Anstey, *The Atlantic Slave Trade and British Abolition 1760–1810* (Atlantic Highlands, N.J.: Humanities Press, 1975), which has fine chapters on the evangelical worldview and evangelical theology; Seymour Drescher, *Capitalism and Antislavery: British Mobilization in Comparative Perspective* (New York: Oxford University Press, 1987), which thoroughly examines the popular mobilization against slavery within its economic and social contexts; Clare Midgley, *Women against Slavery: The British Campaigns 1780–1870* (London: Routledge, 1992), which brings the contribution of women to the center of the stage for the

first time; and Christopher Leslie Brown, *Moral Capital: Foundations of Abolitionism* (Chapel Hill: University of North Carolina Press, 2006), which is an insightful investigation of the roots of British antislavery with a special emphasis on the complex relationship between moral opinion and political action. For a useful survey of the longer historiography of antislavery, see Roger Anstey, "The Historical Debate on the Abolition of the British Slave Trade," in *Liverpool, the African Slave Trade and Abolition,* edited by Roger Anstey and P. E. H. Hair, Historic Society of Lancashire and Cheshire, occasional series, vol. 2 (1976): 157–66.

2. Irv A. Brendlinger, *Social Justice through the Eyes of Wesley: John Wesley's Theological Challenge to Slavery* (Ontario, Canada: Joshua Press, 2006), 169.

3. In singling out the Methodists for special treatment, I do not wish to contradict Drescher's claim that "British abolitionism was to emerge as an ecumenical, and not a sectarian mobilization" (*Capitalism and Antislavery,* 63), but rather to follow the Methodist side of the story for other purposes that will become clear.

4. I am grateful to Brian Clark for helping me clarify the conceptual frameworks represented here.

5. For a more extensive treatment of John Wesley's political attitudes than is possible here, see David Hempton, *Methodism and Politics in British Society 1750–1850* (London: Hutchinson, 1984), 20–54; and Henry D. Rack, *Reasonable Enthusiast: John Wesley and the Rise of Methodism,* 3rd ed. (London: Epworth Press, 2002).

6. The best starting point for this topic is the well-researched and clearly presented book by Brendlinger titled *Social Justice.*

7. Brendlinger, *Social Justice,* 14–15.

8. Lofft: *R. v. Knowles, ex parte Somersett* (1772), Lofft 1, 98 E. R.499, 20. S. T. 1. is a famous judgment of the English Court of King's Bench in 1772 that held that slavery was unlawful in England although not elsewhere in the British Empire. The key judgment was issued by Lord Mansfield, the chief justice of King's Bench.

9. Brendlinger, *Social Justice,* 20–23.

10. John Wesley, *Thoughts upon Slavery* (London, 1774), 16–17.

11. Thomas Coke's journals are particularly revealing of his attitudes toward Africans, slavery, and mission in the Caribbean Islands and the American colonies. See John A. Vickers, ed., *The Journals of Dr. Thomas Coke* (Nashville: Kingswood Books, 2005).

12. *The Works of Hannah More,* new edition in 11 vols., vol.1: *Sacred Dramas and Poems* (London: T. Cadell, 1830), 312.

13. *The Works of Hannah More,*12:324–26.

14. For a recent interpretation of Hannah More's life and writings, see Anne Stott, *Hannah More: The First Victorian* (Oxford: Oxford University Press, 2003). By sponsoring schools with teachers who displayed "methodistical tendencies," Hannah More had to walk a fine line between propagating evangelical seriousness without capitulating to the religion of itinerant ranters. According to Stott, More "maintained a clear distinction between 'these new seceding Methodists' with their 'terrible principles' and Wesley and Whitefield, whom she regarded as fundamentally sound" (242). Needless to say this was a distinction more easily made in sedate correspondence than in the social cauldron of the late 1790s.

15. For an excellent account of how and why American Methodism, especially in the South, slowly capitulated to an acceptance of slavery, see Cynthia Lynn Lyerly, *Methodism and the*

Southern Mind 1770–1810 (New York: Oxford University Press, 1998). For a well-executed account of this period of American Methodist history, see Dee E. Andrews, *The Methodists and Revolutionary America, 1760–1800: The Shaping of an Evangelical Culture* (Princeton, N.J.: Princeton University Press, 2000).

16. For the full text of Hannah More's poem on "The Black Slave Trade," see *The Works of Hannah More*, 2:107–21. For the edition printed by the Methodists along with Wesley's editorial footnote, see *Arminian* 11 (October 1788): 558–60, and (November 1788): 612–16. Brendlinger has reproduced the version printed in the *Arminian* in *Social Justice*, 185–92. Hannah More was of course not the only antislavery writer to use poetry to appeal to popular sensibilities. See J. R. Oldfield, *Popular Politics and British Anti-Slavery: The Mobilisation of Public Opinion against the Slave Trade 1787–1807* (Manchester, U.K.: Manchester University Press, 1995), 133–37. Oldfield makes the point that poetry and other forms of imaginative writing helped spread antislavery sentiment among the professional and middle classes in provincial England. Oldfield also deals effectively with visual culture and popular politics (155–84).

17. *Arminian* 13 (September 1790): 502–3.

18. John Wesley to William Wilberforce, February 24, 1791, in John Telford, ed., *The Letters of the Rev. John Wesley, A.M.,* 8 vols. (London: Epworth Press, 1938), 8:264–65.

19. Samuel Bradburn, *An Address to the People Called Methodists; Concerning the Wickedness of Encouraging Slavery* (Manchester, U.K.: T. Harper, Smithy-Door, 1792). Brendlinger reproduced this text in *Social Justice*, 201–23.

20. Bradburn quoted the exodus of the Israelites from slavery in Egypt and the verse in 1 Timothy 1:10 where slave traders are listed with adulterers, perverts, liars, and perjurers.

21. Bradburn, *An Address to the People Called Methodists,* 18.

22. Drescher suggests that Manchester was a particularly important site for antislavery activity in the early 1790s not only because it had a market-oriented elite but also because it had an uprooted population in search of a myth to elevate their lives. See Drescher, *Capitalism and Antislavery,* 72–73.

23. The best treatment of the relationship between Methodism and the rise of new social and political forces in England is W. R. Ward, *Religion and Society in England 1790–1850* (London: Batsford, 1972). For an account of how the growth of popular radicalism affected the various positions on the future shape of the Methodist polity, in which Bradburn was a key player, see Hempton, *Methodism and Politics,* 55–84.

24. Ward, *Religion and Society,* 29.

25. Ibid., 35.

26. See Brown, *Moral Capital,* 333–89.

27. See Midgley, *Women against Slavery,* 9–40.

28. Paul Wesley Chilcote, *Tell Her Own Story: Autobiographical Portraits of Early Methodist Women* (Nashville, Tenn.: Kingswood Books, 1991), 140.

29. In addition to Midgley, *Women against Slavery,* see Karen I. Halbersleben, *Women's Participation in the British Antislavery Movement, 1824–1865* (Lewiston, N.Y.: Edwin Mellon Press, 1993). Halbersleben argues that women's mobilization against slavery was a relatively safe campaign that nevertheless taught women the skills they were able to employ later in organizations for the achievement of their own rights.

30. Quoted by Roger Anstey in "Religion and British Slave Emancipation," in *The Abolition of the Atlantic Slave Trade,* edited by David Eltis and James Walvin (Madison: University of Wisconsin Press, 1981).

31. See Hempton, *Methodism and Politics,* 116–48. For a more exhaustive account of the Evangelical mission to Ireland, see Desmond Bowen, *The Protestant Crusade in Ireland, 1800–1870: A Study of Protestant-Catholic Relations between the Act of Union and Disestablishment* (Montreal: McGill-Queen's University Press, 1978).

32. For an informed discussion of the political dynamics of this period and their impact on the antislavery issue, see Robert William Fogel, *Without Consent or Contract: The Rise and Fall of American Slavery* (New York: W. W. Norton, 1989), 224–33.

33. Thomas Perceval Bunting, *The Life of Jabez Bunting, D.D.* (London: T. Woolmer, 1887), 562–63.

34. W. R. Ward, *Early Victorian Methodism: The Correspondence of Jabez Bunting, 1830–58* (Oxford: Oxford University Press, 1976), 29.

35. Seymour Drescher, *From Slavery to Freedom: Comparative Studies in the Rise and Fall of Atlantic Slavery* (New York: New York University Press, 1999), 37–40.

36. For a recent assessment of how the slave revolts played into the wider discourse of abolitionism, see Gelien Matthews, *Caribbean Slave Revolts and the British Abolitionist Movement* (Baton Rouge: Louisiana State University Press, 2006). The book seeks to explain "how British abolitionists were able to conduct a nonviolent campaign of social reform while making use of the combustible materials provided by the slaves" (27).

37. This question is addressed head-on in Irv Brendlinger, "John Wesley and Slavery: Myth and Reality," *Wesleyan Theological Journal* 41, no. 1 (Spring 2006): 223–43.

38. For a thorough and insightful treatment of Wesley's theology as it related to the issue of slavery, see Brendlinger, *Social Justice,* 73–128.

39. Abraham Booth, *Commerce of Human Species and the Enslaving of Innocent Persons Inimical to the Laws of Moses and the Gospel of Christ* (London: L. Wayland, 1792).

40. Joseph Priestley, *A Sermon on the Subject of the Slave Trade Delivered to a Society of Protestant Dissenters* (Birmingham, England: Pearson and Rollason, 1788).

41. William Paley, "Speech on the Abolition of the Slave Trade Delivered at a Meeting of the Inhabitants of Carlisle," February 9, 1792, in *The Works of William Paley,* 5 vols. (Cambridge, Mass.: Hilliard and Brown, 1830). For a helpful discussion of the theological ideas expressed by British Protestants against slavery, see Edith F. Hurwitz, *Politics and the Public Conscience: Slave Emancipation and the Abolition Movement in Britain* (London: George Allen and Unwin, 1973), 21–47.

42. For a more sustained treatment of Wesley's theology within a framework of responsible grace, see Randy L. Maddox, *Responsible Grace: John Wesley's Practical Theology* (Nashville, Tenn.: Kingswood Books, 1994).

43. David Brion Davis, *The Problem of Slavery in Western Culture* (New York: Oxford University Press, 1966), 384–87.

44. See J. T. Barker, ed., *The Life of Joseph Barker, Written by Himself* (London: Hodder & Stoughton, 1880). For Barker's career as an antislavery activist, see Betty Fladeland, *Abolitionists and Working-Class Problems in the Age of Industrialization* (Baton Rouge: Louisiana State University Press, 1984), 132–70. For a stimulating account of Barker's less well-known

reconversion to Christianity, along with accounts of other prominent leaders of the secularist movement, see Timothy Larsen, *Crisis of Doubt: Honest Faith in Nineteenth-Century England* (Oxford: Oxford University Press, 2006), 136–72.

45. Other secularist leaders cited by Larsen who later in life reconverted to something approaching orthodox Christianity include William Hone, Frederic Rowland Young, Thomas Cooper, John Bagnall Bebbington, and George Sexton.

46. D. Bruce Hindmarsh, *The Evangelical Conversion Narrative: Spiritual Autobiography in Early Modern England* (Oxford: Oxford University Press, 2005).

47. See the discussion on the importance of hymns for the transmission of the Methodist message in David Hempton, *Methodism: Empire of the Spirit* (New Haven, Conn.: Yale University Press, 2005), 68–74.

48. Selections are taken from some of Charles Wesley's best-known and most enduring hymns. They are all still to be found in the *United Methodist Hymnal* (Nashville, Tenn.: United Methodist Publishing House, 2000).

49. Phyllis Mack, *Heart Religion in the British Enlightenment: Gender and Emotion in Early Methodism* (Cambridge: Cambridge University Press, 2008).

50. For Methodist fortunes in Ireland, see David Hempton, *The Religion of the People: Methodism and Popular Religion c. 1750–1900* (London: Routledge, 1996), 29–48.

51. For a clear explanation of how Roman Catholic emancipation was passed against the will of the English population, see G. I. T. Machin, *The Catholic Question in English Politics, 1820 to 1830* (Oxford: Clarendon Press, 1964).

Slavery, Antislavery, and Moral Progress

A Comparative Historical Perspective

Lamin Sanneh

> There is no unity in the history of institutions, unless one deals with partic-
> ular countries. But there is a grand unity in the history of ideas—of con-
> science, or morality, and of the means of securing it. I venture to say that
> the secret of the philosophy of History lies there: It is the only point of view
> from which one discovers a constant progress, the only one therefore which
> justifies the ways of God to man.
>
> *Lord Acton, 1882*

In the course of field investigations in Senegambia, I once found myself in the
midst of a clerical Muslim community whose ideas on slaves and slavery were in
open conflict with the scruples I had acquired from reading, among others, John
Woolman, Thomas Clarkson, and William Cowper. I suddenly felt ill-equipped and
unprepared, to the ironic interest of these clerics. To much fanfare, after all, I had
arrived in the community trailing an open-minded, objective, scholarly interest in the
history and practices of the clerical center, including slavery. Yet my undeclared reser-
vations and qualms on the subject showed I had something up my sleeve, which was
to depict the slave-owning clerics as cruel and benighted. As a consequence, I faced a
swarm of questions. In the interest of true scholarship, the clerics asked me to reveal
my own views before rigging up elaborate paraphernalia of objective data gathering.
What conscience would allow a scholar to write only about the things of which he
or she approves? Is that how the Western academy views scholarship? How can that
be trustworthy knowledge? *"Kané inuku—m - ma"*—don't hide from us," I was challenged. In that public setting fieldwork suddenly felt like an ambush, and only a
speedy and unreserved acknowledgment on my part stood any chance of allowing me
to salvage my academic mission. The sharp lesson I received about faithful historical
representation made me hope that Clio, the muse of history, would never be a witness against me.

That situation does not let the historian off the moral hook. Given the way the
clerics bristled at mention of the subject, I felt justified in not yielding the ground

entirely. I accepted the challenge to include information on slaves and slavery in my account of Muslim religious practice and even to show how slaves contributed to the prosperous life of religious communities. But I would let stand the moral injunctions and the legal sanctuaries that upheld and burdened the principle of enslavement in Islam. I was struck, for example, by how Muslim informants supplied details on slavery with the confidence afforded by natural entitlement and the weight of objective social institutions. Slavery, I was told, is established in revealed law and upheld by apostolic example, and that is why Muslim legal scholarship apprehends it with the fidelity of divine approval and apostolic conduct and without voiding the numerous qualifications of its practical implementation. Muslim slavery is based on knowledge and fidelity, not on ignorance and disobedience. Slavery is not a negation of religion or a discredit to the righteous life. That was not the way I was used to viewing the subject. So could I do it justice?

Centered in Qur'anic law and in the Sunnah, the idea of slavery is suffused with religious sentiment, which makes legal rectitude and moral conduct about slavery part of the fabric of the ethical life. It is important, however, to remember, as Arnold Toynbee pointed out, that Muslim practice is better characterized as looking to a floor than to a ceiling. Attainment is preferred to idealism.[1] Writing in the ninth century, Ya'qúbí recounted a tradition believed to be *mawálí* propaganda about the famous oration of the Prophet on the occasion of the farewell pilgrimage to the effect that "[all] men are equal in Islam. Men are but the outer margins of the ground that Adam and Eve cultivated. The Arab has no superiority over the foreigner (*'ajamí*) nor the foreigner over the Arab, save in the fear of God. . . . Bring me not your genealogies, but your [good] deeds."[2] A prominent class of *mawálí* who presented a challenge to the theory of equality were blacks whose ancestors, and sometimes who themselves, were imported into Arabia as slaves. The owner's moral life is implicated in how slaves are treated even though sanctions for ill-treatment are not available deterrents to the slave.[3] The rules of treatment, furthermore, offer plenty of room for exculpatory conduct, which the profit motive did a great deal to encourage. In an address signed by Thomas Clarkson as president of the Anti-Slavery Society and presented to Muhammad Ali Pasha of Egypt, E. R. Madden complained that not only was slavery rampant in Egypt but also gross physical injury was inflicted on slaves to increase their commercial value. He spoke of cruel, sanguine, and the most atrocious mutilation of men encouraged by the sultan himself.[4] Not more than a quarter of the slaves subjected to castration survived. Nevertheless, however contrived and self-serving the cultural justification of servitude might be and whatever the pecuniary motives, the institution as such does not rest on any theory of a divinely designated race or culture but on circumstances of time, place, and occasion. Madden made the ironic point to Muhammad Ali that the sultan's support of castrating slaves and defending it as lawful hands the enemies of Islam an advantage they could not have secured on their side of the dispute.

It is perhaps in recognition of the evils inherent in slavery that the Prophet commended manumission as "that which was not an act more acceptable to God" and provided instruments for achieving that end. For Muslim jurists, slavery is not "a constitution of nature," for "the original state of the race of Adam is freedom"—*asl huwa al-hurriyah*.[5] Slavery is an accident of history, place, and circumstance and may therefore be rescinded and in other ways restricted, thanks to the default norm of freedom.[6] Its incorporation into the regular institutions of society surrounds it with the safeguards of ethical conduct rather than rendering it immune to those safeguards, such as they are. By mixing with the slave at home, in the mosque, in the market, on pilgrimage, and in travel, Muslims plant slavery with the seeds of its inhibition and potential dissolution.[7] Slavery is not the total negation of the idea of universal humanity but rather only its social restriction. Ultimately the sentiment that prevented slavery from acquiring a permanent and absolute status was the view that the one God who enjoined it as punishment or as restitution was the one who also provided for its abrogation. Since there can be no contending power to the power of God, slaves belong to the single created order of free men and women. A theology of two natures—slave and free—never took root in canonical Islam in spite of widespread flagrant breach of the rules of enslavement.[8] Unlike the transatlantic experience, slavery and race might be fused in practice but not in principle, because in theory the door is open, however so slightly, to freedom, advancement, and integration. A mixed picture therefore results from trying to apply the law to the vagaries of practice and experience.[9]

Sources on primitive slavery carry the sentiment that slavery acted as a barrier against ultimate wretchedness: mutilation, torture, gratuitous violence, and whimsical power.[10] Any provision for slavery is encumbered with a rule mitigating it rather than one providing an inducement for its propagation. As Lord Acton put it, slavery was a stage to freedom. Cruelty to slaves was subject to legal sanctions. On the economic side Edward Westermarck contended that slavery is an industrial institution embracing compulsory labor beyond the limits of family relations. The interest of the owner in the slave is limited to the working power of the slave. This definition, however, does not reflect the compulsory and uneven nature of the relationship; it relates chiefly to domestic slavery.

It is relevant to the understanding of the circumstantial character of slavery to observe that in origin slavery was rooted in war, with captives forming the bulk of slaves. As defeated enemies captives forfeited their rights and could be killed, as they often were, or else adopted. As an alternative to execution, captivity pointed to manumission, with economic labor an incentive against gratuitous violence. Accordingly the jurists stipulate that mutilation of a slave is grounds for freedom, the implication being that the slave as slave is not mere property and has not forfeited his or her basic right to humanity—God may have allowed slavery, but God created no one a slave. The legal rules regulating slavery stipulate that promises and contracts made by slave owners with their slaves are binding, irrevocable, and notionally enforceable. Typical of such rules is the declaration an owner makes in full health that upon his or her death the slave in question shall be set free: such a slave, known as *mudabbar* because of being granted the license of *tadbír,* may not be disposed of in subsequent probate settlement. "A declaration to grant a slave freedom at the owner's death is made by saying to the slave, 'You are free at my death.' Thereafter the owner has no right to sell the slave or [to] give him away."[11]

The same rule applies to female slaves who have children by the slave master. Such a slave is called *umm walad* and is accorded the status of a *mudabbarah,* that is, she accedes to the rights of a *tadbír.* Indeed the domestic order of slave life is saturated with discretionary concessions and dispensations: undertaking trade or a business venture on behalf of the owner, going on pilgrimage to Mecca, and assuming social or ritual functions normally reserved for free persons, for example, confer the rights of *tadbír.* A slave may also be granted a writ, called a *kitábah,* permitting him or her to purchase freedom on the basis of a mutually agreed sum—such a slave is called a *mukátab* (fem. *mukátabah*). By the terms of a *kitábah* the master is prohibited from having any further sexual relations with the slave.

There are seven forms of manumission: 1) immediate; 2) deferred; 3) partial; 4) by a will; 5) by written agreement; 6) postmortem; and 7) by conceiving and giving birth to the child of a master. There are five reasons for manumission: i) voluntary; ii) for swearing an oath to manumit; iii) for mutilation; iv) for partial freeing; and v) the result of a family relationship.[12] In this way the orthodox canon becomes a Jacob's ladder by which the slave may think to be "admitted to that equal sky," in the words of Alexander Pope in *An Essay on Man.*

Needless to say, these rules have been breached time and again and at will, which creates at the opposite end of the spectrum a far different situation for the victims of the system. Enslavement is not a favor that society does for the slave, and no slave volunteers for the position. Indeed for many it is a dramatic and traumatic way to be hauled into the Muslim world order. Even the means available for achieving one's freedom leave the slave enmeshed in the dragnet of imposed servitude. A slave who is aware of the provisions for manumission still remains beholden to the code and must therefore acknowledge the legitimacy of slavery to be entitled even to the fiction of emancipation. The code socializes the slave to feel slavery to be divinely sanctioned, to feel that the system is just and that moral merit may be obtained by acquitting oneself according to the rules and expectations of servitude. Religious text and social practice thus combined to endorse the culture of servitude, suggesting that slavery sat well with a system of moral enlightenment.

Accordingly for the historian, the really interesting aspect of the legal tracking of slavery is how the rules featured in debates and discussions among Muslims themselves, particularly in cases involving abuse. Slave narratives for that reason are important source material because they contain antislavery sentiments as well as give evidence of socialization in individual cases. Narrative history has its pitfalls, admittedly, but its value for the issue of consciousness and agency cannot be overestimated. In another respect the widespread practice of enslaving Africans in trans-Saharan raids often involved taking Muslim captives in flagrant transgression of the law. Over time threatened Muslim Africans acquired the moral fortitude and backing necessary to attack such indiscriminate slave raids and to challenge their tormentors. In a letter in 1391–92 to the sultan of Egypt, the sultan of the West African kingdom of Borno complained about slave raids into his territory by Arabs from the north in spite of the fact that he and his people were free and Muslim. These Arabs, he lamented, "have devastated all our land, all the land of Bornu. They took free people among us captive, of our kin among Muslims. . . . They have taken our people as merchandise." The Borno ruler appealed for his people to be returned, but to no avail.[13] For such African critics, slavery was the inlet by which the safety of society and the cause of truth were breached.

Thus did Ahmad Bábá turn with an awakened conscience to attack slavery as an evil that stained the image of Islam. An illustrious Muslim scholar, Ahmad Bábá was captured in Timbuktu and exiled to Morocco, where he lived between the years 1593 and 1608. He used the opportunity there to compose a treatise on slavery, *Miráj al-Su'úd*, saying that the slavers brushed aside the stipulations of religion and preyed on innocent Muslim Africans. The convenient but immoral stigma of skin color combined with predatory greed to cloud the slavers' ethical judgment, to the scandal of religious conscience everywhere. The practices involved in pursuing and maintaining the institution of slavery, Ahmad Bábá insisted, were injurious to Africans and corrupting of religion. Dismissing the Hamitic hypothesis of the curse of Noah's children as pure invention, Ahmad Bábá presented a parade of chains of transmission to establish the opinion that no racial connotation can be read into the traditions. Islam, he insisted, is based on the righteous life rather than on race and biology. "There is no difference between one race and another," he asserted.[14]

A nineteenth-century Moroccan scholar, al-Násirí, picked up the racial gauntlet and condemned the practice of enslaving Africans in spite of their being Muslims. He said his country had for far too long been afflicted with the heinous practice of "the indiscriminate enslavement of the people of the Súdán and the importation of droves of them every year to be sold in the market places and country, where men trade in them as one would trade in beasts." People became accustomed to thinking that the Holy Law itself approved enslavement on the ground of color alone. "This, by God's life, is one of the foulest and gravest evils perpetrated upon God's religion."[15] Once slavery has been entrenched in society, evidence of its legitimacy is not hard to establish and is easy to defend.

For that reason, contends al-Násirí, no confidence can be placed in the testimony of slave traders or dealers, who "are even more prone [than regular traders to] lie about their goods when selling them. . . . How could we believe them when we see

that those who import [slaves] or deal in them are men of no morals, no manly qualities, and no religion, and when we know [the evil nature of the] times and see [the
wickedness] of their people?"[16] Without the safeguard of ethical integrity, no reliance
can be placed on the testimonies of slaves themselves, who may be conditioned to lie
and admit to their slave status in order to facilitate a sale and that way escape from a
cruel master. The onus is on Muslims to ascertain whether or not someone has been
enslaved in a lawful manner, as al-Ghazálí (d. 1111) suggested in areas of doubtful
practice. "The clear rule is that the existence of areas of doubt provides the presumption for inquiry," wrote al-Ghazálí.

Muslims could not turn their backs on the scruples with which scripture and the
law saddled enslavement. Even if nothing more than strong doubt existed in the matter, there would be a case for preventive action that would oblige believers "to cease
to have anything to do with an evil which is derogatory to honor and religion. We
ask God to give success to him whom He has charged with the affairs of [His] servants in bringing to an end this wickedness." Implicated in that evil as they were,
Muslims might recall the words of scripture: "Lord, we have wronged ourselves, and
if You do not pardon us and have mercy upon us we shall be among those who suffer [eternal] loss."[17]

The sense of shame and scandal has not, however, made much of a dent on
African enslavement in the Arab world. Progress in moral sentiment, while com-
mendable in itself, was often out of step with developments in practice. Accordingly
slave markets in East and West Africa, Sudan, North Africa, Egypt, and beyond were
thriving well into the twentieth century as confidence in the legitimacy of slavery
remained undiminished even after Western emancipation. The French commandant
of the Saharan oasis town of Timimoun from July 1944 to the end of 1947, F. J. G.
Mercadier, for example, reported on slaves still being seized at the time and secured,
sometimes by means of castration, as they tracked the desolate "middle passage"
across the Sahara.[18] Eunuchs were in such high demand that slavers took risks in neu-
tering them even though the vast majority died as a result.

Running alongside the bitter stream of servile violence is a more agreeable tradition of humane treatment of slaves. The topic is described in great detail in numerous travelers' accounts through the centuries, suggesting a genuinely complicated
picture of the institution of slavery in Muslim society. What seems to persist in many
of the accounts is the sentiment of moral obligation, such as death-bed granting of
freedom with the hope of heavenly reward. The English Jesuit and European diplo-
mat William Gifford Palgrave (d. 1888) described the position of Muslim slaves in
those terms in his *Personal Narrative of a Year's Journey through Central and Eastern
Arabia* (1862–63). In his *Seven Pillars of Wisdom,* Lawrence of Arabia makes related
observations. Similarly Edward Lane in his *Manners and Customs of the Modern Egyp-
tians* set down humane observations on Muslim domestic slavery, as did Douglas
Grant.[19] Yet one is struck in all of this by the relative silence of the slave voice, as if

conscience and agency belong elsewhere as the preserve of others, to be invoked at grave risk to livelihood and liberty.[20]

In contrast, Western slavery and abolition have attracted the attention of Muslim observers, with the interest focused on what was deficient in Western emancipation, including the use of colonial administrative measures to impose abolition on the Muslim world. A member of the Egyptian *'ulamá* commented wryly that when the United States freed its slaves, many fell idle and roamed the streets desperate for something to do and somewhere to belong. At their wits' ends, they returned to their former masters begging to be taken back into slavery.

The same thing happened in Egypt, he claimed, when the British imposed abolition there. Reeling from the social upheaval of sudden emancipation, the British relented and allowed the reinstatement of slavery with the condition that the masters would be forbidden to sell or trade their slaves. All this goes to show, the *'álim* freely allowed, that there was higher wisdom in Islamic law not to mandate abolition but instead to integrate slavery into the structure of a wise and well-ordered society.[21] In the view of such *'ulamá* moral progress is to be measured by the capacity of the religious code to adjust—or to be adjusted—to social changes wrought by other means, which restricts the code to a diagnostic rather than to a prescriptive role in social reform.

It is pertinent to the issue to point out that Tunisia, which was part of the Ottoman dominions, was the first Muslim country to move to suppress the slave trade. Ahmad Bey, the sultan (ruled from 1838 to 1855), promulgated measures in the 1840s to abolish the trade and to emancipate the slaves. After considerable Western pressure and much foot dragging, Egypt in 1877 signed a convention on abolition with Britain. Terence Walz, for example, pointed out in a study how slave markets thrived and were well organized in Cairo through much of the nineteenth century, suggesting the scale of the obstacles to be surmounted to introduce emancipation.[22] Religion's role in historical transformation must be more than providing an opportunistic and mechanistic endorsement of the inevitable, as the *'ulamá* seem to suggest. What flows with the river may not disrupt its flow, but it cannot change its course, and yet in the case of slavery a change of course was a historical imperative.

It is an issue well recognized by the *'ulamá* in other circumstances. In one Muslim's assessment of relations with the West in the context of the loss of Muslim Spain, for example, a related point was made about the importance of moral choice at historical turning points. As one of the last Spanish Muslims to be expelled with his fellow Moriscoes, the writer challenged the new Christian rulers on the sovereign principle of religion. He argued that forced conversion of Christians was forbidden by official policy because it was contrary to the public ordinances of Islam and to Muslim sentiment. He noted that the Christian policy of suppressing Islam violated the very heart of what made a person religious, namely, a free and unfettered conscience. Islam adhered to that rule by limiting itself only to tinkering with the ordinary habits of outward appearance rather than having the inquisitor thrust his hand into people's consciences with the force of penal sanction.

The Morisco might have given the example of the great Jewish scholar Moses Maimonides (1135–1204), who under the puritan Almohads in Spain feigned conversion to Islam and then fled to Muslim Egypt, where he promptly declared himself to be a Jew. A Muslim jurist from Spain pursued him there and denounced him for his apostasy, demanding his execution as a renegade. The case was quashed by al-Qádí al-Fadl 'Abd al-Rahím b. 'Alí, one of the most famous Muslim judges and a prime minister of Saladin (1137–93), the sultan of Egypt. Al-Rahím issued an authoritative legal opinion to the effect that a person who had been converted to Islam by force could not rightly be considered a Muslim, thus voiding the sentence.[23] The story has been vigorously contested by some Jewish writers, although it is relevant to point out that the first writer to mention the story, Ibn al-Qiftí, was a contemporary of Maimonides.[24] At any rate, with pointed reference to the Inquisition, the Morisco probes the principle of toleration based on the primacy of conscience as a defining issue in relations between Islam and the West. Muslims, he admits, do not have clean hands in the matter, as witness their treatment of the Jews. Yet even there Muslims dealt with Jews only "according to justice and equity; but we cannot legally touch their consciences" even when the Jews persisted in their antinomian defiance about being "God's Favourite and Elected People." He challenged the new Spanish Christian powers:

> You can never produce, among us, any bloodthirsty, formal tribunal, on account of different persuasions in points of faith, that anywise approaches your execrable Inquisition. Our arms, it is true, are ever open to receive all who are disposed to embrace our religion; but we are not allowed by our sacred Alcoran to tyrannize over consciences. Our proselytes have all imaginable encouragement, and have no sooner professed God's Unity and His Apostle's mission [than] they become one of us, without reserve; taking to wife our daughters, and being employed in posts of trust, honour and profit; we contenting ourselves with only obliging them to wear our habit, and to seem true believers in outward appearance, without ever offering to examine their consciences, provided they do not openly revile or profane our religion: if they do that, we indeed punish them as they deserve; since their [conversion] was voluntarily, and was not by compulsion. Now, how very different are your ungenerous methods from these, let the world judge. You, not contenting yourselves with forcing people, by the most illegal and most inhumane means in the world, to profess what their own reason will never suffer them to believe, are so far from giving them any encouragement to reconcile their digestion to the nauseous drench you so tyrannically urge down their throats, that you trace pedigrees even up to the tenth progenitor; in which, if your heralds can find a

drop of new Christian blood, the candidate for any profitable employ is impe-
riously and superstitiously told, *Ay vil sangre en la casta, There is base blood in
the stock.* You plead, it is true, a zeal for God's church, but alas! if yours is God's,
which is the Devil's? God is all justice, mercy and bounty. How well you, who
have the presumption to term yourselves His ministers, come up to that character, your actions demonstrate.[25]

Considerations of conscience and slave agency eventually converged in the American
Revolution when Africans were conscripted with the incentive of the offer of emancipation. The Revolution set in train an inexorable human rights movement that
would engulf slavery.[26] In 1772 the Virginia House of Burgesses unanimously agreed
on an address to the king appealing to him "to remove those restraints on the gover-
nors of the colony, which inhibited them from assenting to such laws as might check
so very pernicious a commerce." The address then stiffened into an ominous warning of the coming debacle: "The importation of slaves into the colonies, from the
coasts of Africa, has long been considered as a trade of great inhumanity, and under
its encouragement, we have too much reason to fear, will endanger the very existence
of Your Majesty's American Dominions."[27] In the subsequent period after the Revolution the Virginia legislature debated the question of abolition, to the consternation
of southern slaveholders, one of whom noted with dismay, "The seal has now been
broken; the example has been set from a high quarter." An advocate of the American
Colonization Society (ACS) agreed that the seal had indeed been broken and a new
order begun, "when a slaveholding politician finds himself constrained to write seventy five pages of closely printed argument against the abolition of slavery."[28]

The idea of moral progress was a motivating force in debates about abolition and
emancipation as well as about colonization. Robert Stockton, an architect of the
ACS, said he wished to dissent from those who measured moral progress in terms of
material success because America's greatness was radically different: "What, sir, in the
rearing and advancement of a young, reflecting, and yet enterprising people, are the
real advantages of the age in which we live? Are they, that architecture is rebuilding
her proudest temples; that music swells its unequaled harmony; that painting bids
fair to rival the works of its ancient masters; or that the arts, whether useful or orna-
mental, guided by the light of liberal science, are rapidly striding to perfection? No,
sir; it is because we have before us the experience of many ages, and the philosophy
of so many human experiments and human failures to humble and enlighten us."[29]

In January 1827 Henry Clay rose in the House of Representatives to allay the fears
of his southern compatriots, assuring them that colonization was not detrimental to
their interests while granting the argument of principle that the American Constitution was a universal human rights charter implicitly ranged on the side of liberty for
slaves. The Constitution had lit a fuse for freedom that could never be extinguished,
he asserted. In a letter to the ACS, James Madison echoed Stockton when he said that

he was expressing the devout hope of many fellow citizens "that the time will come, when the dreadful calamity which has so long afflicted our country, and filled so many with despair, will be gradually removed, and by means consistent with justice, peace and the general satisfaction: thus giving to our country the full enjoyment of the blessings of liberty, and to the world the full benefit of its great example."[30] In a resolution proposed to the ACS and adopted, the sponsor, Reverend Slicer, addressed the society specifically on the role he saw Christianity playing in promoting the improvement of Africans. He said that Christian teaching excited sympathy for the suffering and with it deeds of benevolence and humanity. It was the role of churches to challenge Americans to take what he called "a lively, a deep, and an abiding inter-est in the temporal and moral condition of the whole African race." As "partakers of the 'common salvation,' we shall feel a solemn responsibility resting upon us to extend to that benighted and bleeding continent, by every possible means, the bless-ings of Christianity and of civilization."

Slicer believed that the time for restitution had come. Christ died for Africans too, he pleaded. He continued: "Although the tears of the black man have fallen un-heeded, and his sighs have passed in the breeze unheard by his oppressor, yet there is an eye that never sleeps, and an ear that hears 'the sighing of the prisoner'—and there is a common Father in Heaven, 'Who made of one blood all the nations,' and who will avenge the wrong of all his children. The African slave trade, Sir, is the broadest and darkest blot upon the page of this world's history."

A hoodwinked philosophy, Slicer challenged, had set out to pair morality with the contour of the countenance, and to estimate the capacity for knowledge and salva-tion by a scale of inches and by the acuteness of angles, and that way to deny that the children of Mother Africa had any share in the family of Adam and of God. Slicer declared that the time had come when Africans too "*shall be given to the Messiah for his inheritance,* when *the uttermost parts of the earth become his possession.* The word has gone forth and shall not return void; *God shall rebuke strong nations from afar— He shall break the bow, and burn the chariot in the fire*—they shall cast their idols to the moles and bats—'beat their swords into ploughshares, and their spears into prun-ing hooks,' and Ethiopia . . . shall lift up her *confiding hands* to the white man's God and Saviour." Revelation and the omnipotence of God could be trusted for such a decisive moral outcome, Slicer declared confidently.[31]

In many slave communities there was a general disposition to link the war with the specific cause for abolition. In 1774 blacks in Boston offered to fight for the British provided the British would guarantee to free them if they triumphed. The British took the proposal seriously enough to treat it as a matter for high security dis-cussion, though that very confidentiality suppressed any more information about its eventual outcome.[31] In 1775 a group of blacks organized in North Carolina to join the Loyalists in the conviction that if they succeeded, they would "be settled in a free government of their own."[32] In 1778 a slave named Tom, owned by one Henry

Hogan of Albany, New York, was arrested and imprisoned for attempting to incite other slaves to bid for their freedom by joining the enemy side. In July 1780 news was leaked of an impending slave plot in Albany County, New York, to burn the settlement and flee to the British side. In Elizabeth Town, New Jersey, a major slave plot was reported brewing in 1779, aided and abetted by prominent local Tories.[33]

Such widespread and spontaneous outbursts of agitation among slaves indicated that there was widespread sentiment for abolition. Historical opportunity in the form of siding with the British might thus have advanced the cause, but so also might legal action that individual slaves initiated. Thus in 1766 in Massachusetts, John Adams backed the legal appeal of a slave woman who brought action in a court and prevailed. In 1769 another slave sued his master for his freedom in the Nantucket Court of Common Pleas and succeeded. In 1773 the slave Caesar Hendrick brought charges against his being "detained in slavery," as he put it, and won the case with damages and cost. In 1774 the slave of Caleb Dodge of Beverly, just north of Boston, initiated proceedings to obtain his freedom, an action in which he succeeded.

These individual suits were an important avenue of redress on the slave question, and they were resorted to where practicable. Between 1640 and 1865, for example, a total of 591 cases came before the courts in fifteen states and the District of Columbia. Of those cases 279 were won, 224 lost, and 88 unresolved.[34] Figures elsewhere show the same pattern. Of 670 suits for freedom, only 327 were won and 248 lost, with 95 undecided. These suits for freedom were filed in cases in which the slaves were claiming rights in wills that provided for their emancipation.[35] However, the evidence proves that such suits were of limited value, important proof that the slave voice was never completely silenced, but proof too that personal suits could not be an effective or universal answer to the problem. The enterprise and expense involved made personal suits exceptional instruments, and the judgments rendered established no broad principle of universal freedom, with each individual case contested on its merits.[36]

A more useful legal weapon would be to invoke tort law, so in January 1773 a group of slaves petitioned the General Court of Massachusetts to grant them collective relief. "We have no property! we have no wives! we have no children! no city! no country!" they protested.[37] In June 1773 the legislature appointed a "Committee on the Petition of Felix Holbrook, and others; praying to be liberated from a State of Slavery." For their petition the slaves sought the support of the governor, Thomas Hutchinson, but to their disappointment he declined, and the petition languished. Undaunted, the slaves drafted a second petition in May 1774 and sent it to the governor and legislature, describing themselves as "a Grate Number of Blacks who are held in a state of slavery within the bowels of a free and christian Country."[38] Their argument for freedom rested on natural law foundations. They were born free and had never forfeited that freedom by any compact or agreement of their own. On the contrary they had been stolen from their parents, torn from their land, transported against their will, and condemned for life to be slaves in a country that claimed to be Christian. Their enslavement, they pressed, violated natural law norms, moral sentiment, and revealed canon. No species of law or truth could justify slavery. Their freedom should be restored, they insisted, not as a concession but as a right, and restitution by way of land should accompany it. The legislature debated the question but evaded it, stipulating simply that "the matter now subside." The path of collective assignation, like that of individual suits, came to a desultory end.

The Quaker Anthony Benezet wrote in the 1770s that the accounts of travelers in Africa remained a source of much unreliable knowledge since these travelers merely rehashed fabricated accounts, repeating errors from one traveler to another. It takes the report of only one trustworthy observer to expose the unsoundness of such travel accounts. One such report, Benezet said, was by Peter Kolben (1675–1726), a man of learning sent from Prussia to make astronomical observations in South Africa, who, "having no interest in the slavery of the Negroes, had not the same inducement as most other relators, to misrepresent the natives of Africa."[39] Mary Locke emphasizes the importance of such Quaker contribution and in particular takes the work of Benezet as representative of that cause. She offers it as her critical opinion that "there is probably no other man in the period of gradual abolition who did so much for the antislavery movement in America as Anthony Benezet."[40]

It is easy and plausible to construe the issue of freedom in Islam as a matter purely of a slave-ridden culture, with legal instruments fashioned for its implementation. That approach, however, leaves little room for action based on the tribunal of the free conscience and overlooks the sentiments of humanity that saturate the whole field of devotional practice. After all, compulsion in religion is denounced by no less an exalted source than the Qur'an (ii: 256). Indeed the institution of Islam is premised on freedom, with religious obligations ('*ibádát*) a matter of full moral responsibility. The protests mounted in their turn by the king of Borno, Ahmad Bábá, and al-Násirí, for example, against the cavalier enslavement of innocent, defenseless populations, and the complaints by slaves themselves, show that the moral impulse had not wilted completely. When circumstances changed, Muslim leaders favored abandonment of slavery and adopted emancipation.

What the sources have not enabled me to determine with any degree of confidence is the positive role, if any, the Muslim religious code played in contriving and directing the circumstances of emancipation without external Western pressure. The reprimand of my field informants, it may be recalled, was inspired by religious sentiment and showed how attitudes have persisted beyond legal manumission. The argument of David Brion Davis in his essay in this volume, "Slavery, Emancipation, and Progress," to the effect that slavery was not an impediment to ideas of moral progress or even to those of morality seems valid in the Islamic case too. Revealed law and the entire progressive cavalcade of learned jurists inscribed the handicap of slavery into fabric of collective life. The fruits of manumission dispensed with the right hand were no less coveted than the slave booties secured by the bellicose left hand. Both are mandated by the revealed code.[41] From the establishment of the Pax Islamica in Mecca to the rise and expansion of the caliphate slavery remained a recognized social institution in Muslim society. It was no accident that in Muslim law manumission is stipulated only as voluntary and desirable (*matlúb*) rather than as obligatory. Consequently the antislavery sentiment that occurs in much of Islam acquired nothing more than the force of a protest movement.

This prompts a question with relevance for comparative history. Clearly Islam's proximity to the sources of Christian reflection on slavery has not produced a comparable social movement of antislavery moral activism. The diagnostic procedure of the '*ulamá*, we saw, works well in hindsight, but it does little to set the pace for change and reform. Moral reasoning here only traces the path set for it; it does not cut its own track except where it coincides with convenience and opportunity, as the '*ulamá* freely admitted. Can progress in any morally meaningful sense occur in these circumstances without an effect on the code itself? The verdict in one instance of slave-owning clerics that acquiescence to emancipation imposed by the colonial authorities was the price they were willing to pay to save themselves from complete annihilation seems eminently sound.[42] Yet it falls considerably short of the moral stricture that would deem slavery an offense to conscience and to justice.

With respect to the Western antislavery movement the position is no less complex, if somewhat different in tenor and disposition. It is a pertinent question worth raising concerning the fate of the global economic system of the slave trade whether the moral ideas that challenged and ultimately overwhelmed it came from the trade itself. Did material incentives have a hidden and an inexorable moral and humanizing effect on the slave trade, or did such moral ideas originate in sentiments above and beyond the mercantile slavery system, ideas that proceeded from the premise of Christianity as a religion of salvation as Weber defines it? The sunny Enlightenment view that human beings have an inborn will to freedom conflicts with an equally powerful inborn desire for domination, a contradiction that acted to undercut any overweening confidence in natural law remedies. The existence of slavery refutes the notion of freedom as an innate virtue. In its ensconced racial form, slavery was the fatal obstacle that the doctrine of natural perfection could not surmount. Yet by the same token, many who considered themselves virtuous owned slaves and saw little inconsistency in that. Only in the ferment of the antislavery movement and its crucial supporting evangelical scruples did slavery eventually attract the moral odium of international condemnation and rejection that finally contributed to destroying the system. That points to the organizational impetus of the evangelical movement as a key factor in the rise and triumph of antislavery, as David Hempton describes in his essay in this volume, "Popular Evangelicalism and the Shaping of British Moral Sensibilities, 1770–1840."[43]

There was widespread backing for the idea, as William Thornton, the Quaker philanthropist, argued in 1785, that legitimate trade and profit would forge a moral chain to strangle the vicious slave trade to the direct benefit of the long-suffering Africans. Yet experience suggested something else, as Mary Kingsley observed from her research and experience in West Africa. "Conscience," she wrote, "when conditioned by Christianity, is an exceedingly difficult thing for a trader to manage satisfactorily to himself."[44] John Maynard Keynes echoed the idea in his comment about how expedient calculation sits loosely to matters of moral obligation: "The modern capitalist is a fair-weather sailor. As soon as a storm rises, he abandons the duties of navigation and even sinks the boats which might carry him to safety by his haste to push his neighbor off and himself in."[45]

In that mercantile world, slavery flourished by the successful coupling of self-interest and material reward, handing the antislavery movement reason to wrap itself in moral arguments in order to hobble the traffic in human merchandise. Freedom is an attribute of God and, as the Muslim jurists concede, is the original title of the race of Adam. Its denial is an affront to the divine honor, in the words of William Penn.

Notes

1. An Egyptian *'álim*, Muhammad Jum'a 'Abd Alláh, wrote in 1980 that God's "ordinances are not inspired by that which is not in accord with the interests of humanity as a whole. He desires ease for His servants and does not desire hardship for them." He then went on to consider slavery and emancipation, saying that Islam did not force emancipation but worked gradually to usher in changes for which society was prepared. This gradual policy "taught the slave, refined him and perfected him, and raised his status and made him equal with his master. It provided a livelihood for him and then freed him." See the excerpt in John O. Hunwick and Eve Troutt Powell, eds., *The African Diaspora in the Mediterranean Lands of Islam* (Princeton, N.J.: Markus Wiener, 2002), 17–19.

2. Reuben Levy, *The Social Structure of Islam* (Cambridge: Cambridge University Press, 1965), 61.

3. Ibid., 62–63.

4. E. R. Madden, *Egypt and Muhammad Ali, Illustrative of the Condition of His Slaves and Subjects* (London, 1841), excerpt in Hunwick and Powell, eds., *The African Diaspora*, 190.

5. "The basic assumption in regard to the human species is freedom and lack of any cause for being enslaved. Whoever maintains the opposite is denying the basic principle" (Ahmad b. Khalid al-Nasiri of Morocco writing in the nineteenth century, quoted in John Hunwick, "Arab Views of Black Africans and Slavery," http://www.yale.edu/glc/events/race/Hunwick.pdf [last accessed August 25, 2009]).

6. Slavery, writes the Tunisian Muhammad Bayram al-Khámis (d. 1889), is contingent. The term is defined as legal incapacitation in the sense that the slave is disqualified from undertaking duties that a free person could. The institution of slavery is based on the assumption that a person has declined to accept legal responsibility, and it persists in that. "As regards the

general basis of respecting human beings, the slave is not excluded from it, so that he can be fit to return to his original condition of freedom, through being manumitted. . . . Hence one who is already a Muslim cannot be enslaved" (al-Khámis, *Tahqíq fí masʿalat al-riqq*, in Hunwick and Powell, eds., *The African Diaspora*, 15–16).

7. Writing in the nineteenth century, the Dutch scholar Snouck Hurgronje testified that domestic slaves were invariably set free at about the age of twenty because their work would otherwise bring them into daily contact with free and unfree women. Few offices or positions were unattainable to freed slaves, with the consequence that they were well represented among burghers and owners of property and business establishments in Mecca. Hurgronje is cited in Hunwick and Powell, eds., *The African Diaspora*, 166.

8. "For all men are the sons of Adam," declared Ahmad Bábá (quoted in John Hunwick, "Islamic Law and Polemics over Race and Slavery in North and West Africa [16th–19th Century]," in *Slavery in the Islamic Middle East*, edited by Shaun Elizabeth Marmon [Princeton, N.J.: Marcus Wiener, 1999], 51).

9. Ibn Juzayy affirmed: "Whoever intentionally mutilates his slave in a visible fashion, e.g., cuts off his fingertips or the extremity of his ear or the tip of his nose, or if cuts any part of his body, shall be punished and the slave freed without authorization. . . . If someone swears to give his slave a hundred lashes, the slave should rapidly be set free before the beating takes place" (Hunwick and Powell, eds., *The African Diaspora*, 27).

10. Lord Acton, "The History of Freedom in Antiquity," February 26, 1877, http://www.acton.org/research/history-freedom-antiquity (accessed September 4, 2011). See Edward Westermarck, *The Origin and Development of the Moral Ideas*, 2 vols. (London: Macmillan, 1908), especially I: 670.

11. ʾAbdalláh ibn Abí Zayd al-Qayrawání (922–996), *The Risálah*, trans. and ed. Joseph Kenny (Minna, Nigeria: Islamic Education Trust, 1992), 150.

12. Muhammad b. Ahmad al-Gharnátí al-Kalbí, known as Ibn Juzayy (d. 1340), *Qawánín al-ahkám al-sharʿiyya wa-masáʾil al-furúʾ al-fiqhiyya*, in *The African Diaspora*, edited by Hunwick and Powell, 27–28.

13. Bernard Lewis, *Race and Slavery in the Middle East: An Historical Inquiry* (New York: Oxford University Press, 1992), 53.

14. *Miráj al-Suʿúd: Ahmad Bábá's Replies on Slavery*, trans. and ed. John Hunwick and Fatima Harrak (Rabat, Morocco: Institute of African Studies, Université Mohammed V, 2000), 35.

15. Ahmad b. Khálid al-Násirí, in Hunwick and Powell, eds., *The African Diaspora*, 45.

16. Ibid.

17. Qurʾán 7:23.

18. F. J. G. Mercadier, cited in Hunwick and Powell, eds., *The African Diaspora*, 105–6.

19. Dr. Heinrich Barth, *Travels and Discoveries in North and Central Africa: Being a Journal of an Expedition Undertaken under the Auspices of H.B.M's Government in the Years 1849–1855* (5 vols., London: Longmans Green & Co., 1857; repr., 3 vols., London: Frank Cass & Co. Ltd., 1965), 1:439, 527; Douglas Grant, *The Fortunate Slave: An Illustration of African Slavery in the Early Eighteenth Century* (London: Oxford University Press, 1968), chap. 3.

20. One slave, called Griga, described his harrowing experience of enslavement and passing hands until he settled with one master, Si Abdelkader, about whom he testified as follows: "Heaven knows, I can't say I was unhappy living with Si Abdelkader. I was properly fed; I

worked—obviously—but one has to work anywhere doesn't one?" Griga learned the art of pollinating female palm trees. "When I had finished I climbed down, with legs, arms, the whole body scratched to the point of bleeding by the thousands of spikes, and then I went on to the next tree." He explained his capture and induction into Islam, saying that those slaves who did not become Muslims within a few months were prey to harassment from fellow slaves. Although Griga observed the pre-Islamic customs of his African ancestors, he said he admired Muslims for their learning and ability. Eventually his master freed him, but he found himself stranded. He testified: "I, a freed man, was a good deal less fortunate than the slaves, who were fed, clothed and lodged by their master! My fate had not changed in any sense, except on a scrap of paper. I was a sharecropper of the owner of the garden. I was exploited by so-called Muslim scholars doing business in amulets, who tried to force my hand to buy some, so that by means of occult powers or unknown holymen I could change my scarcely enviable fate. In short, for us it is almost misery. We are not free: freedom, inasmuch as it consists of having responsibilities, facing up along to the pitfalls of life, deciding alone what would be good for us or bad, has never been able to change the color of the skin, or the structure of the environment in which one lives. . . . I am as much a slave as the least of slaves, because I am in debt" (Griga, quoted in Hunwick and Powell, eds., *The African Diaspora,* 214f).

21. Hunwick and Powell, eds., *The African Diaspora,* 18.

22. Terence Walz, "Notes on the Organization of the African Trade in Cairo, 1800–1850," *Annales Islamologiques* 11 (1972): 263–86.

23. G. P. Badger, *The Nestorians and Their Rituals,* 2 vols. (London: J. Masters, 1852), 1:133f.

24. A. Berliner, "Zur Ehrenrettung des Maimonides," in *Moses ben Maimon: Sein Leben, seine Werke und sein Einfluss Zur Erinnerung an den siebenhundertsten Todestag des Maimonides,* edited by Wilhelm Bacher et al., 2 vols. (Leipzig: Foch, 1908–14), 2:103ff.

25. Muhammad Rabadan, *Mahometism Fully Explained (Written in Spanish and Arabick in the Year 1603 for the Instruction of the Moriscoes in Spain),* trans. and ed. J. Morgan, 2 vols. (London: E. Curll, W. Mears, and T. Payne, 1723–25), 2:297f, 345f.

26. One of the main publications during the antislavery campaign in the United States was devoted to the human rights aspect of the struggle. See J. D. Weld, "The Bible against Slavery: An Inquiry into the Patriarchal and Mosaic Systems on the Subject of Human Rights," *Anti-Slavery Examiner,* no. 6 (1838). The point was not lost on the proslavery activists of the South, who attacked northern abolitionists for their "nonsensical prating" about "abstract notions of human rights." One such activist proclaimed: "Nothing can be more chimerical [than the claims of northern sentimentalists whose heads were so] filled with visions of equal rights." George Fitzhugh of Virginia affirmed as an article of faith that some men are "born with saddles on their backs and others booted and spurred to ride them, and the riding does them good." He was supported by John C. Calhoun. See Kenneth M. Stampp, *The Peculiar Institution: Slavery in the Ante-bellum South* (New York: Vintage, 1956), 420.

27. *Journals of the House of Burgesses,* April 1, 1772, 131.

28. *Letters on the Colonization Society* addressed to the Hon. C. F. Mercer, Member of the House of Representatives, Philadelphia, April 26, 1832, 22.

29. American Colonization Society, *The African Repository and Colonial Journal,* 68 vols. (Washington, D.C.: Way and Gideon, 1826), 1:14.

30. *Letters on the Colonization Society,* Philadelphia, April 26, 1832.

31. American Colonization Society, *The African Repository and Colonial Journal,* 68 vols. (Washington, D.C.: James C. Dunn, 1838), 14:24–26.

31. Herbert Aptheker, *American Negro Slave Revolts* (New York: Columbia University Press, 1943; repr., New York: International Publishers, 1978), 87.

32. Ibid., 88.

33. Ibid., 89.

34. Marion Russell, "American Slave Discontent in the Records of the High Courts," *Journal of Negro History* 31 (October 1946): 411–34.

35. Ibid., 418–19.

36. Russell wrote that "the length of time required to reach a final decision and the cost of such suits made freedom by this route beyond even the greatest sacrifices of all but a few determined slaves. In *Isaac v. Johnson,* a case begun in 1797, a decision was given in 1816. The deed of liberation in *Manns v. Givens* was granted in 1797; in 1815 the struggle for its recording began; and it was closed in 1836. The case of *Charlton v. Unis* and *Unis v. Charlton,* which appears in the court records of 1847–1855, was initiated in 1826 when a suit for freedom was based upon the declaration that an ancestress had been free in Connecticut or Massachusetts in 1775. *Charlotte (of color) v. Chouteau* appears in Missouri records four times between 1847 and 1862. The cost of the suit for freedom in *Woodfolk v. Sweeper* is given as $743.30" (ibid., 419).

37. Benjamin Quarles, *The Negro in the American Revolution* (New York: W. W. Norton, 1973), 39.

38. Ibid.

39. Anthony Benezet, *Some Historical Account of Guinea, Its Situation, Produce and the General Disposition of Its Inhabitants: With an Inquiry into the Rise and Progress of the Slave Trade* (Philadelphia, 1771; repr., London: J. Phillips, 1788); cited in Olaudah Equiano, *The Interesting Narrative and Other Writings,* edited by Vincent Carretta (New York: Penguin Books, 1995), 272–73. In a later period missionaries were conscious too of the hazards of garnished accounts. One source spoke of the danger that as people actually engaged on the ground, missionaries would be inclined to view their work "in too favourable a light; that they [would] tinge the picture with too bright a glow." The source rejected this, saying instead, "we believe that the very interest which Missionaries feel, and their solicitude for the salvation of the heathen, lead them continually to check themselves, lest they be tempted to place too favourable a construction on what is passing around them; and that they are particularly careful not to make statements, or encourage hopes, which might re-act on themselves or their work in the way of disappointment." The account went on to print the report of a physician who visited a mission station even though he was unconnected with mission work as such. See *Church Missionary Intelligencer* 4, no. 6 (June 1853), report on "The Yoruba Mission."

40. Mary Stoughton Locke, *Anti-Slavery in America: 1619–1808* (Boston: Ginn & Co., 1901), 28. See also Thomas E. Drake, *Quakers and Slavery in America* (New Haven, Conn.: Yale University Press, 1950). This has an exhaustive listing of primary and secondary sources.

41. Qur'an 47:4, 2:172.

42. Lamin Sanneh, *The Jakhanke Muslim Clerics: A Religious and Historical Study of Islam in Senegambia* (Lanham, Md.: University Press of America, 1989), 134–35, 237–38.

43. See also Lamin Sanneh, *Abolitionists Abroad: American Blacks and the Making of Modern West Africa* (Cambridge, Mass.: Harvard University Press, 2001).

44. Mary Kingsley, *West African Studies* (London: Macmillan, 1899; repr., London: Frank Cass, 1964), 128.

45. John Maynard Keynes, "The Resilience of Capitalism," *Atlantic Monthly* 149, no. 5 (May 1932): 521–26.

The Recent Historiography of British Abolitionism

Academic Scholarship, Popular History,
and the Broader Reading Public

Eric Arnesen

The worlds of academic scholarship and popular understandings of our collective past are two distinct, if sometimes related phenomena. In the best of circumstances the work of professional scholars, based on years of painstaking research and conceptualization, finds its way into the hands of those outside the academy. Ideally our research and arguments inform or define not just what our students might think but what the broader public does as well. The "best of circumstances," however, is one of those phrases that might be misleading, for the occasions when our scholarship decisively shapes larger interpretations and understandings occur far less frequently than we would desire. Under more commonly prevailing circumstances, academic historians' work forms a kind of backdrop against which historical popularizers, with access to larger reading markets, can paint their own distinct pictures; to mix my metaphors, our work constitutes building blocks that can be selectively arranged to suit the popularizers' purposes. We, the academic or professional historians, may be indispensable to the enterprise, but we do not have much of a say in determining the uses to which our findings and arguments get put.

To frame the matter in these terms, it can be argued, does a genuine disservice to the popularizers on several grounds. First, unlike academic scholars, popular historians fill a market niche and meet a genuine demand among members of the public for readable works of history. In contrast, academic scholars often make little effort to reach audiences outside of their peers. Admittedly our writing is frequently dense and inaccessible; the debates we engage in are often of limited interest to those who have not spent their lives thinking about the issues we address. In addition, for the most part, we write intentionally for a specific audience—other scholars and students of history. For better or worse, we are specialists (critics might call us overspecialized) whose thematic obsessions, styles of writing, and modes of arguing may be considered appropriate to the academy but inappropriate beyond its walls. Because the work we produce is not intended for broader audiences, it should not be surprising when it does not find its way into the hands of the larger public. In contrast, popular historians reject our scholarly jargon, disregard our internal obsessions and (usually) our analyses, and ignore our historiographical hair splitting. Instead they aim at producing compelling and dramatic narratives that will hold the interest of nonprofessional readers. This requires them to pay much greater attention to the art of storytelling than most academic scholars are willing to devote (or are even capable of devoting). Local color, biographical detail, action, dramatic tension, and bold (in some cases exaggerated) claims dominate their accounts. The results are often fast-paced and readable books that the public can enjoy but professional historians often ignore.

Like academics, popularizers come in many different flavors. Some are rigorous, others sloppy; some are careful in their claims, others irresponsible. That is, like their academic counterparts, there are good popularizers and bad popularizers. At their best, popular historians do their own rigorous research, master the existing historiography, and craft persuasive and often moving narratives in language that (unlike that of many academics) draws readers into their texts and the worlds they create.[1] At their worst they misuse evidence, substitute political agendas for balanced argument, simplify complex material in a reductionist manner, and view the past through the lens of the present.[2] On occasion academic scholars consciously reorient themselves to encroach upon the popularizers' market, publishing books that combine original scholarship (or synthesis) with clear, narrative writing.[3] The heterogeneity of popular history should caution us against painting the genre with too broad a brush.

I would like to raise a distinct issue: the relationship between the scholarship of academic historians and the broader reading public. To put it another way: to what extent do scholars' findings make their way into popular understandings of the past via trade books? When our scholarship is translated for nonacademic audiences, what are the mechanisms of translation and what, precisely, are popular audiences learning? Is there, in fact, a gap—bridgeable or unbridgeable—between the academic world of scholarship and larger audiences? I am an Americanist with no formal training in British history, let alone British abolitionism, but I am a close student of recent popular history and a reader of both scholarly and popular histories of abolitionism on both sides of the Atlantic. My conclusions are straightforward: some of the academic scholars' empirical research does, in fact, find its way into popular histories; scholars provide the essential building blocks for the narratives that the popularizers produce. But something is lost in the process of translation: the larger intellectual concerns about the analysis of meaning, causality, belief, and ideas and ideology tend to be reduced to almost unrecognizable sound bites or simply ignored.

Let me begin briefly on the academic side of the historiographical equation with the treatment of the emergence of the movement to end the British slave trade.[4] Through the early twentieth century British abolitionism represented, to many, a triumph of moral conviction over material interests, to paraphrase John Stuart Mill. "For numerous writers," David Brion Davis has observed, "the history of British antislavery served as a paradigm of how enlightened liberals and reformers struggled in one stage after another to overcome the forces of greed, tyranny, and the most unambiguous symbol of man's inhumanity to man."[5] That model was turned on its head by the mid–twentieth century when the Trinidadian historian/activist Eric Williams and his followers contended that moral conviction was subordinate to and even a cover for material interests. In the case of the abolition of the slave trade, they insisted, Britain's material interests, not humanitarian or religious impulses, governed the course of events: declining profitability in Britain's slave colonies and the rise of manufacturing, with the concomitant imperative for new markets and the reduction in trade barriers, led reformers to attack slavery to ensure Britain's dominance.[6] Although that view long retained currency on the left, a considerable scholarly debate in the 1960s through 1980s effectively challenged the Williams view. David Eltis, Roger Anstey, Seymour Drescher, and others demonstrated that Williams's economic case was empirically flawed. "From the viewpoint of economic self-interest," Eltis argued two decades ago, "British antislavery policy appears wrongheaded enough to qualify for inclusion in Barbara Tuchman's catalog of folly in government."[7]

If Williams has been largely dispatched to the historiographical dustbin, scholars of abolitionism have continued to debate the causes, meanings, and effects of antislavery thought and agitation. Herbert S. Klein put the matter bluntly: "If competition and fear for their declining sugar islands did not drive the British abolition campaign, was it just a moral crusade as earlier scholars argued?"[8] The answers scholars have subsequently provided are, yes and no. Klein himself equated "moral" with possession of a "pro-African stance or belief in the inherent equality of blacks." On both counts white abolitionists fell short. Their deep belief that free labor—"as one of the most crucial underpinnings of modern society"—would lead to "mankind's progress" played to the interests of proponents of free trade and laissez-faire as well as those of British workers. If opposition to the slave trade had a "moral origin," it also was "based on the interests of European workers and capitalists and not on any concern with the African slaves themselves."[9] Framing the origins issue this way, Klein merely nodded in the direction of "moral crusade" while ultimately undercutting the role that morality itself played.

Although historians are generally not so quick to downplay the moral dimension of antislavery, they have long been determined to contextualize it. One "must take greater account of intellectual change in the eighteenth century and study in detail the interplay between the moral purpose of the political nation, muted as it was and long hamstrung by a deep-rooted sense of the national importance of the West Indies, and the high moral purpose, daunting perseverance and political skill, and, for the most part warmly Christian inspiration of the abolitionists," Roger Anstey argued in 1972. "The abolition was principally a moral achievement."[10] Participants in the "Antislavery Debate" of the mid-1980s and early 1990s took as their starting point the arguments on capitalism, hegemony, and abolition in David Brion Davis's 1975 book, *The Problem of Slavery in the Age of Revolution, 1770–1823*. For Thomas Haskell, humanitarian reformers of the late eighteenth century "deserved full credit for their moral insight, their courage in the face of adversity, and their tenacity in uprooting entrenched institutions." Yet those very insights, he insisted, were "called forth by changes in the social and economic conditions of life that, once the stage was set," would have been "almost certainly . . . carried out by other individuals if not by Wilberforce" and others "who actually did the job." The exchange between Davis, Thomas Haskell, and John Ashworth, which brought forth no consensus, ranged widely and creatively on the relationship between capitalism, class interest, ideology, and the emergence of a new humanitarian sensibility.[11]

In 2006 the historian Christopher Leslie Brown productively and provocatively revisited the subject of abolitionism's emergence as both a perspective and a set of political programs. "Although the story" of the rise of early British abolitionism is "well known," he argues in *Moral Capital*, "it remains poorly understood."[12] Tackling the "deceptively simple tale of origins," he contends that abolitionism "did not follow inevitably from enlightened sensibilities, social change, or a shift in economic interests. Nor did it spring forth spontaneously, as an uncaused cause free from circumstance or context." A movement against the slave trade "did not have to happen in Britain," he suggests.[13] Ultimately its emergence was highly contingent, its beginnings tentative. Moral sensibilities did not automatically translate into practice or program, for a "wide gulf" divides "mere perception of a moral wrong from decisions to seek a remedy." Antislavery sensibilities were a necessary precondition for abolitionism's development, but they did not automatically lead to an abolitionist movement. At the outset of his study he insists, "Antislavery values were not enough in the eighteenth century, or after. The decision to act involved more than thinking of slavery as abhorrent, although clearly this was crucial. Somehow this particular moral wrong had to become important and urgent enough to drive individuals and groups to confront entrenched institutions."[14] Abolitionism, he declares, "requires an explanation," a belief that leads him to focus on how antislavery ideas "translated into effective action."[15]

Rejecting classic formulations emphasizing providential design and the role of the heroic core of religiously driven leaders of the abolitionist movement—the "Saints" of the Clapham Sect—Brown reminds us that the movement "involved far more than the small circle of propagandists and elite politicians whom the first chroniclers tended to lionize." Sharing the credit (if not center stage) are the enslaved, whose resistance "helped put the legality of slaveholding in Britain on trial," on the one hand, and a "mobilized abolitionist public" that "helped ensure that the slave trade and slavery remained a political issue," on the other hand. Ultimately the movement's success "depended on a wider variety of actors than the older studies tended to allow."[16] Brown, however, also distances himself from the debates over capitalism, hegemony, evangelicalism, and humanitarianism that occupied much scholarly attention in the 1980s and 1990s. "The fit between antislavery values and their religious principles is well established," he concurs.[17] But that cannot explain timing or form; ideological frameworks are "conditions, not causes. If they predisposed, they did not dispose." The grand backdrop of grand concepts—capitalism's rise, the Enlightenment, free labor ideology—are overly broad: "We learn that certain individuals had certain ideas and that these ideas circulated extensively in the late eighteenth century but not what moved people to take specific initiatives at particular moments."[18]

Among Brown's contentions are the centrality of the American Revolution in rendering slavery problematic and politically important in "ways that it had never mattered before," turning the slave system "into a symbol, not just an institution, the source of self-examination" and prompting a dramatic rethinking of the "relation between empire and slavery."[19] On another level British military policy toward slaves of the advocates of American independence—the offering of freedom to those willing to fight against the Revolution and then of protection and removal to those who did so once the war had ended—also played a role. Moral purpose "emerged from an entirely amoral set of decisions," he argues. British commanders "did not set out to undermine North American slavery. Yet, once they started the process, they found little incentive to reverse course."[20] Brown also seeks to restore a proper appreciation of "Evangelicals' motivations,"[21] a subject he feels has been neglected in recent accounts. Not all Evangelicals embraced antislavery, of course. What requires explanation, Brown argues, is "not only why [specific] Evangelicals championed abolition . . . but, more generally, why Evangelicals took to politics at all, why a new ethos developed that enlarged the traditional concern with saving souls into a broader effort to reshape the nation and the empire."[22] Some turned to antislavery out of deep frustration with West Indian slaveholders' hostility to the propagation of the Gospel among the enslaved; their initial concern was not abolition but the spreading of the Gospel and a program of Christian reform in the Caribbean. Brown makes clear that slave trade abolition "for the Evangelicals always was an end in itself, never merely an instrument."[23] At the same time abolitionism operated for the Evangelicals as "an opening wedge, a Trojan horse that might breach the walls of infidelity for the cause of godliness,"[24] legitimizing their entry into a political arena, investing the devout with "political standing," and serving as an "opening salvo in a wider campaign against nominal Christianity that they advanced at once on several fronts."[25]

In addressing the question of popular history, it is necessary first to establish the larger cultural and political context in which this genre operates. In the United States the subject of race—in the American past and present—is an ever-present concern. All questions lead to the present, while contemporary political conflicts draw upon understandings (or misunderstandings) of the past. What "we understand today as racism is largely a legacy of the slavery that formally ended nearly a century and a half ago," James Oliver Horton and Lois E. Horton have argued. "The history of slavery continues to have meaning in the twentieth century—it burdens all of American history and is incorporated into public interpretations of the past."[26] Indeed Ira Berlin has observed that recent years have "witnessed an extraordinary engagement with slavery. . . . Without question, slavery has a greater presence than at any time since the end of the Civil War."[27] Concretely understandings of the past and political agendas in the present inform debates over how to present America's slave past in textbooks, documentaries, museums, and historical sites; apologies (or lack thereof) over slavery; affirmative action; and reparations, to cite but a few examples. For Berlin, the "extraordinary engagement with slavery" has sparked "a rare conversation on the American past—except, of course, it is not about the past" but rather about "a search for social justice on the critical issue of race. . . . There is a general, if inchoate, understanding that any attempt to address the question of race in the present must also address slavery in the past."[28] Yet not everyone would agree that the "conversation," as Berlin calls it, is actually taking place. In her book *African Voices of the Atlantic Slave Trade,* the historian Anne C. Bailey finds a "deafening silence on the subject of slavery and the Atlantic slave trade." The reluctance to address the slave past that she perceives extends not just to whites but to blacks as well. That, to her mind, requires explanation. "What is behind this silence? How can a period of more than three hundred years in some areas on the continent . . . be almost collectively forgotten?" African Americans and Africans exhibit a "kind of shame associated with slavery": some of this pertains to a taboo on discussing slave origins of individuals, while some of it surrounds the "involvement of some Africans in the sale of others in the Atlantic slave trade." Whatever the explanation, in assembling voices of the slave trade she hopes to fulfill the traditional academic function of adding to our "body of knowledge." Perhaps more importantly, she writes with "a social function in mind": to create a "kind of catharsis" that "in its best sense moves us to positive action."[29] If Bailey might not agree with Berlin about the centrality of slavery to contemporary American discussions, she shares with him the conviction of its political relevance for today.

On the matter of the "presence of" or "engagement with" slavery in today's political conversations, Berlin is more on target than Bailey, at least in the United States. That engagement takes multiple, public forms: museum exhibits, public-television documentaries, municipal laws requiring companies doing business with cities to document their involvement with slavery (my home city of Chicago has precisely such a law), the repeated furors on college campuses demanding acknowledgment of educational institutions' own dependence on slavery, and a spate of books aimed at popular audiences. But what Americans know about early American slavery or the British campaign against the slave trade is thin indeed. Several recent trade books have refocused readers' attention on that earlier period. In the remainder of this essay

I turn to several recent examples of "popular history" to examine how the antislavery impulse is treated and how contemporary scholarly concerns and findings are reflected, or deflected, in them.

To the extent that Americans know much about slavery before the antebellum era or the abolition of the slave trade, it is likely to come by way of an autobiography encountered at the undergraduate university level: *The Interesting Narrative of the Life of Olaudah Equiano, or Gustavus Vasa, the African, Written by Himself.*[30] A best seller in the late eighteenth century that economically sustained its author and served as an important weapon in the abolitionists' crusade against the slave trade, *The Interesting Narrative* is today a staple on reading lists in courses in history, English, and African American studies departments in the United States. It should not be a surprise that the book, since its rediscovery, has become a standard part of the curriculum, for Equiano's story can be said "to have it all." The book covers a wealth of subjects: West African societies in the mid–eighteenth century; the Middle Passage; slavery in the Americas; transatlantic travel and maritime culture; religion; and early abolitionism. Of particular importance is the simple fact of voice: Equiano the African offers a first-hand account of slavery, freedom, and racism in the eighteenth century, a period from which such voices are rare and hard to hear. The narrative was "one of the first anti-slavery books by a former slave,"[31] which alone would guarantee its importance. However, for the purposes of undergraduate education, it is the first-person testimony about the horrific character of the trade and the brutality of the slave system, on the one hand, and the agency of a slave-turned-freedman-turned-abolitionist, on the other, that gives the book its central appeal.[32]

The publication of Vincent Carretta's biography *Equiano the African: Biography of a Self-Made Man*[33] raises new historical and interpretive questions that have yet to be fully assimilated into pedagogical practices. The punch line of Carretta's book centers on the authenticity of a crucial aspect of Equiano's biography: his birthplace. If, as Carretta argues, evidence suggests that Equiano was born not in Africa, as he claimed, but in South Carolina, then the status of his firsthand observations is called into question. "The available evidence suggests that the author of *The Interesting Narrative* may have invented rather than reclaimed an African identity," he writes. If this new evidence is accurate, "he invented his African childhood and his much-quoted account of the Middle Passage on a slave ship." However, the possibility, or likelihood for Carretta, of an intentional misrepresentation of autobiographical fact does not diminish the narrative's significance. After all, Carretta argues, "Every autobiography is an act of re-creation, and autobiographers are not under oath when they are re-constructing their lives. Furthermore, an autobiography is an act of rhetoric." In addition, and crucially, Equiano's words were penned for the greater good of abolition: "the anti-slave-trade movement needed precisely the kind of account of Africa and the Middle Passage that he, and perhaps only he, could supply. An African, not an African American, voice was what the abolitionist cause required." That is what he provided. In doing so the role he assumed thus "earned him the right to claim an African name."[34]

Carretta's, of course, is hardly the last word on how we judge the narrative's importance. In a lively exchange in the pages of *Historically Speaking*, Trevor Burnard concludes that "Equiano cannot remain a central figure in the reconstruction of the Atlantic world unless the doubt that Carretta has cast upon his authenticity as an African disappears." Paul Lovejoy steps into the debate in an effort to challenge Carretta's biographical revisionism and reestablish Equiano's African origins.[35] But I would speculate that however or even if the debate is resolved, the outcome is likely to have little bearing on Equiano's utility for classroom instruction. Equiano "gave a voice to the millions of people forcibly taken from Africa and brought to the Americas as slaves," Carretta insists.[36] Given the paucity of such voices, our contemporary, understandable need to showcase those voices that do survive will probably guarantee that the narrative remains a popular primary document. I would also venture that current political realities will lead more scholars to accept Carretta's views than to reject them.

What, then, of the genuine trade books aimed at large, nonacademic audiences? In this section I will briefly examine two important and widely acclaimed books by award-winning authors: Adam Hochschild's *Bury the Chains: Prophets, Slaves, and Rebels in the First Human Rights Crusade;* and Simon Schama's *Rough Crossings: Britain, the Slaves and the American Revolution.*[37] Each book has reached a sizable popular audience that the vast majority of scholars could never dream of attaining. As they are perhaps the only books on their subjects that most in the nonacademic audience will encounter, it is useful to examine closely their approaches with an eye toward these two related questions: What, precisely, is the public learning? And, to what extent are the fruits of academic scholarship making their way beyond the academy's walls?

Professional historians encountering Hochschild's *Bury the Chains* will find a familiar story, albeit one that is more dramatically and compellingly told than in university press books. Hochschild may break no new empirical ground on the subject of the abolition of the slave trade and the institution of slavery in the British Empire, but as he is a thoroughly engaging writer, his accomplishment lies in poignantly transporting his modern-day lay readers to a world that, as historians instinctively grasp but popular readers may be forgiven for not always knowing, was in many ways vastly different from our own. Just over two centuries ago the institution of chattel slavery was not only alive and well but also served as the economic basis not just of the states in the American South but of the English, French, Spanish, and Portuguese empires in the Americas as well. At the end of the eighteenth century, Hochschild reminds readers, much of the planet's population was composed not of free independent laborers but of slaves or serfs toiling under compulsion and pain of cruel punishment. Bondage, not freedom, was "normal." Slavery, with a history stretching back millennia, was legal, largely unquestioned, and generally legitimate. From the late fifteenth through the late nineteenth centuries, a "huge armada" of European vessels, "spread out in time as well as space," completed as many as thirty-five thousand transatlantic voyages transporting eleven million slaves to the colonies in the Americas. Before the British ended their participation in the international slave trade in 1807, their ships alone were responsible for the capture and forcible relocation of over three million Africans.[38]

This was, Hochschild argues, "a universe that took slavery for granted," so much so that even religion did not necessarily lead to its questioning. In the late eighteenth and early nineteenth centuries, the Church of England not only contributed nothing to the small but growing antislavery movement but also itself maintained plantations in Britain's Caribbean colonies, deriving significant income from the forced agricultural labor of Africans. In Hochschild's hands the life of John Newton serves as an effective vehicle for graphically illustrating the evils of the slave trade and the normalcy of human bondage among Christians. Newton, an Anglican minister and writer of hymns, accumulated considerable experience in the slave trade in his youth, first when he was involuntarily swept up by a British naval impressment gang and later as a sailor and eventually as a captain of a slaving vessel. In that latter capacity he participated in more than his share of brutality against enslaved Africans. But Newton was also an intensely religious man who recorded in copious detail his experiences at sea, both dramatic and mundane, and his own state of mind. Though he considered himself a sinner, he focused on blasphemy, not his inhumanity toward his prisoners. If he believed that God continually intervened at crucial moments in his life and even spoke to him, "John Newton seems never to have heard God say a word to him against slavery."[39] Only decades later when he was in his sixties, long after he had left the sea and risen in the ministerial ranks, did he add his voice to the growing antislavery critique.

Two distinct groups of protagonists drive Hochschild's narrative. The first are the small number of intrepid moralists and religious dissenters (the "prophets" of his subtitle) who broke sharply with the proslavery prevailing wisdom of their society and forged an unprecedented movement with the establishment of the Society for Effecting the Abolition of the Slave Trade. In so doing they launched what would become a fifty-year campaign against the transatlantic traffic in human beings and eventually against human bondage itself. Initially viewed as "oddballs" or "at best as hopelessly idealistic,"[40] Hochschild explains, they confronted considerable public indifference and powerful political opposition. Yet against tremendous odds—"against the odds" is a recurrent theme of popular books dealing with reformers and revolutionaries—their crusades against the slave trade prevailed within two decades and against slavery itself within an additional three. The second, vastly larger group was composed of slaves and slave rebels who highlighted the moral issues of slavery and raised cost of maintaining it. Equiano is, not surprisingly, the black abolitionist whose story Hochschild weaves into his narrative; only in the final chapters do the slave "rebels" of his subtitle briefly make their appearance.[41] With those gestures Hochschild makes clear that he does not see abolitionism as a "great gift to poor slaves by a group of pious, benevolent men."[42] Together the abolitionists and the slaves drove home the point that an economic and social system based on the legal ownership of one human being by another was untenable.

Given its long history and its utter pervasiveness, what is most astonishing to Hochschild is how quickly the slave trade and slavery ended. By the 1830s there was no mistaking the significance of what had transpired: In the world's largest empire, the legal ownership of one human being by another had formally been outlawed, a momentous achievement for justice in human history, no matter how incomplete the broader process of emancipation.[43] How did that happen? Hochschild reinforces the older understanding of antislavery as a noble and ultimately triumphal story affirming a clear sense of human progress toward a more just and equitable world by earnestly reviving the earlier belief in the centrality of a small number of activists and politicians to the success of antislavery. To them should go much of the credit for ending the slave trade. "If one were to fix one point when the crusade began," he argues, "it would be the late afternoon of May 22, 1787, when twelve determined men sat down in the printing shop at 2 George Yard, amid flatbed presses, wooden trays of type, and large sheets of freshly printed book pages, to begin one of the most ambitious and brilliantly organized citizens' movements of all time."[44] He is hardly unmindful of the "long chain of events, large and small, [that] led to that meeting." But he is largely unconcerned with any of the debates occupying the attention of scholars. The prehistory of the new abolitionist movement lay less in transatlantic religious currents, the development of capitalism, humanitarianism, the ideology of free labor, or the like than in specific individuals whose experiences converted them to an antislavery perspective.

Hochschild did not merely revive an older narrative tradition; he gave his story a new twist. Those who fought against the slave trade had created "the greatest of all human rights movements" and "one of the most ambitious and brilliantly organized citizens' movements of all time."[45] With an eye fixed firmly on the present, with its plethora of single-issue associations and various causes, Hochschild was deeply concerned with the art of political organizing. Early antislave trade activists pioneered a variety of tools "used by innumerable civic organizations ever since." They collected and disseminated considerable information about the trade, published various updates and appeals for financial support, drew upon the Quakers' extensive organizational network, participated in countless mass meetings, and worked closely with sympathetic members of Parliament to introduce their legislative reforms. With their distribution of the pottery designer Josiah Wedgwood's "Am I Not a Man and a Brother?" design, portraying a chained, kneeling African with arms lifted high, the movement made the "first widespread use of a logo designed for a political cause."[46]

British abolitionists put slavery and the slave trade squarely before the public eye. The "nature of the slave-trade needs only to be known to be detested," Granville Sharp once observed, while Thomas Clarkson similarly insisted that "it was only necessary for the inhabitants" of Britain to know the details about this "enormous evil" for them to "feel a just indignation against it."[47] Academic historians (Brown being the most recent, but with many preceding him) would readily reject these claims, as they had long noted that knowledge of slavery's brutality hardly evinced widespread moral qualms before the late eighteenth century. Hochschild seems to endorse the stance of Sharp and Clarkson, and he is deeply impressed with the tireless devotion of the first English abolitionists to bringing the facts of the slave trade to the public's attention. He recounts in detail the efforts of Clarkson, one of his book's heroes, as he traveled across England in search of concrete knowledge, interviewing sailors on slaving vessels about the inhuman conditions on board their ships; the staggering mortality of slaves and sailors; and the everyday brutalities suffered by Africans during the Middle Passage. Clarkson also assembled a collection of props—what he termed his "little collection of African productions"[48] such as spices, cloth, rare woods, and pepper as well as thumbscrews, chains and manacles, and other pieces of equipment used in the imprisonment and torture of slaves. These made for powerful visual accompaniments to his dramatic antislavery speeches. With the publication in 1789 of the two-volume autobiography of the former slave Olaudah Equiano, the all-too-rarely heard voice of the enslaved finally reached a significant audience. Equiano took to the road in an eighteenth-century version of the book tour, addressing tens of thousands in Britain as he promoted his book and condemned the slave trade and slavery. His narrative quickly became a best seller in his adopted country. However, leading white abolitionists, at best paternalistic toward Africans and their descendants, expressed "peculiarly little interest in the testimony of any of the thousands of former slaves in Britain," Hochschild observes. There are "no records of any of them appearing on speakers' platforms with abolitionists at this time" or efforts by white abolitionists to record their stories. Hochschild, echoing Klein and others, acknowledges that white activists saw themselves as "uplifting the downtrodden, not fighting for equal rights for all,"[49] but he oddly declines to pursue their relationships with black Britons or to explore their larger racial ideologies or sentiments.

How and why did the abolitionist band eventually succeed? Hochschild offers incomplete answers to this long-debated question. Credit can be given, he argues, to the "brilliant planning" and organizational skills of the small band of dedicated leading abolitionists. These men "mastered one challenge that still faces anyone who cares about social and economic justice: drawing connections between the near and the distant."[50] That is, with slavery confined to British colonies thousands of miles away, abolitionists successfully brought home a compelling and dramatic portrait of the horrors of slavery and the slave trade through their pamphlets, tracts, speeches, and the like. Numerous developments facilitated the dissemination of the abolitionists' ideas: the rapid development of a highway system that made transportation faster and easier; improvements in the British postal system; a proliferation of newspapers, coffeehouses, debating societies, libraries, and bookstores; and the flourishing of an uncensored political culture. Unquestionably these contributed to the spreading of abolitionist arguments and sentiments and rendered political organizing an easier task. To this list Hochschild added a growing popular aversion to naval impressment, which in effect turned otherwise free-born British men into slaves when they were scooped up off the streets and forced to labor on military or commercial vessels. "People are more likely to care about the suffering of others in a distant place if that misfortune evokes a fear of their own," he argues. It was the "long public struggle" against impressment that "psychologically set the national stage for the much larger battle over slavery."[51]

In the end Hochschild insists that the success of abolitionism involved the "historic, pioneering mobilization of public opinion, via boycotts, petitions, and great popular campaigns, all powerfully reinforced by the armed slave revolts."[52] But like many (if not all) academic works, his narrative focuses not on the grassroots but on the leaders. Hochschild provides tantalizing glimpses of a popular enthusiasm for the abolitionist cause. Abolition committees composed of working-class and middle-class Britons alike were formed in countless communities throughout the British Isles. Three hundred thousand men and women participated in a boycott of slave-grown sugar. Women's antislavery societies conducted door-to-door canvasses, turned out large crowds to protest meetings, organized boycotts of merchants selling slave-produced sugar, raised needed funds, and in essence "formed the cement of the whole Antislavery building," in one male abolitionist's words. But these were not really Hochschild's concern.[53]

His concern was the power of "human empathy" and a sincere belief that "a small group of thoughtful, committed citizens can change the world. Indeed, it is the only thing that ever has."[54] These last words are those of Margaret Mead, whose sentiment Hochschild endorses. However, this, academics might respond, is not necessarily the best way to understand the politics of abolitionism. Hochschild read back onto the past our current modes of liberal political organizing a little too enthusiastically. His abolitionist crusade's reliance on full-time activists, mobilization of networks of supporters, and emphasis on publicity and empathy resemble in key ways the approaches adopted by professionally staffed associations and nongovernmental agencies tackling such important issues as world hunger, poverty and inequality, environmental degradation, and international human rights today.

That resemblance goes only so far. Hochschild's approach obscures the broader transatlantic currents stimulating the opposition to slavery. Focusing on the person-alities of individuals and the tactics they pioneered and employed, *Bury the Chains* is decidedly *not* an exploration of ideas and ideologies—about race, slavery and freedom, or democracy and capitalism—or of the broader social, economic, and political forces shaping their protests. Hochschild's decision to focus almost exclusively on leaders makes for a dramatic and powerful story, but in neglecting to take greater advantage of the wealth of scholarship on abolition, it also limits our understanding of antislav-ery's emergence, growth, success, and shortfalls.

The pursuit of dramatic narrative and biographical detail also drives Simon Schama's *Rough Crossings: Britain, the Slaves and the American Revolution.* Schama is a master of the grand historical narrative. The prolific Columbia University historian's books on such wide-ranging subjects as the seventeenth-century Dutch, the French Revo-lution, Rembrandt, and most recently the history of Britain have reached wide audi-ences in and out of the academy. In *Rough Crossings,* which was the recipient of the National Book Critics Circle Award for Nonfiction in 2006, he focuses on the age of revolution of the late eighteenth century to explore what he terms "the sin of the Great Contradiction."[55] The American Patriots who trained their rhetorical guns on the British, invoking the language of rights, liberty, and freedom as powerful weapons in their unprecedented crusade for political freedom from British oppression, were themselves responsible for denying an even more fundamental freedom to the 20 per-cent of the colonial population who were enslaved. "However intoxicating the heady rhetoric of 'rights' and 'liberty' emanating from Patriot orators and journalists," argues Schama, the Revolution was, particularly in the South, "first and foremost, mobilized to protect slavery."[56]

In their enduring fascination with the Revolution, Americans tend to prefer their Founding Fathers as larger-than-life figures whose heroism and wisdom continue to speak to us through the ages. When confronted with the inconvenient truth of the "Great Contradiction," many (if not all) prefer to look the other way or dismiss those who insist upon it as being too politically correct. From the perspective of hundreds of thousands of slaves in the colonies, liberty had a far more tangible definition than the one advanced by white Patriots. The American Revolution—or more specifically, British efforts to crush it—promised them a chance at freedom that their colonial masters denied them.

To his credit, Schama engages in none of the Founding Fathers worship evident in many popular histories of the era; nor does he sanctimoniously or anachronisti-cally belabor the point of white American racism (though his accounts are chilling and depressing). Instead he puts his storytelling skills to good use by re-creating a variety of worlds that include the political circles of British abolitionists, brutal warfare on the North American continent, small and scattered communities of free blacks in Nova Scotia, harrowing transatlantic ocean voyages, and life on the West African coast. If American Patriots come across looking hypocritical and brutal, Schama does not substitute the British for his story's heroes, for their track record too left much to be desired.

His heroes, rather, are black loyalists and a handful of white British abolitionists. Schama skillfully weaves together their two interrelated stories. First, he poignantly traces the experiences of black loyalists—enslaved men and women who cast their lot with the British against the advocates of American independence and in many instances fought on behalf of the Crown. Second, he recounts the relentless efforts by a core of British abolitionists to assist the black loyalists in creating new lives—first in Canada and then in Sierra Leone. Schama's source material is far richer for the British white reformers, whose political exploits and personal lives he reconstructs in vivid detail. He titles each of the book's two sections, perhaps unnecessarily, after his principal white protagonists: the antislavery crusader Granville Sharp, the highly colorful figure at the center of the emerging abolitionist network in London; and John Clarkson, younger brother of the more prominent abolitionist Thomas Clarkson, who undertook the transport of disappointed black loyalists in Canada to a new colony in Africa. Yet in the end Schama manages to do literary justice to the former slaves, whose survival under inhospitable circumstances and determination to realize the freedom they had been promised he successfully conveys.

Slaves in the North American colonies had good reasons for preferring the British to their American owners, Schama makes clear. Ideological currents questioning slavery, although still in their infancy, had crossed the Atlantic, planting in more than a few slaves' minds the "idea of British freedom [as] a germ of hope."[57] More important was the 1775 British offer of freedom, initially made by Lord Dunmore, Virginia's last colonial governor, to slaves of rebel owners who would assist the Crown in suppressing unruly colonists. Dunmore's offer was born of military necessity, not abolitionist motives, Schama observes. "Yet from opportunist tactics, some good might still arise."[58]

Vast numbers of slaves concurred, taking up Dunmore's and other British commanders' offers. "Twenty-five thousand blacks—a quarter of South Carolina's slave population, and a third of Georgia's—left the plantations in what was by far the greatest exodus from bondage in African-American history until the Civil War and Emancipation." Others flooded into British-controlled New York. Slaves "knew exactly what they were doing."[59] The British, Schama makes clear, were hardly saints. After all, British involvement in the "Accursed Thing," the slave trade, was substantial, and British colonies in the Caribbean were wholly dependent on slavery. Moreover countless suffered for their decision—when they were not reenslaved or executed as traitors by the white Americans who recaptured them, those making it to British lines died in large numbers from disease or at times were forced to labor for the British under harsh conditions.

The British lived up to some of their promises, evacuating thousands of black loyalists from New York and Charleston, for example, and resettling them in Nova Scotia. But they reneged on others, failing to provide the land promised to them in Nova Scotia and Sierra Leone. Schama evocatively describes ex-slaves suffering in both of those places, while at the same time he gives voice to their democratic strivings and nascent political sensibilities. He makes clear a simple point: the tragedy of the black loyalists' fate should not obscure the broader significance of their passage from slavery to freedom. As political actors they challenged the Patriots' hypocrisy, adopted notions of British liberty as their own, and repeatedly acted on them, even when the British seemed intent on denying their relevance.

If Schama's tale stands as a sharp counterpoint to popular celebrations of the American Revolution, it is also a tale well known to academic historians, whom Schama readily credits. Many pieces of the historical story he assembles have, to a significant extent, been told before by Sylvia Frey, Benjamin Quarles, Gary Nash, and Graham Russell Hodges, to mention just the American side of the story.[60] His achievement has been to produce a compelling and dramatic narrative. But that accomplishment, I would suggest, comes at a cost. Like Hochschild, Schama was not particularly concerned with offering an analysis of cultural, religious, or economic developments. As is the case with *Bury the Chains,* readers—academic or general—looking for insights into the emergence and spread of antislavery thought or the reforming impulses of evangelical Christianity will find it necessary to supplement *Rough Crossings* with additional reading. Even in the hands of a highly skilled academic author writing for popular audiences, biography and unfolding human drama are the organizing principles. The larger, more difficult issues and questions that animate academic scholarship find little place, it seems, even in the better works in this genre.

Can it be otherwise? Are the issues that absorb academic historians' attention so arcane or inscrutable that they cannot pass over from the scholarly journals or the university press books to the trade divisions of large publishing houses? It would be unrealistic to expect a book such as Christopher Leslie Brown's *Moral Capital* to make its way onto the best-seller list. It was never intended for nonacademic audiences. Written with a high level of detail concerning treatises and tracts, offering close textual scrutiny, and avoiding the dramatic (though not the biographical), *Moral Capital* appropriately takes other scholars and informed students as its audience.

But is it asking too much to hold popularizers and their publishers to a higher standard than the one many of them currently meet, one that reflects the genuine "state of the field"? Should popular histories do more than draw selectively from established scholarship to craft stories that popular audiences have come to expect?

There are enough good trade books in history that *do* meet the standard to suggest that the demand is not an unreasonable one. Academic historians and popular historians have much to teach one another. If those of us in the academy hoping to reach beyond university walls can fruitfully learn about more graceful and literary writing, so too can popular historians be expected to be more attentive to the complexities of the past about which they write.

NOTES

1. See, for example, Nick Kotz, *Judgment Days: Lyndon Baines Johnson, Martin Luther King Jr., and the Laws That Changed America* (Boston: Houghton Mifflin, 2005).

2. Examples of problematic "trade books" in history include Myra MacPherson, *"All Governments Lie": The Life and Times of Rebel Journalist I. F. Stone* (New York: Scribner's, 2006); and Stephan Talty, *Mulatto America: At the Crossroads of Black and White Culture; A Social History* (New York: HarperCollins, 2003).

3. Two outstanding examples of academic scholars crossing over into popular or trade-book history are Melvin Ely, *Israel on the Appomattox: A Southern Experiment in Black Freedom from the 1790s through the Civil War* (New York: Knopf, 2004) [on Ely's accomplishments, see Eric Arnesen, "In-Between Peoples," *New Republic* (January 1–15, 2007)]; and James Oakes, *The Radical and the Republican: Frederick Douglass, Abraham Lincoln, and the Triumph of Antislavery Politics* (New York: W. W. Norton, 2007). Other fine works by academic historians writing for popular audiences include Heather Cox Richardson, *West from Appomattox: The Reconstruction of America after the Civil War* (New Haven, Conn.: Yale University Press, 2007); Scott Reynolds Nelson, *Steel Drivin' Man: John Henry, the Untold Story of an American Legend* (New York: Oxford University Press, 2006); Michael Kazin, *A Godly Hero: The Life of William Jennings Bryan* (New York: Knopf, 2006); Richard Slotkin, *Lost Battalions: The Great War and the Crisis of American Nationality* (New York: Henry Holt, 2005); Kevin Boyle, *Arc of Justice: A Saga of Race, Rights, and Murder in the Jazz Age* (New York: Henry Holt, 2004); and Linda Colley, *The Ordeal of Elizabeth Marsh: A Woman in World History* (New York: Pantheon, 2007). Kai Bird and Martin J. Sherwin's Pulitzer Prize–winning book, *American Prometheus: The Triumph and Tragedy of J. Robert Oppenheimer* (New York: Knopf, 2005), is the product of a collaboration between an academic historian and a popular historian. On the subject of academic historians writing for broader audiences, see Eric Arnesen, "Historians and the Public: Premature Obituaries, Abiding Laments," *Historically Speaking* 9, no. 2 (November/December 2007): 2–5.

4. "For at least eighty years after the American Civil War," David Brion Davis wrote, "the triumphant achievements of the British abolitionists were interpreted in Britain and then in much of the English-speaking world as irrefutable evidence to support the view, as phrased by the philosopher John Stuart Mill, that 'the spread of moral convictions could sometimes take precedence over material interests'"; see Davis, *Inhuman Bondage: The Rise and Fall of Slavery in the New World* (New York: Oxford University Press, 2006), 238. Also see Davis, *Slavery and Human Progress* (New York: Oxford University Press, 1984), 109–10. "For a century after British emancipation," Seymour Drescher observed over two decades ago, "its historical context was virtually unchanged." Emancipation was treated as a "national and imperial triumph. . . . The reigning historians of England and of Abolition . . . agreed that emancipation had elevated all mankind to a higher moral plane. The national memory was refreshed by a roll call

of the gallant band of Saints." See Seymour Drescher, "The Historical Context of British Abolition," in David Richardson, *Abolition and Its Aftermath: The Historical Context, 1790–1916* (London: Frank Cass, 1985), 3–4. See also Herbert S. Klein, *The Atlantic Slave Trade* (Cambridge: Cambridge University Press, 1999), 183–87.

5. Davis, *Inhuman Bondage,* 239.

6. "The capitalists had first encouraged West Indian slavery and then helped to destroy it," wrote Eric Williams in *Capitalism and Slavery* over six decades ago (1944; repr., New York: Capricorn Books, 1966), 169. As for "the 'Saints,'" Williams argued that although they engaged in "one of the greatest propaganda movements of all time," their "importance has been seriously misunderstood and grossly exaggerated by men who have scarified scholarship to sentimentality and, like the scholastics of old, placed faith before reason and evidence" (178). Although the specifics of Williams's work have been thoroughly challenged, the impact of *Capitalism and Slavery* is hard to overstate. It "had forever stigmatized the humanitarian narrative," Christopher Leslie Brown recently concluded. He continued, "By the 1970s, few academic historians cared to write about 'selfless' men engaged in a 'virtuous crusade.'" That stigma was hardly permanent, for the humanitarian narrative has resurfaced prominently in the writings of popular historians and in film. See Christopher Leslie Brown, *Moral Capital: Foundations of British Abolitionism* (Chapel Hill: University of North Carolina Press, 2006), 16.

7. David Eltis, *Economic Growth and the Ending of the Transatlantic Slave Trade* (New York: Oxford University Press, 1987), 7; Seymour Drescher, *Econocide: British Slavery in the Era of Abolition* (Pittsburgh: University of Pittsburgh Press, 1977); Seymour Drescher, *The Mighty Experiment: Free Labor versus Slavery in British Emancipation* (New York: Oxford University Press, 2002), 4–5. See also Roger Anstey, "Capitalism and Slavery: A Critique," *Economic History Review,* n.s., 21, no. 2 (August 1968): 307–20; David Brion Davis, "Capitalism, Abolitionism, and Hegemony" and "The Benefit of Slavery," in David Brion Davis, *In the Image of God: Religion, Moral Values, and Our Heritage of Slavery* (New Haven, Conn.: Yale University Press, 2001), 217–18 and 205–16, respectively.

8. Klein, *The Atlantic Slave Trade,* 185.

9. Ibid.

10. Roger Anstey, "A Re-Interpretation of the Abolition of the British Slave Trade, 1806–1807," *English Historical Review* 86, no. 343 (April 1972): 331–32.

11. See the exchange between John Ashworth, David Brion Davis, and Thomas L. Haskell in Thomas Bender, ed., *The Antislavery Debate: Capitalism and Abolitionism as a Problem in Historical Interpretation* (Berkeley: University of California Press, 1992). The book is based on an earlier debate in the pages of the *American Historical Review.* The Haskell quote is from Thomas L. Haskell, "Capitalism and the Origins of the Humanitarian Sensibility, Part 1," in *The Antislavery Debate,* ed. Bender, 135.

12. Brown, *Moral Capital,* 1.

13. Ibid., 211.

14. Ibid., 1–3.

15. Ibid., 18, 17.

16. Ibid., 21–22. "With an expanded concept of politics," he later argued, "the 'Saints,' as contemporaries derisively tagged the Clapham Sect, emerge merely as one of many groups committed to antislavery projects at the end of the eighteenth century" (334). For an account about American abolitionism that similarly focuses on "how and why a group of abolitionists

embraced political action," see Bruce Laurie, *Beyond Garrison: Antislavery and Social Reform* (New York: Cambridge University Press, 2005), 1.

17. Brown, *Moral Capital,* 19.

18. Ibid., 20. It "is hard to see how the familiar explanatory categories—'Enlightenment,' 'Evangelicalism,' 'Quakerism,' 'capitalism,' 'humanitarianism,' and the like—could make sense of the sudden rise in political activism in the late 1780s" (ibid., 23).

19. Ibid., 27, 240.

20. Ibid., 312.

21. Ibid., 335.

22. Ibid., 341. "The most recent generation of scholarship typically has found it hard to embrace the Evangelicals. Frequently, and not incorrectly, these modern assessments tend to characterize the pious reformers as a repressive and reactionary elite. The reputed limits of Evangelical philanthropy have become almost legendary" (ibid., 377).

23. Ibid., 388.

24. Ibid., 387.

25. Ibid., 389.

26. James Oliver Horton and Lois E. Horton, introduction, in *Slavery and Public History: The Tough Stuff of American Memory,* edited by Horton and Horton (New York: New Press, 2007), x.

27. Ira Berlin, "Coming to Terms with Slavery in Twenty-First-Century America," in *Slavery and Public History,* edited by Horton and Horton, 1–2.

28. Ibid., 1, 3.

29. Anne C. Bailey, *African Voices of the Atlantic Slave Trade: Beyond the Silence and the Shame* (Boston: Beacon Press, 2005), 1, 10, 11, 13, 24. Bailey's handling of this issue reveals the persistent difficulties of discussing African involvement. "Often this participation is examined in a vacuum outside of the context of the very real and dynamic external European and American forces that played a key role in the trade from demand to supply. The reality is that in the operations of the Atlantic slave trade, five of the six legs of the trade were exclusively controlled by external forces in America and Europe. . . . Furthermore, this issue of African agency is also often raised without much discussion of the ways in which some African societies resisted both internal and external forces and protected their communities from the trade. For these and other reasons, a natural defensiveness may arise when this subject is broached" (15).

30. "Every American schoolchild learns how slaves fled Southern plantations, following the North Star on the Underground Railroad," Adam Hochschild notes at the outset of his *Bury the Chains: Prophets, Slaves, and Rebels in the First Human Rights Crusade* (Boston: Houghton Mifflin, 2005), 3. But, he continues, "England is where the story really begins, and for decades it was where American abolitionists looked for inspiration and finally for proof that the colossally difficult task of uprooting slavery could be accomplished."

31. Robert Allison, "Introduction: Equiano's Worlds," in *The Interesting Narrative of the Life of Olaudah Equiano Written by Himself* (Boston: Bedford/St. Martin's, 1995), 1. "Equiano experienced virtually every kind of slavery and every part of the slave experience: capture in Africa, the 'middle passage' from Africa to the Americas, plantation labor in Virginia and the West Indies, and ultimately service on a slave-trading ship between North America and the Caribbean. He was one of the few to survive and to write about the experience" (1).

32. Allison, introduction; Werner Sollors, introduction, in Olaudah Equiano, *The Interesting Narrative of the Life of Olaudah Equiano, or Gustavus Vassa, the African, Written by Himself,* edited by Werner Sollors (New York: Norton, 2001). Coverage of the emergence and nature of abolitionist sentiment is *not* a likely reason for course adoption, and in the necessarily brief scholarly introductions by editors of Equiano's book, the roots—intellectual, political, and religious—of abolitionism are touched on only briefly.

33. Vincent Carretta, *Equiano the African: Biography of a Self-Made Man* (Athens: University of Georgia Press, 2005). The more recent paperback edition has been published by Penguin, guaranteeing far greater distribution.

34. Ibid., xiv, xviii, xvii, 367.

35. In "Olaudah Equiano, the South Carolinian? A Forum," *Historically Speaking* 7, no. 3 (January/February 2006), see Vincent Carretta, "Does Equiano Still Matter?" (2–7); Paul E. Lovejoy, "Construction of Identity: Olaudah Equiano or Gustavus Vassa?" (8–9); Trevor Burnard, "Goodbye, Equiano, the African" (10–11); Jon Sensbach, "Beyond Equiano" (12–13); and Vincent Carretta, "Response to Lovejoy, Burnard, and Sensbach" (14–16). The forum was reprinted in Donald A. Yerxa, ed., *Recent Themes in the History of Africa and the Atlantic World* (Columbia: University of South Carolina Press, 2008), 81–118. Also see Paul E. Lovejoy, "Autobiography and Memory: Gustavus Vassa, alias Olaudah Equiano, the African," *Slavery and Abolition* 27, no. 3 (December 2006): 317–47.

36. Carretta, *Equiano the African,* xvii–xviii.

37. Hochschild, *Bury the Chains;* Simon Schama, *Rough Crossings: Britain, the Slaves and the American Revolution* (New York: HarperCollins, 2006). One further example is Steven M. Wise, *Though the Heavens May Fall: The Landmark Trial That Led to the End of Human Slavery* (Cambridge, Mass.: Da Capo Press, 2005), a book on the subject that is perhaps the least informed by modern scholarship. The book's subtitle is part of a trend that authors or publishers too readily participate in—establishing the significance of their subject by exaggerating its importance or attributing to it vast causal or explanatory powers. In following the model of many trade books, Wise combines two narrative approaches: biography and the dramatic narrative event. The former includes detailed sketches of the famous and the relatively unknown—James Somersett (sometimes Somerset), Olaudah Equiano, Granville Sharp, Charles Steuart, and Lord Mansfield—while the latter includes the 1772 Somersett decision (and the events leading up to and following its delivery). Wise's final chapter, "The Beginning of the End of Human Slavery," briefly traces Sharp's subsequent career on behalf of abolition. Sharp, along with Wilberforce, Clarkson, "and a handful of others," went on to form the "society for the Abolition of the Slave Trade [*sic*]" and continued to work with "other antislavery committees, including one formed by Quakers, and the Clapham Sect, a small group of intensely religious, deeply committed philanthropists." Virtually nothing more is said about how the campaign against the slave trade and slavery evolved. But, he concludes, "Somerset delivered a wallop to the system from which it never recovered, though it had plenty of fight left"; Mansfield's judgment "proved just the opening salvo in a legal barrage that, within a century, splintered all of human slavery's bulwarks." In the book's final sentence Wise, without explanation, makes the final leap: "Meanwhile, Somerset's principles have begun to radiate beyond humanity, as some lawyers are insisting today that at least the most cognitively complex nonhuman animals should no longer be treated as slaves" (223, 225). For a discussion of

the Somersett case, which appeared after the publication of Wise's book, see the articles in "Forum: Somerset's Case Revisited," *Law and History Review* 24, no. 3 (Fall 2006).

38. Hochschild, *Bury the Chains,* 2, 28.

39. Ibid., 110, 29.

40. Ibid., 213.

41. In a series of fast-paced, if brief chapters, Hochschild dramatically recounts the violent confrontations between slaves and masters in sugar-producing St. Domingue in the 1790s and early 1800s, Demerara in 1823, and Jamaica in 1832. These slave uprisings, as numerous scholars have shown, terrified colonial whites, provoked considerable repression, raised un-avoidable questions about the costs of maintaining a slave empire, and raised the hopes of slaves and free blacks elsewhere in their quest for freedom. At a minimum, Hochschild argues, they "altered the idea of what was possible" (Hochschild, *Bury the Chains,* 296).

42. Hochschild, *Bury the Chains,* 350.

43. As Davis notes in *Inhuman Bondage,* "Sad to say, in a present-day world that seems to be governed by clashing self-interests and material forces, where we have learned that idealis-tic rhetoric usually cloaks nationalistic purposes or even far more diabolical schemes, it has become increasingly difficult to explain collective actions that profess to be driven by virtuous ideals or a desire to make the world a better place. . . . Today we are far more cynical" (232). In making his case Hochschild refreshingly reveals little of the cynicism of recent decades over the inadequacies of antislavery accomplishments. He would undoubtedly agree with Davis, who notes, "From any historical perspective . . . [abolitionism brought about] a stupendous transformation. . . . From the distance of the late twentieth century . . . the progress of eman-cipation from the 1780s to the 1880s is one of the most extraordinary events in history" (Davis, *Slavery and Human Progress,* 108).

44. Hochschild, *Bury the Chains,* 3.

45. Ibid., 113–14, 3.

46. Ibid., 128.

47. Ibid., 364.

48. Ibid., 115–16.

49. Ibid., 133.

50. Ibid., 213, 5.

51. Ibid., 222, 225.

52. Ibid., 350.

53. Ibid., 327. Davis has noted that "we still have more to learn about the local activists who organized meetings, disseminated tracts, and solicited petition signatures" (Davis, *Inhu-man Bondage,* 246). On British abolitionism as a broader social movement, see Seymour Drescher, "Whose Abolition? Popular Pressure and the Ending of the British Slave Trade," *Past and Present* 143 (May 1994): 136–66; J. R. Oldfield, *Popular Politics and British Anti-Slavery: The Mobilisation of Public Opinion against the Slave Trade, 1787–1807* (Manchester, U.K.: Manchester University Press, 1995); and Clare Midgley, *Women against Slavery: The British Campaigns, 1780–1870* (London: Routledge, 1992).

54. Hochschild, *Bury the Chains,* 364, 7.

55. Schama, *Rough Crossings,* 14.

56. Ibid., 67.

57. Ibid., 57.

58. Ibid., 7.

59. Ibid., 105, 11.

60. See, for instance, Sylvia R. Frey, *Water from the Rock: Black Resistance in a Revolutionary Age* (Princeton, N.J.: Princeton University Press, 1991); Graham Russell Hodges, *Root and Branch: African Americans in New York and East Jersey 1613–1863* (Chapel Hill: University of North Carolina Press, 1999); Benjamin Quarles, *The Negro in the American Revolution* (Chapel Hill: University of North Carolina Press, 1996); Sidney Kaplan and Emma Nogrady Kaplan, *The Black Presence in the Era of the American Revolution,* rev. ed. (Amherst: University of Massachusetts Press, 1989); and Gary B. Nash, *Race and Revolution* (Madison, Wis.: Madison House, 1990). Three other recent books warrant mention: Leslie Harris, *In the Shadow of Slavery: African Americans in New York City, 1626–1863* (Chicago: University of Chicago Press, 2003); David Waldstreicher, *Runaway America: Benjamin Franklin, Slavery, and the American Revolution* (New York: Hill and Wang, 2004); and Thelma Wills Foote, *Black and White Manhattan: The History of Racial Formation in Colonial New York City* (New York: Oxford University Press, 2004).

The Lessons of History

Generalizations, Traditions, and Inspirations

C. Behan McCullagh

Many historians want to deny that history has any lessons for the present. There are two common reasons for their denial. The first is summed up in the words of L. P. Hartley that such historians are fond of quoting: "The past is a foreign country; they do things differently there."[1] Not only does the past differ from the present, they say, but also it is important for historians to recognize the differences and refrain from interpreting past events on the basis of their present significance. To suppose that the past has lessons for the present seems to suppose that the two have much in common, ignoring the features of past events that make them unique. To emphasize the uniqueness of past events is, of course, to overlook what they have in common with the present. The best way to display their present relevance is to explain and illustrate it in detail, which this essay will attempt to do.

The second reason why historians deny the relevance of past events to the present is that they are generally aware of the failure of philosophers of history to discover any generalizations or trends in history that are universally valid. Old Testament assertions that those who honor God will be blessed and those who do not do so will be cursed have proved false—unless the blessing is understood in terms of personal spiritual transformation or the rewards and punishments are meted out at some Judgment Day in the future. The optimism of the Enlightenment, when many believed that the application of reason to human affairs would result in greater freedom and happiness, the so-called Whig interpretation of history, was destroyed in the twentieth century when reason improved the instruments of destruction causing unimaginable suffering. Rather than look for general trends in history, it seems wiser to admit that every age is governed by its own tendencies, and that it is wrong to suppose that those governing the present age prevailed in the past.

It is true that there are no interesting universal lessons of history. But there are some historical generalizations, trends, and paradigms that are of intense interest in the present, as we shall see. These are not universally valid but are true under certain general conditions, and it is reasonable to believe that they are true wherever such conditions exist, even in the present.

Past events relate to the present in many different ways. Not all will be discussed here. For example, past events are the source of a whole range of obligations that individuals and institutions have acquired or inherited.[2] This essay investigates ways in which knowledge of the past can better the lives of people in the present. There are three important ways it can do so, and each is quite different.

To plan intelligently for the future, we rely on general knowledge of the ways in which individuals and institutions behave. Much of this knowledge we acquire from our everyday experiences, but sometimes the general beliefs we hold are a bit speculative and not entirely correct. History can present individual cases that drive historians to qualify, or even reject, some of the generalizations they had taken for granted. This is the first way in which history can be of assistance in the present.

The second way history can help us is by revealing the origin and value of various institutions and traditions we have inherited: military, legal, educational, and so on. Conservatives tend to be quite uncritical about traditions, frightened of change. To assess the value of our traditions rationally, however, it is vital to discover why they arose and what functions they have performed, for good or ill. Historical knowledge is indispensable for this task.

Third, individuals are sometimes inspired to emulate historical figures whose lives they admire. If they value virtues such as courage, generosity, patience, and so on, they can be moved by studying past paragons of virtue to acquire more of those virtues themselves. That benefits not only them but also the people they encounter.

These three ways in which people can benefit from knowledge of history are so important to people's lives in the present, wherever and whenever the present might be, that they deserve much more attention than they have received. Indeed I think that those who plan what history students study have an obligation to select topics relevant to present general knowledge, institutions, and concerns, which will help the students cope better with the world around them.

Before studying the three ways in which historical knowledge can better people's lives, we must clarify the senses of betterment we have in mind. Most people of goodwill hold certain states of affairs to be intrinsically good: such as prosperity, freedom, justice, peace, self-respect, and love. It is little wonder that historians are drawn to subjects related to these: economic history, political history, constitutional and legal history, the history of international affairs and war, social history, and the history of human relations, be they communal, family, or sexual relations. Individuals rank these goods in different orders. Some judge prosperity to be the source of all happiness and will ignore problems of injustice to achieve it. Those who prefer justice will sacrifice the prosperity of some, through taxes and other constraints, for the benefit of all. Some want peace at any price and will sacrifice quite a lot of money to arm and train soldiers and police, and limit freedom of speech and assembly, to obtain it.

No particular order of goods will be assumed here. The aim is to demonstrate the three ways in which people today can further some or all of those goods by drawing upon their knowledge of history. For example, the study of generalizations considers some that relate to people's prosperity and others about the extension of freedom; the analysis of traditions shows how one can better understand why slavery was outlawed and how the defense of property can yield injustice; and third, the section on inspiration suggests ways in which dispositions to act well can be stimulated.

Causal Generalizations

It is well known that historians employ general theories of human behavior to explain past events. If the theories are of a familiar, commonsense kind, then historians are scarcely aware of their role. For instance, historians will commonly look for people's reasons for acting, assuming that humans, being rational, normally act for reasons. The reasons might involve pursuit of a desired goal or conformity to an accepted rule or the expression of a valued principle. When such reasons cannot be found, historians will normally judge the action irrational and investigate emotions that might have caused it. The use of these widely shared theories of human action is so automatic that historians are scarcely aware of them.

Explanations of group behavior can follow these theories of rational or emotional actions, but sometimes there are aspects of the events being explained that they do not capture and contrasts for which they cannot account. Marx, for example, saw class interest underlying much historical behavior and decided that rational justifications that legitimated many actions were cases of false consciousness that did not represent the real causes of those actions at all. Historians who find this theory illuminating employ it by looking for class interests that may be furthered by group behavior, thinking that those interests could have motivated it. Other well-known theories of unconscious motivation are Freud's theory of instincts and Foucault's theory of power. All these theories account for features of people's behavior that are not explained by everyday theories of behavior.

Another source of special general knowledge is the devising of rational strategies and policies in certain common circumstances, be they political, military, or economic. One can often explain a range of actions by showing that they implement a rational policy in the circumstances. The policy might not be fully understood by the agents, who are merely following rules or conventions. But the rational significance of their behavior can be detected by those familiar with the strategy that underlies those rules. It is not widely acknowledged that the generalizations about individual and social behavior assumed by historians are sometimes tested and refined by the study of particular historical cases. This is the first way in which history can provide lessons of value to people today.

Does the history of the movement in Britain for the abolition of the slave trade provide any lessons that will improve historians' theoretical assumptions? Before addressing this question directly, let me say something about the nature of the causal generalizations being referred to. The causal generalizations of interest to historians are those that enable them to identify causes and effects. Causes are events of a certain kind that in normal circumstances are necessary for other events of a certain kind, their effects, to occur and that produce a tendency of some strength or other for their effects to occur.

Causal generalizations sum up our general knowledge of causes and effects. Often there are several different kinds of event that can bring about a certain kind of effect, a disjunction of causes, and our general knowledge sums them up. When one of those causes is present but no others are, we judge the presence of that cause to have been necessary for the effect, not universally necessary but necessary in the particular circumstances under consideration, so that in the absence of that cause the effect would not have occurred. Similarly sometimes an event can have a range of different outcomes, usually judged to have different probabilities, and in policy making these all have to be taken into account so that the unwanted effects can be prevented.

Indeed because an event can often have a variety of effects, investigators are interested in qualifying causal generalizations so that their predictive powers are increased, or to put it another way, they become more accurate. For instance in a normal capitalist economy, if you increase the price of a commodity, demand for it will tend to fall. However, if the price of a commodity increases but that commodity is essential for life, for example salt, then demand for it will not fall—unless the price for it exceeds people's ability to pay for it, in which case demand will fall. And so on. In practice it is impossible to anticipate every condition that will affect the effect of a cause. Therefore it is simpler to say that causes are events that trigger a disposition or tendency for a certain effect to occur, but that such a tendency might be offset by other tendencies at work in a situation. For instance, the tendency to refrain from buying something because it is too expensive can be offset by a stronger disposition to buy it because it is essential for life.

It is quite difficult to specify the background conditions under which causal generalizations will be true. Generalizations about human nature are sometimes universal but often culture-specific. Those about military, political, and economic outcomes apply only to situations of kinds that existed in some places for some years, but not in every society at every time. Clearly for history to be useful to us, we must examine the truth or falsity of generalizations in historical situations of the kind that is presupposed in formulating them.

What theories can be illuminated by the history of the movement in Britain to abolish the slave trade? Historians who want to confine their analysis of the past to everyday generalizations will deny that any theories are relevant. A narrative account of the growth of that movement among the Quakers and Evangelicals, its propaganda, organization, and petitions to Parliament, would seem to involve no particular theory at all over and above commonsense theories of human behavior. The ideas about slavery promulgated by the Quakers, by John Wesley and John Newton, and by William Wilberforce and his Evangelical friends served to stir compassion among the populace for slaves. Furthermore some philosophers of the Enlightenment saw liberty "as a natural and fundamental right" and noted that slavery was a severe obstacle to individual happiness.[3] These statements triggered widespread compassion for slaves, and compassion triggered the movement for abolition. What more needs to be said?

The generalizations that underpin simple narratives of this kind are of an everyday sort. Most relate people's beliefs, values, goals, and passions to their actions. Generalizations of more interest are commonly employed in three contexts. The first is in supplying deeper, often unconscious motives for actions, which explain tendencies of people's behavior that cannot be otherwise accounted for.[4] The second is in accounting for coordinated actions by a number of individuals by describing how certain institutions motivated and organized their behavior. The third common function of historical generalizations is to provide contrastive explanations for why one action or event occurred rather than some other that might have been expected in the circumstances. We have evidence of generalizations serving all these functions in debates about the causes of the abolition of the slave trade.

The motives driving those who campaigned to end the slave trade were religious and humanitarian. Traditionally Christians, following Saint Paul, had condoned slavery, but Quakers and Evangelicals became convinced that it was contrary to God's will. Philosophers who declared that everyone had a right to freedom and the pursuit of happiness implied that slavery was immoral. Such ideological explanations seem sufficient to account for popular opposition to slavery. But those familiar with Marx's writing cannot help suspecting that ideological conviction is not enough to explain the widespread support for the antislavery movement, and that class economic interests played a part too. Thus David Brion Davis, having listed many of the cultural activities that furthered the antislavery movement, goes on to ask, "What were the more material considerations which helped both to shape the new moral consciousness and to define its historical effects?" He explains: "The needs and interests of particular classes had much to do with a given society's receptivity to new ideas and thus to the ideas' historical impact."[5] In a more recent publication Davis focuses particularly on the majority of members of Parliament (MPs) in both houses who opposed Wilberforce's motions for many years, presumably in defense of their economic interests. To explain their final change of heart, Davis suggests, one must be able to show that abolition was to their economic advantage. He wrote, "Clearly it is one thing to find various noneconomic motives among British abolitionists, the media, and the public they succeeded in mobilizing, and quite another to believe that majorities of hardheaded M.P.'s would vote for measures that they knew could lead to economic disaster, undermining the colonial plantation economy that by 1805 accounted for about one-fifth of Britain's total trade."[6] The generalization Davis employs here is that ideological motives are not enough to move people concerned about the economy to adopt a measure likely to harm it, and if they do so, they must recognize, perhaps unconsciously, that the measure is somehow to the country's economic advantage.

In fact Davis's explanation of the success of the abolitionist movement has been qualified over the years in response to ever more detailed information about its history. In his earlier work Davis outlined a theory about the economic disadvantages of slavery that he rather vaguely assumed to be widely respected and influential in winning support for the abolitionist cause. Eric Williams, in *Capitalism and Slavery* (1944), had assumed that abolition of slavery was in the economic interests of Britain—something most historians now dispute. Davis's theory was much subtler. Adam Smith had argued in *The Wealth of Nations* (1776) that free people, unlike many slaves, work hard in order to earn the money they need to purchase the goods they require. Prosperity would come to those who worked hard, and to those who employed others to work hard on their behalf. He wrote, "A person [like a slave] who can acquire no property, can have no other interest but to eat as much and to labor as little as possible."[7] Moreover free labor is self-sustaining, whereas slaves have to be bought and cared for, which is much more expensive. So it was in the interests of capitalists to have a free workforce. In addition to these economic advantages, Davis noted an eighteenth-century interest in the dignity of labor, when hard work and thrift were seen as evidence of personal virtue. Davis concluded, "No doubt the [antislavery] movement unconsciously reflected the interests and aspirations of the English middle class."[8]

Not everyone is convinced of the Marxist theory that people are unconsciously motivated by their class interests. Challenged to produce evidence that members of the antislavery movement were so motivated, Davis was unable to do so. But he defended the theory nevertheless by referring to several famous examples of its truth. He wrote, "As historians, we do need to recognize the reality of deceptive or biased consciousness—of collective rationalizations, sometimes consciously crafted, that serve identifiable interests and help convince individuals of their own innocence and virtue. . . . Modern history, from the Holocaust and Vietnam War to the peril of Star Wars and nuclear annihilation, teems with examples of individual and collective self-deception."[9] In this case the historical facts do not prove his theory true or false. Thomas L. Haskell remarked on "the absence, even in principle, of any empirical evidence that would permit us to distinguish between the unconsciously intended consequences that the self-deception explanation requires and the unintended consequences that make up so much of what happens in human affairs."[10]

No one doubts that if the MPs consciously believed it was to their economic advantage to free the slaves, they would have done so. What can be doubted is (1) whether they ever held that conviction and (2) whether there were no alternative reasons, namely political ones, that moved them. If economic motives for abolition cannot be found and alternative political ones existed, then economic motives were not necessary in the circumstances to motivate the abolitionists and so did not cause them to act as they did.

Davis's theory was criticized on both counts by the detailed work of Seymour Drescher. To Davis's credit, he has acknowledged the need to qualify his views. As was indicated in the quotation above, Davis now acknowledges that concern about the economic significance of abolition was largely confined to the West Indian lobby and the government and did not extend to the whole of the middle class. Drescher has shown that the government and many MPs doubted that abolition would bring economic benefits. On the contrary they were very concerned that without slave labor, production in the West Indies of sugar, cotton, coffee, and tobacco would fall. To assist the slaveholders in adjusting to the change, the British government provided compensation of £20 million as well as a period of compulsory apprenticeship by former slaves, who would have to continue working for four years after gaining their freedom. The MPs regarded emancipation of the slaves as "a mighty experiment" of whose outcome they were quite uncertain. In response to these facts Davis has turned from an economic explanation to one that stresses the importance to MPs of "a sense of self-worth created by dutiful work,"[11] an ideological rather than an economic explanation.

Assuming that ideological convictions were not enough to motivate a majority of MPs, an additional economic motive is credible only if no alternative, more plausible motive is available. Given the widespread popular support for the antislavery movement, evidenced in the numerous petitions to Parliament against it, both Drescher and Davis have identified a political motive for its success. Parliamentarians probably supported abolition to appease their constituencies.

A second field of generalizations of interest to historians is that of social organization. Seymour Drescher concluded a recent book by asserting, "The true taproot of antislavery lay in its successful mass political mobilization around a fundamentally uneconomic proposition."[12] The number of pamphlets and petitions produced during the campaign to abolish the slave trade, and later to abolish slavery itself, was huge and the number of signatories enormous. Their influence on public opinion, and on MPs, was presumably considerable. To explain this massive coordinated campaign, historians have described the political structures and practices that organized it.

The assumption underlying this explanation is the simple one that coordinated political campaigns require organization and cannot be explained on ideological grounds alone. Drescher, whose interest was in economics, did not explain the process of "mass political mobilization" to which he referred, and Davis chastised him for his failure. "At times," Davis wrote, "Drescher writes as if 'mobilization of opinion' were a self-sufficient force."[13] In fact, as he explains, it was the product of a complex network of organizations.

The movement began in the 1750s with the Philadelphia Meeting of Quakers urging members to free slaves and to cease importing them. After the American Revolution the Philadelphia Quakers urged the Quakers in London to take up the cause, which they did. Their organization was impressive. Committees were formed to arrange petitions, publications, and articles. A few Anglican Evangelicals, as they were known, were caught up in the movement, notably Granville Sharp, James Ramsay, Thomas Clarkson, and William Wilberforce, the latter two forming another committee with Quaker abolitionists. Davis has described the Quakers' network of contacts, made through business and the church, by means of which members were encouraged to adopt the church's policy.[14]

In this case no sophisticated theory of rational political organization has been employed. Common sense dictates that the movement required widespread ideological conviction, effective motivation, steering committees to plan and coordinate activities, and money to finance all these activities. There are doubtless theories about the ways these things can be produced and about the conditions of their success, and reference to these theories might have enriched the explanations given by historians. It might be enlightening to test such theories against the remarkable extensive organization of the antislavery campaigns.

A third function of interesting generalizations is to explain why one event occurred rather than another of a different kind that might well have been expected in the circumstances. These I call "contrastive explanations." They are unlike "genetic explanations," which describe events that increased the probability of an outcome with no particular contrast in mind.[15]

The English journalist William Cobbett attacked Wilberforce for wishing to help slaves overseas while ignoring the plight of the poor laboring classes in Britain. He said, "So often as they agitate this question, with all its cant, the relief of 500,000 blacks; so often will I remind them of the one million two hundred thousand white paupers in England and Wales."[16] The question is sometimes asked, why did Wilberforce, so full of Christian compassion, not do more for the oppressed in his own country? Or, to bring out the contrast more clearly, why did he devote so much of his life to relieving slaves overseas rather than work to relieve the plight of the poor on his own doorstep? Davis offers an ideological explanation, employing a generalization about a set of beliefs that he judged sufficient to motivate attitudes of the kind Wilberforce held. Abolitionists regarded slaves as unfree, whereas the British poor were indeed free, if subject at times to harsh discipline. Slavery was regarded as immoral, whereas harsh treatment of free men, women, and children was a matter of less concern.[17] Patrick Cormack dug a bit deeper and discovered a conservative disposition in the reformers, who feared that reform in England could lead to social turmoil, as it had in France during the revolution, and so were reluctant to disturb the status quo at home.[18] Notice that their conservatism does not explain why the reformers attacked slavery. It explains only why they were reluctant to press hard for widespread social reform at home.

The generalizations that historians produce to explain particular historical facts are usually instances of broader generalizations that are still relevant today. For instance, a conviction that God loved the African slaves as well as their white owners was sufficient to motivate many people to agitate for the abolition of slavery. This generalization would still be relevant to religious communities where slavery is practiced today. But in most of the world slavery is outlawed, and the only generalization relevant today is the more general one, that the conviction that God loves even those at the bottom of the social ladder is likely to move people who hold it to care for them, so long as other desires do not overwhelm their compassion.

Similarly the generalization that the organization of the Quaker community facilitated the coordinated outcry against slavery is not particularly relevant today. But a more general statement is: that for mass protest movements to succeed, they must be carefully organized and promoted. In addition the generalization that men who feared a repetition of the anarchy of the French Revolution were reluctant to press for widespread social reform seems remote from present concerns. But generalizations such as "those who fear the consequences of political reform will probably oppose it" still have relevance.

The study of the antislavery movement confirmed these very broad generalizations, giving us more confidence in their truth. It has also cast some doubt on the assumption that actions that impact upon the economy are always done for economic advantage. William Lecky's much-quoted declaration that "the crusade of England against slavery may probably be regarded as among the three or four perfectly virtuous acts recorded in the history of nations"[19] expresses the conviction that there was not a shred of self-interest among its motives. There was probably a degree of political expediency behind the vote of many MPs, but certainly no economic self-interest.

Traditions

Alasdair MacIntyre's analysis of cultural traditions in his book *After Virtue* (2nd ed., 1985) is a revelation. He explains that the values we share today are promoted by institutions and are manifest in the practices of virtuous members of those institutions Those values have been arrived at by members of the institutions over past years, usually in response to situations that called for a concerted response. For instance, respect for knowledge and understanding is promoted by universities, and that respect is manifest in the practices of conscientious academics in their teaching and research. Knowledge and understanding centuries ago focused on religious dogma, but over time universities, impressed with the success of scientific methods of inquiry, decided that they should be adopted as much as possible in all disciplines. So the knowledge and understanding that universities promote today are based on reason rather than faith. MacIntyre puts it thus: "So when an institution—a university, say, or a farm, or a hospital—is the bearer of a tradition of practice or practices, its common life will be partly, but in a centrally important way, constituted by a continuous argument as to what a university is and ought to be or what good farming is or what good medicine is. Traditions, when vital, embody continuities of conflict."[20]

The institutions to which people belong encourage a variety of practices, ways of doing things, and these practices have been adopted as means of furthering the goods to which the institution is committed. Thus scholars are required to defend their assertions by offering evidence of their truth. This practice is designed to promote knowledge rather than mere opinion. MacIntyre writes of goods such as knowledge being "internal to" the practices. The practices people adopt are often defined by the role they take within an institution, for instance the role of student, teacher, researcher, librarian, and so on. The goods to which an institution is dedicated are also enshrined in the rules that members of the institution are expected to follow. By adopting the roles and following the rules of an institution, members sometimes promote certain goods without being aware of doing so.

MacIntyre concludes, "What I am, therefore, is in key part what I inherit, a specific past that is present to some degree in my present. I find myself part of a history and that is generally to say, whether I like it or not, whether I recognize it or not, one of the bearers of a tradition."[21] It is a revelation to discover that people's behavior today is largely a product of the institutions to which they belong and the traditions that those institutions have inherited. Once this is understood, for the benefit of society it is vital that the traditions expressed in the practices of its institutions are evaluated. Were they designed for the benefit of all or just a few? Have they yielded those benefits or have they done more harm than good? Are there any traditions superior to those dominant in society today? History itself supplies the answer to each of these questions.

To understand why institutions adopted the values and practices they have, it is best to see what circumstances and arguments led to their adoption in the first place. One of the rules we have inherited is the law that slavery is illegal. This law is upheld by the courts, which are supported by police and penal institutions. Today there is a tendency among most members of law-abiding states to decry slavery. However, for centuries it was accepted by quite civilized societies. So why is it now so abhorred when it might have economic advantages? There is no better way of discovering why it is abhorred than by studying the movement that led to its abolition. Historians of the abolition movement do our communities a great service by setting out the reasons for which slavery was widely and then universally condemned. The arguments used against it then might well hold against anyone tempted to condone slavery today.

It must be allowed, of course, that the theological reasons for which the Quakers and Evangelicals opposed slavery were by no means the only grounds for doing so. Today people without a religious faith would probably be so appalled by the treatment of slaves as to want it outlawed on humanitarian grounds alone. To deepen one's understanding of the value of an institution, it is wise to study not just the reasons for which it was instituted but also the reasons people have given for supporting it down the years.

To judge the value of a law, it is important to discover not just the reasons for adopting it but also the effects of upholding it in society. Not all laws are just in practice. Here is a striking example. In the late eighteenth century enclosures of common land and growing industrialization produced an increase in poverty and crime. To reduce this, rather than relieve the plight of the poor, legislators increased the penalties for even minor offenses, especially against property. "Thus one Act imposed the death penalty for the theft of hares, rabbits, fish, for cutting down trees, wounding cattle, or setting fire to any house, barn, haystack or wood."22 Those who were not executed for such offences were sent as convicts to Australia. Here we have a historical tendency to try to reduce crime by imposing punishments so severe as to be quite unjust—that is, out of all proportion to the offense.

When we read of these consequences of the policy, we can see that it is not a tendency that should be encouraged. Wilberforce was aware of this. He wrote, "The barbarous custom of hanging has been tried for too long, and with the success that might have been expected. The most effectual way to prevent the greater crimes is to punish the smaller, and by endeavoring to repress the general spirit of licentiousness which is the parent of every kind of vice."23 This conviction lay behind his appeal, through William Pitt and Archbishop Moore, for King George III to reissue the traditional proclamation he had made on his accession to the throne in 1760, "for the Encouragement of Piety and Virtue and for the Preventing of Vice, Profaneness and Immorality." This the king did in June 1787, adding a long preamble expressing his concern at the impiety and licentiousness of the nation. Wilberforce encouraged people to take the proclamation seriously, and it did stimulate many magistrates and others to encourage reform. Indeed Garth Lean ascribes a new tradition of public accountability to Wilberforce, writing that he and his friends "pioneered a new political integrity in an age of corruption and did much to transform the House of Commons from a club which cared for the interests of its Members into an assembly responsible for great issues of the common weal."24 This is a tradition that MPs need to be reminded of from time to time.

The strength of people's dispositions often varies. Not everyone condemns slavery, even in the West. Some have adopted Nietzsche's philosophy that deplores pity for those in need as debilitating, as it drains one's energy and resources. He wrote that pity makes suffering contagious! Furthermore Nietzsche cited evolutionary theory to argue that it is only natural for the strong to exploit the weak and for the weak to suffer and die. Those with Christian or humanitarian commitments are likely to oppose slavery strongly, but others such as Nietzsche might be less concerned about it. History teaches not just the reasons for current common dispositions but also the motives people had, and still have, for opposing them.

Incidentally, to estimate the strength of a person's tendency to behave in a certain way in certain circumstances, one must know not just the strength of that disposition when it exists unopposed but also the strength of other dispositions the person has that do in fact oppose it. History teaches that slavery can work to the economic advantage of slave owners, so the temptation to enslave people could easily emerge again. Indeed it has, for instance when firms enslave illegal workers from overseas, whom they pay a pittance, by threatening to expose their illegal status to the authorities. Most people employing laborers today would avoid slavery. In most cases the workers would complain of their treatment, and the consequences would be dreadful, ruining a business that could do quite well with free labor. It is when the workers can be compelled to be silent that slavery becomes economically attractive.

Just as some individuals behave illegally, so too do some institutions. In countries where slavery is outlawed, the police and courts will prosecute slave owners, so long as members of the police force and the magistrates are not corrupt. As MacIntyre explained, for institutions to deliver the goods to which they are nominally committed, their members must be virtuous. In some cases public officials accept bribes to "look the other way," to ignore illegal activities. In societies where the bribery of public officials is unchecked, slave owners have only to pay them and then can carry on their businesses with impunity.

Our residual Whig faith in rationality and progress often leads us to assume that the traditions of our society today are superior to those it had in the past. But that is not always true. Historians can reveal traditions in the past that were better than ours today. In so doing they alert us to ways our present institutions and practices could be reformed.

An important agent of the abolition of the slave trade was the British Parliament. What is striking about it from a modern perspective is the relative freedom of members to support whatever position they wished. Today members of Parliament in the Westminster system are required to support the policy of their party or of their leader in the speeches they make and the votes they cast. But although the leaders of the Commons, William Pitt and Charles James Fox, supported Wilberforce's motions against the slave trade, the majority of members defeated them for many years. In the end, under Lord Grenville, freedom of conscience yielded the majorities needed for reform.

At times MPs today would like the freedom to vote according to their individual convictions, but the tradition of party discipline that has evolved over time prevents irresponsible opposition to bills that are clearly in the national interest. Still it is worth comparing the freedom enjoyed by MPs in the eighteenth century with that of MPs today to discover which practice is generally more beneficial.

So history can tell us which traditions are worth preserving and which do more harm than good, and it can even teach us about traditions that have been lost but could well be restored. A community that is ignorant of the history of its institutions is unable to appreciate the value of the ideals and practices they promote. History teachers have an obligation, I believe, to teach students the origins of the great civilizing traditions of their culture and of the other cultures the children are likely to encounter. One of the more corrupt premiers of an Australian state admitted he had no idea of the doctrine of the separation of powers. No wonder he ran the executive, legislative, and judicial branches of government from his office! Widespread ignorance of the doctrine meant that even the electorate scarcely noticed the loss of checks and balances that the independence of those institutions is meant to maintain.

Inspirations

Patrick Cormack introduced his biography of Wilberforce with these words: "The story of his life can still be an inspiration to a Christian politician."[25] Precisely what is meant by "inspiration" here? The word is used in several different senses, which can readily be illustrated. The most inspiring person in human history was probably Jesus of Nazareth. He has been an inspiration to his followers in three ways. First, there have been those who admire his teaching and his way of life and try to follow them themselves. In this case inspiration involves a value judgment about an aspect of the subject, a cognitive act, and then a determination to emulate that aspect in one's own life, an act of will. In the Christian church Calvinists and Evangelicals commonly find inspiration from Jesus in this way. I suspect that Wilberforce, who constantly checked how well he measured up against the standards set by Jesus, was inspired by him in this way.

A second kind of inspiration involves one's emotions as well as one's judgment. Some are moved not just by Jesus' teaching and example but also by his attitudes, his compassion and love, his forbearance, his determination and courage. As they hear the stories of his life, they exercise their imagination and empathy and find those attitudes quickened in themselves. On Good Friday some reflect at length upon the passion of Christ and are moved by his faithful obedience to what he believed to be God's will and by the depth of God's forgiveness and love that his sacrifice displays. They find the same dedication and love quickened in themselves.

More prosaic examples of this kind of inspiration are experiences of being stirred by speakers espousing causes one shares, concerning subjects such as war and the environment and, if you like, being aroused by accounts of sexual congress. In all these cases one not only approves of what is being said or done but finds one's emotions quickened as well.

I have been inspired by the words and life of Martin Luther King Jr., as I am sure many have. He not only sought justice for African Americans but also worked for brotherhood between whites and blacks. He not only wanted to mobilize protests against racial discrimination but was also passionately concerned to preserve the protestors from the spiritual corruption of hatred. I admire his teaching. His life is a model too: withstanding hatred and attacks of all kinds, resisting the temptation to adopt more violent forms of protest, persisting year after year with his crusade, never giving up hope for a better community. That commitment, perseverance, and courage move me to emulate them as best I can.

The third kind of inspiration is one in which a person attempts to live like the one who inspires him or her. It is characterized by the repeated question, what would X have done in these circumstances? There is an attempt to assume the whole personality of the inspiring other and to let it dictate one's thoughts and actions. In Christian practice this kind of identity is achieved by a spiritual transformation, described as dying to oneself and living in response to the spirit of Jesus. At one stage Saint Paul wrote, "We possess the mind of Christ" (1 Corinthians 2:16). Nonreligious examples are easy to find, however. People commonly say, "What would my mother have done?" "How would Judge X have ruled?" "What strategy would General X have adopted?"— and so on.

In 2006 Australia's prime minister Kevin Rudd was elected leader of the parliamentary Labour Party in Australia's federal parliament. Shortly before his election he spoke of his admiration for Dietrich Bonhoeffer, "the man I admire most in the history of the twentieth century."[26] As is well known, this Lutheran pastor and theologian spoke as a Christian leader against the Nazi regime in Germany. He supported a plot for the assassination of Hitler and was executed just before the war ended. In the course of his talk Rudd referred to "the searing intensity of Bonhoeffer's gaze, cast across the decades into our own less dramatic age: the need for the church to speak truthfully, prophetically and incisively in defiance of the superficiality of formal debate in contemporary Western politics."[27] He went on to ask, "How would Bonhoeffer respond to militant Islamism and the broader challenge of international terrorism today? . . . Bonhoeffer's voice, speaking to us through the ages, would ask this simple, truth-based question: what is causing this phenomenon? He would also caution against inflammatory rhetoric that seeks to gain political advantage, rather than to respond substantively and find a way forward."[28] He concluded his speech by saying, "I believe that today Bonhoeffer would be traumatised by the privatised, pietised and politically compliant Christianity on offer from the televangelists of the twenty-first century. Bonhoeffer's vision of Christianity and politics was for a just world delivered by social action, driven by personal faith."[29] Clearly Rudd is inspired by Bonhoeffer, and so far his work as leader has expressed the convictions voiced here.

Wilberforce, like Bonhoeffer and Rudd, believed that Christians should let their faith influence their political life, by helping to shape their policies and by inspiring their commitment to them. I suspect that most of those who find Wilberforce inspiring do so in the first sense. They admire his convictions and attitudes and become determined to apply them in their own lives. Rudd's relation to Bonhoeffer is much deeper. Bonhoeffer speaks to Rudd across the years and shapes his thinking today. Here is inspiration of the third kind, the most profound of all.

Clearly what inspires people depends on their present values, passions, and concerns. Those who are appalled by slavery and judge it to be monstrously immoral will not only approve of Wilberforce's dogged crusade against it but also be moved by it. The wider such values and passions are shared, the more people will be inspired by him. But because they are not universally shared, he will not be a universal source of inspiration, though we might think he should be.

It is perhaps worth adding that some lives are lessons in how not to live. Rather than inspiring us to do better, they warn us of ways in which people can do harm. Other lives are ethically neutral but reveal possibilities of life that we have not encountered, and perhaps never even considered. There are several different ways in which historical biographies can instruct us.

It should be noted that people can be inspired by social movements, not merely by individuals. The success of the Solidarity movement in Poland in defeating an entrenched government, for example, has inspired other organizations working for social justice. I wonder whether Quakers have been inspired to act on behalf of other downtrodden people by the success of their movement to abolish slavery.

Conclusion

The past differs from the present in ever so many ways. But people's general patterns of behavior in the past do not always differ from our own. The closer a past society is to the culture and institutions of our present one, the more tendencies they and we will have in common. That is why history can provide an invaluable window onto the nature and value of traditions and practices we have inherited.

First of all it can help us assess the accuracy of our present knowledge of how people are likely to respond in certain circumstances. We saw, for example, that the Marxist assumption that political change is motivated by economic self-interest is not always true. But the history of the abolitionist movement supports the belief that simultaneous widespread political protest requires a great amount of organization. By comparing roughly similar cases historians can detect important qualifications to generalizations currently held. I have not examined this process here, but it is another way in which people can draw lessons from history.[30] Whereas the first section of this essay considered how a knowledge of history can help one judge the truth of generalizations about the dispositions of individuals and institutions to act in certain ways in certain circumstances, the second section showed how history can help people judge the value of such dispositions. The dispositions that govern people's behavior are largely passed on by tradition. One can assess their value by examining the reasons for which they were originally adopted, by judging the actual consequences of exercising them, and by comparing them with alternative patterns of response that might have been better. Such judgments provide a justification for strengthening those institutions we have inherited that are of value and for reforming those that are not. In the third section on inspiration, we saw three ways in which people can strengthen in themselves the dispositions they admire in others: by deliberate acts of imitation; by empathetic sharing of their emotions; and by identifying with the personalities of the persons they admire. These are some of the more important ways people today can benefit from a study of the past.

NOTES

1. L. P. Hartley, *The Go-Between* (London: Hamilton, 1953), 9.

2. See Janna Thompson, *Taking Responsibility for the Past: Reparation and Historical Justice* (Cambridge, U.K.: Polity Press, 2002).

3. David Brion Davis, "The Problem of Slavery in the Age of Revolution, 1770–1823," in *The Antislavery Debate: Capitalism and Abolitionism as a Problem in Historical Interpretation,* edited by Thomas Bender (Berkeley: University of California Press, 1992), 22, 28; the quotation is from 28.

4. See C. Behan McCullagh, *The Logic of History* (London: Routledge, 2004), 177–84.

5. Davis, "The Problem of Slavery," 25.

6. David Brion Davis, *Inhuman Bondage: The Rise and Fall of Slavery in the New World* (Oxford: Oxford University Press, 2006), 244–45.

7. Adam Smith quoted in Seymour Drescher, "Free Labor vs Slave Labor: The British and Caribbean Cases," in *Terms of Labor: Slavery, Serfdom, and Free Labor,* edited by Stanley L. Engerman (Stanford, Calif.: Stanford University Press, 1999), 57.

8. Davis, "The Problem of Slavery," 81.

9. David Brion Davis, "Reflections on Abolitionism and Ideological Hegemony," in *The Antislavery Debate,* ed. Bender, 167.

10. Thomas L. Haskell, "Capitalism and the Origins of the Humanitarian Sensibility, Part I," in *The Antislavery Debate,* ed. Bender, 123.

11. Davis, *Inhuman Bondage,* 248.

12. Seymour Drescher, *The Mighty Experiment: Free Labor versus Slavery in British Emancipation* (Oxford: Oxford University Press, 2002), 236–37.

13. Davis, *Inhuman Bondage,* 246.

14. Davis, "The Problem of Slavery," 39–64.

15. McCullagh, *The Logic of History,* 172–76.

16. Cobbett quoted in Patrick Cormack, *Wilberforce, the Nation's Conscience* (Basingstoke, U.K.: Pickering, 1983), 115.

17. Davis, "The Problem of Slavery," 63.

18. Cormack, *Wilberforce,* 117.

19. Lecky quoted in Davis, *Inhuman Bondage,* 249.

20. Alasdair MacIntyre, *After Virtue,* 2nd ed. (London: Duckworth, 1985), 222.

21. Ibid., 221.

22. Garth Lean, *God's Politician: William Wilberforce's Struggle* (London: Darton, Longman and Todd, 1980), 70.

23. Wilberforce quoted in ibid., 73–74.

24. Ibid., 75–76, 170–71.

25. Cormack, *Wilberforce,* 12.

26. Kevin Rudd, "Faith in Politics," *Monthly* 16 (October 2006): 22.

27. Ibid., 27.

28. Ibid., 29.

29. Ibid., 30.

30. For a number of examples, see C. Behan McCullagh, *The Truth of History* (London: Routledge, 1998), 270–89.

II

Moral Progress in Specific Historical Contexts

Science, Religion, and Modernity
Early Modern Science and the Idea of Moral Progress

PETER HARRISON

In his inaugural lectures delivered at Harvard University in the years 1935–36, the pioneer historian of science George Sarton confidently announced, "The history of science is the only history which can illustrate the progress of mankind." "In fact," he went on to say, "progress has no definite and unquestionable meaning in other fields than the field of science."[1] For most historians and philosophers of science, this bold view has become a victim of the progress of their respective disciplines.[2] Yet Sarton's contention that science is uniquely progressive—in contrast to such areas of human endeavor as the arts, literature, religion, philosophy, and ethics—remains remarkably widespread.[3] His confidence in the progressive nature of science, moreover, was by no means unprecedented, and it drew on a long tradition that had its origins in the Enlightenment and which received robust expression in the philosophy of Auguste Comte, whom Sarton regarded as a kind of founding father of the history of science. Indeed the association of science with human advancement goes back even further to the beginnings of modern science in the seventeenth century. During this period, however, the idea of scientific progress was not divorced from the more "subjective" realm of moral and religious values, and "the advancement of learning," to use Francis Bacon's expression, was premised on a particular vision of moral advancement.

The broad thesis sketched out in this essay is that what we encounter from the seventeenth century was both a new conception of science and a new conception of moral progress, and that these were intimately related. The idea of scientific advancement that emerged for the first time in the seventeenth century owed something to discussions that were taking place in the realm of moral philosophy. Indeed the social legitimacy of the new science was dependent to a large degree on the emergence of this new conception of moral progress.

Natural Philosophy, Science, and *Scientia*

The current generation of historians of science tends to be scrupulous in its use of actors' categories for the various approaches to the study of nature in particular periods of history. Historians typically avoid using the anachronistic term "science" when referring to systematic investigations of natural order in the premodern and early modern periods. Instead they use expressions that contemporaries used to describe their own activities—"natural philosophy," along with "natural history," "mixed mathematical sciences," astronomy, astrology, alchemy, physic, and so on.[4] While a fastidious insistence on the use of actors' categories may at times seem to concede too much to the current trend of anti-Whig history, this practice has been of enormous importance in providing insights into the intellectual world of the early modern period, and into the connections between formal approaches to the study of nature, on the one hand, and other aspects of human endeavor such as religion and ethics, on the other. As a consequence of these new sensitivities, it has become clear that natural philosophy is very different from modern science, and that one important difference lies in the role that moral and religious considerations played in natural philosophy. For example, the English Franciscan philosopher Roger Bacon (1214–94) contended that natural philosophy ultimately had a moral orientation: "all speculative philosophy has moral philosophy for its end and aim."[5] Under the prevailing disciplinary taxonomy, speculative philosophy comprised theology, mathematics, and natural philosophy. We hear echoes of this sentiment four centuries later in Isaac Newton's observation, set in the *Opticks* (1704), that one of the goals of natural philosophy—the activity Newton considered himself to be engaged in—was to enlarge the bounds of moral philosophy and ultimately to shed light on the nature of the "first cause"—God.[6] Considerations of this sort have led historians to the conclusion that natural philosophy, on account of its religious and moral orientation, differs significantly from modern science. Cambridge historian of science Andrew Cunningham has gone so far as to say that the natural philosophy was about "God's achievements, God's intentions, God's purposes, God's messages to man."[7]

I do not wish to suggest, however, that Roger Bacon and Isaac Newton shared a common vision of the goals of philosophy, in spite of the continuity implied by their shared use of the term "natural philosophy" and their insistence on its moral orientation. A key difference lies in Newton's confidence that, as he put it, the bounds of moral philosophy might be "enlarged." This suggests, in turn, that he believed moral philosophy to be a cumulative enterprise and hence capable of being enlarged. Newton's idea seems to have been that what makes this possible is advancement in the auxiliary discipline of natural philosophy. In order to understand the significance of this difference between Roger Bacon and Isaac Newton, we need to give consideration to changing conceptions of the nature and goals of philosophy itself.

In the past decade there was a growing interest among historians of ideas in the conceptions of philosophy in the classical and medieval periods. One of the more influential writers on this topic, the French intellectual historian Pierre Hadot, has suggested that whereas we typically imagine ancient and medieval philosophy to have been conducted in a manner broadly similar to what transpires in the modern university departments of analytical philosophy, in fact ancient philosophers were primarily concerned with "spiritual exercises" and "a way of life." Past philosophical activity, on this understanding, was focused less on doctrines and arguments to do with epistemology and ontology and aimed instead at moral formation. It follows that many contemporary historians of philosophy have systematically misconstrued ancient philosophy by considering philosophical doctrines and arguments to have been the end of philosophy rather than means of personal transformation.[8] Others have advanced views similar to Hadot's or have elaborated these claims in various ways.[9]

As a branch of philosophy, natural philosophy may be assumed to have shared some of the "spiritual" goals of philosophy. In our own age, when science has largely eschewed questions of meaning and value, it is difficult to image how in the past the study of nature might have served the ends of philosophical formation. However, if we attend carefully to what past thinkers said about their "scientific" activities, a case can be made that natural philosophy, no less than philosophy proper, was addressed to the question of the pursuit of the good life. That case cannot be made here, but even a cursory consideration of the evidence will, I hope, point to the plausibility of such a claim. Consider these examples from antiquity. Epicurus recommended "endless pursuit of the study of nature" because of his conviction that such study "contributes more than anything else to the tranquility and happiness of life."[10] Epicurean physics was thus intended to serve Epicurean ethics. The skeptics, both Academic and Pyrrhonic, can also be understood as engaged in the quest to achieve wisdom of a similar kind. The Pyrrhonic skeptic is one who, through the suspension of judgment (*epoche*), attains peace of mind or "unperturbability" (*ataraxia*). Natural science, logic, and ethics were studied only because they contributed to this state of tranquillity.[11] In a similar vein the astronomer and mathematician Claudius Ptolemy contended that study of the mathematical regularities of the heavens "makes its followers lovers of this divine beauty, accustoming them and reforming their natures, as it were to a spiritual state."[12]

Once we understand the goals of natural philosophy in this light, we gain important new insights into some of the classic episodes in the history of philosophy and science. The famous Condemnation of Aristotle, issued by the bishop of Paris in 1277, has typically been understood as a reaction against those Aristotelian doctrines that were held to be inconsistent with Christian teaching. While it is true that a number of such doctrines are identified in the 219 propositions, it can be argued that the primary issue was the Aristotelian conception of the philosophical life and the claim that it was superior to the prevailing understanding of the Christian life.[13] Tellingly the very first propositions to be censured are these: "That there is no more excellent state than to study philosophy"; and "That the only wise men in the world are the philosophers."[14] Similarly the revolution in the sciences that took place over the course of the sixteenth and seventeenth centuries may be characterized, at least in part, as a series of attempts to revise the goals of natural philosophy—goals that had previously been subordinated to this broader understanding of philosophy as a formative process.[15] Much of the recent skepticism about the category "the scientific revolution" has rightly focused on the fact that there was at this time neither "science" as we understand it nor a revolution. Yet it is possible to identify a significant change in conceptions of the goals of philosophy and natural philosophy at this time, and this, it can be argued, accounts for the common sentiment among seventeenth-century writers that they were witnesses to a momentous change in the realm of learning. On this understanding, the Copernican revolution that saw a rejection of the Ptolemaic cosmos was accompanied by a parallel rejection of the Ptolemaic understanding of the moral goals of mathematical and philosophical investigation.

Ideas about the formative role of the contemplation of nature were not difficult to incorporate into a framework of medieval theology that tended to emphasize the priority of the contemplative life and which held that God's wisdom and power were evident in the created order. They were also consistent with a Christianized Aristotelian moral philosophy that had become dominant from the thirteenth century. In this framework virtues were understood as habits or dispositions that were acquired through practice. Aristotle, of course, had known nothing of the Christian virtues of faith, hope, and love, but these "theological virtues" were now added to an existing taxonomy of mental habits that already included moral and intellectual virtues. One of the latter was "science" (scientia), understood as a personal quality rather than a body of knowledge. Bringing together the idea of philosophy as moral formation and a conception of virtue as an inner disposition acquired by repeated practice, we can see that the practice of natural philosophy in the Middle Ages had as a primary aim the development of particular intellectual virtues. Natural philosophy, as one of the three speculative sciences, was aimed at producing a particular kind of person, namely, one possessed of the intellectual virtues. Witness Thomas Aquinas on the intellectual virtue scientia: "In like manner, science can increase in itself by addition; thus when anyone learns several conclusions of geometry, the same specific habit of science increases in that man. Yet a man's science increases, as to the subject's participation thereof, in intensity, in so far as one man is quicker and readier than another in considering the same conclusions."[16]

"Science" was thus a mental habit that was gradually acquired through the practice of scientific demonstration. This basic conception applied to all the sciences, including their queen, theology. The science of theology, according to John Duns Scotus, produces a habit that perfects the intellect: "The intellect perfected by the habit of theology apprehends God as one who should be loved."[17] Scotus's point was that the science of theology was to be understood as a means of perfecting the intellect and predisposing it to the act of loving God. These connotations of scientia were well known in the Renaissance and persisted until the seventeenth century. Thomas Holyoake's Dictionary (1676) states that scientia, properly speaking, is the act of the knower and secondarily the thing known. The entry also stresses the classical and scholastic idea of science as "a habit of knowledge got by demonstration."[18] The progressive nature of science, on this understanding, lies in the fact that through repeated practice the individual can become more proficient at particular mental operations.

The point I wish to extract from all this, without simplifying matters too much, is that in the ancient and medieval intellectual worlds the primary locus of progress—scientific and moral—was the individual. The main scope for improvement lay in the progress of the soul, rather than in the commonweal. The study of nature, as a branch of philosophy, was subordinated to this end. Much of this was to change over the course of the seventeenth century. Indeed, as I have already suggested, while the so-called scientific revolution of the seventeenth century has often been understood in terms of the appearance of new scientific doctrines and methods, a case can be made that a more fundamental development during the period was the introduction of a new and progressive conception of natural philosophy.[19]

The New Science and Human Progress

The seventeenth century is often identified as the period during which individuals first entertained the idea of progress in history, although many thinkers were rather ambivalent about the idea of progress.[20] Historians are also divided about whether this was the first appearance of the idea of progress in the West.[21] There can be no doubt, however, of a new, progressive conception of natural philosophy in the seventeenth century. Its first and indeed foremost proponent was Francis Bacon. In a number of writings addressed to the reform of philosophy and the advancement of learning, Bacon challenged the traditional understanding of philosophy and its goals. Knowledge, he insisted, should be sought "not for the quiet of resolution but for a restitution and reinvesting (in great part) of man to the sovereignty and power . . . which he had in his first state of creation."[22] He was later to write that "the true ends of knowledge are not . . . for pleasure of the mind . . . but for the benefit and use of life, and that they perfect and govern it in charity."[23] Two biblical motifs lie behind these contentions about the goals of knowledge. The first was the idea that Adam's original vocation in his prelapsarian state had been to exercise dominion over the beasts. While much of this original power had been lost as a consequence of Adam's disobedience, Bacon imagined the goal of natural philosophy to be that of reestablishing a dominion over things that had been lost because of the Fall.[24] For much of the Patristic period and the Middle Ages, Adamic dominion had been read as referring to a control over the "beasts within," understood as unruly passions and sensual desires. This was in keeping with both the common practice of allegorical interpretation and the idea of philosophy as personal transformation.[25] A second biblical allusion is to Saint Paul's warning that "scientia inflat caritas vero aedificat" (knowledge puffeth up, but charity edifieth).[26] Bacon wanted to insist that while some knowledge may well puff up the knower with pride—and he had in mind here the supposedly contentious, inwardly focused knowledge of the scholastics—this could never be true of charitable knowledge that was aimed at promoting the good of others. Knowledge may be perverted, but only "if it be severed from charity, and not referred to the good of men and mankind."[27] The application of knowledge to human welfare—its promotion of the good of others rather than just the edification of the individual—was a prophylactic against the first of the deadly sins, pride.

A second emphasis in the Baconian conception of natural philosophy concerns the importance of the active life and the need to conjoin action and contemplation. There had been a long-standing distinction in the West, originating with the Greeks, between the active and contemplative lives.[28] In both Greek and Christian traditions there had been a strong tendency to favor the contemplative life. Aristotle had contended that the particular excellence of human beings lies in their capacity for rational reflection, and hence while social life requires some to be involved in the active life, the true end of human existence lies in contemplation (which is also the sole activity of God). This classical emphasis was reinforced in Christian literature by a common interpretation of the Gospel narrative of Mary and Martha, in which the contemplative Mary is deemed to have chosen the better part.[29] In addressing this traditional divide, Bacon did not deny the importance of contemplation, but he was to insist that contemplation must give rise to action: "the rule of religion, that a man should know his faith by his works, holds good in natural philosophy too. Science also must be known by works."[30]

A third feature of Bacon's new conception of natural philosophy concerns its corporate and cumulative nature. The "perfection of the sciences," Bacon insisted, will come "not from the swiftness or ability of any one inquirer, but from a succession [of them]."[31] Natural philosophy is not about private contemplation; neither is it a closed fraternity of adepts dealing with secret information. It is instead a public activity, practiced in a communal setting, and capable of incremental advance as generations of philosophers add to the store of useful knowledge. There is clear contrast between this notion of the "increase" of science and Aquinas's individualistic conception of how science is cumulative: "science can increase in itself by addition; thus when anyone learns several conclusions of geometry, the same specific habit of science increases in that man."[32]

In sum, for Bacon, philosophy was no longer understood as a solitary, contemplative practice that aimed primarily at the spiritual formation of the individual but was instead an active, outward-looking, and corporate enterprise that aimed at the mastery and manipulation of nature. Knowledge becomes common stock and accumulates over time as a consequence of the cooperative endeavors of individuals who are guided by a set of established methods. The growing body of knowledge that results is applied to the material problems of human welfare. This was not totally divorced from earlier ideas about self-improvement, for what Bacon was attempting in all of this was to connect the classical and medieval ideals of spiritual formation with the goal of the improvement of the human estate—in Bacon's succinct summary:

"The improvement of man's mind and the improvement of his lot are one and the same thing."[33]

This new conception of philosophy attracted both imitators and detractors. A number of scientific societies that sprang up in the seventeenth century self-consciously modeled themselves on Baconian principles. These included the French Académie Royale des Sciences, the Italian Accademia della Tracia, and the Royal Society. Individual natural philosophers articulated a similar ideal of natural philosophy as scientific knowledge accumulated over time and directed toward the public good. René Descartes, for example, complained that Aristotelianism was distinguished only by the fact that it had remained virtually unchanged for millennia. "The best way of proving the falsity of Aristotle's principles," he argued, "is to point out that they have not enabled any progress to be made in all the many centuries in which they have been followed." By way of contrast, those who followed Cartesian principles were supposed to progress incrementally toward a perfect philosophy. As Descartes modestly described it, "moving little by little from one truth to the next, they . . . in time acquire a perfect knowledge of all philosophy, and reach the highest level of wisdom." This was a matter not merely of personal fulfillment but of social progression.[34] Like Bacon, Descartes espoused a communal and cumulative philosophical program: "And I judged that the best remedy [for the ills of philosophy] was to communicate faithfully to the public what little I had discovered, and to urge the best minds to try and make further progress by helping with the necessary observations, each according to his inclination and ability, and by communicating to the public everything they learn. Thus, by building upon the work of our predecessors and combining the lives and labours of many, we might make much greater progress working together than anyone could make on his own."[35]

Descartes' contemporary Blaise Pascal, who disagreed with his compatriot on much else, gave eloquent expression to this new progressive philosophical ideal. In his preface to the *Treatise on the Vacuum,* in an argument for the progress of the sciences, Pascal asked the reader to envisage the commonwealth of learning as in some ways analogous to the older model of the individual scholar. Imagine, he wrote, "the whole succession of men, during the course of many ages . . . as a single man who subsists forever and learns continually."[36] Henceforth knowledge would not be limited to the capacity of the single mind, but would be a public commodity to which all may contribute and from which all may benefit.

In England fellows of the newly formed Royal Society spoke in similar terms of the new philosophy. In an essay on the "usefulness" of experimental natural philosophy, Robert Boyle rehearsed a number of the arguments first advanced by Bacon. The new approach to nature, he argued, both increased the individual's devotion to God and enabled the performance of charitable works on a much larger scale. In the finding of natural philosophy, there are "divers things deliver'd, which may tend to enlarge Man's power of doing Good: By them, in the whole, both our Honour to

God, and our Charity to our Neighbors." Experimental philosophy, he opined, encompasses "the Substantial part of all the most Noble, not only Human but Christian Vertues, both Speculative and Practical."[37] Another early fellow of the society, the Anglican divine Joseph Glanvill, published in 1668 the apologetic *Plus Ultra,* which bore the subtitle "The Progress and Advancement of Knowledge since the Days of Aristotle." Aristotle's philosophy, he complained, was "inept for New discoveries; and therefor of no accommodation to the *use* of *life.*"[38] In the essay "Modern Improvements of Useful Knowledge" he went on to note that the Royal Society was founded on the Baconian premise "that *Nature* being *known,* it may be *master'd, manag'd,* and *used* in the Services of Humane Life."[39]

While the merit of projects to reorient philosophical activity toward practical and public goods may in retrospect seem obvious, at the time they were not uncontroversial. One example of this was the dispute that erupted in England during the second half of the seventeenth century over the "usefulness" of the new philosophy.[40] Works such as Glanvill's *Plus Ultra* aroused the ire of supporters of Aristotelianism and of the more traditional, virtue-based idea of philosophical advancement. The classicist Meric Casaubon was one who expressed serious doubts about the usefulness of the new style of philosophizing. The best effect of philosophy, Casaubon insisted, was to "promote virtue and godliness" and to "moralise men." In general, he wrote, those activities that "promote the goodness in the soul are to be lauded above those who promote material welfare." He mockingly pointed out that the Baconian aims of the Royal Society—to provide for the conveniences of the present life—were better achieved by brewers and bakers than by natural philosophers, who by implication should concern themselves with more elevated matters.[41] While Casaubon and those who shared his views are now often portrayed as conservative reactionaries vainly attempting to hold back the inevitable tide of progress, when we consider them in the light of the traditional understanding of natural philosophy, we can see that in fact they represent a serious and long-standing view about the ultimate goals of human knowledge, one that should not be lightly dismissed.[42] As for the controversy itself, it points to a divide that in the nineteenth century would become a permanent feature of the culture of the West—the partitioning of intellectual territory between the sciences and the humanities.

Science as Philanthropy

The term "philanthropy" first entered the English lexicon at the turn of the seventeenth century. It should now come as little surprise that the term was coined by Francis Bacon.[43] While the word was familiar to readers of Greek, Bacon thought it worth appropriating and investing with new meaning: "I take goodness in this sense, the affecting of the weal of men, which is that the Grecians call philanthropia; and the word humanity (as it is used) is a little too light to express it. Goodness I call the habit, and goodness of nature, the inclination. This of all virtues, and dignities of the mind, is the greatest; being the character of the Deity."[44]

Interestingly Bacon retained an emphasis on the interior *habitus* but supplemented it with the outward-looking reference to the good of the commonwealth. We may wonder why, given the comprehensive taxonomy of virtues already available to Bacon, he thought it necessary to introduce one more, particularly since he later equated philanthropy with "the theological virtue Charity."[45] One plausible explanation would be that Bacon wanted an expression that would convey something of a new philosophical program that was oriented toward human welfare. In retrospect we might judge Bacon's neologism to have been unnecessary, for "charity" is now no longer understood primarily as the first of the Christian virtues but refers instead to public beneficence or, as a noun, to welfare organizations. In fact the gradual shift in the meaning of "charity" is emblematic of a more fundamental change that also saw the virtue *scientia* reified into "science"—now a body of doctrines arrived at through the application of a particular method. For Bacon, an important new justification for the pursuit of natural philosophy was that if it were prosecuted correctly, benefits would flow to the human race. In essence his model of natural philosophy was that it was a philanthropic activity. Moral and scientific progress in his scheme of things were one and the same thing.

It must be said, in conclusion, that this broad narrative about how changing conceptions of the goals of philosophy were related to the emergence of a new progressive understanding of science is at best a partial account. There are at least two other, perhaps better-known, narratives that intersect with this one. One of these concerns the gradual demise of an ethics of virtue in the modern period and its replacement by what we would now call consequentialist, emotivist, and deontological alternatives. The story of the decline of virtue ethics, as compellingly related by Alasdair MacIntyre, is usually not thought to be directly relevant to the history of science.[46] In the light of the preceding discussion, it seems that the history of moral philosophy is something from which historians of science can profitably learn. It is also worth pondering whether the emergence of some kind of consequentialist moral framework is a necessary prerequisite for a conception of moral progress in history.

A second missing narrative concerns the more conventional history of ideas of progress. A key ingredient of the Baconian science of the revolutionary period in England was a millenarian vision of history and a strong belief that the efflorescence of scientific activity was a necessary prelude to the end of the world.[47] While this strong chiliastic understanding of history became less popular after the Restoration, there were still significant associations between the idea of scientific advancement and providential conceptions of history. It was commonly asserted, for example, that the reformation of religion was destined by Providence to be accompanied by a reformation in the realm of learning.[48] When the eighteenth-century philosophes appropriated the idea of progress and integrated it into their account of human enlightenment, they tended to be silent about the religious motivations and goals of the earlier pioneers of the new science. Indeed the most prominent Enlightenment prophet of progress, the Marquis de Condorcet, posited a negative relation between progress and religion, identifying religion as an obstacle to the advancement of the human spirit.

The grain of truth in these later interpretations is that the progressive understanding of natural philosophy that made its appearance in the seventeenth century did involve a rejection of certain aspects of the classical-Christian philosophical ideal. But for most of the key agents, this rejection was motivated by what they saw as a more genuinely Christian vision of the aims of philosophy. The "rise of science" as a progressive enterprise involved the attempted liberation of both ethics and natural philosophy from their thraldom to "pagan" Aristotelianism and the replacement of this putatively corrupt medieval model with a more authentic understanding of the Christian vocation. It was the capacity of the new philosophy to present itself as a legitimate form of Christian life, rather than its self-evident "scientific" superiority to previous systems of philosophy or its technological benefits, that accounts for its unique status in the modern West. As the historian of science Stephen Gaukroger has perceptively remarked in his recent book on the rise of science in the West: "Christianity took over natural philosophy in the seventeenth century, setting its agenda and projecting it forward in a way quite different from that of any other scientific culture, and in the end establishing it as something in part constructed in the image of religion."[49]

NOTES

1. George Sarton, *The Study of the History of Science* (Cambridge, Mass.: Harvard University Press, 1936), 5.

2. For representative discussions of progress in science, see Larry Laudan, *Progress and Its Problems: Towards a Theory of Scientific Growth* (Berkeley: University of California Press, 1977); Philip Kitcher, *The Advancement of Science: Science without Legend, Objectivity without Illusions* (Oxford: Oxford University Press, 1993); Thomas S. Kuhn, *The Structure of Scientific Revolutions* (Chicago: University of Chicago Press, 1962); I. Niiniluoto, *Is Science Progressive?* (Dordrecht: D. Reidel, 1984); A. Jonkisz and L. Koj, eds., *On Comparing and Evaluating Scientific Theories* (Amsterdam: Rodopi, 2000); Rom Harré, ed., *Problems of Scientific Revolutions: Progress and Obstacles to Progress in the Sciences* (Oxford: Oxford University Press, 1975); and J. L. Aronson, R. Harré, and E. C. Way, *Realism Rescued: How Scientific Progress Is Possible* (London: Duckworth, 1994).

3. For the perspective of scientists, see Steven Weinberg, *Dreams of a Final Theory* (New York: Vintage, 1994); Brian Greene, *The Elegant Universe* (New York: Vintage, 2000); John Maddox, *What Remains to Be Discovered* (New York: Touchstone, 1998); and John Horgan, *The End of Science* (New York: Broadway, 1997).

4. See, for example, Andrew Cunningham, "How the *Principia* Got Its Name: Or, Taking Natural Philosophy Seriously," *History of Science* 29 (1991): 377–92; Peter Dear, "The Mathematical Principles of Natural Philosophy: Toward a Heuristic Narrative for the Scientific

Revolution," *Configurations* 6 (Spring 1998): 173–93; Margaret Osler, "Mixing Metaphors: Science and Religion or Natural Philosophy and Theology in Early Modern Europe," *History of Science* 35 (1997): 91–113; and Christoph Luthy, "What to Do with Seventeenth-Century Natural Philosophy? A Taxonomic Problem," *Perspectives on Science* 8 (Summer 2000): 164–95.

5. Roger Bacon, *Opus Majus of Roger Bacon,* trans. Robert Burke, 2 vols. (Philadelphia: University of Pennsylvania Press, 1928), 1:72. Under the Aristotelian classification, natural philosophy along with mathematics and theology made up the speculative sciences. Bacon's point may also have been related to controversies about this classification, and specifically whether theology was a practical or speculative science.

6. Isaac Newton, *Opticks,* Query 31, 405.

7. Andrew Cunningham, "Getting the Game Right: Some Plain Words on the Identity and Invention of Science," *Studies in the History and Philosophy of Science* 19, no. 3 (1988): 384. For discussions of Cunningham's views, see Edward Grant, "God and Natural Philosophy: The Late Middle Ages and Sir Isaac Newton," *Early Science and Medicine* 6, no. 3 (2000): 279–98; Peter Dear, "Religion, Science, and Natural Philosophy: Thoughts on Cunningham's Thesis," *Studies in History and Philosophy of Science* 32A (2001): 377–86; Andrew Cunningham, "A Response to Peter Dear's 'Religion, Science, and Philosophy,'" *Studies in History and Philosophy of Science* 32A (2001): 387–91; and Peter Harrison, "Physico-Theology and the Mixed Sciences: The Role of Theology in Early Modern Natural Philosophy," in *The Science of Nature in the Seventeenth Century,* edited by Peter Anstey and John Schuster (Dordrecht: Springer, 2005), 165–83.

8. Pierre Hadot, *What Is Ancient Philosophy?* (Cambridge, Mass.: Harvard University Press, 2002); Pierre Hadot, *Philosophy as a Way of Life* (Oxford: Blackwell, 1995).

9. Berold Thomassen, *Metaphysik als Lebensform: Untersuchungen zur Grundlegung der Metaphysik im Metaphysikkommentar Alberts des Grossen* (Münster: Aschendorff, 1985); Alexander Nehamas, *The Art of Living: Socratic Reflections from Plato to Foucault* (Berkeley: University of California Press, 1998); Martha Nussbaum, *The Therapy of Desire* (Princeton, N.J.: Princeton University Press, 1984); John Sellars, *The Art of Living: The Stoics on the Nature and Function of Philosophy* (Aldershot, U.K.: Ashgate, 2003); Richard Sorabji, *Emotion and Peace of Mind: From Stoic Agitation to Christian Temptation* (Oxford: Oxford University Press, 2003); John Cottingham, *Philosophy and the Good Life* (Cambridge: Cambridge University Press, 1998); John Cottingham, *The Spiritual Dimension: Religion, Philosophy, and Human Value* (Cambridge: Cambridge University Press, 2006); H. Hutter, "Philosophy as Self-Transformation," *Historical Reflections/Réflexions Historiques* 16, nos. 2 and 3 (Summer and Fall 1989): 171–98; R. Imbach, "La Philosophie comme exercice spirituel," *Critique* 41 (March 1985): 275–83.

10. Epicurus, *Letter to Herodotus,* in Diogenes Laertius, *Lives and Opinions of Eminent Philosophers,* 10.24.

11. Sextus Empiricus, *Outlines of Scepticism,* 1:viii–ix.

12. Claudius Ptolemy, *Ptolemy's Almagest,* trans. G. J. Toomer (Princeton, N.J.: Princeton University Press, 1998), 37.

13. David Piché, ed., *La condemnation parisienne de 1277: Texte latin, traduction, introduction et commentaire* (Paris: Vrin, 1999). For alternative interpretations, see John F. Wippel, "The Condemnations of 1270 and 1277 at Paris," *Journal of Medieval and Renaissance Studies*

7 (1977): 169–201; John E. Murdoch, "Pierre Duhem and the History of Late Medieval Science and Philosophy in the Latin West," in *Gli studi di filosofia medievale fra otto e novecento*, edited by Alfonso Maier and Ruedi Imbach (Rome: Edizioni di Storia e Letteratura, 1991), 253–302; and Edward Grant, "The Condemnation of 1277: God's Absolute Power, and Physical Thought in the Late Middle Ages," *Viator* 10 (1979): 211–44.

14. Condemnation of 1277, quoted in Edward Grant, "Science and Theology in the Middle Ages," in *God and Nature: Historical Essays on the Encounter between Christianity and Science*, edited by David C. Lindberg and Ronald L. Numbers (Berkeley: University of California Press, 1986), 55.

15. Peter Harrison, "Was There a Scientific Revolution?," *European Review* 15, no. 4 (2007): 445–57.

16. Thomas Aquinas, *Summa theologiae* 1a2ae.52, 2. See also his *Summa theologiae* 1a2ae.54, 4; 1a.89, 5; 1a2ae.50, 4; 53, 1; 54, 4; *Summa contra gentiles* I.61; II.60; II.78; and *On the Virtues in General*, A. 7, Obj. 1.

17. John Duns Scotus, *Ordinatio* prol.5.1–2, nn. 314, 332 *Opera Omnia*, ed. C. Balíc et al. (Vatican City: Typis Polyglottis Vaticanis, 1950–), 1:207–8, 217, quoted in Richard Cross, *Duns Scotus* (Oxford: Oxford University Press, 1999), 9.

18. "Scientia . . . Knowledge, learning, skill, cunning, properly the act of him that knoweth, secondly the state of the thing known, . . . thirdly an habit of knowledge got by demonstration, Arist 7. Ethic. 3. fourthly any habit of the understanding" (Thomas Holyoake, *A Large Dictionary in Three Parts* [London: W. Rawlins, 1676], *vscientia* [unpag.]). A longer but similar definition is given in Eustachio e Sancto Paulo, *Summa Philosophiae Quadripartita* (Paris: Chastellain, 1609), 1:230–31, in *Étienne Gilson: Index Scholastico-Cartésien* (Paris, 1912; repr., New York: Franklin, 1964), sec. 408. See also Charles Lohr, "Metaphysics," in *Cambridge History of Renaissance Philosophy*, edited by C. Schmitt and Q. Skinner (Cambridge: Cambridge University Press, 1988), 632; and Heiki Mikkeli, *An Aristotelian Response to Renaissance Humanism: Jacopo Zabarella on the Nature of Arts and Sciences* (Helsinki: Finnish Historical Society, 1992), 27–29.

19. "Scientific revolution" has become a contentious category, partly because it assumes a revolution in science rather than natural philosophy. For arguments that a new conception of natural philosophy emerged at this time, see Stephen Gaukroger, *Francis Bacon and the Transformation of Early Modern Philosophy* (Cambridge: Cambridge University Press, 2001); Harrison, "Was There a Scientific Revolution?"; and the contributions of Harrison and Gaukroger, in *The Philosopher in Early Modern Europe*, edited by C. Condren, S. Gaukroger, and Ian Hunter (Cambridge: Cambridge University Press, 2006).

20. While such expressions as "new philosophy," "new astronomy," and "new physic" were common, new philosophical doctrines were often presented as revivals of ancient models. Hence the new atomic and corpuscular theories were described as "Epicurean," the Copernican model as "Pythagorean," and so on. Whole systems of philosophy, such as those of Descartes, could even be described as the recapitulation of an ancient Judeo-Christian wisdom first elliptically set out by Moses in the book of Genesis. Rather than describing their innovations as revolutionary, proponents of novel ideas often used such terms as "revival," "reformation," and "instauration."

21. Sydney Pollard, *The Idea of Progress: History and Society* (London: Watts, 1968), chap. 1; Robert Nisbet, *History of the Idea of Progress* (New York: Basic Books, 1980); E. L. Tuveson,

Millennium and Utopia: A Study in the Background of the Idea of Progress, 2nd ed. (New York: Russell and Russell, 1964); John Passmore, *The Perfectability of Man,* 3rd ed. (Indianapolis: Liberty Fund, 2000), chap. 10. On progress in antiquity, see Ludwig Edelstein, *The Idea of Progress in Classical Antiquity* (Baltimore: Johns Hopkins University Press, 1964); and E. R. Dodds, *The Ancient Concept of Progress and Other Essays on Greek Literature and Belief* (New York: Oxford University Press, 1973).

22. Francis Bacon, *Valerius Terminus,* in *The Works of Francis Bacon,* 14 vols., ed. James Spedding, Robert Ellis, and Douglas Heath (London: Longmans, 1857–74), 3:222.

23. Francis Bacon, *Great Instauration, Preface,* in *The Works of Francis Bacon,* ed. Spedding, Ellis, and Heath, 4:21.

24. "For man by the fall fell at the same time from this state of innocency and from his dominion over creation. Both of these losses however can even in this life be in some part repaired; the former by religion and faith, the latter by arts and sciences. For creation was not by the curse made altogether and forever a rebel, but . . . is now by various labours . . . at length and in some measure subdued to the supplying of man with bread; that is to the uses of human life" (Francis Bacon, *Novum Organum,* bk. 2, sec. 52, in *The Works of Francis Bacon,* ed. Spedding, Ellis, and Heath, 4:247).

25. Peter Harrison, "Subduing the Earth: Genesis 1, Early Modern Science, and the Exploitation of Nature," *Journal of Religion* 79 (1999): 86–109; Peter Harrison, "Reading the Passions: The Fall, the Passions, and Dominion over Nature," in *The Soft Underbelly of Reason: The Passions in the Seventeenth Century,* edited by S. Gaukroger (London: Routledge, 1998), 49–78.

26. 1 Corinthians 8.1 (Vulgate/Authorized Version).

27. Francis Bacon, *Advancement of Learning,* edited by Arthur Johnston (Oxford: Clarendon Press, 1974), 8.

28. C. Butler, *Western Mysticism: The Teaching of Augustine, Gregory and Bernard on Contemplation and the Contemplative Life,* 2nd ed. (New York: Haskell House, 1966); M. E. Mason, *Active Life and Contemplative Life: A Study of the Concepts from Plato to the Present* (Milwaukee: Marquette University Press, 1961).

29. Luke 10:38–42; Augustine, Sermon 104, "Discourse on Martha and Mary, as Representing Two Kinds of Life," in *Works of St. Augustine,* ed. John Rotelle, 20 vols. (New York: New City Press, 1991–), 3:4, 83; *The Trinity* I.iii.20–21. See also Anne-Marie La Bonnardière, "Les deux vies: Marthe et Marie (Luc 10, 38, 42)," in *Saint Augustin et la Bible,* edited by Bonnardière (Paris: Beauchesne, 1986), 411–25.

30. Francis Bacon, *Redargutio Philosophiarum* (1608), in B. Farington, *The Philosophy of Francis Bacon* (Liverpool: Liverpool University Press, 1964), 92f.; Francis Bacon, *Advancement,* in *The Works of Francis Bacon,* ed. Spedding, Ellis, and Heath, 3:294.

31. Francis Bacon, *De sapientia veterum,* in Bacon, *The Works of Francis Bacon,* ed. Spedding, Ellis, and Heath, 4:753. Cf. Francis Bacon, *Parasceve,* in ibid., 4:252.

32. Aquinas, *Summa theologiae* 1a2ae. 52, 2. Cf. 1a2ae. 54, 4.

33. Bacon, *Redargutio Philosophiarum* (1608), in Farington, *Philosophy of Francis Bacon,* 93. This contention parallels in some respects the idea expressed by the Renaissance humanist Francesco Piccolomini, that while the spiritual perfection of man lay in contemplative philosophy, the perfection of society required a philosophical engagement with civil science that could bring about a corresponding perfection of society. As James Hankins has expressed the

general proposition, "the purpose of polity is to perfect human nature by maximizing the scope for virtue and rationality." See Heiki Mikkeli, *An Aristotelian Response to Renaissance Humanism: Jacopo Zabarella on the Nature of the Arts and Sciences* (Helsinki: Suomen Historiallinen Seura, 1992), chap. 2; Nicholas Jardine, "Keeping Order in the School of Padua," in *Method and Order in the Renaissance Philosophy of Nature,* edited by Eckhard Kessler, Daniel Di Liscia, and Charlotte Methuen (Aldershot, U.K.: Ashgate, 1997), 183–209; and James Hankins, ed., *Renaissance Civil Humanism* (Cambridge: Cambridge University Press, 2000), intro., 9. Bacon makes a similar claim for natural philosophy rather than polity.

34. René Descartes, *Principles of Philosophy,* in Descartes, *The Philosophical Writings of Descartes,* trans. John Cottingham, Robert Stoothoff, and Dugald Murdoch, 2 vols. (Cambridge: Cambridge University Press, 1984), 1:188, 180.

35. René Descartes, *Discourse on the Method,* in Descartes, *Philosophical Writings,* 1:143.

36. Blaise Pascal, *Minor Works,* trans. O. W. Wright, Harvard Classics, vol. 48 (New York, Collier, 1909–14); see www.bartleby.com/48/3/ (accessed September 14, 2011). The analogy was commonplace in the seventeenth century but dates back to the Roman historian L. Annaeus Florus (fl. A.D. 100) and may also be found in Augustine, *City of God* 10.14. See William Freedman, "Swift's Struldbruggs, Progress, and the Analogy of History," *Studies in English Literature: 1500–1900* 35 (Summer 1995): 457–72. The image was later used by John Draper and Auguste Comte, whose views influenced Sarton.

37. Robert Boyle, *The Usefulness of Natural Philosophy,* in *The Works of the Honourable Robert Boyle,* 6 vols., ed. Thomas Birch (London, 1772; repr., Hildesheim: Georg Olms, 1966), 3: 193.

38. Joseph Glanvill, *The Vanity of Dogmatizing* (London: E. C. for H. Eversden, 1661), 178.

39. Joseph Glanvill, *Essays on Several Important Subjects in Philosophy and Religion* (London: J. D. for J. Baker and H. Mortlock, 1676), 36.

40. Michael Heyd, "The New Experimental Philosophy: A Manifestation of 'Enthusiasm' or an Antidote to It?," *Minerva* 25 (Winter 1987): 423–40; Ian Stewart, "Books and How to Use Them," *History of Science* 40 (June 2002): 233–44; Richard Serjeanston, ed., *Generall Learning: A Seventeenth-Century Treatise on the Formation of the General Scholar by Meric Casaubon* (Ithaca, N.Y.: Cornell University Press for Medieval and Renaissance Texts and Studies, 1999), intro.

41. Meric Casaubon, *A Letter of Meric Casaubon, D.D. &c. to Peter du Moulin D.D., Concerning Natural Experimental Philosophie* (Cambridge: William Mordgen, 1669), 31, 5f. Similar remarks may be found in Henry Stubbe, *Legends No Histories: or a Specimen of Some Animadversions upon the History of the Royal Society . . . Together with the Plus Ultra Reduced to a Non-Plus* (London, 1670); and Henry Stubbe, *Campanella Revived* (London, 1670). See James R. Jacob, *Henry Stubbe, Radical Protestantism and the Early Enlightenment* (Cambridge: Cambridge University Press, 1983).

42. For Casaubon as a reactionary, see M. R. G. Spiller, *"Concerning Natural Experimental Philosophie": Meric Casaubon and the Royal Society* (Heidelberg: Springer-Verlag GmbH, 1980). Cf. Michael Hunter, *Science and the Shape of Orthodoxy: Intellectual Change in Late Seventeenth-Century Britain* (Woodbridge, U.K.: Boydell Press, 1995), chap. 11.

43. For the history of the term, see Marty Sulek, "Philosophia and Philanthropia—A Cultural History of the Inter-relations between Philosophy and Philanthropy, from the Pre-Socratics to the Post-Moderns" (Master's thesis, Indiana University, 2006).

44. Francis Bacon, "Of Goodness and Goodness of Nature," in *Essays,* in Bacon, *The Works of Francis Bacon,* ed. Spedding, Ellis, and Heath, 6:403. The Vulgate edition of the Bible translated the Greek *philanthropia* as *humanitas;* hence Bacon's reference to the fact that "humanity" was an inadequate translation.

45. Bacon, *Essays,* in Bacon, *The Works of Francis Bacon,* ed. Spedding, Ellis, and Heath, 6:403. For Bacon's treatment of charity in relation to good works, also see his *Meditationes Sacrae,* in Bacon, *The Works of Francis Bacon,* ed. Spedding, Ellis, and Heath, 7:244. On Bacon's philanthropy, see Brian Vickers, "Bacon's So-called 'Utilitarianism': Sources and Influences," in *Francis Bacon: Terminologia e Fortuna nel XVII Secolo,* ed. Marta Fattori (Rome: Edizione dell'Ateneo, 1984), 281–314; and Masao Watanabe, "Francis Bacon: Philanthropy and the Instauration of Learning," *Annals of Science* 49 (March 1992): 163–73.

46. Alasdair MacIntyre, *After Virtue* (South Bend, Ind.: University of Notre Dame Press, 1981).

47. Charles Webster, *The Great Instauration: Science, Medicine, and Reform, 1626–1660* (London: Duckworth, 1975); Robert G. Clouse, "Johann Heinrich Alsted and English Millenarianism," *Harvard Theological Review* 62, no. 2 (1969): 189–207; Howard Hotson, *Johann Heinrich Alsted 1588–1638: Between Renaissance, Reformation, and Universal Reform* (Oxford: Clarendon, 2000); Patrick Curry, *Prophecy and Power: Astrology in Early Modern England* (Cambridge: Cambridge University Press, 1989); Christopher Hill, *Antichrist in Seventeenth Century England* (London: Oxford University Press, 1971).

48. For a good overview of early modern conceptions of history and their relation to natural philosophy, see Rob Iliffe, "The Masculine Birth of Time: Temporal Frameworks of Early Modern Natural Philosophy," *British Journal for the History of Science* 33, no. 4 (2000): 427–53.

49. Stephen Gaukroger, *The Emergence of a Scientific Culture: Science and the Shaping of Modernity, 1210–1685* (Oxford: Oxford University Press, 2006), 23.

Is There Moral Progress in History?

The Old Kantian Question Raised Yet Again

ALLAN MEGILL

I propose to assess the question of moral progress in history, which was famously raised by Immanuel Kant in the late eighteenth century and which remains relevant now in the context of the question of the public and political uses of history. The question of progress in history occupied Kant's mind for an extended period, and he dealt with it in three essays. The first of these was his "Idea for a Universal History with a Cosmopolitan Purpose," which appeared in a Berlin newspaper, *Berlinische Monatschrift*, in November 1784, a month before the publication in the same newspaper of his far more famous essay, "What Is Enlightenment?" He raised the question again in January 1786 in a second essay, "Conjectures on the Beginning of Human History," also published in the *Berlinische Monatschrift*, and finally in a chapter, "A Renewed Attempt to Answer the Question: 'Is the Human Race Continually Improving?,'" written in 1795, that appeared in his book *The Contest of the Faculties* in 1798.[1] In sum Kant seriously attended to the question of human progress. It should be added that his thoughts on progress were closely related to his thinking about issues of ethics. This fact is hardly surprising, given that he was working on ethical issues at the same time that he turned to the question of progress. Kant's *Groundwork of the Metaphysics of Morals* was published in 1785 and *Critique of Practical Reason* in 1788.

Kant on History

Kant's reflections on history had much to do with his negative reaction to an ambitious work by his former student J. G. Herder, *Ideas on the Philosophy of the History of Mankind*, the first part of which was published in early 1784. Herder attempted to argue that a tendency toward progress is built by God into the substance of nature, and that this progressive tendency extends into human history as well. The poetically speculative character of Herder's *Ideas* offended Kant's sense of epistemological propriety, and in 1785 he published two critical reviews of Herder's work in which he said so. Yet Kant, who had spent many laborious years charting the limits of human knowledge, did not want to reject the progressive hopes that he saw so poorly and awkwardly presented in Herder's work. Kant's aim in his "Idea for a Universal

History with a Cosmopolitan Purpose" was to show how one might conceive of history in a progressive way while not exceeding the limits of human reason and understanding.

Kant put forward his idea of progress suppositionally, contending that "the history of the human race as a whole can be regarded as the realization of a hidden plan of nature to bring about . . . [a] perfect political constitution as the only possible state within which all natural capacities of mankind can be developed completely." The ultimate end would be "a perfect civil union of mankind," in the form of a federation of free states (50). Kant acknowledged that his proposed history—in which the "unsocial sociability" of human beings generates a competitiveness that pushes them to develop their talents and to embark on "a continuing process of enlightenment" (44)—was a philosophical idea, and he denied that he intended "to supersede the task of history proper, that of empirical composition" (53). But Kant suggested that even though it lacks empirical justification, such a view of history as he proposed—one that assumes "a plan of nature" lying behind human history—has the advantage of "open[ing] up the comforting prospect of a future in which we are shown from afar how the human race eventually works its way upward to a situation in which all the germs implanted by nature can be developed fully, and in which man's destiny can be fulfilled here on earth" (52–53).

Kant was a subject of the deeply authoritarian state of Friedrich der Große. Herder's reflections on progress were the occasion for Kant's first publications on this topic, but the deep reason for the attention Kant devoted to it was clearly his discontent with the Friedrichian state and his desire to imagine some sort of escape from it. In all three of his essays on history he put forward a progressive view of history. To be sure, in his "Idea for a Universal History" (1784) and "Conjectures on the Beginning of Human History" (1786), he presented his progressive view as no more than a useful conjecture. He assumed that if people imagine a progressiveness in history, they will be stimulated to work for human improvement and that this will help make progress real.

In the final essay, "A Renewed Attempt to Answer the Question" (1795), Kant went half a step further. Here he suggested that there are three ways of interpreting history in relation to the question of progress: we can see history as regressing, as being marked by an alternation between progress and regress, or as progressing; he called these, respectively, the terroristic, abderitic, and eudaemonistic views of history. Kant contended that we have no empirical grounds for favoring any one of these views over the others. As he put it, "the problem of progress cannot be solved directly from experience." Yet he also contended that "there must be some experience or other" that "might suggest that man has the quality or power of being the cause and . . . the author of his own improvement" (180, 181). In looking at his own time, Kant found such an empirical indicator in "the attitude of the onlookers" of the greatest event of his time, the French Revolution. Observers who had nothing to gain from the revolution greeted it with enthusiasm—even in Prussia, where such enthusiasms were dangerous. The sympathy of these onlookers for the French Revolution, Kant held, could have been caused only by a "moral disposition within the human race," the presence of which gives ground for believing that human history is progressive (182).

In the light of our own situation today, how ought we to assess Kant's conception of historical progress? First, it must be said that Kant's hope for the future is surely exemplary, as is his commitment to human freedom—a freedom that he equated with obedience, that is, with obedience to an ethical law that we ourselves have chosen. The German historian and historical theorist Reinhart Koselleck has seen in Kant's thinking the manifestation of something new that arose in the eighteenth century, namely, a divergence of the "horizon of expectation" from the "space of experience." Koselleck's claim, stated in less technical terms, was that the late eighteenth century saw the emergence of a new conviction that the future might well be generically different from the past, rather than the same old thing as before.[2] In Kant's eyes, as in the eyes of many others, the radical events that began in France on July 14, 1789, authorized this new view.

There seems little doubt that events in France prompted Kant to suggest in his 1795 essay that "a prophetic historical narrative of things to come" can have a priori justification if "the prophet himself occasions and produces the events he predicts" (177). So far as I know, no one before Kant linked the writing of a historical narrative with the production of new historical events that would be in conformity with that narrative. This is a really interesting line for Kant to have taken. But is it a line that we ought to want to follow? To be sure, Kant was right in asserting that a prediction regarding the future will come true if a human agent is able to make it true. He was also right in a more general and important sense—that is, in his insistence on holding open a gap between experience as we know it now and what we might be able to expect in the future. Maintaining a gap between experience and expectation is a precondition for any willed change that diverges from past and present norms. Within some present-day contexts, one sometimes encounters the assumption that because things usually operate in such-and-such a way now, they will of course operate in the same way in the future. But what usually happens (or usually did happen) is not necessarily the template for the future. Here Kant's position is both right and salutary.

I have a serious problem, however, with Kant's "prophetic" historian, who "produces the events he predicts." I am put in mind of the first volume of Isaac Deutscher's gripping (but also credulous) biography of Leon Trotsky, *The Prophet Armed;* of course Trotsky soon became *The Prophet Unarmed* and then *The Prophet Outcast.*[3] Like Thucydides, the man who became head of the Red Army turned in his retirement to the writing of history—in this case to the writing of his gripping (and tendentious) *History of the Russian Revolution.* It would have been more suitable to my purposes had Trotsky's rival Stalin written a history more substantial (and less ghost-written) than the *History of the Communist Party of the Soviet Union.* But the general point remains the same: we have already seen an attempt to turn a prophetic history into real history, one that operated by forcing the present to conform to that history's prescriptions. We call this prophetic history "dialectical materialism." We are perhaps justified in thinking that, on balance, the attempt to actualize dialectical materialism was a disaster for Russia and for the world. Is there something perhaps wrong then with the aged Kant's notion that a eudemonistic reading of history is likely to have a helpful role to play for the present? I am inclined to think that there is.

In fact there are three things wrong with the question to which Kant's eudemonistic view of history is an answer. First, the question presupposes the validity of the assumption that there is such a thing as a single process of history. Second, the question founders on the complexities and contradictions that surround the term "moral." Third, the assumption that belief in "moral progress in history" is likely to contribute to moral action in the present is unsupported. In this essay I leave aside the first and third issues. The first issue has been extensively discussed in the literature already.[4] The third issue would take me too far afield. So I focus on the second issue, which is highly relevant to the question of the role and uses of historical writing today.

Should Historians Talk about Morality in History?

If we are to speak of morality in relation to the work produced by historians, we need to think about what we mean by the term "moral." It is possible to identify four different things to which moral, morality, ethics, and related terms can refer. First, at the most descriptive level "moral" can designate the customary modes of behavior that prevail within a group, abstracted from any judgment as to ethical value: for example, in some societies people stand very close to each other when engaged in conversation, and in other societies they stand at some distance; this is simply the way things are. Various terms have been invented to designate this sense of the moral: for example, Heidegger's term *das Man* ("the one"; "the they") and Bourdieu's *habitus.* There are also traditional terms, most notably the French term *les moeurs.* For the purposes of the present essay I prefer the term "mores" because it designates something neutral and yet has a close linguistic relation to the word "moral."[5] Second, "the moral" can refer to the views within a society concerning which ways of acting are worthy of ethical praise or blame. Third, it can refer to actions carried out by human beings to which ethical praise or blame can be attached. These second and third meanings of "the moral" have a normative dimension and thus are to be distinguished from the nonnormative attitude that we usually adopt toward mores. We can refer to the second meaning of "the moral" under the designation moral codes and the third meaning under the designation morality, understanding here that we mean actual morality, or morality in action. A fourth meaning of "the moral" refers to the grounding or justification of particular moral codes and moral action. The classic instance of "the moral" in this sense is Kant's categorical imperative. We can call this sense of "the moral" ethics.[6] We thus end up with four senses of the moral: mores, moral codes, morality, and ethics.

The question, is there moral progress in history?, collapses under the weight of these different senses of the moral. It also collapses because of the impossibility of identifying a single process that is the process of history, but that is another story. The collapse of the "moral progress" question forces us to turn to another, more productive question: Is it legitimate for historians to think of historical events as having an ethically normative dimension at all? Many historians, from Leopold von Ranke onward, have held that it is not.[7] The question is really one as to whether morality—I mean actual morality, "morality in action"—can be regarded as existing in history or whether it is a mere chimera or else, simply, something that historians ought not to talk about. Clearly there is no doubt about the existence of mores, and there is also no doubt that moral codes exist. The problem has to do with actual morality, for the historian can hardly regard any action in history as an instance of actual morality unless it can be shown that the action in question was substantially motivated by ethical considerations, as distinguished from self-interest. For example, if the behavior of those British evangelical Christians who in the late eighteenth and early nineteenth centuries agitated for the abolition of the slave trade and subsequently for the abolition of slavery itself arose out of a calculated self-interest, or as a natural efflux of the mores of Quakerdom, or from a new, capitalist orientation toward time, or from some other aspect of their normal way of living (mores), historians might conclude that their behavior had long-run socially beneficial consequences. But it would be difficult to regard that behavior as morality in action.

The issue of motivation is crucial. But here we run up against an irreducible limit of historiography, namely, its inability to plumb what in embarrassingly nonhistoriographical language we might call "the deepest reaches of the human soul." Historians can argue as much as they want about what really motivated the abolitionists—whether it was moral commitment, disguised self-interest, a desire to assert British imperial power, the impact of an emergent new capitalist orientation to time, or so on—but at the end of the day an irreducible element of uncertainty remains, in spite of the historical evidence that can be deployed. At this point one is grateful for the talents of the novelist, who, unlike the historian, has license to enter into the otherwise inaccessible interior consciousness of her characters and to represent that consciousness in language that readers will find gripping or uninteresting, plausible or implausible without having to attend to any "facts of the matter" that do not suit her purposes.

The historian cannot do this—cannot plumb this level of motivation—without violating the rules of the discipline. At most, like Natalie Zemon Davis in her account of the illiterate peasant woman Bertrande de Rols in *The Return of Martin Guerre,* the historian can only canvass the different possibilities, while stopping short of claiming to know what was going on in the minds of the historical protagonists in question.

To be sure, less difficult issues of motivation are open to the historian, who can plausibly claim to know, for example, that Caesar crossed the Rubicon because he desired to challenge the authority of the Roman senate, even though there may be no explicit documentary evidence that would establish this claim. But the question, was ethical motivation determinative in such and such case?, is exceedingly difficult to answer in a historiographically justified way, given how hidden ethical motivation is and how susceptible past accounts of motivation are to lying, self-deception, and the play of unconscious influences.

Accordingly it might well be held that historians ought not to talk about (actual) morality at all. I have already noted Ranke's hostility to moral judgment in history. We can attribute his adoption of this stance to two factors: his willingness to leave moral judgment to the Lutheran God to whom he deferred; and his (justified) sense that the previous "moralizing" tradition—the tradition of *historia magistra vitae*—had allowed its concern with offering moral lessons to impair the project of coming to understand what had actually happened in the past.[8] But we do not need to hearken back to Ranke to see in historiography an aversion to questions of moral judgment. To offer moral judgments one needs in the first place to assume that morality (as distinguished from mores) is possible. No one denies that mores exist: indeed mores are the prime object of the so-called new cultural history, which is arguably the dominant orientation in history writing today.[9] Historians—and sociologists and anthropologists—are confronted by the question, does morality exist? Some hold that it does not, or that if it does, it is not relevant to historiography. Foucault's notion of power is the articulation of precisely such a position. As is often the case with Foucault, he clarifies an issue by taking an extreme position with regard to it. In effect Foucault authorizes a darkly ironic, cynicizing view of history and of the human field in general, a view in which everything is seen as an exercise of power, including the most highly elevated ethical and humanitarian claims.[10]

Against Ethical Reductionism

Foucault offers what I take to be an a priori ethical reductionism, by which morality is reduced to mores. However, there is at least one metahistorical argument that militates against such a reduction. It is a condition of possibility of the discipline as it has developed over the last two hundred years that historians not assume that humans are totally determined beings incapable of free motivation. If soi-disant historians held such a view, they would not be historians at all but would instead be oriented toward the discovery of theories that would explain and predict human behavior—a project that presupposes that human beings are essentially unfree. Yet at the same time historians do not regard human beings as completely free, since their discipline requires that they engage in the painstaking investigation of the conditions under which human action takes place. If human beings were completely free, the historian's long grubbing in the archives would be an entirely unnecessary torture. In other words, free-floating intelligence would not need to be historically investigated, while the historical investigation of deterministically governed beings would be pointless, given that human behavior would be explicable in nomothetic terms, as deriving from the workings of scientific laws. It is my contention that the discipline of history is marked by an unresolving dialectic between determinism and freedom in which neither has primacy and both are clearly present.[11]

Since historians assume the possibility of human freedom, they must also assume the possibility of ethical motivation, and hence of morality, in human life. To be sure, this does not mean that we are going to find the categorical imperative working its way in the world. Clearly Kant thought of ethics in starkly ideal terms, and in reaction against what one might call "Kant's ethical rigorism" one might be inclined, rather, to see human beings as exercising their thinking capacity for purely pragmatic ends—for example, for the intended betterment of their material lives. Under such a view human beings would not be ethical beings at all and actual morality would not exist.

However, we do not need a pure Kantian ethics in order to think of human society as having at least a tincture of the ethical. In what, absent any access on the historian's part to Kant's realm of ethical noumena, might this tincture of the ethical consist? I want to suggest that something like actual morality is often found when there is a commitment to principle, even when the principle is not as purely ethical as the categorical imperative. The crucial point here is that a principle, even when it is not strictly ethical, has the advantage of taking people away from the demands of the particular and limited time and space within which they stand. In so doing it offers a quasi freedom from the demands of self-interest and from the determinism of the immediate situation. It also offers the possibility of a kind of quasi morality.

Consider the case of the slave James Somersett (sometimes Somerset), who in 1769 was brought by his master from Virginia to England and who in October 1771 ran away. His owner had him recaptured and put on a ship that was set to sail for Jamaica, where the captain was to sell him on his owner's behalf. However, Somersett had defenders in England, who obtained a writ of habeas corpus requiring that his owner bring him before the Court of King's Bench. The upshot was that, in his famous decision of 1772, Lord Chief Justice William Murray, Lord Mansfield, declared, "Whatever inconveniences . . . may follow from a decision, I cannot say this case is allowed or approved by the law of England; and therefore the black must be discharged." So Somersett went free.[12]

How, from an ethical point of view, ought the historian to describe Lord Mansfield's decision? Clearly Mansfield's decision was an instance of what we can think of as principled action. But under what specific category ought we to classify it? To the degree that Lord Mansfield's decision was simply the product of the legal thinking prevailing at that time, we might think of the decision as doing nothing more than clarifying British mores concerning slavery that were already embedded in the legal system. But such a view is not quite adequate to Lord Mansfield's decision. The case did have to go to court: Somersett's self-proclaimed owner and his supporters did contend that he owned Somersett. Lord Mansfield might be seen as "only" articulating the applicable mores in this case, but note the form of the articulation: here is how British custom ought to be interpreted. So mores morph into morality.

What allows this shift? It is the implied existence of an ethical realm. Kant, the great theorist of the ethical, made it absolutely clear that the ethical is separate from "the convenient." In fact the Kantian ethical operates only when ethical agents put "convenience" aside in what they do and govern their actions according to the universal moral law. Lord Mansfield did not have the ethical purity and elevation that Kant demanded in his *Groundwork of the Metaphysics of Morals,* but his decision, in diverging from the immediately given situation, falls within a domain that is akin to that of morality. Would that the same sort of principled action were more clearly visible in such places as U.S. military prisons and in the U.S. Department of Justice at the time that I wrote this in 2007. But the key point here, I contend, is that historians ought to recognize and acknowledge such quasi-moral action when they discern it in the past. In so doing they conform to a time-tested disciplinary principle while at the same time holding a mirror to the present.

NOTES

1. I cite Kant's essays in the convenient English translation by H. B. Nisbet: Immanuel Kant, *Political Writings,* 2nd, enl. ed., ed. Hans Reiss, trans. H. B. Nisbet (Cambridge: Cambridge University Press, 1991). Page references will appear parenthetically in the text of this essay.

2. Reinhart Koselleck, "'Space of Experience' and 'Horizon of Expectation': Two Historical Categories," in Koselleck, *Futures Past: On the Semantics of Historical Time,* trans. Keith Tribe (Cambridge, Mass.: MIT Press, 1985), 267–88.

3. Isaac Deutscher, *The Prophet Armed: Trotsky, 1879–1921; The Prophet Unarmed: Trotsky, 1921–29*; and *The Prophet Outcast: Trotsky, 1929–1940* (Oxford: Oxford University Press, 1954, 1959, 1963).

4. See especially Jean-François Lyotard, *The Postmodern Condition: A Report on Knowledge,* trans. Geoff Bennington and Brian Massumi (Minneapolis: University of Minnesota Press, 1984). The issue is discussed in Allan Megill, *Historical Knowledge, Historical Error: A Contemporary Guide to Practice* (Chicago: University of Chicago Press, 2007), chap. 9, "'Grand Narrative' and the Discipline of History," 165–87.

5. The linguistic relation between *moeurs* and *moral* is entirely appropriate. I have been referring to the first sense of "the moral" as ethically neutral, but the *mores* of a society surely have *normatively* moral (ethical) implications. This indeed is a central claim made by the tradition of "virtue ethics." The *mores* of a people, time, and place are thus susceptible to normatively oriented analyses, in which the question posed is: to what extent do *mores* of this type sustain an ethical order? Obviously this is more a philosopher's than a historian's question. On virtue ethics, see Alasdair MacIntyre, *After Virtue* (Notre Dame, Ind.: University of Notre Dame Press, 1981).

6. The morality/ethics distinction that I articulate here is different from, for example, Hegel's distinction between morality (*Sittlichkeit*) and ethics in his *Elements of the Philosophy of Right* (1821). Different authors have used these terms in different ways.

7. Leopold Ranke, preface to the first edition of *Histories of the Latin and Germanic Nations* (1824), in Ranke, *The Theory and Practice of History,* ed. Georg. G. Iggers and Konrad von Moltke, trans. Wilma A. Iggers and Konrad von Moltke (Indianapolis, Ind.: Bobbs-Merrill, 1973), 135–38, at 137.

8. See Reinhart Koselleck, "Historia Magistra Vitae: The Dissolution of the Topos into the Perspective of a Modernized Historical Process," in Koselleck, *Futures Past,* 21–38.

9. See Megill, *Historical Knowledge, Historical Error,* chap. 10, "Coherence and Incoherence in Historical Studies: From the *Annales* School to the New Cultural History," 188–208.

10. See especially Michel Foucault, *Discipline and Punish: The Birth of the Prison,* trans. Alan Sheridan (New York: Vintage, 1977).

11. Consider, for example, Fernand Braudel, *The Mediterranean and the Mediterranean World in the Age of Philip II,* trans. Siân Reynolds, 2 vols. (New York: Harper & Row, 1972 [original French ed., 1949]). In large measure the book is "about" the geographical determinisms driving human life in the sixteenth-century Mediterranean world. Yet, as Paul Ricoeur has pointed out, Braudel's work makes sense *as history* only because that geography was the locus within which human beings, from Philip II on downward, pursued their projects. See Ricoeur, *Time and Narrative,* vol. 1, trans. Kathleen McLaughlin and David Pellauer (Chicago: University of Chicago Press, 1984), 206–17.

12. There is extensive literature on the Somersett case. The best account is George Van Cleve, "*Somerset's Case* and Its Antecedents in Imperial Perspective," *Law and History Review* 24, no. 3 (Fall 2006): 601–45, which is followed by commentaries by Ruth Paley and Daniel J. Hulsebosch, with a reply by Van Cleve. It should be noted that Mansfield's decision was delivered orally and there is no official written record of it. The wording I quote here is authorized by the report by Lofft: *R. v. Knowles, ex parte Somersett* (1772), Lofft 1, 98 E. R. 499, 20. S. T. 1.

III

Is Moral Progress Possible?

A Long-Term Economic Perspective on Recent Human Progress

GARY M. WALTON

T he year 1750 does not usually evoke images of great prosperity or of revolution-ary progress, but in fact the mid–eighteenth century was a historical turning point of economic advance.[1] Organizational and technological changes in that period allowed growing numbers of people to move from mere subsistence activities to thoughts and actions that furthered economic, political, and social progress. This monumental turning point in human existence is often missed because of the way we perceive the past.

History of the Masses

It is an interesting exercise to reflect on a historical episode, perhaps from the Bible or from Shakespeare or from some Hollywood epic. For most of us, the stories we recall are about great people or great episodes: tales of love, war, religion, and other dramas of the human experience. Kings, heroes, or religious leaders—in castles, on battlefields, or in cathedrals—engaging armies in battles or discovering inventions or new worlds readily come to mind. Glorifying the past is a natural instinct.[2]

There were so-called golden ages, such as ancient Greece, the Roman era, China's Sung Dynasty, and other periods and places where small fractions of societies lived in splendor and reasonable comfort, and when small portions of the population some-times rose above levels of meager subsistence.[3] But such periods of improvement were never durably sustained.[4] Taking a long, broad view, the lives of almost all of our dis-tant ancestors were utterly wretched. Except for the fortunate few, humans every-where lived in abysmal squalor. To capture the magnitude of this deprivation and sheer length of the road out of poverty, consider this time-capsule summary of humanity from Douglass C. North's 1993 Nobel address:

> Let us represent the human experience to date as a 24-hour clock in which the beginning consists of the time (apparently in Africa between 4 and 5 mil-lion years ago) when humans became separate from other primates. Then the beginning of so-called civilization occurs with the development of agriculture

and permanent settlement in about 8000 B.C.E. in the Fertile Crescent—in the last three or four minutes of the clock. For the other 23 hours and 56 or 57 minutes, humans remained hunters and gatherers, and while population grew, it did so at a very slow pace.

Now if we make a new 24-hour clock for the time of civilization—the 10,000 years from development of agriculture to the present—the pace of change appears to be very slow for the first 12 hours. . . . Historical demographers speculate that the rate of population growth may have doubled as compared to the previous era but still was very slow. The pace of change accelerates in the past 5,000 years with the rise and then decline of economies and civilization. Population may have grown from about 300 million at the time of Christ to about 800 million by 1750—a substantial acceleration as compared to earlier rates of growth. The last 250 years—just 35 minutes on our new 24-hour clock—are the era of modern economic growth, accompanied by a population explosion that now puts world population in excess of 5 billion (1993).

If we focus on the last 250 years, we see that growth was largely restricted to Western Europe and the overseas extensions of Britain for 200 of those 250 years.[5]

Any brief explanation of the major forces and events lifting larger and larger portions of the world's population to levels of good health and decent material comfort suggests a degree of presumption that even a Cheshire cat's grin could not hide. While acknowledging many problematic issues of measurement and interpretation, we proceed without apology directly and selectively to the historical evidence. Long-term measures of population size, length of life, infant mortality, body heights and weights, income per person, and many other such indicators of well-being, whatever the quibbles over exactness, are perfectly clear. So are the geographic and national identities of the places inventions and improvements came from and where declines of poverty started and spread.

The Decline of Poverty: Where and When

Figure 1 (below) shows world population over the past ten thousand years, along with noteworthy inventions, discoveries, and events. The graph conveys a literal explosion of the world's population in the mid–eighteenth century. Shortly before the United States won its independence from Britain, the geographical line bolts upward like a rocket, recently powering past six billion humans alive on earth. Advances in food production from new technologies, commonly labeled the second agricultural revolution, and from the utilization of new resources (for example, settlements in the New World) coincide with this population explosion. Also noteworthy is the intense acceleration in the pace of vital discoveries. Before 1600 centuries elapsed between vital discoveries. Improvements and the spread of the use of the plow, for example,

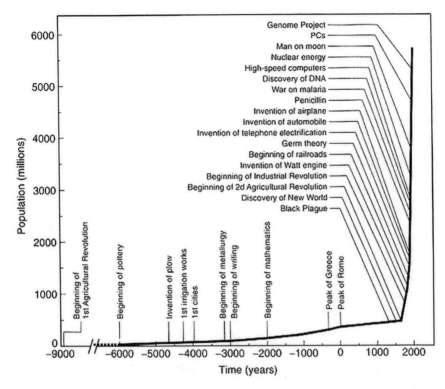

FIG. 1. The growth of the world population and some major events in the history of technology. From Robert W. Fogel, "Catching Up with the Economy," *American Economic Review* 89 (March 1999): 2. Courtesy of the American Economic Association and Robert W. Fogel

first introduced in the Mesopotamian Valley around 4000 B.C.E., changed very little over the next five thousand years. Contrast this with air travel. The first successful motor-driven flight occurred in 1903 by the Wright Brothers. In 1969, a mere sixty-six years later, Neil Armstrong became the first man to step foot on the moon.[6]

Before 1750 chronic hunger and malnutrition, disease, illness, and early death were the norm, and it was not just the masses who ate poorly; as Nobel laureate Robert Fogel (1999) reports: "Even the English peerage, with all its wealth, had a diet during the sixteenth and seventeenth centuries that was deleterious to health. Although abundant in calories and proteins, aristocratic diets were deficient in some nutrients and included large quantities of toxic substances, especially alcoholic beverages and salt."[7]

For most people, poor diet was not a matter of bad choices but rather the absence of choices, the fact of scarcity. Exceedingly poor diets and chronic malnutrition were the norm because food production seldom rose above basic life-sustaining levels.

Meager yields severely limited energy for all kinds of pursuits, including production. Most people were caught in a food-energy trap, and low food supplies and inadequate diets were accompanied by high rates of disease and low rates of resistance.[8] Remedies from known medical practices were almost nil.

The maladies of malnourishment and widespread disease are revealed in evidence on height and weight. The average height of men at maturity from economically advanced nations gained four to five inches from the mid–eighteenth century to the mid–twentieth century. Today the average American adult man stands five inches taller than mid-eighteenth-century Englishmen. The average Dutchman, the world's tallest, stands seven inches taller. A typical Englishman in 1750 weighed around 130 pounds and an average Frenchman about 110, compared to about 175 for U.S. males today.[9] It is startling to see the suits of armor in the Tower of London that were worn for ancient wars; they vividly remind us of how small people of long ago really were.

The second agricultural revolution, beginning in the mid–eighteenth century, and the industrial revolution, which soon followed, first in England and then in France, the United States, and other Western countries, initiated and sustained the population explosion, lifting birth rates and lowering death rates. Table 1 summarizes research findings on life expectancy at birth for various nations, places, and times. This and other empirical evidence[10] reveal that for the world as a whole, it took thousands of years for life expectancy at birth to rise from the low twenties to around thirty years in the mid–eighteenth century. Leading the breakaway from a past of early death and malnutrition, poor diet, chronic disease—for example, chronic diarrhea[11]—and low energy were the nations of Western Europe. From Table 1 we see that by 1800 life expectancy in France was just under thirty years and in Great Britain about thirty-six, levels that China and India had not reached one hundred years later. By 1950 life expectancy in England and France was in the high sixties, while in India and China it was only about forty.

Table 1. Years of life expectancy at birth

Place	Middle Ages	Select Years	1950–55	1975–80	2002
France		~30 (1800)	66	74	79
United Kingdom	20–30	~36 (1799–1803)	79	73	78
India		25 (1901–11)	69	53	64
China		25–35 (1929–31)	39	65	71
Africa			41	48	50
World	20–30		46	60	67

James Lee and Wang Feng, "Malthusian Models and Chinese Realities: The Chinese Demographic System, 1700–2000," *Population and Development Review* 25, no. 1 (1999): 33–65; S. H. Preston, "Human Mortality throughout History and Prehistory," in *The State of Humanity*, edited by Julian L. Simon (Malden, Mass.: Blackwell, 1995), 30–36; E. Anthony Wrigley and Roger S. Schofield, *The Population History of England, 1541–1871: A Reconstruction* (Cambridge, Mass.: Harvard University Press, 1981); World Resources Institute, *World Resources Database Diskette, 1998* (Washington, D.C.: WRI, 1998); and United Nations Development Program, *Human Development Report 2002* (New York: Oxford University Press, 2002).

When life expectancy data are adjusted for quality by subtracting years of ill health (weighted by severity), "healthy-active life expectancy" indexes reveal years totaling seventy, sixty-two, and fifty-three in the United States, China, and India respectively in 1997–99.[12] These "quality life spans" are substantially more than these countries' total life expectancies fifty to one hundred years ago.

In the period before 1750, surviving childhood was problematic. Infant mortality was high everywhere; depending on time and location, between 20 and 25 percent or more of babies died before their first birthdays. By the early 1800s infant mortality in France, and probably England, had dipped below the 20 percent level, rates not reached in China and India and other low-income developing nations until the 1950s. For Europe, North America, Australia, and New Zealand, this rate is now under 1 percent, but it remains at 4 percent in China, 6 percent in India, and 9 percent in Africa.[13] Accompanying the declines in infant mortality were striking declines in maternal mortality. For example, U.S. data show infant rates falling from 100 to 7 per 1,000 live births (1915 to 1996), with maternal rates plummeting from 220 to 7.6 per 100,000 live births.[14] The high losses of infants and mothers in birth reflect more than just lives lost. They also reflect more pregnancy time over a woman's life and more time futilely spent in caring for children who died before their first birthdays, both time uses implying production losses.

Tables 2 and 3 provide another long-term perspective on the escape from poverty and early death, in the form of evidence on real income per person, albeit inexact, for periods long ago. The gradual rise of real income over the past one thousand years was led by Europe. By 1700 Europe had broken into a clear lead, rising above the level of per capita income it shared earlier at lower levels with China, which was the most advanced empire/region circa 1000.

Table 2. Real gross domestic product per capita in 1990 dollars

	1000	1500	1700	1820	1900	1952	2003
Western Europe	$427	$772	$997	$1,202	$2,892	$4,963	$19,912
USA			$527	$1,257	$4,091	$10,316	$29,037
India			$550	$533	$599	$629	$2,160
China	$450	$600	$600	$600	$545	$537	4,609
Africa	$425	$414	$421	$420	$601	$928	1,549
World	$450	$566	$615	$667	$1,262	$2,260	$6,477

Angus Maddison, *Development Centre Studies, the World Economy: Historical Statistics* (Paris: Organisation for Economic Cooperation & Development, 2003); and Angus Maddison, "World Population, GDP and Per Capita GDP, 1–2003 A.D.," 2007, http://www.ggdc.net/maddison/ (accessed September 6, 2011).

While the rest of the world slept, and changed little economically, Europe and England's colonies in America advanced. By the early 1800s the United States had pushed ahead of Europe, and by the mid-1900s citizens of the United States enjoyed incomes well above those of Europeans and many multiples above people living elsewhere. The real impact of regional differences in economic growth is apparent when we realize that the poor nations of today—such as Zaire, Ethiopia, Tanzania, Bangladesh—have per capita income levels comparable to those in Europe five hundred to one thousand years ago. Even by 2011 they have not attained levels of well-being experienced by western peoples at the time of the American Revolution (see Table 3).

Table 3. GDP per capita then and now (1990 $)

	1820	1870	1900	1950	1973	2003
Western European Countries						
Austria	1,218	1,863	2,882	3,706	11,235	21,232
Belgium	1,319	2,692	3,731	5,462	12,170	21,205
Denmark	1,274	2,003	3,017	6,943	13,945	23,133
Finland	781	1,140	1,668	4,253	11,085	20,511
France	1,135	1,876	2,876	5,271	13,114	21,861
Germany	1,077	1,839	2,985	3,881	11,966	19,144
Italy	1,117	1,499	1,785	3,502	10,634	19,150
Netherlands	1,838	2,757	3,424	5,996	13,081	21,479
Norway	801	1,360	1,877	5,430	11,324	26,033
Sweden	1,198	1,662	2,561	6,739	13,494	21,555
Switzerland	1,090	2,102	3,833	9,064	18,204	22,242
United Kingdom	1,706	3,190	4,492	6,939	12,025	21,310
Western Offshoots						
Australia	518	3,273	4,013	7,412	12,878	23,287
New Zealand	400	3,100	4,298	8,456	12,424	17,564
Canada	904	1,695	2,911	7,291	13,838	23,236
United States	1,257	2,445	4,091	9,561	16,689	29,037
Selected Asian Countries						
China	600	530	545	439	838	4,609
India	533	533	599	619	853	2,160
Bangladesh				540	497	939

	1820	1870	1900	1950	1973	2003
Burma	504	504		396	628	1,896
Pakistan				643	954	1,881
Selected African Countries						
Côte d'Ivoire				1,041	1,899	1,230
Egypt	475	649		910	1,294	3,034
Eritrea & Ethiopia				390	630	595
Ghana		439		1,122	1,397	1,360
Kenya				651	970	998
Nigeria				753	1,388	1,349
Tanzania				424	593	610
Zaire				570	819	212

U.S. Bureau of Census, *Statistical Abstract of the United States 1999* (Washington, D.C.: U.S. Census Bureau, 2000), 97.

An Institutional Road Map to Plenty

From these per capita income estimates and other evidence, and from North's fascinating time-capsule summary of human existence, it is clear that the road out of poverty is new. It has been traveled by few societies: Western Europe; the United States, Canada, Australia, and New Zealand (Britain's offshoots); Japan, Hong Kong, and Singapore; and few others. What steps did Western Europe and its "offshoots" take to lead humanity along the road to plenty? Why is China, the world's most populous country (almost 1.3 billion), now far ahead of India (second with 1 billion) when merely fifty years ago both nations were about equal in per capita income and more impoverished than most poor African nations today? Is there a road map leading to a life of plenty, a set of policies and institutional arrangements that developing nations can adopt to replicate the success of advanced modern economies? An honest answer to this question is disappointing. Economic development organizations such as the International Monetary Fund, the World Bank, and countless scholars who have committed their professional lives to the study of economic growth and development are fully aware of the limited theoretical structure yet pieced together. The heartening news is that while we cannot map out a clear highway to wealth, there are clear road signs to point us in the right direction and away from cliffs.

Well known is the fact that a nation's total output is fundamentally determined (and constrained) by its total inputs, measured in terms of natural resources, labor force, stock of capital, and entrepreneurial talents; and by the productivity of those inputs, measured as the output or service produced per input(s). However, to measure standards of living we rely on output (or income) per capita, rather than total output, and for changes in income per capita, productivity advance dominates the story. For example, if a nation's population increases by 10 percent and the labor force and other inputs also increase by 10 percent, output per capita remains essentially unchanged unless productivity increases. Two hundred and fifty years ago, and for many centuries preceding that, most people (80–90 percent of the labor force) everywhere were engaged in agriculture, with much of it being subsistence, self-sufficient, noncommercial farming. Today that proportion is under 5 percent in most advanced economies (3 percent in the United States). During this two-and-one-half-century transition, people grew bigger, ate more, and worked fewer hours and days in greater safety and comfort.[15] The sources of productivity advance that have raised output per farmer (and per acre) and allowed sons and daughters of farming people to move into other (commercial) employments and careers and into cities include advances or improvements in technology (knowledge), specialization and division of labor, economies of scale, organization and resource allocation, and human capital (education and health). These determinants are especially useful when analyzing the rates and sources of economic growth for single nations, but less satisfactory in explaining why productivity advances and resource reallocations have been so apparent and successful in some parts of the world but not in others.

To explain why some nations grow faster than others, we need to look closely at the way nations apply and adapt these sources of productivity change. To use this perspective, we need to assess the complex relationships of the laws, rules, and customs of a society and its economic performance.[16] For example, the dissolution of the Soviet Union and the difficulties of building market-based economies there have made us acutely aware of the importance of the rules of economic and social interaction. Likewise in Afghanistan and Iraq we are continually reminded of both the difficulty and the necessity of gaining popular acceptance of changes designed to promote peaceful exchange and economic growth.

Consider just one of the sources of productivity change, technological change, and how it is intimately tied to the institutions, laws, rules, and customs of a society. A new technology can introduce a whole new product and service, such as the airplane and faster travel, or it can upgrade and improve an existing one; we have come a long way from the Model A Fords of the 1930s to today's luxury BMWs and state-of-the-art hybrid fuel technologies. A new technology can also affect the cost of production; the introduction of relatively light but strong aluminum changed the cost of producing a whole range of goods and services, from soft-drink cans to airplanes.

In short, technological changes can be thought of as advances of knowledge that raise or improve output or lower costs. They often encompass both invention and/or modifications of new discoveries, called innovation. Both require basic scientific research and then further trial and error and study to adapt and modify the initial discoveries and put them to practical use. The inventor or company pursuing research bears substantial risk and cost—including the possibility of failure and no commercial gain. How are scientists, inventors, entrepreneurs, and others encouraged to pursue high-cost, high-risk research ventures? How are these ventures coordinated and moved along the discovery/adaptation/improvement path into commercially useful applications for our personal welfare?

This is where laws and rules, or institutions as they are called, help us better understand the causes of technological change. They establish, positively or negatively, the incentives to invent and innovate. Patent laws, first introduced in 1789 in the U.S. Constitution, provided property rights and exclusive ownership to inventors for their patented inventions. This pathbreaking law ultimately spurred creative and inventive activity, albeit not immediately. As legal interpretations extended exclusive ownership rights to ideas including the right to sell, a market for new, patented ideas emerged, with inventors often selling their patents to people who specialized in finding commercial uses of new inventions. The keys here are the laws and rules, the institutions, that lay out the incentive structures that generate dynamic forces for progress in some societies and stifle creativity and enterprise in others. In advanced economies laws provide positive incentives to spur enterprise and help forge markets using commercial, legal, and property rights systems that allow new scientific breakthroughs (technologies) to realize their full commercial-social potential. Properly constructed institutions generate productivity advances through specialization and division of labor, allowing universities, other scientific research institutions, corporations, and other business entities (and lawyers and courts too) to cooperate through interrelated markets (production and exchange) hastening the growth and spread of technological advances.[17] Setting the institutions right and sustaining institutional changes that realize gains for society as a whole are fundamental to the story of growth. The ideologies and rules of the game that form and enforce contracts (in exchange), protect and set limits on the use of property, and influence people's incentives in work, creativity, and exchange are the key institutional components paving the road out of poverty.

Examining the successful economies of Europe, North America, and Asia suggests a partial list of the institutional determinants that allow modern economies to flourish:

- the rule of law, coupled with limited government and open political participation;
- rights to private property that are clearly defined and consistently enforced;
- open, competitive markets with freedom of entry and exit, widespread access to capital and information, low transaction costs, mobile resource inputs, and reliable contract enforcement; and an atmosphere of individual freedom in which education and health are accessible and valued (see Table 1).

North's study of economic progress confirms that "it is adaptive rather than allocative efficiency which is the key to long-term growth."[18] The ability or inability to access, adapt, and apply new technologies and the other sources of productivity advances is fundamentally determined by a society's institutions. Institutions can open doors of opportunity or throw up roadblocks. In addition institutional changes often come slowly (customs, values, laws, and constitutions evolve), and established power centers and special vested interests and religious beliefs sometimes deter and delay changes conducive to economic progress. How accepting is a society of risk and change when change creates losers as well as winners[19] or transgresses religious beliefs?

The Decline of Poverty: Contemporary Trends

Despite various impediments to positive institutional change in many nations, heightened competition spurred by the information revolution and spread of political and economic participation worldwide bode well for people previously cut off from the path out of poverty. In this regard it is important to emphasize that economic growth, where it has taken hold, has benefited all layers of society. In the United States the rise in material affluence was so great and widespread in the twentieth century that individuals the government currently labels "officially poor" have incomes surpassing those of average Americans in 1950 and all but the richest (top 5 percent) in 1900. The poverty income level in the United States, about one fourth the U.S. average, is far higher than average per capita incomes in most of the rest of the world. To show how widespread the gains from economic growth have been, table 4 lists items owned or used by average households in the United States in 1950 compared to below-poverty-threshold Americans today. Air-conditioned homes with electricity, refrigerators, flush toilets, television, and telephones are common even among poor Americans. Indeed American households listed below the poverty level today are more likely to own color television sets than is an average household in Italy, France, or Germany. In short, the substantial gap among income classes as measured by income and especially wealth becomes much narrower when measured by basic categories: food, housing, and items and services for comfort and entertainment. In the United States there are more radios owned than ears to listen to them.

Table 4. Ownership by poor households (2001)
vs. ownership by all U.S. households (1950)

	All U.S. households (1950)	Below poverty level (2001)
Dishwasher	2	34
Clothes dryer	2	56
Washing machine	47	65
Air-conditioning	12	76
Automobile	19 (1960)	73
Telephone	73 (1960)	88 (1997)
Television	10	97
Refrigerator	80	97
Flush toilet	76	99 (1997)
Electricity	94	99 (1997)

U.S. Bureau of the Census, *American Housing Survey for the United States in 1997;* U.S. Bureau of the Census, "Housing Then and Now," www.census.gov/hhes/www/housing/census/histcensushsg.html (accessed September 6, 2011); *Historical Statistics of the United States,* Series Q 175.

Lest the relative wealth of the American poor seem an exception, it is important to note that the path out of poverty is now being traveled by greater and greater proportions of the world's population. While the one dollar per day (current real purchasing power) threshold value, used by economists and other development specialists as an absolute standard of extreme poverty, is in sharp contrast to the relative wealth of America's poor, it should not distract us from the reality that poverty in the world is declining. Figure 2 shows that the share of the world population living in extreme poverty—that is, below the one dollar per day threshold—has been falling for almost two centuries. The long decline pictured in figure 2 bears the good news that the battle against poverty made headway even as world population grew. Figure 3 shows that in recent decades the decline in proportion has finally led to a decline in absolute numbers. There are fewer poor people in the world today than there were twenty years ago.

Conclusions

Recent declines in the number of the world's poor are primarily a result of institutional improvements in Asia, especially in China and India. Since 1980 more than 200 million people have moved above the poverty threshold measure. The policy shifts allowing private holdings of land in China and greater freedom to create commercial enterprises to produce and exchange goods are revolutionizing life there. These changes were formally institutionalized in 2004 by constitutional changes bolstering private property rights and again in 2007. In contrast, the number of poor people in Africa continues to grow, as insecure property rights and weak regimes of law and order discourage investment, production, and exchange throughout much of the continent.

There has been phenomenal growth rate in economies that have moved away from centrally-planned, closed economic systems, to open, globally integrated systems (see table 5 for a static ranking of countries by measures of openness to international trade).[20] The comparison to both advanced rich nations and to those which, by design or lack of opportunity, have not globalized is striking. The faster growth rates of nations entering into the world market system is positive news, holding out the very real possibility of poorer nations "catching up" to the material comforts enjoyed by the advanced/rich nations, even as the less globalized fall farther behind.

This positive conclusion rests on both actual growth rates and population size. Stanley Fischer's analysis of the growth rates of nations, unaccounted for population size, demonstrates that richer nations grow more rapidly on average than poorer nations. But when population size is taken into account, there is a catching up, especially in

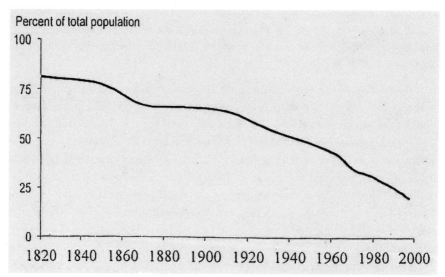

FIG. 2. Share of world population in poverty, 1820–1998. David Dollar, consignment research paper for the Foundation for Teaching Economics, Davis, Calif., 2003.

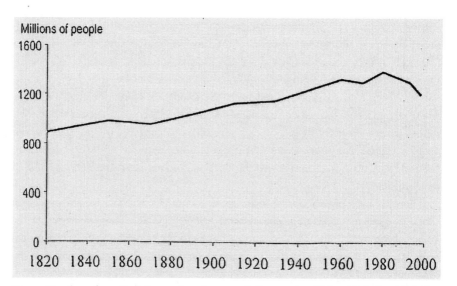

FIG. 3. Number of people living on less than one dollar per day, 1820–1998. David Dollar, consignment research paper for the Foundation for Teaching Economics, Davis, Calif., 2003.

Asia, where institutional economic change has been notable. Populous China and now India are following Hong Kong, Singapore, Japan, Taiwan, and South Korea out of poverty. The catching up process in Asia, however, is in sharp contrast to the situation sub-Saharan Africa, which constitutes one of the great institutional challenges of the twenty-first century.[21]

Recent research by Haber, North, and Weingast emphasizes this point especially with regard to political institutions in Africa.

> Economists have made an impressive start on the types of economic institutions needed to support efficient markets, but have not made equal strides in devising political institutions that will accomplish that objective. It took a Sekou Touré, or a Hastings Banda, five minutes of despotism to undo the finest economic theory. . . .
>
> In effect, solving the development problem in Africa requires the crafting of political institutions that limit the discretion and authority of government and, more saliently, of individual actors within the government. No simple recipe for limiting government exists.[22]

Devising political systems that divide power—either by checks and balances among branches or components of one level of government or by federalism creating competition among layers of government—holds promise for the needed economic institutional support of enterprise and markets. The daunting challenge for poor nations is to craft better political institutions and to promote the rule of law, rather than the more arbitrary rule of whim.[23] This challenging transition is vital because "history offers us no case of a well-developed market system that was not embedded in a well-developed political system."[24]

Regardless of the fact that some areas of the world are still struggling (and failing in some cases) to move onto and along the road out of poverty by getting the institutions right, greater and greater numbers of humans are living longer, in greater ease and comfort, and with more dignity. It is noteworthy that two hundred years ago, scholars, most notably Malthus, were preoccupied with the challenge of feeding the poor, while in advanced countries today the main challenges are fighting obesity and caring for the aged. Although revolutions, natural and man-made catastrophes, and war can imperil regions, the economic evidence and historical record provide ample reason to expect that the global progress launched by open markets and individual freedoms secured by rule of law around 1750 will continue indefinitely. The creative powers inherent in secure, stable, competitive, open-market systems are the wellspring for optimism about the future of humanity.

Table 5. Education, average number of years (c. 1820 to 1992)

	France	USA	Japan	India	China
1820		1.75	1.5		
1870		3.92	1.5		
1913	6.99	7.86	5.36		
1950	9.58	11.72	9.11	1.35	1.6
1973	11.96	14.85	12.9	2.6	4.09
1992	15.69	18.4	14.78	5.55	8.93

Source: Indur M. Goklany, "Economic Growth, Technological Change, and Human Well-Being," in *It's Getting Better,* edited by Terry L. Anderson (Palo Alto, Calif.: Hoover Institution, Stanford University, 2003), 65. Courtesy of the Hoover Press

Table 6. Rankings of nations from least to most globalized, 2005

Least Globalized		Most Globalized	
60 Iran	45 Argentina	30 Poland	15 Czech Republic
59 India	44 Thailand	29 South Korea	14 Norway
58 Indonesia	43 Saudi Arabia	28 Greece	13 Australia
57 Egypt	42 Nigeria	27 Japan	12 United Kingdom
56 Bangladesh	41 Sri Lanka	26 Italy	11 New Zealand
55 Brazil	40 Mexico	25 Spain	10 Finland
54 Turkey	39 Senegal	24 Slovak Republic	9 Austria
53 Venezuela	38 Morocco	23 Panama	8 Sweden
52 China	37 Ukraine	22 Hungary	7 Denmark
51 Peru	36 Tunisia	21 Portugal	6 Canada
50 Russia	35 Taiwan	20 Germany	5 Netherlands
49 Colombia	34 Romania	19 Slovenia	4 United States
48 Pakistan	33 Chile	18 Malaysia	3 Switzerland
47 Kenya	32 Uganda	17 France	2 Ireland
46 South Africa	31 Philippines	16 Israel	1 Singapore

Source: Federal Reserve Bank of Dallas, 2005

NOTES

1. I am grateful to Douglass C. North for his advice and encouragement to write this chapter. I am also grateful for very helpful discussions and commentary from the late Milton Friedman, Paul Romer, Lee Alston, Philip Coelho, Joel Mokyr, Dan Benjamin, David Dollar, Roger Ransom, Pat Fishe, Surrey Walton, Jerry Hume, Donald Raiff, Chris Wright, Smokey Murphy, Donna McCreadie, Gene McCreadie, Mike Copeland, Ken Leonard, Nicholas Koukopolos, Jim Klauder, and Kathy Ratté on the issues and topics herein. My gratitude also goes to Joyce Gordon, Yvonne Liebig, and Heather Carkuff for clerical assistance and to Lisa Chang for all her work.

2. Such glorification is long-standing: "The humour of blaming the present, and admiring the past, is strongly rooted in human nature, and has an influence even on persons endued with the profoundest judgment and most extensive learning" (David Hume, "Of the Populousness of Ancient Nations," in *Essays Moral, Political, and Literary,* 2 vols., edited by T. H. Green and T. H. Grose (London: Longmans, Green, 1875), 1:443.

3. For select accounts, see Charles Murray, *Human Accomplishment: The Pursuit of Excellence in the Arts and Sciences, 800* B.C.–1950 (New York: HarperCollins, 2003).

4. For example, see Winston Churchill's description of life in Britain during and after the Roman era in his *History of the English-Speaking Peoples,* vol. 1 (New York: Dorset Press, 1956).

5. Douglass C. North, "Economic Performance through Time," *American Economic Review* 84 (June 1994): 359–68. For additional demarcations, see Jared Diamond, *Guns, Germs, and Steel: The Fates of Human Societies* (New York: W. W. Norton, 1999), chap. 1.

6. For a sober reflection on the hundred most important people ever and their inventions, creations, and achievements, see Michael H. Hart, *The 100: A Ranking of the Most Influential Persons in History* (New York: Citadel Press, 1994).

7. Robert W. Fogel, "Catching Up with the Economy," *American Economic Review* 89 (March 1999): 1–21.

8. Minimum daily energy requirements to engage in light work and maintain body weight and health require between 1,720 and 1,960 calories per day. Per capita estimates of 1,750 for France in 1790 and 2,060 in England have increased to well over 3,000 today. Averages in 1950 of 1,635 in India and 2,115 in China compare to 2,466 and 2,972 respectively in 1998. See Indur M. Goklany, "Economic Growth and the State of Humanity," PERC Policy Series, April 2001, http://www.perc.org/pdf/ps21.pdf (accessed 9/7/2011).

9. See Robert W. Fogel, "Economic Growth, Population Theory, and Physiology: The Bearing of Long-Term Processes on the Making of Economic Policy," *American Economic Review* 84 (June 1994): 369–95; and Robert W. Fogel, *Escape from Hunger and Premature Death, 1700–2100: Europe, America, and the Third World* (New York: Cambridge University Press, 2004).

10. S. H. Preston, "Human Mortality throughout History and Prehistory," in *The State of Humanity,* ed. Julian L. Simon (Malden, Mass.: Blackwell, 1995), 30–36.

11. See Fogel, "Economic Growth."

12. World Health Organization, *The World Health Report 2000* (Geneva: WHO, 2000).

13. World Resources Institute, World Resources Database Diskette, 1998–99 (Washington, D.C.: WRI, 1999); United Nations Development Program, *Human Development Report 2000* (New York: Oxford University Press, 2000).

14. U.S. Bureau of Census, *Statistical Abstract of the United States 1999* (Washington, D.C.: U.S. Census Bureau, 2000), 97.

15. For the dramatic growth of human time available for leisure and other (nonwork) discretionary uses since 1880, see Fogel, *Escape from Hunger and Premature Death,* 1–30, 68.

16. Douglass C. North, *Understanding the Process of Economic Change* (Princeton, N.J.: Princeton University Press, 2005).

17. For elaboration, see Nathan Rosenberg and L. E. Birdzell Jr., *How the West Grew Rich* (New York: Basic Books, 1986); and Joel Mokyr, *The Lever of Riches: Technological Creativity and Economic Progress* (New York: Oxford University Press, 1990).

18. North, "Economic Performance through Time," 359–68.

19. Joseph A. Schumpeter, *The Theory of Economic Development* (Cambridge, Mass.: Harvard University Press, 1934).

20. See David Dollar and Paul Collier, *Globalization, Growth and Poverty: Building an Inclusive World Economy* (New York: Oxford University Press, 2002).

21. Stanley Fischer, "Globalization and Its Challenges," *American Economic Review* 93, no. 2 (May 2003): 11–12.

22. Stephen Haber, Douglass C. North, and Barry R. Weingast, "If Economists Are So Smart, Why Is Africa So Poor?" *Wall St. Journal* (July 30, 2003): A12.

23. Douglass C North, John Joseph Wallis, Barry R. Weingast, "A Conceptual Framework for Interpreting Recorded Human History," NBER Working Papers 12795, National Bureau of Economic Research, Inc, 2006.

24. Haber, North, and Weingast, "Why Is Africa So Poor?"; Robert Guest, "A Survey of Sub-Saharan Africa," *The Economist* (January 17, 2004): 1–16.

Reflections on Religion, Historical Progress, and Professional Historians

Bruce Kuklick

A commitment to historical progress is a relic of the period when history and the supernatural were more entangled than they now are. I do not believe there is any progress in history, but it is foolish to think this position can be proven. In their implicit commitment to the naturalistic study of the past, professional historians have helped to make my position respectable, but the guild has also helped to subvert coherent inquiry into the issue. The purpose of this essay is to expound on these ideas and the tensions in my own view, which is resolutely antisupernatural.

The Presuppositions of Critical History

Throughout the middle of the nineteenth century a revolution took place in historical thinking, centered in what was known as the Higher Criticism of the Bible. While its influence is still pervasive, historians have largely lost an understanding of the intellectual issues at stake.[1] The Lower Criticism prevalent to that time had examined the ancient sources of the Bible to find the most authentic accounts and to see what the texts really said. On the contrary, the Higher Criticism asked unforgivingly if what the texts stated or presupposed was true. German scholars in particular came to treat the Bible as they would any other book they would engage with if they were testing its claims to truth and additionally figuring out the manner of its composition. In analyzing the truth of biblical narratives in the New Testament, scholars came to be rightfully skeptical of the virgin birth, Jesus' feeding of the multitudes, and his resurrection from the dead. This skepticism was notoriously associated with the *Leben Jesu* (1835, 1836) of David Friedrich Strauss. The learned did not believe that miracles occurred in their own culture, and what was possible in their experience became the criterion for what might occur in all possible experience. The scholar did not attack the integrity of the biblical authors, who may have believed in miracles. Indeed higher critics made an effort to understand these authors in the context of their own time, perhaps to empathize with their prescientific ideas or their concessions to archaic local prejudice. In a full account of the meaning of texts scholars also needed to conjecture about what was really going on when, say, the crucifixion of Jesus was described. Maybe Jesus was still alive after he came down from the cross. Maybe he was dead but the body was stolen. Historians recognized that the norms governing the credibility of testimony from another era might differ from the norms that govern acceptance of such testimony in the present. Historians recognized that present norms must govern their understanding. Perhaps in the fourteenth century the learned might take at face value a biblical source that told them that Jesus rose from the dead. By the nineteenth century scholars would question these sources in terms of their better belief about what might be going on when eyewitness reports by committed followers of Jesus related that he had died but come back to life.

So first the Higher Criticism attacked the truth of certain assertions made in the Bible. The critics then raised issues about how parts of Scripture were assembled. Students usually associate this development with the Old Testament scholarship of Julius Wellhausen, who published *Geschichte Israels* in 1878 and gave full expression to what was called the "Documentary" or "Source Hypothesis." Wellhausen looked at the Pentateuch, the first five books of the Bible. How had their supposed author, Moses, assembled them? Exploring the way the documents were composed, Wellhausen questioned the integrity of these five books and finally argued that they were patched together from other sources. The most easily assimilated argument of Wellhausen and his followers insisted that since the Pentateuch spoke of the death of Moses, it strained credulity to assume that he wrote the books. Something was wrong with the view that someone could author a text proclaiming his death.

The learned used the best scholarly tools at their disposal and their reasoning powers to see if they could warrant basic biblical contentions. The same sort of rationality was at work in their efforts to learn how various revered writings came to be assembled in the Bible. The fundamental assumption of the Higher Criticism was that what occurred in the past was not radically dissimilar from what occurred in the present. What investigators believed could possibly happen in the contemporary period was a measure of what was acceptable as what could have happened in the past, no matter what the Bible or other venerated sources told us. The past was brought to the bar of present standards of veracity. If we understood today how two separate texts might be blended together in one extant text, we could see how this might happen in the past. If we did not believe in miracles today, we could not believe in them in the past. The nineteenth century dealt ordinary Western religious commitments a devastating blow. They all had postulated divine intervention in nature, the supernatural. Central to the Higher Criticism was the notion that the impossibility of supernaturalism in the present made it an equally unacceptable explanation for the past. The belief in inviolate laws of nature became supreme. History became a naturalistic discipline.

At a less elevated level, historians in their reasoning became more aware of the universal and common experiences of peoples. Historians became less gullible about travelers' tales, fantastic stories, and wild reports. They dissected evidence, and a commentator was more likely to ask, what is it that is actually going on here? The principles that emerged in the Higher Criticism were especially hard on time-honored religious belief, but additionally a professional ethos materialized. It premised that historians work with a certain notion of "getting it right."

Van A. Harvey has tellingly emphasized this aspect of the Higher Criticism: that the special morality of the historian or scholar is at issue.[2] My duty is to establish the grounds of belief not on what I wish or hope for, not on what I have learned from various authorities, not on faith, but on what can best be established as true. I will call this development the rise of the will to truth in scholarship. It is pitiless, because it puts evidence to the torture. The method is indeed without mercy to our beliefs, and it especially brought to the bar previous explanations of human acts that had called upon the divine.

It is surely true that historical writing over the last one hundred years is replete with bias and evidence of the milieu in which it was written. Some of these failings are no doubt due to conscious trimming on the part of the historian, the imperfect imbibing of the morality of the Higher Criticism. Some failings are due to laziness, pressures of time, and all those variables that explain why we fall short of an ideal. I chalk up some to prejudices and presuppositions of which scholars were not, or are not, aware. Even so, as a form of knowledge, this sort of history is better than myths, legends, storytelling, journalism, or the religiously inspired construction of the past that critical history replaced.

The Higher Criticism brought together two concerns of the era that we at least can distinguish. Substantively the Higher Criticism denigrated the role of the supernatural in the study of the past. Methodologically it elevated present standards of truthfulness and an obligation to use them in examining what had transpired in the past.

While historians today in the academy are bearers of the Higher Criticism, they are usually (I have found) ignorant of its development and not always flawless carriers of its imperatives. Almost all professionalized historians rule out the supernatural in the study of the past, but they do so reflexively, and sometimes the excision is at odds with their own religious beliefs. Many historians in the West are conventionally religious. They are often Jews or Christians who in some measure affirm a spirituality that has its basis in some supposed supernatural historical truths. They are uncomfortable about this affirmation and avoid it in their history writing. Score a point here for how one of the elements of critical history has become part of a commitment absorbed in graduate school training.

With regard to the methodological aspect of the Higher Criticism, the basic issue of what I have called the will to truth often puzzles many practitioners. In talking about their research, as opposed to just doing it, they often get confused. If I intend to tell the truth about some historical problem, I may be naive and oblivious to some assumptions that undergird my enterprise. But what I will be doing will differ from what those commentators who desire to justify certain policies in the past, to warrant a certain present political campaign, to forward certain social or religious ideals, or even to tell a gripping story are doing. What is it that someone rationally does in intending to tell the truth? It is different from predicting the consequences that might result from what is said, or from contributing to some supposed social good, or from a calculation of the expediency of the effort. As a historian I may be self-deluded in many ways, but what I will be doing if I intend to tell the truth about the past will be different from what others are doing, if they are, say, endorsing democracy in the United States or sponsoring true religion in Pakistan.

This principle of the Higher Criticism certainly expresses professional ideals, but it has been imperfectly absorbed theoretically. Historians are committed to honesty in their research effort. They also have their own moral proclivities, and they are aware that history is not physics. They often self-consciously acknowledge their subjectivity. Graduate students frequently tell me, "I am committed to social justice," and they join this piety about their vocation—it is certainly not a real commitment on the part of most of them—to some sophomoric philosophical relativism. The result is a mixed-up credo that says we are truthful, that the evidence restricts us, but also that BLAH, BLAH, BLAH limits our findings. The BLAH, BLAH, BLAH is a placeholder for almost anything, but in the left-liberal academy it is usually something like "our commitment to democracy" or "our commitment to feminism." This credo, however, muddles several things. The historians who tell us that their fundamental commitment is to promote egalitarianism or multiculturalism are often proud that they are so conscious of their locus in the world, and it is all to the good to be self-conscious. But one's blindest spots—or those of one's culture—are far deeper. We cannot own up to them so easily, and the self-congratulation of some historians in this respect is troubling.

Critical history recognizes that we write from our own locus in time. We are temporal creatures, and there is no atemporal spot from which we might work. Certain assumptions, some probably very deep and unrecoverable to us, govern our efforts. But if we practice critical history, if our idea is to tell the truth about the past, then our labors will have a different character from those of people who are differently minded about what they want to do.

Being a judge is different from being a lawyer, although this is not to say that judges are without a social place. There is a difference between a critical commitment to history and the confounded commitment that one finds espoused by some historians who are, in a flawed way, reflecting on historical writing. Nonetheless, although professional historians are not much good at telling us what goes on in the practice, they have absorbed the practice. Their deficiencies are more in the realm of the philosophy of history than in their writing of history proper. In fact in their writing I find that historians are able to detach their individual principles from their historical interpretations. For example, they do not in any serious way prejudice their understanding of the 1960s by their commitment to feminism in the 2000s. Being able to swim differs from being able to explain how to swim. Historians can swim even if they cannot explain what they are doing in swimming.

The fundamental ideas of critical history that I have spelled out are no longer explicitly taught, but they firmly survive in professional training and writing. Critical history has surely damaged supernaturalism. The sense of the morality of the historian has proved remarkably enduring, despite the misunderstandings that arise when historians explicate what they are about.

In 1874 in his "The Presuppositions of Critical History,"[3] the philosopher Francis Herbert Bradley gave the Higher Criticism a stunning philosophical culmination—Bradley was an explainer of swimming, not a swimmer himself. He focused both on the commitment to tell the truth and on the natural shape of the truth. The most significant Anglo-Hegelian metaphysician, Bradley argued that we inevitably try to figure out what was true of the past in terms of our best sense of what would pass muster in the present. Contemporary authority, our own experience of the way the world worked, must be the background to our grasp of the past. More important, Bradley tried to discern "our best sense of the way the world worked." He intimated that if this sense changed, then so would our standards of historical explanation. Unpacking the criteria of contemporary authority, Bradley concentrated on the disappearance of the supernatural in his era. He emphasized that historical understanding must proceed on the assumption that human beings operated in a world governed by natural law. The prized truths of contemporary scientific investigation and the Darwinian revolutions were front and center for Bradley in the late nineteenth century. Within this antisupernatural context he adumbrated the structure of the reasoning that historians use in weighing evidence to come to conclusions.[4]

For Bradley, the will to truth in history is synonymous with antisupernaturalism. Our scientific standards are and must be naturalistic. Bradley understood that our norms must govern our understanding of the past. But, he also presumed, norms that made supernaturalism acceptable had been permanently discarded. Critical history methodologically made the will to truth central; the method would inevitably rule out the supernatural—an achievement of substance. But there is a lot going on in allying the commitment to truth telling to naturalism, and as I have suggested, the two are distinct. Things change, and warrants for belief that are now acceptable may not be so in the future. If not, the way we would reach conclusions about what had happened in the past would be amended. For Bradley, this discovery is true a priori: the standards that we must use in writing our histories are our contemporary standards. We cannot use warrants other than those that are accepted in the professional world today, unless we want to give up the claim to be responsible historians. The reason that supernatural historical explanations were once acceptable, say, in the fourteenth century is that supernaturalism itself was acceptable in the fourteenth century.

A nasty question here is, who constitutes the "we" I have been deliberately using so cavalierly? The "we" refers to a relatively small community of professional historians whose predecessors have inculcated in us the principles of critical history. That is, Bradley presumes that there is one monolithic professional community that has a unified array of standards, and it is in fact the case that an antisupernaturalist crowd has indeed been professionally supreme in Western historical writing since the end of the nineteenth century.

My analysis of the decline of Edwardsean Calvinism in American intellectual circles may differ from that of many committed Christian historians. But both this group and I would disallow an explanation that sees in the decline God's irritation at Congregationalists as opposed to Presbyterians, although this might be what the Presbyterian Christian truly believes. George Marsden, one of these Christian historians, has allowed that as a university-based historian he is willing to play by these rules of the academic game. Yet, he says, Christians should not regard these rules as of ultimate importance. If I as a nonbeliever go to my mother's church, I will take very seriously the injunction by the minister to "bow our heads in prayer": I do it perhaps out of a serious moral respect and also surely to avoid a fight. Historians of faith abide by the professional rules, but if they are Christians, they have their own private views of what was going on when Jesus was brought down from the cross.

Things can get worse from my point of view. Richard Bushman is a respected historian and a Mormon who has kept his beliefs under wraps in mainstream publications. It turns out that he has a more or less secret life, writing essays on the history of his own faith that take for granted some of its supernatural truths. The essays got collected in *Believing History*. He tells us what he thinks really happened in Palmyra, New York, in the late 1820s, when Joseph Smith founded the Mormon religion. For any who do not know, an angel delivered golden plates to Smith, and before they were lost he translated them into the Book of Mormon. Among other things the translation relates stories about ancient battles between Lamanites and Nephites for supremacy on the American continent before the arrival of the Europeans. As a believer, Bushman gives his historian's benediction to these battles, as well as to the tale of the delivery of the golden plates. These things never happened. To believe them is lunatic, madcap. Yet here we have a professional who feels confident enough in his beliefs to assert them for the general consumption of his peers.[5]

The professional "we" is not much of a fortress. Today supernaturalism is unacceptable in the historical community only because it is generally unaccepted. The belief that our naturalistic worldview must be dominant is itself limited. The force of Bradley's work is just that he spells out its presuppositions. But even if *we* cannot think it away, even if *we* refuse to believe what is not believable to *us*, what happens if the *we* and the *our* and the *us* alter?

One reason that history gets rewritten is that our sense of an acceptable warrant changes as time passes. The contemporary becomes the past. The present brings new authority to bear on what has transpired. Beliefs change not just because of the discovery of new information but also because of alterations in the norms governing what is believable, our criteria of what make for sound belief. In this sense it is a mistake to focus on the animus of critical history against traditional Christianity: for Bradley, the Higher Criticism was not a set of antireligious conclusions or any substantive conclusions. One can imagine that sometime in the future supernaturalism might again dominate discussion. In that case there would be a reconstrual of the Bible more in line with what had been said before the writing of Strauss and Wellhausen. Critical history was the coming to clear consciousness of the way historians reasoned about history. They could not avoid bringing the past to the courtroom of present conceptions of believability. What they credited about the past conformed to what was appropriate in the present. In my imagined future, populated perhaps by supposed supernatural interventions that contemporaries found acceptable, New Testament miracles might look a lot better than they do today.

Without something more Bradley's analysis is only a factual description of the ethos of a professional community, of a set of practices at a given time. Bradley's analysis, however, did have "a more." As a progressive evolutionist of sorts and a Hegelian, Bradley implied that the cosmos was a form of absolute consciousness and that the growth of this consciousness was somehow displayed in time. There were also social props to this metaphysics, more than props if you are a social historian— the triumphs of the British Empire, the Victorian belief in progress, and the supposition that Oxford, where Bradley taught, represented an eternal sort of tolerant, open society that promoted belief of his sort. Bradley thought that present-day knowledge always enhanced what had gone before. No reversion to supernaturalism would occur, and in our knowledge of the past, a constant reconsideration and improvement that derived from advances in the present would emerge. Progress in knowledge of the past went hand in hand with the progress of contemporary knowledge. Our criteria for historical belief would become more refined in the future; our science would get better, and some form of naturalism would prosper. So—if we follow Bradley— historical knowledge evolves in a somewhat linear fashion. This is the unstated vision that gives Bradley's point of view its power and makes his analysis more than an anthropological account of some local scholarly customs. The quasi-Hegelian metaphysics intimates how historical practice will improve. The metaphysics guaranteed that naturalism would not conflict with the historian's will to truth. However, without the certainty that his metaphysics provides, I can see a space between the historians' will to truth and the commitment to naturalism.

Well over one hundred years after Bradley we may still be convinced that science advances, but certainly we are less convinced that the cultures that honor science can survive. My royal professional "we" pertains only to ostensible naturalists in the historical profession. Even today there are some historians who, like Marsden, play by the dominant rules but do not think that these rules need give us the full truth about human life; there are many historians who without much thought doff their churchgoing life when they go to work; and there are oddballs who, like Bushman, do not even play by the rules. What happens to history in a planet-of-the-apes culture? Less apocalyptically, what would happen to historical knowledge if dominant human cultures rejected science and again adopted supernaturalism? What happens to critical history in Iran? There are no good, compelling answers to these questions.

To put the problem another way, Bradley's critical history is laden with tensions. It has promoted an admirable practice that outlaws the supernatural, but at the same time critical history needs what amounts to a spiritual metaphysics to sustain it theoretically. Critical history requires something close to the supernaturalism it rules out. Bradley's questionable naturalism arose from a Hegelian point of view that many scholars have identified with religious speculation and complicated philosophical defenses of some cousins of Western theism. It is no secret that nineteenth-century German and British idealism is a close relation of traditional Christianity. Bradley's critical history is unstable. It calls for Hegelian emphases to maintain its will-to-truth naturalism, but just such emphases can sabotage the naturalism.

Progress and Professional History

For Bradley, the writing of history progresses because we get closer to historical truth. This progress occurs because there is a concomitant improvement or progress in the human story—life is somehow getting scientifically and morally better. Over the long term we can, I think, see the bond between these connected but distinct notions of progress to a religious orientation to the universe. For Bradley and his philosophical peers, their philosophical analyses were a kind of Christian spiritualism purged of irrational dross. For there to be progress in the human story entails that there are agreed-upon goals of human effort. In some ambiguous way these goals tend to be realized over time, though they may never be achieved at any given time. Progress in the writing of history correlated with the progress of humanity. You can tweak these characterizations of progress in many ways, and they will still be satisfactory to me. It is crucial that purpose is a category intrinsic to our understanding of the world and of history. Scientists and historians can investigate the world only with teleological concepts. This premise pretty clearly passed over from the Western religious tradition to critical history.

Just as Bradley both undercut and relied on Christian accents, professional concerns today, again in ways that are not fully consistent, continue to depend on but undermine the teleology. Professional historical practice is in fact a bulwark of naturalistic approaches that rule out any overriding or agreed-upon purpose. Yet some of the theories of many current practitioners—I will call them perspectivists—irregularly cast doubt on this naturalism.

Consider the standard arguments about the futility of what is called "the master narrative." It used to be thought, the claim is made, that there might be one overall story. It was premised that all the monographic work of individual historians, scurrying around in the archives, might find its niche in some inclusive scheme that would be History, with a capital H. But we now know, the reasoning continues, that there is no such thing as a master narrative. Similar considerations are at issue in the various attacks on "essentialism," whereby it is argued that there is no defining trait that must be captured in any legitimate historical treatment of a topic. Then there are the proponents of cultural studies in history who assert that we are left with an irreducibly indefinite number of conflicting meanings in our investigations of the past. It is not difficult to make fun of these postmodern impulses, and many Anglophone philosophers have. But despite the fact that perspectivist historians are better at doing what they do than they are at philosophizing about it, the plethora of unintegrated or unsynthesized historical accounts should give us pause. They are indications about what is going on in our fractured professional community.

All of the people who argue that there is no master narrative presuppose that their own position is false. In examining their reasoning I employ a version of what I call a transcendental argument. This is a fancy adjective borrowed from the philosophy of Immanuel Kant. He used the word, roughly, to talk about principles that describe the most fundamental aspects of the framework of our beliefs. Transcendental arguments loosely connected to Kant are popular with some philosophers nowadays. I use the phrase to talk about arguments that show the falsity of a view because, in expounding the view, its defenders trust in ideas the view denies.[6]

It is amiss to say that there cannot be one overall account. To say this implies that we can have a stance that will enable us to say that no account can be definitive. How can you deny a master narrative, unless you are in a position to see that such a narrative must fall short? How can you say that there are an irreducibly indefinite number of options in elaborating a historical account of a topic unless you have a place to stand that is able to see that the options are indefinite, in which case your standing place is better than that of your peers? Listen to Allan Megill, who ought to know better: "Nietzsche's assertion in *On the Genealogy of Morality* is correct: down here on earth, 'there is only a perspective seeing, only a perspective 'knowing.'"[7] Now how would Megill know that it is "correct" that we can achieve only perspectival accounts? He thinks he can occupy a position from which he can see that everyone else is operating from a more limited point of view. He presumes conditions that refute his or Nietzsche's perspectivism.

In avowing perspectivism would-be historian-theorists leave themselves open to the devastating criticism that they positively imply the existence of a grand, comprehensive standpoint, a view from nowhere. Megill's theoretical posture above, for example, hints at a view contingent upon the existence of a supratemporal absolute. As an orientation, perspectivism, which is a fierce form of contemporary naturalism, leads to the erosion of the natural.

The Historical Profession

Here is the complex constellation of issues that all historians might be better off explicitly facing. Some historians are contemptuous of belief, and some are even suspicious of writing religious history—unless it is the history of peculiar folk beliefs. Even most historians who are churchgoers would not dream of introducing their religious beliefs into their history. That is, there is little in historical practice that suggests working historians have much of a sense of overall historical progress or of the intrusion of supernatural into history. But for the last 175 years no one has formulated a philosophical vindication of history's underlying naturalist conventions that does not uneasily amalgamate naturalistic claims and supernatural assumptions. One finds this uneasy amalgam in Bradley. In talking about perspectivism, a lot of historians are not just dismissive of progress but also wary of historical truth. Yet when perspectivists enunciate their various ideals, they assume a structure that defeats perspectivism and elevates something more.

Here is my problem. On the one hand, I believe that there is no progress in the human story and thus no religious dimension to it. But I am not foolish enough to think I can prove this, for the proof presupposes a location from which I would be able to look at the whole of history and see it as not measuring up. Achieving such a position would reintroduce the religious considerations that I want to rule out. At best I can be unconvinced of attempts to show that there is historical progress. On the other hand, I also believe that some histories are better than others, that some historians probe more deeply into the past and are more likely to get it right. That is, I do believe in something like historical truth, even if I am uncertain about our ever having obtained it; at least I believe that proofs for perspectivism must fail. My hope that there is historical truth is at odds with my doubts about progress. If there is historical truth to be found, why would I believe this unless there were confirmation of its existence—that is, confirmation that our work got closer to what went on in the past?

To make my points I have made Bradley a more straightforward Hegelian than he really was, but it is well to observe that he took up all these issues in a more complex way. Mind, thought, consciousness, and purpose were for Bradley inescapable and irreducible aspects of the world. Their formative, shaping dimension was a necessary constituent of reality. Without mind, no world, and so mind must finally lend coherence to the cosmos. But Bradley was also something of a skeptic. All human minds were prone to confusion and the proliferation of partial insights, and we could not expect definitive or even clear answers to a lot of important questions.

As a philosopher concerned about the nature of reality, Bradley thought that historical understanding was a specific dimension of a more general understanding of the real, and so his tentative skepticism also applied to our grip on the past. Although he believed historical knowledge progressed, he hesitated about how much we could grasp of this progress. We cannot understand progress in finite time, and how it might happen was unintelligible to our intellects. We are in fact faced with conflicting attributions of meaning, indicators of warring temporal perspectives.

Bradley is getting at something like this. Human beings do, indeed must, think in historical terms. History is of the nature of stories, of narrative. We always construe our lives and those of others and the life of our culture in such terms. Now stories have a point, and we cannot conceive that history does not have a point. If all intelligent life were destroyed today forever—if history were to end—we would probably conceive its end as the conclusion to a failed enterprise; or we might say only that human history has ended, and there will be a past of the universe, even if there is no one to write about it. For Bradley, the idea is that we cannot conceive its end. Stories imply a storyteller who stands outside the story and for whom the story has some meaning or other. Historians are, of course, human storytellers. But even supposing that the business of human history writing is over implies that a consciousness grasps that it is over. History is at least a mandatory category of human understanding, and for Bradley that implies, somehow, an indefinitely extended series of consciousnesses or a greater-than-human consciousness.

Our necessary ways of thinking about the past entail that if we ponder human stories at all, they must have directionality and meaning that consciousness grasps. But how this occurs, says Bradley, is beyond our ability to understand. Our reasoning powers are not the shipwreck of understanding, but our brains simply get lost when we try to press any further.

There is thus for Bradley something nonrational in allowing that we have to think historically and still urging that such thinking ends merely with fragmentary and disputed meanings. If storylike thought is part of the furniture of the mind, if we reinstate it even in denying it, how can it be so unsatisfactory? We have a puzzle or, better, a mystery of some large significance. We are required to think about ourselves historically but cannot fully comprehend what is involved in such thinking.[8] Bradley at lasts rests in a sort of faith.

I would like to point us in the direction of a Bradley-like skeptical faith. The trouble with Megill's perspectivism is that he thinks he can show it to be true. Perspectivism may be true, but we cannot show that it is. To try to prove it involves its overthrow. On the other side, the transcendental argument does not guarantee that we actually have a comprehensive (and thus antinatural) standpoint. The argument guarantees only that we can reject claims that say we do not have such a standpoint. The transcendental argument is a useful tool to underscore the historical hope we need to have to function as historians, but it is an argument that falls short of establishing any firm transtemporal outlook.

This position accepts in respect to history the modest stance that Kant adopted in respect to all knowledge of the "phenomenal" world. Historians cannot have accounts that we can say are ultimate. We can never say we have reached historical truth, a final, best history about a subject. We can never say that we have clutched the past and that this part of history is nailed down. That is, no standpoint can serve as what Kantians call a constitutive ideal. A sufficient grasp of the past never constitutes our historical practice.

This belief in the past and historians' connection to it, however, can serve to regulate their conduct. We do presume that there is a past always ready to check our pretensions and that there is a future in which present historical assertions are called to account. The past forever serves as a reservoir of evidence to correct limited interpretations, to remind historians that they just cannot make it up, and to put us on notice that our limited outlooks are inadequate. The future opens out without exact limits as the time in which to make assertions answerable to evidence.

In actual historical studies historians who may be perspectivists in their not-so-thought-out theorizing use the modes of reasoning that have come to dominate professional history. They demonstrate the prejudices of supposedly neutral scholarship; they point out discrimination against certain kinds of historians. They show that certain kinds of data have been overlooked or that previously examined data must be looked over again. This group of commitments and beliefs is what I would term a regulative ideal. Historians can hope that it is legitimate, for no one could ever prove that it was unjustified.

Historians tremble between their knowledge that they operate from a limited point of view, that they are trapped in time, and their instinct that there is always something more. They are confined to the partial but cannot rule out attempts to get to the impartial and thus the timeless aspects of their enterprise. They are caught between the natural or temporal and the transtemporal or divine. They often make a hash of how to conceive this disjunction. I probably have. We get at the nerve of historical knowledge by examining this area of trembling. We can hope that our limited temporal location somehow connects up with a more enduring framework, but how it connects up is unclear.

I used to think that we might move forward, even progress, if we thought more seriously as historians about this no-man's land. But I am now more certain that we are better off accepting a skepticism of Bradley's sort or the only modest hopefulness of Kant. Historians of religious faith, for whom I have some esteem, and even those who go over the edge, such as Richard Bushman, make the mistake of thinking they can improve history by somehow introducing into it what they believe are the real, nonnatural causes of things. Better to recognize that history is a limited form of knowledge and that we need to resist the temptation, as historians, to overreach its boundaries. At the same time, for me at least, issues of historical knowledge are so compelling just because the knowledge exists on the permanent frontier between an acceptable naturalism and something more.

NOTES

1. This discussion has its genesis in "On Critical History," in Bruce Kuklick and Darryl G. Hart, eds., *Religious Advocacy and American History* (Grand Rapids. Mich.: Eerdmans, 1997), 56–64, but extends and alters that argument.

2. Van A. Harvey, *The Historian and the Believer: The Morality of Historical Knowledge and Christian Belief* (New York: Macmillan, 1966).

3. Reprinted in Francis Herbert Bradley, *Collected Essays,* 2 vols. (Oxford: Clarendon Press, 1935), 1:1–70.

4. Harvey, in *The Historian and the Believer,* 43–67, outlines how this takes place, what the norms of reasoning are, and how the warrants worked in the mid–twentieth century (and still do today).

5. Richard Bushman, *Believing History* (New York: Columbia University Press, 2005). The reader might also examine the exchange in *Books and Culture* (March/April 2005): 6–7, with Bushman, Mark Noll, and me.

6. Paul Boghossian, in *Fear of Knowledge: Against Relativism and Constructivism* (Oxford: Oxford University Press, 2006), 52–57, does not like this "traditional" argument but finds another closely linked one that does the same job.

7. Allan Megill, *Historical Knowledge, Historical Error* (Chicago: University of Chicago Press, 2007), 107–8.

8. The preceding relies on "The Presuppositions of Critical History" and my interpretative reading of Francis Herbert Bradley, *Appearance and Reality* (London: Allen & Unwin, 1893; 2nd ed. with appendix, 1897), esp. 359–400, 455–552.

Revisiting the Idea of Progress in History

The Perspectives of Herbert Butterfield, Christopher Dawson, and Reinhold Niebuhr

Wilfred M. McClay

W e have become uneasy with the very concept of progress. We are not prepared to give it up entirely; that would be nearly inconceivable. Peel away the ironic surface of even the most insouciant postmodern pose, and you find revealed, startling as a ghost, some brightly colored and long-forgotten fresco, a gaudy metanarrative of progress still silently at work, shaping our choices of ends and means and norms. There are many such hidden frescoes still at work today. The West is still remarkably committed to the idea of purposive action and resistant to the lure of fatalism, perhaps because rebellion against the binding power of necessity forms the very core of Western identity.

A culture like ours has enormous progressive inertia. It does not necessarily have to acknowledge the existence of its earlier commitments to be propelled or guided by them for a very long time. Nor can it dispense with the underlying frescoes without also dispensing with all of the surfaces that have been painted over them. We have no intention of doing that. But we do not feel quite as ready as we once were to endorse the idea of progress without always employing the protective mechanisms of qualifiers or sneer quotes. This is perhaps the most obvious evidence of the depth of our unease.

If we are honest with ourselves, we have to admit that we still believe implicitly in the possibility of something that one could legitimately call "progress." This is nigh unto inescapable. Even our occasional efforts to sound fatalistic in our speech betray all the things that such speech silently presumes: that as free and purposeful beings we cannot help projecting certain ideals or goals, if even only short-range or proximate ones, into the inchoate future. This is particularly so in the United States, where every lamentation has a way of turning into a jeremiad, and thereby into a form of moral exhortation, the polar opposite of fatalism.[1] The language of true fatalism would be silence, and that is not what we are hearing.

However, our compulsive belief in progress is being challenged constantly by the honesty of our unbelief. Hence when we speak of progress, it is often "progress" that we speak of. The use of "sneer" quotes is often a way of pretending to be superior to the concept being quoted, and to those who would be so naive or mendacious as to use the words without critical distance. But their use may also be a way of frankly confessing one's inability to get beyond straddling an issue or even a way of evading the law of noncontradiction, by both asserting and not asserting something at the same time—a way of saying tacitly what was once said biblically: "Lord I believe; help thou my unbelief" (Mark 9:24).

The idea of progress in history—the liberating song of the Enlightenment, the grand choral ode of the nineteenth century, the marching music central to the rise and dominance of the modern West—has gradually become problematic to us. The skepticism runs deep. Not only is it our faith in the inevitability of progress that we question but also the very idea that we would have any sure means of judging what progress is, if it indeed does occur. Some of this can be attributable to intellectual fashion, or cultural boredom, or the occasional metastasizing of the Western self-critical impulse into a raging self-hatred.

The nub of the problem arises not out of psychology but out of historical reality. The idea of progress, after all, received its first, and perhaps profoundest, shock in the response to World War I. That conflict's unprecedented, cataclysmic scale of destruction, its having arisen for the most obscure reasons and then having been carried along seemingly unstoppably by its own horrifying momentum, made a mockery of the great progressive assumption: that the growth of knowledge, social organization, and human control over forces of nature would lead steadily and inevitably to greater harmony, prosperity, rationality, and well-being.

The idea of progress has been on shaky ground ever since, and its detractors have found no want of additional evidence in support of their case. The rise of maniacal and murderous regimes in the heart of civilized Europe, the many brutalities of World War II, the advent of nuclear and other weapons of inconceivable destructive power, the intense and troubling moral self-examination that came with the end of the great European colonial empires (and continues in those societies today, with the growing social tensions posed by postcolonial migration), the massive global inequities in the use of resources and distribution of wealth, and the growing fear that the planet cannot provide the means to sustain Western standards of social and economic life—all of these concerns have added to the weight borne by the West in its reconsideration of the idea of progress. Some see as a sign of profound civilizational demoralization the growing specter of "demographic winter" in the West, as the birthrate in country after country in the developed West plunges beneath replacement levels.[2]

It sometimes seems as if progress has all along been accompanied by a doppelgänger, a shadow side, a reversal of Hegel's famous "cunning of reason," which has sought to make the works of reason all conduce to the benefit of unreason and to make all that we had thought to be progress into something regressive. Such sweeping pessimism is, in a sense, far too easy and regards too lightly such triumphs as the abolition of the African slave trade, whose anniversary we have just observed, or the many material improvements, such as manifold advances in medicine and nutrition, that have brought longer and fuller lives to countless persons all over the globe. Yet it is plausible to argue that what we call "progress in history" has not brought moral progress along with material progress. It is plausible to assert that what progress we have made in freeing humankind from the constraints of material necessity has also increased the possibilities for human transgressiveness and wanton cruelty and destructiveness on larger and larger scales. In addition it has estranged us further from nature and perhaps also inhibited the development of resilient individuals who are also capable of sustaining love, empathy, and self-giving. In this starker view what would appear to be steady progress has actually, in human terms, been steady degradation.

This last statement surely goes too far. But at the very least one can say that the expansion of human agency, of the growing ability to master the material terms of our existence, has been an ambivalent achievement, one that does not necessarily bring moral improvement or human happiness. Far from bringing inevitable moral improvement, it may even severely impede the moral life, which derives not from a sense of mastery but rather from the acceptance of a life encircled by limitations and interdictions.[3] Far from bringing inevitable happiness, it may even bring on a kind of bottomless despair from which there is no exit, since there is no remaining excuse for one's failings and no escape from one's putative mastery into the absolving fog of irresponsibility, let alone forgiveness. The more we are exclusively in control, the more we are exclusively to blame. The less willing we are to be judged, the less able we are to be forgiven.

Being asked, as we are in this collection of essays, to engage "big questions" also obliges us to stick out our necks. Let me do so now, or continue to do so, in explaining my choice of topic. It is my conviction that we believe in the idea of progress, and we need to be able to do so and to do so more fully and confidently and unapologetically than we now do. We need that belief in progress in order to continue to be what we are, to sustain the things we cherish, and to exercise our moral freedom in the profoundest way available to us: by giving of ourselves for the well-being of others, including the careful and generous stewardship of the world resources, with a view to the generations of men and women to come. One might say, more succinctly, that the belief in progress, the narrative structure of the progressive idea, is so thoroughly inscribed in our cultural makeup that we cannot conceive what we would be without it. There are, so to speak, no alternative images beneath the fresco—a fresco is, after all, a work of art painted into the very substance of the wall. Dedication to a goal outside of and beyond ourselves serves—if I may be permitted one more use of painterly metaphor—in something like the same capacity as the vanishing point in Renaissance linear perspective, the external point of reference by which the whole picture is brought into a comprehensive and harmonious order, a wholeness that would otherwise be unavailable to it.[4]

For these and other reasons, the idea of Progress is a big idea that we cannot do without, and that we can ill afford to hold in disdain. But we need to find better ways of talking about it and thinking about it, ways of chastening it, restraining it, and protecting it against its excesses. It can survive as a big idea, but perhaps only if it is not too big. What this may mean is that progress needs to be liberated from being Progress, from the kind of nineteenth-century faith in Progress that posited it as a substitute for religion, with a secular and immanent eschatology.

The need to sustain the idea of progress, in the face of all its problems, was also the underlying theme of the sociologist Robert Nisbet's grand and gloomy book published at the tail end of the gloomy 1970s and entitled *History of the Idea of Progress*.[5] The chief innovation of Nisbet's book was its argument that the idea of progress is not exclusively modern but had ample antecedents in many ancient and medieval authors and texts. But it is perhaps more noteworthy for my purposes to point out that Nisbet strongly connected the health of the idea of progress with the health of the Western religious tradition. "Any answer," Nisbet wrote, to the question of "the future of the idea of progress in the West" is going to require an answer to a prior question: "what is the future of Judeo-Christianity in the West?" It was, he argued, a prior belief in the dimension of the sacred in human existence that gave authority to "ideas of time, history, development, and either progress or regress." Only on the basis of such confidence in the existence of such divine patterning could the West come to be confident that there was also such patterning in the history of the world.[6]

Nisbet was not a conventional religious believer, but he is hardly the only one to have come to similar conclusions about the role of religion in forming many of the most crucially important secular ideas. The German philosopher Jürgen Habermas has said similar things in recent years. "For the normative self-understanding of modernity," he said in a recent interview, reported by Richard Wolin, "Christianity has functioned as more than just a precursor or a catalyst. Universalistic egalitarianism, from which sprang the ideals of freedom and a collective life in solidarity, the autonomous conduct of life and emancipation, the individual morality of conscience, human rights, and democracy, is the direct legacy of the Judaic ethic of justice and the Christian ethic of love."[7]

Although it is important to note that Habermas's focus here is on equality rather than "progress" and that he remains firmly committed to strictly secular standards of discourse and judgment, the features he names as by-products of the belief in universalistic egalitarianism are the very same features that a robust Western belief in the idea of progress would wish to claim for itself. It is also worth noting that, according to Wolin, Habermas's perspective on these matters has been crucially informed by his dialogues with Joseph Cardinal Ratzinger, now Pope Benedict XVI, and by his growing concern over the moral implications of unconstrained biological engineering and human cloning—problematic fruits of an uncritical idea of scientific or technological progress and one in which the formulation of strictly secular grounds for the imposition of limits has been slow and uncertain in coming.[8]

So the question arises whether the perspective offered by the traditional biblical religious heritage of the West, by what Nisbet called "Judeo-Christianity," has not only been an originating source for the idea of progress but also is and remains a source for the critique of that idea's hypertrophy. More simply put, does a reconsideration of the idea of progress from the standpoint of Western religion hold the prospect of giving us resources for a better understanding of that idea?

To begin exploring this problem I have in what follows selected for examination three important English-language books published at roughly the same time, during the middle interwar years: Herbert Butterfield's *The Whig Interpretation of History* (1931); Christopher Dawson's *Progress and Religion: An Historical Inquiry* (1929); and Reinhold Niebuhr's *Moral Man and Immoral Society* (1932). These were arguably the most important works produced by their authors, men whose work was centrally concerned with discovering the reasons why the idea of progress in history had become so problematic and what was to be done about it. Each author operated in such a way as to permit the examination of history on a very large scale. Each understood World War I as a mortal challenge to the once-regnant metanarratives regarding progress in history. However, each one understood the challenge in a different way, with different conclusions and different implications for the future of the idea of progress. In addition each author came to the subject grounded in religious commitments that would be brought to bear, directly or indirectly, on the subject at hand. In some sense the relationship between the Christian cultural legacy and the idea of progress was the subject each of them was engaging. Yet the uses to which they put Christianity varied strikingly, as did their answers to the questions posed above.

Herbert Butterfield was one of the most eminent figures of British academic life in the early and middle parts of the twentieth century, teaching for over fifty years on the faculty at Cambridge (1928–79), where he was Master of Peterhouse, vice chancellor of the university (1959–61), and Regius Professor of Modern History (1963–68).[9] He was a scholar of remarkably wide-ranging interests and published influential books in such fields as the history of science, eighteenth-century constitutional history, and international politics, among other subjects. His small book on the "Whig interpretation" of history is probably his most enduring contribution and one of the handful of truly influential books in the field of Anglo-American historiography.[10]

In it Butterfield defined "Whig" history (using the term somewhat idiosyncratically) precisely in terms of its alignment of the story of the past strictly with the dictates of the idea of progress and the present's imperious need to understand itself as a progressive advance upon the past. What he called "Whig history" referred to "the tendency of so many historians to write on the side of Protestants and Whigs, to praise revolutions provided they have been successful, to emphasize certain principles of progress in the past and to produce a story which is the ratification if not the glorification of the present."[11] Butterfield stood firmly against such tendencies, which seemed to him gross oversimplifications of the past and betrayals of the rightful task of the historian. The historian should prescind from making such arguments, he thought, and choose for himself a more modest role, answerable to a different set of canons. No mere mortal historian had a right, or had sufficient knowledge, to be making the kind of final moral judgments about historical actors and movements that Butterfield saw and criticized in, for example, the writings of Lord Acton.

Instead Butterfield sought a historiography that would take losers just as seriously as winners and, instead of tracing a line of triumphant truths culminating in the dominant conventional wisdom of the present, would seek deliberately to distance itself from Acton's smug view that "history is the arbiter of controversy" and firmly reject the self-satisfied idea that the way things have turned out is, in some sense, the way they should have. The historian played a different kind of role, trying to study the past without insisting upon its reference to the present and without playing the arbiter, the "avenging judge" who was engaged in dispensing "verdicts." Instead the historian had a broader civilizing task. He should be trying to cultivate the intellectual and moral discipline required to "enter into minds that are unlike our own," to make sympathetic contact with the full range of human experience and cognition, to "see all lives as part of the one web of life," and to take "men and their quarrels into a world where everything is understood and all sins are forgiven." It was a kind of God's-eye view to which he aspired, one in which a deliberate attempt was made to set aside the dominant moral claims and sympathies of one's own era—not out of a misplaced relativism but out of a carefully thought-out set of judgments about the limits of what historians could do and the peculiar set of virtues to which they should aspire.[12]

Such a view was, in a way, a precursor to the great flowering of social history and history "from the bottom up" that has transformed American historical writing over the past four decades. It also clearly reflects the influence of Butterfield's active Methodist religious faith, with its insistence on respecting equally the historical experience of all persons and not merely those who were granted fortunate outcomes and fortunate alignments in their lives. All were equally creations of God; all fell equally within his providential reach; all had an intrinsic importance and value; all would be judged by God alone. We should not presume that the events and outcomes that we find to be of note are, in fact, noteworthy sub specie aeternitatis. To cultivate such inclusiveness of vision is a kind of spiritual discipline; to achieve it, even in only small and intermittent measure, is a kind of godliness.

One might have guessed that his strong Christian convictions would have caused Butterfield to seek eagerly for the traces of God's hand in history. Yet that was not the case. Butterfield was quite severe in denouncing the idea that historians had it in their power to acquaint themselves with the operations of Providence. That was stepping over the line, from being godly to being godlike. Such was precisely the error committed by the Whig historians, who were too confident that they knew where "History" was "going" and that their judgments about questions of importance and nonimportance corresponded with those of the Deity. Butterfield thought it a massive arrogation for the historian to think that he had even the remotest capacity for such high-level teleological judgments. That was simply not his job. Moreover it was beyond his ken or that of any mere mortal.

Paradoxically then it was not out of programmatic skepticism but precisely out of Butterfield's robust religious beliefs, including his eschatological confidence in God's Providence, that he was able so easily to insist that the historian has to forswear any attempt to make final moral claims about the deeds and the consequences of human history. Comprehensive providential understanding, just like vengeance, should be yielded up unto the Lord, and for exactly the same reasons. The best that the mortal historian can hope for, or aspire to, is an impartial record of what happened, with all its complexities and ambivalences. History is not an oracle. Instead Butterfield thought that it had to be regarded with suspicion, as an ambitious upstart always willing to give itself over as a hireling or harlot, beholden to unsavory worldly alliances. Hence its judgments are never to be trusted as final or ultimate. "In other words," he said in his deceptively simple concluding words, "the truth of history is no simple matter . . . and the understanding of the past is not so easy as it is sometimes made to appear." The idea of progress, particularly as the Whig historians employed it, was in his view a terrible and dangerous simplifier, which puffed up ordinary men into prophets and dispatched other men, particularly those who had the misfortune to be history's losers, to oblivion.[13]

There is much to be said for the generosity and epistemological modesty of Butterfield's position, which sought, quite simply, to exclude the idea of progress from having any decisive influence on the proper practice of historiography. It corresponds well with the general stated ethos of the historical profession as it exists today, if not always necessarily the profession's actual practice. Yet this position, which for taxonomic purposes I will call the exclusionary stance, does not do justice to the seriousness of the problem. In the end it treats the idea of progress as dispensable even as it relies on the continued existence of the idea, as embodied in Whig historiography, as an antagonist, and hence an organizing principle. So accustomed is it to the rock-solid existence of the Whig hegemony against which it rebels, that the exclusionary stance does not take seriously the possibility that in the absence of such an ordering principle, Western history might have no good way to reorganize itself.

In addition it seems to leave out of account one of the chief culture-forming distinctivenesses of Judeo-Christianity: its understanding of divine history and human history as intersecting stories and not merely parallel or disparate ones. It would be wonderfully simplifying if one did not have to take account of this complexity, and secular historians, of course, do not have to. But the Judaism and Christianity of the Bible are faiths whose God takes a strong and active interest in doings of nations and the outcomes of historical events, and occasionally intervenes in them, sometimes quite dramatically. This Deity also delights in reversals and overturnings, making the first last and the last first in ways that often entirely subvert the world's paradigms. But he does not always or invariably do these things. Sometimes he does the opposite. Hence although Christians can have no expectation that there will be a sure correspondence between worldly success and metaphysical success, neither can they expect that the two will always be at odds.

What then was one to do with such a quirky, unpredictable, uncategorizable Providence? It seems that Butterfield did something rather similar to what the analytic philosophers of his day were doing: asserting that because nothing can be said with clarity and precision about God's activity in history, nothing should be said about the subject at all.[14] It was a perfectly reasonable move for any secular academic to make, and while a less obvious one for an avowedly Christian academic, nevertheless one that made considerable intellectual and moral sense, with an admirably ascetic integrity to it.

To be fair it should be pointed out that Butterfield showed a keen awareness that there was some kind of necessary intersection for Christians of divine and human history, and he laid that proposition out with clarity and eloquence in his impressive, civilized 1950 study *Christianity and History,* a work now long out of print and sadly almost unavailable.[15] This work is well worth reading, by Christians and non-Christians alike, as a classic statement of the civilizing effects of the historical imagination and a glimpse into the mind of a great and humane scholar. Yet it has to be said that *Christianity and History* did almost nothing to show readers how the Christian scholar might understand and explain the specific aspects of that intersection. Instead the most powerful statements in the book tended to reinforce the separation of the two realms, rather than encourage their mingling, and to make the Christian view of history something highly individual, even subjective, in character. Approvingly citing Ranke's statement that "every generation is equidistant from eternity," Butterfield expanded on the point: "So the purpose of life is not in the far future, nor, as we so often imagine, around the next corner, but the whole of it is here and now, as fully as ever it will be on this planet. It is always a 'Now' that is in direct relation to eternity—not a far future; always immediate experience of life that matters in the last resort—not historical constructions based on abridged text-books or imagined visions of some posterity that is going to be the heir of all the ages. . . . If there is a meaning in history, therefore, it lies not in the systems and organizations that are built over long periods, but in something more essentially human, something in each personality considered for mundane purposes as an end in himself" (66–67).

Even more powerful, but also perhaps more unsettling to some, are his concluding words: "I have nothing to say at the finish except that if one wants a permanent rock in life and goes deep enough for it, it is difficult for historical events to shake it. There are times when we can never meet the future with sufficient elasticity of mind, especially if we are locked in the contemporary systems of thought. We can do worse than remember a principle which both gives us a firm Rock and leaves us the maximum elasticity for our minds: the principle: Hold to Christ, and for the rest be totally uncommitted" (145–46). In other words, in place of Progress with a capital P one should instead embrace the Rock with a capital R, which is perhaps another way of saying that ultimate truth is, finally, outside of the reach of historical inquiry.

There is a great deal to be said for Butterfield's formulation, and in today's environment many mainstream academics with religious commitments, perhaps even most of them, find that a choice to prescind from genre-mixing inquiries still makes a great deal of professional and personal sense. But such a stance does not give us any help in the task with which we began, that is, seeing whether there is a way that the perspectives provided by the great Western religious traditions might play a role in helping us to better understand, and perhaps reinvigorate or reappropriate, the idea of progress in history. On the contrary, Butterfield's position merely reinforces our distance from the very idea of progress in history. It does not merely problematize the relation between the two but rules the question of their connection permanently out of bounds, a knowledge too noumenal for phenomenal beings.

Christopher Dawson offers a very different kind of example as an Oxford-educated independent scholar who had converted to Roman Catholicism in his twenties and who never enjoyed the comforts of a regular academic appointment.[16] He was, then, something of an outsider compared to the ultra-insider Butterfield, but not entirely so, for he managed to cut his own impressive swath across the intellectual history of his time. He was widely respected for the broad learning and profound synthetic insight of his many books, as was amply evidenced by his selection in 1947–49 to present the prestigious Gifford Lectures, from which his important book *Religion and the Rise of Western Culture* was derived, as well as his election as a Fellow of the British Academy and his appointment as the Charles Chauncey Stillman Chair of Roman Catholic Studies at Harvard Divinity School from 1958 to 1962.[17] In addition he was an important (and warmly avowed) influence on T. S. Eliot, among others, and a member in good standing of some of the same Anglo-Catholic intellectual circles in which Eliot ran. Dawson had many admirers, and his bold and imaginative syntheses displayed the kind of expansive range and interpretive flair that one associates with such "big thinking" contemporaries as Arnold Toynbee and Oswald Spengler.

Progress and Religion: An Historical Inquiry appeared in 1929 and was explicitly composed as a response to the confidence-shattered aftermath of World War I.[18] That conflict had, he remarked, led many people to "despair of the future of Europe" and to adopt "fatalistic theories of the inevitability of cultural decline"—again the very inverse of the idea of progress.[19] Dawson agreed that the idea of progress was deeply imperiled, and he felt the full weight of that fact. But he attributed that imperilment not to the bouleversement wrought by the war but to a wrong turn that modernity had made much earlier, in believing that it was possible to detach the idea of progress from its religious roots and make the idea of progress itself into the focal point of a secular religious or quasi-religious faith.

Religion was, for Dawson, the core institution of any and every culture. That something like an active religion had to be present at the center of a functioning culture was amply demonstrated, he thought, by the history of comparative religions. The existence of a culture demanded it. "Every living culture," Dawson argued, "must possess some spiritual dynamic, which provides the energy necessary for that sustained social effort which is civilization." In other words, every vital society must possess that organizing core, and the characteristic religion of a society "determines to a great extent its cultural form." Therefore the entire process of studying social and cultural developmental change has to begin and end not with a treatment of economic or political factors but with a consideration of the animating faith, the cultus around which the culture was organized, since that is the source and destination of everything else that transpires in it.[20]

Such concerns informed his understanding of the current crises, including the diminished condition of the idea of progress. The West as we know it was for Dawson the product of the confluence of two factors: the religious tradition deriving from Judeo-Christianity; and the scientific tradition that derived (ultimately) from ancient Greece. Dawson saw the two factors as entirely complementary when properly understood. The second had proven to be enormously powerful and pervasive in its influence, not only in the realms of science proper but also in the development of Western philosophy, law, and modern political and social organization. Yet for Dawson it was the first, the religious factor, that constituted the truly "dynamic" force in Western civilization, the organizing spark and propulsive engine that supplied the energy and direction for the West. Hence the "Religion of Progress," an understanding of progress that had removed progress from its relationship to religion and established it as a strictly secular force, would continue to have vitality only so long as it was able to draw on the religious tradition that it had, explicitly or implicitly, rejected. But in the end it had no independent force of its own and was doomed to fail when the inertial momentum had faded.[21]

By shunting aside its religious basis and making Progress into a false object of worship, the modern West had cut itself off from the chief sources of nourishment for its very roots and made Progress into something potentially monstrous and uncontrollable. It is important to stress that this harsh judgment was not born of hostility to science on Dawson's part or a desire to seek its repudiation. On the contrary, he saw modern science as an extraordinary human achievement and grasped the mutually beneficial relationship that could, and should, exist between religion and science. However, that relationship ceases to exist when one force succeeds in overwhelming the other, and the essential benefits of complementarity are lost. "Without religion," he observed, "science becomes a neutral force which lends itself to the service of militarism and economic exploitation as readily as to the service of humanity." "Without science," however, "society becomes fixed in an immobile, unprogressive order." Both are necessary, for it is "only through the cooperation of both these forces that Europe can realize its latent potentialities and enter on a new phase of civilization."[22] As those rather upbeat final words should imply, Dawson was, unlike Butterfield, actually a quite enthusiastic believer in the career of the idea of progress, so long as the idea could once again become rightly understood, as it had not been over the past two centuries. "The religious impulse must express itself openly through religious channels," he insisted, rather than "seeking a furtive, illegitimate expression in scientific and political theories." There should be no disguises and no tacit premises. The West must acknowledge that "our faith in progress and in the unique value of human experience rests on religious foundations, and that they cannot be severed from historical religion and used as a substitute for it, as men have attempted to do during the last two centuries."[23]

When properly understood again, however, the idea of progress would face few intrinsic limits to the levels of development that might be hoped for from it. Indeed there were passages in *Progress and Religion* that sounded positively giddy and utopian, imbued with a kind of high Hegelian optimism that was as far as could be imagined from the sober limits imposed by a religion historically grounded in the doctrine of original sin. For example, consider these two sentences near the book's conclusion: "the progressive intellectualization of the material world which is the work of European science is analogous and complementary to the progressive spiritualization of human nature which is the function of the Christian religion. The future of humanity depends on the harmony and co-ordination of these two processes."[24] The Europe of the future would be something dramatically new, dramatically different, he thought, from both the immobility of the East and the sterile materialism of the current West. It would promise an elevation of the human being to a more and more purely spiritual level of being, which would pave the way for a more and more durable international unity, as "the spiritual element," rather than the political or economic ones, became "the mainspring of our whole social activity."[25] Like many other postwar observers, Dawson was convinced of the need for a European union. But he was convinced that only the Christian tradition could provide the foundation for "the social unification that [Europe] so urgently needs."

We can well imagine what Dawson would have thought about the much-controverted question of whether the European Union's draft constitution should have included mention of Christianity. In fact, however, his vision of European union was not political at all. It would be not a "theocratic state" but rather "a spiritual community," whose centripetal energy "transcends the economic and political orders."[26] The thrust of Dawson's work, then, could hardly have been more different from that of

Butterfield's. Where the former stressed the inappropriateness of imposing ideas of progress upon accounts of political and social events, the latter sought to insist on the impossibility of properly understanding political and social events without reference to precisely such ideas. Where Butterfield saw little or no position of culture-forming influence for the historian, Dawson saw instead an enormous task and a vital role. Where Butterfield wanted to keep the eternal and the temporal separate, Dawson saw the West as precisely that part of the world, and the Western story as precisely that part of human history, in which those realms had been shown to intersect and in which the possibility of such separation had been decisively refuted. The Christian worship of the God-man, of "the Divine Humanity" expressed in the person of Christ, held the key to the reconciliation of opposites. "The Christian," said Dawson, "and he alone, can find a solution to the paradox of the inherence of eternity in time, and of the absolute in the finite, which does not empty human life and the material world of their religious significance and value."[27] There is an undeniable richness and suggestive depth to this analysis, even for the non-Christian historian. Dawson saw Christianity not merely as a set of doctrines or theological assertions, or a set of private individual desiderata, but even more as the foundational principle of a whole society, the organizing force of an entire way of life. We might classify his, then, as a foundational understanding of the relationship between religion and historical practice, and between religion and a society's view of the idea of progress.

Even if it could be demonstrated with Euclidean precision that all of human history so far had afforded not a single example of a vital culture that was not built around a religion, then who was to say that the time had not come when such an innovation would at last be possible, just as heart transplants and transatlantic flights and instantaneous global communications and other formerly unimaginable things were now possible? Why should historical precedent be taken to overmaster historical possibility? Secular modernity had never claimed to be able to justify itself by pointing to its long line of historical antecedents. Instead it was precisely its departure from that long line of antecedents that constituted its most powerful appeal. Why could not the overcoming of the need for religion be itself taken as a profound evidence of progress?

Was not Dawson's appeal to the functional role of religion, like all such arguments, subject to the complaint that it traded in the social usefulness of religion rather than its truth? Let us think of Christianity not principally as a potentially effective agent of cultural formation and a good way to organize and manage a culture, but more narrowly as a set of assertions about the nature of God and the nature of the world we live in. What was there in Dawson's argument as I have described it above that would suggest reasons why historic Christianity would be deserving of a fresh look from the secular world and another chance to be culturally dominant within it? It is one thing to argue that the Christian faith is socially beneficial and even intellectual and morally plausible, but quite another to argue that it is true. Unless men and women are convinced of the truth of the Christian faith, how can it have the culture-forming role that Dawson described—how can it even be a "religion" in Dawson's sense, that organizing force that constitutes a social world? To argue for the resurrection of religion because it is the dynamic core of the culture of the West and the proper partner for (and opposite number to) science is, at bottom, to make an argument from utility, from the standpoint of consequences rather than truth.

It is possible then that if the exclusionary stance claims too little, the foundational stance seeks too much—too much in the way it wishes to conjoin religion with the idea of progress, which of course for Dawson meant progress rightly understood. Instead of allowing us to draw freely upon religious perspectives for purposes of clarification and discernment, the foundational stance insists that the idea of progress can never again be understood properly unless it is once again seen through the eyes of the historical Christian faith—which for Dawson was inevitably the Roman Catholic faith, Protestantism having been for him ultimately a cause and symptom of the secularism of the present moment. In order to survive, the idea of progress would have to be reincorporated into a fundamentally religious worldview, and a particular one with a particular institutional grounding. This may well be the case, but it transposes the problem of the idea of progress into an entirely different key from the one with which we began. A problem of insight has been turned into a problem of faith.

Finally, like all declension narratives, which are, so to speak, the black sheep of the Whig narrative family, Dawson's account suffers from its tendentiousness, its tendency to preordain results and interpret decline as a result of a mistaken judgment or an intellectual or moral lapse, rather than as the result of a historical dynamic that may itself have an important place—even if only a provisional one, like a structure of temporary scaffolding—in the larger unfolding historical narrative. History is not just an unfolding Logos. It also is full of serendipities and contingencies and trivialities and unexpected finds, which often turn out to be matters of enormous consequence. It is in precisely such matters that Butterfield's epistemological modesty would seem likely to serve us better and equip us for fresh understanding. "Either Europe must abandon the Christian tradition and with it the faith in progress and humanity," Dawson sternly declared in the concluding pages of *Progress and Religion,* "or it must return consciously to the religious foundation on which these ideas were based." This foundation, he further insisted, "cannot be severed from historical religion and used as a substitute for it, as men have attempted to do during the last two centuries."[28] However, this challenging formulation, while undeniably powerful and thought-provoking, also begs the question of exactly what the "tradition" and the "historical religion" are and what it would mean to "return consciously" to them—matters about which there is notoriously little agreement even among Christians.

A third and rather different perspective on the subject comes from arguably the most prominent American public theologian of the twentieth century, Reinhold Niebuhr.

He enjoyed an unusually long and productive career, churning out innumerable books, articles, reviews, sermons, speeches, pamphlets, and other writings in the years between World War I and the Vietnam War. He was not merely a theologian and scholar of distinction but also a public intellectual of the first order who addressed himself to the full range of contemporary concerns. He had a mind of enormous scope and ambition, and there is hardly an issue of importance—political, social, economic, cultural, or spiritual—that he did not discuss in his many works.[29] His early formation was as a liberal Protestant of strongly progressive sympathies. Yet his explosive 1932 book *Moral Man and Immoral Society* was a salvo directed at progressivism's central belief in the malleability and perfectibility of human nature.[30] In so doing he established himself as one of America's most notable internal critics of American progressive thought, breaking thereby not only with such distinguished contemporaries as John Dewey but also with a long line of predecessors stretching back to the likes of Herbert Croly and Edward Bellamy. It became the burden of his career to present the Christian faith as the carrier of progressive ideals and as a tough-minded but essential corrective to them.

Born in 1891 in rural Missouri, he was the son of a German immigrant pastor affiliated with a tiny Protestant denomination known as the German Evangelical Synod. He inherited from his father a strong sense of theological vocation and a keen interest in social and political concerns. As a consequence of that influence as well as his two years at Yale Divinity School, Niebuhr began his career as a devotee of the Social Gospel, the movement within liberal Protestantism that located the Gospel's meaning in its promise as a blueprint for progressive social reform, rather than in its assertions about the nature of supernatural reality. Social Gospelers were modernists who played down the authority of the Bible and the historical creeds, insisting that the heart of the Christian Gospel should be understood symbolically and expressed in the language and practice of social reform. In Walter Rauschenbusch's words, "we have the possibility of so directing religious energy by scientific knowledge that a comprehensive and continuous reconstruction of social life in the name of God is within the bounds of human possibility." The Kingdom of God was not reserved for the beyond but rather could be created in the here and now by social scientists and ministers working hand in hand.[31] This sounded like the makings of an organizing spark, but Niebuhr soon grew impatient with it. He found the progressive optimism undergirding the Social Gospel to be naive about the intractable fallenness of human nature, and therefore inadequate to the task of explaining the nature of power relations in the real world. What Christianity called "sin" was not merely a by-product of bad but correctible social institutions. "Sin" identified something inherent in the human condition, some deep and uncorrectable disorder in the structure of the human soul, something social institutions could never completely reform. The doctrine of original sin was, at bottom, empirically valid simply because it reflected the observable truth about human behavior as it actually was and did so far better than any of the alternatives on offer. It required an enormous leap of faith to conclude that men are perfectible, while it requires only open eyes to conclude that they are perverse.

Nor did Niebuhr accept the belief of so many American progressives that the individual was improved and morally uplifted by being "socialized," by being incorporated into the moral solidarity of social groups and thereby lifted out of the moral anomie of individual self-seeking. In *Moral Man and Immoral Society*, Niebuhr turned the Social Gospelers' emphasis on its head, arguing that there was an inescapable disjuncture between the morality of individuals and the morality of groups, and that the latter was generally inferior to the former. Individuals could transcend their self-interest only rarely, but groups of individuals, especially groups as large as nation-states, almost never could.

In a word, he argued that groups generally made individuals morally worse rather than better, for the real glue that held human groups together was something more complicated than shared ideals. The larger the group, the greater the hypocrisy, the less genuine the altruism, and the less humane the moral outlook. This became particularly complicated in questions of the nation, where some of the most admirable sentiments may feed the most unworthy goals. "Patriotism," he observed, "transmutes individual unselfishness into national egoism" and grants the nation moral carte blanche to do as it wishes. "The unselfishness of individuals," he mused, "makes for the selfishness of nations." That is why the idea of solving the social problems of the world "merely by extending the social sympathies of individuals" was so completely vain.[32]

Thus Niebuhr dismissed as mere sentimentality the progressive hope that the sources of individual sin could be overcome through intelligent social reform, and that America could be transformed in time into a loving fellowship of like-minded comrades holding hands beside the national campfire. Such a dismissive view of his progressive contemporaries was, to be sure, something of a caricature and unfair exaggeration made for polemical effect.[33] But it served to provide an effective contrast to Niebuhr's own approach, which insisted relentlessly on the harsh and inescapable facts of fallen life.

These harsh facts, however, did not mean that Niebuhr gave up on the possibility of social reform and the possibility of progress. On the contrary. Christians were obliged to work actively for progressive causes and for the realization of social ideals of justice and righteousness. Fatalism and complacency were not allowed. But in doing so they had to abandon their illusions, not least in the way they thought about themselves. The pursuit of good ends in the arena of national and international politics had to take full and realistic account of the unloveliness of human nature and the unlovely nature of power. Christians who claimed to want to do good in those arenas could count on getting their hands soiled, for the pursuit of social righteousness would inexorably involve them in acts of sin and imperfection, not because the end justifies the means but because the fallenness of the world militates against the moral purity of any purposive action. Even the most surgical action creates collateral damage, the responsibility for which cannot be waved away.

However, the Christian faith just as inexorably called its adherents to a life of perfect righteousness, a calling that gives no ultimate moral quarter to dirty hands. The result would seem to be a stark contradiction, a call to do the impossible. Niebuhr insisted, though, that the Christian understanding of life embraced both parts of that formulation. Man is a sinner in his deepest nature. But man is also a splendidly endowed creature formed in God's image, still capable of acts of wisdom, generosity, and truth and still able to advance the cause of social improvement. All these assertions were true, in his view. All had an equivalent claim on the Christian mind and heart. In insisting upon such a tense, complex formulation, Niebuhr was correcting the idea of progress, but he was by no means abandoning it.

These ideas would continue to be developed in subsequent years. In his own Gifford Lectures of 1939, later published in two volumes as *The Nature and Destiny of Man* (1941–43), Niebuhr offered a magisterial *tour d'horizon* of the entirely intellectual and spiritual history of the West, and in the process he addressed more directly the idea of progress.[34] His vision there incorporated insights that were highly reminiscent of both Butterfield's and Dawson's perspectives but enmeshed in a pensive and self-critical view that was very much Niebuhr's own, and that we here will call the reflexive stance.

As Niebuhr saw it, the Christian worldview had always understood history to be meaningful, but with its meaning sometimes discovered inside the crosscurrents of history and sometimes entirely outside them, a fact that for him made the interpretation of history a hazardous but necessary undertaking. The secularized idea of progress, however, had as its guiding principle belief in an immanent Logos that was no longer regarded as transcendent but was thought of as operating in history, bringing its disorder gradually under the dominion of reason, making chaos into "cosmos." Like Dawson, he understood this idea of progress as having originated under the wing of Christian theology and eschatology; the very language was the biblical language of creation in Genesis and in the Gospel according to John. But the idea had been transformed and "liberated" during the Renaissance by two crucial post-Christian innovations, each of which discloses the emergence of a characteristic Niebuhrian theme.

First, this new understanding of progress presumed that "the fulfillment of life" could occur without the supernatural interventions of "grace" and that the laws of reason and nature would serve as "surrogates for providence," giving "meaning to all of history." As for the questions of power that were at the heart of *Moral Man and Immoral Society,* the new view simply did not take those questions to be important, precisely because it assumed that the Logos would "inevitably bring the vitalities of history under its dominion." Over and against the idea that the Fall had rendered all of reality and particularly human reality out of joint with itself and beyond the reach of natural or human rescue, the new understanding sought to render all of reality as one potentially harmonizable continuum.[35]

A second and related point was that the thinkers of the Renaissance, while coming to regard history as dynamic, failed to see that the dynamism of history was twofold in character and double-edged. It assumed, Niebuhr wrote, that "all development means the advancement of the good." However, in so assuming, it failed to recognize that "every heightened potency of human existence may also represent a possibility of evil." Here we return to one of the concerns with which we began, the sense that even a great progressive advance may contain within the potential for bringing about an equally great calamity. As Niebuhr explained it, everything that has its being within history is "involved, on every level of achievement, in contradiction to the eternal." This contradiction reflects the inevitable tendency of every comprehensive understanding of the meaning of history "to complete the system of meaning falsely" in a way that makes either the individual or the group "the premature centre, source, or end of the system."[36] All modern interpretations of history, Niebuhr thought, show this tendency; and here his words are strongly reminiscent of Butterfield's: "They identify their own age or culture, or even their own philosophy, with the final fulfillment of life and truth and history. This is the very error which they have not taken into account or discounted in their basic principle of interpretation." Niebuhr then goes on to add his characteristic reflexive dimension: "It is not possible for any philosophy to escape this error completely. But it is possible to have a philosophy, or at least a theology, grounded in faith, which understands that the error will be committed and that it is analogous to all those presumptions of history which defy the majesty of God."[37]

In short, for Niebuhr, modern interpreters of historical progress have been right in conceiving history dynamically and taking a broader and more generous view of history's fertile and various possibilities. But they have conceived the dynamic aspects of history too simply. "They hope for an ever increasing dominance of 'form' and 'order' over all historical vitalities," he charged, "and refuse to acknowledge that history cannot move forward towards increasing cosmos without developing possibilities of chaos by the very potencies which have enhanced cosmos."[38] In other words, we are never out of the woods, so to speak, and the danger only increases as we progress. Man's capacity for evil advances apace with his progress toward the good; hence the greater the progress, the greater the need for vigilance and the greater the need for some metaphysical check on human pride.

In *The Irony of American History* (1952), Niebuhr explored how this same tension manifested itself in a consideration of America's role in the world.[39] Published at the height of the cold war, *The Irony of American History* was a stinging attack on communism—and at the same time a stinging indictment of American moral complacency and a warning against the moral failings to which that complacency made America vulnerable. Once again Niebuhr was fighting on two fronts at once. Indeed, despite his passionate and unyielding opposition to the Communist cause, Niebuhr also believed that the United States resembled its antagonist more than it cared to imagine, and much of the book is devoted to making that case. Americans rightly complained of the Communists' dogmatic commitment to "philosophical material-ism," the notion that mind is the fruit of matter and culture the fruit of economics. But as Niebuhr pointed out, Americans could be said to be equally committed to materialism in practice. Here is a statement that rings even truer today than in 1952: "Despite the constant emphasis upon 'the dignity of man' in our own liberal culture," Niebuhr contended, "its predominant naturalistic bias frequently results in views of human nature in which the dignity of man is not very clear."[40] So, he believed, the nation needed to be more rigorously self-critical in its exercise of its power.

Niebuhr said something more. He added that America also had to act in the world and do so effectively. Indeed it had no choice but to do so. Just as the sinful and imperfect Christian is obliged to work intently for the cause of good, despite his in-capacities and imperfections, so a morally imperfect America was and is obliged to employ its power in the world. Opting out is not an option; or rather, it is an option that is just as morally perilous as the alternatives it would avoid. Niebuhr put it this way: "Our culture knows little of the use and abuse of power; but we [now] have to use power in global terms. Our idealists are divided between those who would renounce the responsibilities of power for the sake of preserving the purity of our soul and those who are ready to cover every ambiguity of good and evil in our actions by the frantic insistence that any measure taken in a good cause must be unequivocally virtuous."[41] Needless to say, Niebuhr rejected both of these options, which corre-spond roughly to attitudes of moralistic isolationism and amoral Realpolitik. He con-tinued thus: "We take, and must continue to take, morally hazardous actions to preserve our civilization. We must exercise our power. But we ought neither to believe that a nation is capable of perfect disinterestedness in its exercise, nor become com-placent about particular degrees of interest and passion which corrupt the justice whereby the exercise of power is legitimatized."[42]

Niebuhr concluded *The Irony of American History* by invoking the example of Abraham Lincoln, whose second inaugural address near the end of the Civil War exemplifies the doubleness of vision for which a Niebuhrian statesman should strive. Lincoln's great speech was notable for its unwillingness to demonize or diminish the soon-to-be-defeated enemy and for its tempering of moral resoluteness by a broadly religious sense of a larger, imponderable dimension to the struggle. "Both sides," Lincoln famously declared, "read the same Bible, and pray to the same God. . . . The prayers of both could not be answered; that of neither has been answered fully. The Almighty has His own purposes." The vantage point of a God who loves all his crea-tures was vastly greater than that envisioned by any fallible human cause.[43] Again one is reminded of the *humanitas* and humble restraint underlying the exclusionary his-toriographical stance of Herbert Butterfield. But it is also important to recognize that nothing in Lincoln's words suggested even a hint of faltering in the ultimate goal of destroying the Confederacy and reuniting the nation. Lincoln's awareness of the broader perspective invoked in his speech did not prevent him from taking strong action in the world based on his own ideas of what constituted progress. Yet the speech suggests not only Lincoln's great charity for the enemy but also his keen awareness of the arrogance, blindness, or triumphalism to which his own side was susceptible, flaws that might beget precisely the ironic effects that Niebuhr feared and deplored. This reflexiveness carries a price. Lincoln may not have been entirely innocent of such flaws, and the fact that his conduct of the war necessarily involved him in inflicting wounds that would be painfully slow to heal only underscores the truth of his words.

The combination of moral resoluteness about the immediate issues with a religious awareness of another dimension of meaning and judgment must be regarded as almost a perfect model of the difficult but not impossible task of remaining loyal and responsible toward the moral treasures of a free civilization while yet having some religious vantage point over the struggle.[44] There was no better example, Niebuhr thought, of the "dual aspect" to history's dynamism than the United States, where so many manifest strengths could also become dangerous weaknesses. America's "quest for happiness," he wrote, is suffused in irony precisely because it has been so triumphant. The United States "succeeded more obviously than any other nation in making life 'comfortable.'" But it has "tried too simply to make sense out of life, striving for harmonies between man and nature and man and society and man and his ultimate destiny, which have provisional but no ultimate validity." This has had an ironic result. "Our very success in this enterprise," he observed, "has hastened the exposure of its final limits."[45] The "naturalistic bias" that has produced a condition in which even the very genetic foundations of human personhood are increasingly viewed as malleable on the deepest level has indeed led to a view of human nature "in which the dignity of man is not very clear."

Niebuhr understood the doctrine of original sin—which he believed to be at the core of the Christian understanding of human nature, with its dualities and tensions—as central to American democracy. As he often said in various places and ways, man's capacity for goodness and justice makes democracy possible, and his susceptibility to sin and injustice makes democracy necessary. The tension between the two should be regarded as perpetual and mutually necessary, a perfect embodiment of the tense and necessary relationship between an optimistic idea of progress and a pessimistic view of human nature. The doctrine of original sin, while surely an enemy of Progress, is the best guarantor of the possibility of the marginal improvement of the human race, that is, progress rightly understood, since it offers us a truthful and realistic view of the crooked timber of humanity and prepares us rightly to live with a disjunction between the idea and the act, with the fact that we must strive, however imperfectly, for objectives whose fulfillment we may never see. "Nothing which is true or beautiful or good makes complete sense in any immediate context of history," wrote Niebuhr in *The Irony of American History;* "therefore we must be saved by faith."[46]

Of the three writers here under consideration, I suspect that Niebuhr may well be the one with the most to offer us in thinking about how a religious perspective can shed light on the present condition and future prospects of the idea of progress. His "reflexive" outlook takes account of the virtues of both Dawson's and Butterfield's works by acknowledging that the idea of progress is deeply rooted in the Christian Weltanschaauung and in Christian culture but also by insisting that the misuses of the idea, including the overconfident identification of man's purposes with God's, are paradigmatic examples of sin at work—and by insisting that the dynamic of progress in history, while genuine, is also by its very nature full of moral peril for us precisely because of the kind of beings we are.

Niebuhr's reflexive outlook also evades some of the defects in the other two authors' views. The exclusion of all moral or progressive criteria from the study of history, as Butterfield would seem to advocate, may be enormously enriching in the short term; however, in the longer run it robs us of the uses of history as a source of moral orientation, since God's intentions, which are the only sure source of ultimate truth, are seen to operate entirely outside of the patterns of historical perception and validation. Yet Dawson's identification of the dynamic of progress entirely with the vantage point of "historical and traditional Christianity" and his imagined telos of "spiritualization" that envisions the eventual transformation of man within history perhaps render history's meanings too immanent and thereby ask far too much of history, even as they fail to face up to the sheer incorrigibility of human nature. They perhaps fail to reverse the immanentizing of the eschaton that progressive secularism presumed.

Moreover Niebuhr's view does not require of us a conversion to Christianity but rather asks only that the Christian view of the human condition and of human nature be taken seriously as a model for ways of thinking about progress in history. He suggested that we distract ourselves and impoverish our potential self-understanding if we treat the doctrine of original sin strictly as a question of the historicity of the events related in the opening chapters of the book of Genesis. View it instead, he argued, as a quite accurate way of describing how people actually behave and have always behaved. Treated simply as a heuristic device, it may lead us far more fruitfully than psychologies that fail to connect our virtues and our vices quite so fully.[47] That original sin is for the individual, the "duality of history's dynamic" is for the idea of progress in history; the second is merely the amplification of the first. What the nineteenth century lacked was a sense of the perilousness of progress. We now understand the peril. We have "progressed" this far, to such a level of self-understanding. But now we risk being overwhelmed by that sense of peril. Having discovered that

Progress is not a god, we are now inclined to deny its existence entirely. This seems unwise and unserious, for we do still believe in progress in some form. What we need is a chastened but strengthened understanding of the idea of progress, and of the possibility of genuine human altruism, that has the capacity to hold together a strong sense of both the promise and the peril that our efforts in the world inevitably entail.

Such an understanding needs to put paid to the myths of human plasticity and begin with a subtler sense of what sorts of beings we are. It should affirm that we humans are creatures of enormous creativity and capacity for love and rational discernment and yet acknowledge that we are creatures harboring depths of utter perversity and wanton destructiveness, the kind of creatures who are capable of appallingly hard-hearted deafness to the anguish of others and who, for example, will spray paint graffiti on masterpieces and anonymously vandalize the computers of people we will never meet just for the sheer fun of it. It should recognize that both are always present possibilities.

Progress in history has turned from a complacent march into a tense tightrope walk. We can see now that every step we take not only carries us further along, which makes us proud, but also makes a possible fall more calamitous, which makes us terrified. We cannot afford to stop, but we also cannot afford to fall. So we must be careful where we step and how we step, and we must consider where we are going. To do so with the right set of expectations, it would help greatly to have a clearer and more realistic idea of just what kinds of strange and willful but also noble and imaginative creatures we humans are. Any idea of progress, secular or religious, that does not consider both will be of little help to us.

NOTES

1. Cf. the title essay in Perry Miller, *Errand into the Wilderness* (Cambridge, Mass.: Harvard University Press, 1956), 1–15: "If you read [the Puritan jeremiads] all through, the total effect, curiously enough, is not at all depressing: you come to the paradoxical realization that they do not bespeak a despairing frame of mind. There is something of a ritualistic incantation about them; whatever they may signify in the realm of theology, in that of psychology they are purgations of soul" (8–9).

2. Representative reflections on this issue include Philip Longman, *Empty Cradle: How Falling Birthrates Threaten World Prosperity and What to Do about It* (New York: Basic Books, 2004); George Weigel, *The Cube and the Cathedral: Europe, America, and Politics without God* (New York: Basic Books, 2005); and http://www.demographicwinter.com/ (accessed September 7, 2011).

3. This is a consistent theme of Philip Rieff, *The Triumph of the Therapeutic: Uses of Faith after Freud* (Chicago: University of Chicago Press, 1966); and *My Life among the Deathworks: Illustrations of the Aesthetics of Authority* (Charlottesville: University of Virginia Press, 2006).

4. Samuel Y. Edgerton Jr., *The Renaissance Rediscovery of Linear Perspective* (New York: Harper & Row, 1975), esp. 25–43.

5. Robert Nisbet, *History of the Idea of Progress* (New York: Basic Books, 1980).

6. Ibid., 352–57.

7. Quoted in Richard Wolin, "Jürgen Habermas and Post-Secular Societies," *Chronicle of Higher Education* (September 23, 2005): B16.

8. Ibid.; Joseph Cardinal Ratzinger and Jürgen Habermas, *Dialectics of Secularization: On Reason and Religion* (San Francisco: Ignatius Press, 2006).

9. For biographical and other insights, see C. T. McIntire, *Herbert Butterfield: Historian as Dissenter* (New Haven, Conn.: Yale University Press, 2004). Also extraordinarily valuable, particularly as a thorough meditation on Butterfield's view of Providence, is Keith C. Sewell, *Herbert Butterfield and the Interpretation of History* (Basingstoke, U.K.: Palgrave Macmillan, 2005).

10. The most readily available edition in the United States is Herbert Butterfield, *The Whig Interpretation of History* (New York: W. W. Norton, 1965), which follows pagination of the 1931 British edition exactly.

11. Ibid., v.

12. Ibid., 1–8.

13. Ibid., 129–32.

14. I am thinking here, for example, of the famous statement attributed to A. J. Ayer: "Theism is so confused and the sentences in which "God' appears so incoherent and so incapable of verifiability or falsifiability that to speak of belief or unbelief, faith or unfaith, is logically impossible," quoted in Karen Armstrong, *A History of God: The 4000-Year Quest of Judaism, Christianity, and Islam* (New York: Knopf, 1994), 379.

15. Herbert Butterfield, *Christianity and History* (New York: Scribner's, 1950). See, for example, his insightful discussion of the relationship between religion and history on pp. 1–8.

16. Biographical details are in Cristina Scott, *A Historian and His World: A Life of Christopher Dawson* (New Brunswick, N.J.: Transaction, 1991).

17. Christopher Dawson, *Religion and the Rise of Western Culture* (London: Sheed & Ward, 1950).

18. Christopher Dawson, *Progress and Religion: An Historical Enquiry* (London: Sheed & Ward, 1929); new American edition, with introduction by Mary Douglas (Washington, D.C.: Catholic University Press, 2001).

19. Ibid., 3. All references are to the 2001 edition of *Progress and Religion*

20. Ibid., 3–4.

21. Ibid., 140–58.

22. Ibid., 191.

23. Ibid., 188.

24. Ibid., 190.

25. Ibid., 192.

26. Ibid., 191–92.

27. Ibid., 189.

28. Ibid., 188.

29. For biographical details, see Richard Wightman Fox, *Reinhold Niebuhr: A Biography* (New York: Harper & Row, 1987); and Charles C. Brown, *Niebuhr and His Age: Reinhold Niebuhr's Prophetic Role and Legacy* (Harrisburg, Pa.: Trinity Press International, 2002). My own interpretation of Niebuhr's work, and particularly his book *The Irony of American History,* draws heavily on my essay "The Continuing Irony of American History," which appeared in *First Things,* no. 120 (February 2002): 20–25.

30. Reinhold Niebuhr, *Moral Man and Immoral Society: A Study in Ethics and Politics* (New York: Scribner's, 1932).

31. Walter Rauschenbusch, *Christianity and the Social Crisis* (New York: Macmillan, 1907), 209.

32. Ibid., 91.

33. Jon Roberts's essay in this volume strongly defends the very progressive and liberal outlooks that Niebuhr criticized while pointing out precisely the ways in which he was tendentious and unfair.

34. Reinhold Niebuhr, *The Nature and Destiny of Man,* 2 vols. (New York: Scribner's, 1941–43).

35. Ibid., 2: 165–66.

36. Ibid., 2: 166–67.

37. Ibid., 2: 167.

38. Ibid., 2: 168–69.

39. Reinhold Niebuhr, *The Irony of American History* (New York: Scribner's, 1952).

40. Ibid., 6.

41. Ibid., 5.

42. Ibid.

43. Ibid., 171.

44. Ibid., 172.

45. Ibid., 63.

46. Ibid.

47. An intriguing initial exploration of this very idea, using the conceptual framework of original sin as an anthropological principle, is George M. Marsden, "Human Depravity: A Neglected Explanatory Category," in *Figures in the Carpet: Finding the Human Person in the American Past,* ed. Wilfred M. McClay (Grand Rapids, Mich.: Eerdmans, 2007), 15–32.

IV

Moral Progress in Specific Christian Traditions

American Liberal Protestantism and the Concept of Progress, 1870–1930

JON H. ROBERTS

For too long students of American religious thought have tended to interpret the perspectives of liberal Protestants with regard to human nature, human history, and the prospects of realizing the Kingdom of God from the perspective of some of liberalism's harshest critics.[1] During the late 1920s and 1930s partisans of neoorthodoxy chastised liberal Protestantism for its naive view of human nature, its uncritical embrace of the reigning culture, and its shallow, overly optimistic view of progress.[2] Since that time numerous historians have echoed that view. To be sure some have attempted to provide a more balanced perspective. In 1963, for example, William R. Hutchison demonstrated the existence of "a vital and articulate tradition of liberal self-criticism" throughout the period after World War I, and he urged readers to approach liberal Protestants "with a minimum of preconceptions about what these people are supposed to have believed."[3] For the most part, however, historians have tended to ignore Hutchison's cautionary admonitions in favor of castigating American liberal Protestants as naive partisans of a facile culture-religion. T. J. Jackson Lears, for example, asserted that liberal Protestantism "signalled the submergence of religion in secular modes of thought."[4] Protestant liberalism, Lears contended, was characterized by a "pattern of evasive banality" that "came to terms with modernity by denying its darker side."[5] James R. Moore has concluded that liberals "adulterated Darwinism with the concept of inevitable material, social, and spiritual progress."[6] Eugene McCarraher has written dismissively of the "bland Esperanto of liberal Protestantism."[7] Gary Dorrien, the author of a well-received three-volume study of the history of American liberal Protestantism, has suggested, "The rationale for not taking sin realistically was built into liberal rhetoric about it from the beginning."[8] Liberals, Dorrien declared, "only belatedly" called into question "whether they had granted too much authority to modern culture."[9]

There is no question that liberal Protestants in the United States adopted more positive and optimistic views of human nature and human society than did the more theologically conservative Christians with whom they were contending. This does not mean, however, that they were endorsing an undiscriminating program of cultural assimilation. As a number of historians have discerned, one way of approaching the question of whether American liberal Protestants provided a perspective on the human condition that differed not only from that of conservatives but also from that of more secular thinkers is to examine the way in which they thought about the concept of progress. In this essay I hope to disclose what we might call the "morphology" of the liberal Protestant concept of progress and to describe the conditions under which proponents/exponents of that concept believed that progress was able to occur. The chronological framework for my analysis is the period between 1870 and 1930. This period, which marked the high point of the liberal tradition within American Protestantism, is admittedly a rather extensive slice of time, but this problem is mitigated by the fact that my interpretation emphasizes continuity rather than change. I reject, for example, the notion that World War I occasioned a significant change in the way that American liberal Protestants thought about progress. I should also note that I have limited my discussion to partisans of "mainstream" Protestant liberalism—to those liberals who made a conscious effort to associate their views with Christian tradition. I have not discussed the work of "modernists" who were less intent on remaining gospel-centered than on embracing modernity and more wedded to an empirical approach to religion that veered quite noticeably in the direction of naturalism.[10] In addition I have sought to allow liberal Protestants to speak for themselves about God, human nature, and prospects for progress as much as possible in the hopes of disclosing their principal rhetorical gestures and argumentative strategies.

There was little in the inception of the liberal Protestant theology emerging in the United States during the course of the 1870s that suggested either a jaunty self-confidence or a commitment to secular perspectives. It is true that partisans of the "New Theology" were sufficiently confident about contemporary developments and their relation to Christianity to dissent from traditional formulations of Christian theology. Much of the intellectual energy galvanizing their work, however, was generated by an undercurrent of anxiety that advances in humanity's understanding of the natural world and human history posed a serious challenge to the credibility of Christianity.[11] Convinced that "a full adjustment between reason and Christianity is steadily to be sought" and that "the total thought of an age ought to have the greatest possible unity," partisans of the New Theology took the position that theological reconstruction to bring Christian doctrinal formulations in line with the conclusions of modern science and historical scholarship was imperative.[12] In turn their conviction that theological change was needed in their own day lent credence to the idea that Christians must continually be prepared to alter doctrines in response to the broader experience of humanity. That idea became a defining motif of American liberal theology in the period after 1870.[13]

The conviction that it is necessary to integrate Christian theology within the larger culture was one of the impulses that most clearly set liberals apart from more conservative Protestants. Conservatives held that a merciful God had provided an ignorant and sinful humanity with a clear, comprehensive, and inerrant guide to salvation in the Scriptures. The use of "commonsense principles" in interpreting the scriptural text, they maintained, would yield truth concerning the fundamental elements of God's scheme of redemption. From this perspective conservative Protestants denied that progress in theological understanding was a reasonable expectation. Luther Tracy Townsend, a Methodist theologian at Boston University, thus held that "science, philosophy, archaeology, and all the correlated sciences, have added not one new fundamental truth to our theological knowledge, and have changed nothing."[14] In justifying this claim, Townsend asserted that "the writers of the Bible advanced so far into the field of pure theology, and revealed so much, that, from the nature of the case, theology cannot discover an essentially new truth, and cannot in this respect be a progressive science."[15] This perspective encouraged many conservatives to interpret theological change as a movement away from truth. Stuart Robinson, pastor of the Second Presbyterian Church in Louisville, Kentucky, thus suggested that "while secular science must grow up slowly from ignorance to perfectness, the science of theology starts from infallible revealed truth at first, and its changes as it passes through the hands of fallible men are generally in the direction of corruption."[16]

Although partisans of the New Theology and the numerous mainstream liberals who succeeded them joined conservatives in closely associating the process of understanding the nature of the encounter between God and human beings with the idea of divine revelation, their view of both the sources and the dynamics of that revelation was predicated on ideas concerning the nature of both God and human nature that differed dramatically from the views of conservative Protestants. In their discussions of the nature of God, for example, liberals joined other Christians in emphasizing the need to employ the terms "transcendence" and "immanence" alike in describing the relationship between God and the spatio-temporal order, but they placed much greater emphasis than did conservatives and most other Christians prior to 1870 on the doctrine of divine immanence. This emphasis was the product of several considerations that played a special role in the liberal worldview. For one thing, liberals recognized that an ever-growing number of phenomena that had once been ascribed to divine supernatural intervention were now described in terms of natural processes. This prompted them to abandon the idea of a sharp dichotomy between the natural and the supernatural and to insist that natural processes simply described the ways in which an immanent Deity chose to act. In fact it was not at all uncommon within liberal Protestant circles during the late nineteenth and early twentieth centuries for theologians, clergy, and even scientists to maintain that beyond the realm of human activity, the actual source of all causal efficacy was God. From this perspective, they reasoned, as the Andover theologian Francis Howe Johnson put it, "the agency of God in creation can never be negatived, or obscured, but only more clearly revealed, by the unveiling of the processes by which He works."[17]

Commitment to the doctrine of divine immanence also manifested itself in liberals' discussions of the encounters between God and human beings. In discussing past encounters, liberals gave special emphasis to the ongoing interaction of God with humanity that had long played a central role within the Christian worldview. Convinced that "history is neither conceivable nor realizable without the divine," they affirmed the presence of "Deity indwelling in the historical process."[18] "All History, rightly understood," an Episcopalian clergyman with liberal inclinations wrote in 1890, "is also a Bible" in the sense that "its lessons are God's divine methods of slowly exposing error and of guiding into truth."[19]

In contrast to secular thinkers, liberal Christians embraced a teleological view of historical process. To be sure, liberals acknowledged, even emphasized, the important role that contingency played in history and the ability of human beings to frustrate God's purposes. Nevertheless they were convinced that the process of historical development disclosed the gradual unfolding of a divine plan for the redemption of humanity. The preeminent evidence for the existence of such a plan, they maintained, was Jesus, "the highest expression of the mind and heart of the Infinite in reference to man."[20] In 1879 Newman Smyth, a clergyman who was forthright in his support for the New Theology, described Jesus as "the most perfect possible impartation and revelation in human form of the very life of God with the world and in the world."[21] William Newton Clarke, a Colgate theologian who in 1898 published the first systematic treatment of the New Theology, agreed, declaring that "God's richest, most spiritual, and most effective self-expression to men was made in Christ,—in what he was, in what he said and did, and in the fact that God gave him to the world."[22] For most liberals, the ongoing encounter that had taken place between an immanent Deity and humankind in the past served as suggestive evidence that God continued to interact with human beings through the medium of religious experience.[23] That view prompted a professor at Union Theological Seminary to reason that "as God is immanent in the life of man[,] divine revelation comes from within, not from without. The religious man looks into his own experience for the disclosure of divine truth."[24] Indeed the idea that religious experience disclosed through the "Christian consciousness" served to validate doctrines and provide the basis for the "theology of any age" became one of the reigning tenets of American liberal theology.[25]

The emphasis that liberals gave to the idea that God played an active, even pervasive, role within the created order had the effect of broadening their conception of the nature of revelation. To be sure, they continued to affirm that "the Bible gives the theologian materials for his science."[26] They coupled that affirmation, however, with the insistence that all aspects of human experience, not merely the Scriptures, should be seen as sources of divine revelation.[27] Alexander V. G. Allen, a professor of church history at the Episcopalian Theological School in Cambridge, Massachusetts, gave voice in 1882 to a view that became increasingly common among liberals when he declared that the doctrine of divine immanence "has given a new meaning and value to outward nature, and it has lent sanctity to all that concerns man in his history and development."[28] Because the Bible served as a unique repository of truths relating to the life and teachings of Jesus, most liberal Protestants continued to view it as a "unique book, uniquely precious" as a source of revelation.[29] If, however, most liberal Protestants did not entirely abandon Protestantism's traditional claim that the Bible constituted a unique source of authority, they nevertheless felt compelled to emphasize as never before the value of nature, history, and contemporary religious experience as vehicles of God's revelation to humanity.[30] In the wake of this more comprehensive view of divine revelation, the boundary between the "sacred" and the "secular" inevitably became less rigid.[31]

In thus calling attention to the ubiquitous activity of God in nature, history, and the religious experience of contemporary Christians, liberal Protestants were affirming that sources of divine revelation existed that supplemented the Word of God found within the pages of the Bible. No less important, they were also expressing their view that interaction between God and the created order was dynamic rather than static. Revelation was therefore not to be thought of as a fixed entity; rather it was an ongoing process.[32] Just as important, liberals emphasized that humanity's apprehension of spiritual truth also underwent significant change.[33] Even the Scriptures themselves, the prominent liberal clergyman Lyman Abbott suggested, could best be understood as a historical record "of the growth of man's consciousness of God."[34] From this perspective liberals reasoned that theological change was inevitable. Doctrinal reconstruction would be necessary for as long as God continued to provide human beings with fresh sources of insight. "Theologizing," the Andover Seminary professor George Harris declared, "must always go on."[35]

In principle the claim that time and place played important roles in determining the nature of theological affirmations might have led liberal Protestants to embrace a view of religious truth that was both relativistic and culture-bound. Liberals emphasized, however, the existence of religious absolutes. The most important of these were truths disclosed through the teachings, person, and religion of Jesus. In Jesus, liberals believed, one encountered "the heart of what we call the Christian revelation."[36] That conviction prompted them to insist that, as Charles Augustus Briggs, a biblical critic who became militant in his support of a number of liberal theological perspectives, put it, "a Christian man must follow His teachings in all things as the guide to all truth."[37] A similar view prompted a Connecticut liberal clergyman to assert that "no matter to what heights reason may climb, no matter to what culture the human spirit may attain, Christ as the culmination, the fullness of the divine Word set forth in the Scriptures, will still be far on, infinitely above all human achievement, the glorious and ever-living Word. And He, as found in the Scriptures, and as apprehended and interpreted by the common Christian consciousness of each successive age, will be, as He should be, the *ultimate* criterion of all truth."[38]

The life and teachings of Jesus were not the only elements in Christian theology that endured the vicissitudes of cultural change; there were other "abiding truths" fundamental to the scheme of redemption.[39] Liberals maintained that the task of theologians in each generation was to impart those truths through the use of terminology and concepts that accurately reflected the experience of their age.[40] The very logic of the idea that periodic doctrinal reformulation would be necessary in order to respond to ongoing changes in divine revelation and human understanding necessarily impelled the proponents of liberal theology to resist dogmatizing about which Christian beliefs would ultimately survive the winnowing effect of cultural change. This did not prevent most liberals from assuming, however, that such fundamental elements of the Christian worldview as the existence and personality of God, the special status of human nature, the reality of divine creation, and the central importance of the drama of salvation within human history would remain secure from alterations occasioned by new insight.[41] That assumption reflected the effort of liberal Protestants to retain what they viewed as essential truths of the Christian tradition even while expressing those truths in the language of contemporary modes of thought. That assumption, when it found expression in their insistence that abiding truths existed, helped to shield them from the charge that they had utterly abandoned a commitment to absolutes.

Even if their confidence that the life and teachings of Jesus and other truths would survive all challenges is acknowledged, however, it is still the case that most liberal Protestant thinkers in the United States who discussed the nature of theology placed at least as much emphasis on change as on stability. Indeed this is a major reason why many liberals were decidedly unenthusiastic about the idea of formulating creeds. It is not that liberals were indifferent to theology or even to doctrine; on the contrary they acknowledged that theology was "a direct and legitimate outgrowth of Christianity."[42] Their consciousness of the need to be able to adjust doctrinal formulations to new advances in knowledge and understanding, however, made them skittish about "bring[ing] the whole truth of the Faith within the bounds of a system."[43] It is therefore not surprising that the first systematic exposition of theology from the perspective of the liberalism that had emerged after 1870 did not appear until almost the very end of the nineteenth century, when William Newton Clarke published *An Outline of Christian Theology* (1898). Even Clarke was at pains to emphasize that "the danger of over-systematizing in theology is a serious one, and is ever present," at least in part because "present forms of doctrine cannot be final, any more than were those that went before."[44] Human experience, which served as the data for theological reflection, was by its very nature a function of time and space. Hence, while their possession of the life and teachings of Jesus gave Christians reason to believe that

Christianity was the "final religion," this did not prevent them from asserting that "absoluteness and finality," as one Andover Seminary professor put it, "do not belong to Christian theology."[45]

The emphasis that liberal Protestants gave to the idea that theology was in "constant need of readjustment" implied that like other realms of understanding, it remained "very incomplete and fragmentary in its knowledge of facts and laws, very uncertain and liable to change in its speculations and theories."[46] Notwithstanding that view, partisans of the liberal theological perspective remained optimistic that the outcome of theological reformulation promised to bear rich fruit, for their understanding of both the nature of divine revelation as an ongoing divine activity and the history of humanity's gradually increasing understanding of that revelation convinced them that "there is a widening comprehension of Christianity through the ages."[47] Within the nineteenth century alone, one proponent of the New Theology pointed out, "improved scientific and historical methods of inquiry" had led to "great and gratifying progress" in theological discourse.[48] George Trumbull Ladd, a clergyman who went on to become a professor of philosophy and psychology at Yale, gave voice to an idea that was commonly held by liberal Protestants when he suggested that since "theology is a science with all the characteristics which belong to the conception of a science," humanity's understanding of religious truth is "inherently progressive."[49] Indeed, Ladd asserted, "this conception of theology as a progressive science underlies our statement of the possibility of a new theology."[50] Although liberals resisted the temptation to equate each instance of theological change with an increase in spiritual insight, they were inclined to regard the failure to recognize that progress had been made in apprehending spiritual truth as tantamount to an unwillingness to acknowledge God's interest in the outcome of human history. After all, they asserted, progress in theological understanding was at least partly the result "of the presence and energy within the church of the promised Spirit of truth."[51]

Many liberals inferred from their examination of modern historical scholarship and scientific inquiry alike that gradual development constituted the means God had consistently chosen to accomplish divine ends.[52] Theodore T. Munger, for example, declared in 1886 that "unity exists not only because one God created all things, but because He works by one process, or according to one principle. As knowledge broadens and wider generalizations are made, we find a certain likeness of process in all realms that indicates one law or method; namely, that of development or evolution."[53] That method, Munger asserted, had led to the emergence of ever "finer and higher forms."[54] For the numerous liberals who shared Munger's progressive interpretation of the evolutionary process, it seemed quite reasonable to affirm that "in some important respects the gospel is better understood now than it ever has been before."[55] No less important, past experience strongly suggested that "all of revelation that has gone before is but as seed for the future."[56] Christianity was by its very nature, William Adams Brown maintained, "a progressive religion."[57]

The claim that theology was a progressive enterprise can be viewed as a kind of intellectual compensation for liberal Protestants' acknowledgment of the impossibility of arriving at final and complete understanding of Christian doctrine. Some indication of the importance of such compensation can be inferred from the fact that many partisans of the New Theology identified their position as "Progressive Orthodoxy." The Union Theological Seminary professor Arthur Cushman McGiffert provided the appropriate juxtaposition of the lack of finality with progress in the realm of theology when he observed in 1915, "We expect our children to look back, perhaps with tolerant amusement, at much that we have held most dear, or have most plumed ourselves upon. We not only expect it but we rejoice in it, for we no longer think that we are in possession of absolute truth and final wisdom. We count confidently upon their knowing and doing more and better than we have known and done. For this belief in evolution is no mere conviction that change, not fixity, is the rule of existence. It does not substitute a new chaos for the old cosmos. It assumes not a meaningless flux of advancing and receding forces, but progress, in some degree at least, definite and constant."[58] The belief that the essential elements of the divine-human encounter had become more clearly understood over time provided liberal Protestants with another bulwark against the idea that theological revision could be interpreted as a purely relativistic undertaking.

Historians and theologians who have called attention to liberal Protestantism's allegiance to the larger culture clearly have a point. Liberals were convinced that in an era of unbelief and growing indifference to the Christian Gospel, it was incumbent on those who remained loyal to that Gospel to demonstrate its power and its credibility to people of their generation. In taking on that task, liberal apologists believed that a "sympathetic knowledge" of the dominant characteristics of their age became an essential prerequisite.[59] It thus seemed clear, as Lewis French Stearns put it, that "each period must draw the material of its theology out of its own profound convictions, mold it by its own intellect, and utter it in its own words."[60]

That prescription did not imply, as critics have frequently charged, that liberals were guilty of an overweening preoccupation with cultural assimilationism. On the contrary the allegiance of most of them to the zeitgeist was sharply circumscribed. The same apologetic impulse that convinced them of the need to formulate theology in ways that would bring it into accord with the latest knowledge and insights available to them also led most of them to emphasize the importance not of embracing the secularization of the sacred but of sacralizing the secular in an effort to bring "the kingdoms of this world" within "the kingdom of the Lord Jesus Christ."[61] That emphasis reflected the conviction of most liberal Protestants that the reconstruction of theology, however laudable, was simply a means to the larger end of redeeming individuals and society. Progress in understanding religious truth meant little if it did not lead to regeneration.

The way in which liberal Protestants in the United States thought about the spiritual prospects of humanity reflected their resolutely teleological view of natural and human history. That view prompted them to interpret evolution as a progressive and purposeful process. Like more conservative Christians, liberal Protestants tended to assume that the chief value of the natural world was that it served as the stage on which the drama of salvation was performed.[62] But in contrast to more conservative Christians, who opposed the transmutation hypothesis at least in part because they believed that it devalued human beings, liberals were convinced that the evolutionary process should be seen as the means that a providential Deity had employed in bringing about the emergence of "man, the crown of creation."[63] No less important, they held that the appearance of a species endowed with attributes conferring on members of that species a special relationship with the Creator marked a crucially significant and fundamentally new departure in the history of the cosmos.[64] The "main current" of the evolutionary process now centered on "the realm of mental and moral forces" and was oriented toward generating the "completed free individual."[65]

Although liberals commonly interpreted the evolutionary process in anthropocentric terms, most of them were more intent on affirming the unique nature and privileged status of human beings than on discussing the specific means that God had employed in creating them. Still the sustained discussion and sometimes heated debate over the validity of the theory of organic evolution did prove useful, for it impelled liberals to devote sustained attention to issues relating to the nature and status of humankind and the place of humanity within the overall scheme of things. In addressing those issues, liberals continued to place great emphasis on the scriptural affirmation that human beings had been created in God's image. That affirmation, which had long played a prominent role in Christian tradition, grounded a number of convictions that were of central importance within liberal theology. For one thing, it served as the springboard from which Christians made a number of important affirmations about the nature of God. Lewis French Stearns, a theologian at the Congregational seminary in Bangor, Maine, inferred from the idea that human beings had been created in God's image that they are "in finiteness what God is in infinitude." Hence, he asserted, "we can know God only through man."[66] That conviction proved especially important in lending credibility to the doctrine of a personal God, a doctrine that had come under heavy fire from scientific naturalists, Spencerians, and others who rejected the attribution of personality to God. Liberals believed that the natural world provided data attesting to many of the attributes of its Creator, but in establishing "the personality of Deity," they asserted, it was necessary to look to "our own consciousness."[67]

If liberals valued the doctrine that human beings had been created in God's image for its usefulness in justifying the acceptance of important assertions about the nature of God, they also held that the doctrine yielded important information about human nature. Noting that the basis of the "principle of revelation" is "that one mind is made in the image of the other, and therefore capable of similar processes of thought and feeling," liberals concluded that the fact that members of the human species bore God's image was precisely what enabled them to apprehend "the deepest and truest revelations of God."[68] More broadly the idea that human beings had been created in the image of God grounded the conviction of American liberal Protestants that they possessed an "inherent sanctity" and a unique redemptive relationship with the Creator.[69] Convinced that just "as every true conception of God must be in a sense anthropomorphic, so every true conception of man must be in a sense theomorphic," Stearns concluded that the special ontological relationship existing between God and humanity entitles human beings to "participate in the divine eternity."[70] More succinctly George Harris declared that "all arguments for immortality are eventually reduced to this one argument of kinship with God."[71]

Implicit in affirmations of humanity's kinship with the Creator was the question of which particular attributes human beings possessed that reflected the image of God. In addressing that question, liberal Protestants joined with other Christians in concluding that the elements of human nature that "resemble and reflect divinity, and indicate our celestial origin" were the mental faculties—faculties that were variously described as self-consciousness, intelligence, imagination, memory, feelings, will, and the capacity for moral impulses.[72] The term that liberals typically used in describing those attributes of mind was "personality." Indeed during the period between 1870 and 1930 that term became one of the most revered and frequently used in the lexicon of liberal Protestant theology.[73] Proponents were quick to use "personality" to describe God, human beings, and the special relationship that those spiritual beings maintained with each other.

The well-known clergyman George A. Gordon, noting that a theistic interpretation of reality was predicated on the idea that human minds encountered the divine mind in both the physical and the moral universe, gave a sense of the centrality of the concept of personality within liberal cosmology when he declared in 1908 that theism could be viewed as an interpretation of the cosmos in accordance with the principle of personality.[74] William Newton Clarke suggested that "complete personality exists in God alone."[75] William Adams Brown, Roosevelt Professor of Systematic Theology at Union Theological Seminary and author of an influential summary of Christian thought from a liberal perspective, associated the claim that "God is spirit" with the idea that the Deity "is moral personality, having reason, conscience and freedom."[76] The conviction that personality should be seen as "the crowning attribute of man" played an equally important role in shaping liberal Protestants' approach to human nature.[77] Those Christians rejected the views of more secularly inclined progressives who found nothing wrong with treating human beings as manipulable objects, for they regarded personality as sacred—indeed the most sacred element within the created order.[78] William Newton Clarke, for example, suggested that as the spiritual element within human nature that bears the "image or likeness of God," personality should be regarded as "the goal and crown of the evolution of the race."[79] Harry Emerson Fosdick, the best-known liberal clergyman in the United States between the two world wars, regarded the high value that Jesus placed on personality as "his most original contribution to human thought."[80] Indeed, Fosdick held that belief in the "divine origin, spiritual nature, infinite worth, and endless possibilities" of personalities constituted the very essence of the Gospel.[81] "Take it or leave it," Fosdick declared in one of many passages that he wrote on the subject, "that is what Christianity is about. That is its guiding star and its dynamic faith. Personality, the most valuable thing in the universe, revealing the real nature of the Creative Power and the ultimate meaning of creation, the only eternal element in a world of change, the one thing worth investing everything in, and in terms of service to which all else must be judged—that is the essential Christian creed."[82]

During the period between 1870 and 1930 liberal Protestants extolled the Christian Gospel not only for affirming the infinite value of human personality but also for providing human beings with the resources needed to develop personality's full potential. One of the quarrels that proponents of liberal theology had with the theological formulations embraced by more orthodox Christians was that they seemed to lack what Shailer Mathews described as "a regenerating power in the modern world."[83] In contrast to the numerous secular liberals, who frequently envisioned human fulfillment as the product of "socialization" and "acculturation," liberal Protestants emphasized the need for the kind of "self-transcendence" that could occur only in response to the "moral and religious experience of the power of the gospel."[84] Fosdick, for example, asserted, "The deepest elements in human personality are truncated and incomplete until they have expanded into religion."[85]

Like most other Protestants, liberals maintained that God initiates the process that culminates in salvation. The liberal exposition of divine grace centered on the idea that human nature "has been vitiated by sin" and "thus rendered incapable, without a radical change in character, of ever coming to perfection."[86] The initiative for that "radical change of character" came from an immanent Deity acting primarily through the person and teachings of Jesus to enable humans who were willing to open their hearts to experience a "new birth," forsake sin, and achieve redemption.[87]

In describing this process of salvation, liberal Protestants emphasized several often-overlapping themes. Many inferred from their conviction that an intimate association existed between religion and morality that Christian life involved a process of moral development initiated by and ultimately the product of an encounter with the life and precepts of Jesus. Acting in response to that encounter, individuals began their pilgrimage with "a sense of the reality of sin," then moved on to repentance, and ultimately underwent a "moral transformation" that enabled them to approach "a new ideal, that of the character of Jesus."[88] Walter Rauschenbusch suggested that "the creation of re-generate personalities, pledged to righteousness, is one of the most important services which the church can render to social progress."[89]

In view of the emphasis given by liberal Protestants to the idea that human beings had been made in the image of God, it is not surprising that they concluded that "the divine standard of character must be accepted as our standard."[90] In practice, the way that human beings could most effectively "enter into the perfection of their Father in Heaven," liberals maintained, was through the "imitation of Christ."[91]

By the early twentieth century, although liberal Protestants continued to stress the moral value of religion, their increasing allegiance to the idea that the "final test" of any worldview was its ability to minister to human needs prompted many of them to take the view that imitation of Christ would yield much more than character development.[92] By providing human beings with "the most glorious interpretation of life's meaning that the sons of men have ever had," the life and teachings of Jesus enabled individuals who embraced them to acquire "the fruit of the Spirit—love, joy, peace, long-suffering, kindness, goodness, faithfulness, meekness, self-control."[93] In other words commitment to the Gospel, with "its insight into life's meanings, its control over life's use, its inward power for life's moral purposes," had the effect of conferring on individuals a "fresh influx of inward power" that resulted in "transformed and tri-umphant" personalities.[94]

At the end of the day, however, while liberals were certainly intent on touting the "therapeutic" advantages of religion, they also made a point of closely relating accept-ance of the Gospel to humanity's encounter with the divine. An appreciation of the life and work of Jesus—"humanity's consummate flower" and the "perfect reli-gious personality"—inevitably "brings us back to God" by enabling human beings to ascend the realm of the flesh "into the region of the spirit." For liberal Protestants, that ascension constituted redemption.[95]

If belief in the sacredness of personality provided the framework for liberal Protes-tant discussions of the importance of the Christian Gospel, it also served as the underlying rationale for liberal Protestant discussions of the need to "Christianize" the social order. Henry Churchill King, a theologian who served as the president of Oberlin College, recognized this when in 1901 he credited "the growing sense of the worth of personality, helped particularly by the immensely deepened knowledge of 'the other half,'" with developing "the *social conscience* of our time."[96] By the last decade of the nineteenth century the work of social scientists, coupled with interac-tions between liberal clergy and their parishioners, had convinced many proponents of liberal theology in the United States of the plasticity of human nature and the salience of social interaction in shaping human personality.[97] From this perspective those Christians concluded that the dislocations attending the development of indus-trial capitalism did not simply represent a social problem; they also threatened the spiritual development of multitudes of individuals who lived in oppressive social environments. It seemed increasingly obvious to liberals who thought in those terms that the only way to give God a "fair chance" to redeem those individuals was to alter those environments.[98] The numerous liberals who committed themselves to a set of ideas that came to be known as the "Social Gospel" typically described that project of environmental reform in terms of working toward the establishment of the "Kingdom of God."[99]

A sustained treatment of the Social Gospel lies beyond the scope of this essay. For our purposes it will perhaps be sufficient to emphasize two points. First, partisans of the Social Gospel were convinced that Christianity constituted the essential agent in generating the inspiration and the courage to undertake the reformation of society. Noting that important alterations of society required "the high elation and faith that come through religion," Walter Rauschenbusch maintained that it was imperative that Christianity "now add its moral force" to the other elements in society that were "making for a nobler organization of society."[100] What gave Rauschenbusch special reason to hope for success in the efforts of Christians to promote social justice was his conviction that "for the first time in religious history we have the possibility of so directing religious energy by scientific knowledge that a comprehensive and continuous reconstruction of social life in the name of God is within the bounds of human possibility."[101] Second, the logic of the Social Gospel discouraged its proponents from making sharp distinctions between the regeneration of individuals and the promotion of a more just and loving social order. Washington Gladden, sometimes referred to as the father of the Social Gospel, expressed a view that was commonly held by liberal Protestants eager to promote the Kingdom of God when he declared that "the end of Christianity is twofold, a perfect man in a perfect society."[102]

In attempting to accomplish that end, however, liberals made it clear that they valued the reformation of social structures and institutions primarily because they believed this would, in Rauschenbusch's words, "guarantee to all personalities their freest and highest development."[103] Indeed the intimate connection between social reform and the redemption of individual personality was a constant theme of liberal Protestant discourse in the period between about 1890 and 1930. Harry Emerson Fosdick, for example, held that the "attitude of Jesus toward personality"—the conviction of Jesus "that there are extraordinary possibilities in ordinary people and that if the doors of opportunity are thrown open wide enough surprising consequences will come from unlikely sources"—constituted "one of the major springs of Western democracy."[104] In turn the "development of democracy," wrote Harry F. Ward, a professor of Christian ethics at Union Theological Seminary, in 1919, should be seen as "a process of the continued emancipation and expansion of personality."[105]

Not surprisingly, because they evaluated life in terms of the sanctity of personality, liberal Protestants proved to be relatively indifferent to conceptions of the material advancement of society that were central to more secular conceptions of progress. Liberals, in fact, were convinced that the "profound need for a spiritual interpretation of life was not "satisfied" by such conceptions.[106] Rather they tended to view redemption as the appropriate criterion for evaluating the progress of individuals and the establishment of the Kingdom of God as the appropriate yardstick for measuring social progress. The creation of a "spiritual society . . . in which love shall be the bond of union, and humility the test of greatness," not the promotion of prosperity, was their ultimate goal.[107]

Liberal Protestants commonly maintained that an examination of human history disclosed a great deal of progress in the success of the Gospel in bringing about the redemption of individuals and the larger society. In 1895, for example, Washington Gladden wrote exuberantly that "the thought of the world is gradually being freed from superstition and prejudice; the social sentiments are being purified; the customs are slowly changing for the better; the laws are gradually shaped by finer conceptions of justice. There are reactions and disasters, but taking the ages together the progress is sure."[108] A few years later George A. Gordon echoed this remark but put an even more explicitly Christocentric spin on it when he suggested that "upon the whole, and over the wide expanse of time, the historic movement is slowly but surely away from the brute, and upward to the attainment of manhood according to the measure of the stature of Christ."[109] Gordon asserted, "The depths that have been left behind and the heights that have been gained fill the mind with amazement."[110] Examining more recent history, Harry Emerson Fosdick declared in 1922 that Christianity had probably made more progress in the previous half century than at any time in all of its history.[111]

One explanation for the splendid record of spiritual progress, liberals maintained, could be found within human nature. In contrast to Christians who emphasized human depravity, partisans of Progressive Orthodoxy and their successors maintained that human nature "is adapted to realize the Christian end."[112] Convinced that "man was created as the child of God, and the sonship that was established by the creative act could never be destroyed," liberals reasoned that while sin served to alienate human beings from God, "in regeneration the Father touches one who never ceased to be his offspring."[113]

In the final analysis, however, those liberals recognized that human beings were dependent for their very existence, as well as for their place within the scheme of redemption, on the will of a divine Creator. That recognition prompted them to acknowledge that "the spring of human progress"—as one ardent proponent of the New Theology from Boston put it—"is not in man, but in God."[114] One of the implications that American liberal Protestants drew from their belief in the loving Fatherhood of God was that "God understands man and sympathises with him and longs to do him good."[115] That perspective prompted William Newton Clarke to maintain that the act of regeneration could best be viewed as "the fulfilling of his original intention that man should be in the fullest sense his son."[116] George A. Gordon inferred from his conviction that "it is the will of God that all men should be saved" that it was "for that his gracious power is organized in life and in history, for that he works, and for that he must always work."[117] William Adams Brown made a similar point about the redemption of society. He suggested that all divine activity was "directed to a single end; namely the establishment of the kingdom of God, which is 'righteousness and peace and joy in the Holy Ghost.'"[118]

If, however, liberals believed that the spiritual progress that had occurred in human history was rooted in God's intentions for the created order, they also emphasized, unlike many secular thinkers, that such progress was not inevitable. Herbert Spencer, for example, held that progress, which he identified as the ever greater adaptation of organisms to their environment, "is not an accident, but a necessity."[119] Spencer's necessitarianism prompted Lester Frank Ward, an American partisan of scientific naturalism who embraced many of Spencer's other metaphysical views, to complain that the "extreme scientific view" of progress had the effect of depriving human beings of any control over their destinies.[120] In spite of the fact that liberal Protestants embraced an understanding of the ultimate nature of reality that could hardly have been more different from that of Ward, they shared his hostility to the idea of removing the factor of human agency from discussions of historical change, for it conflicted with their view that the ability to exercise free will constituted one of the salient characteristics of personality.[121] That view prompted Newman Smyth to assert that with the emergence of humanity a new factor had been introduced into the evolutionary process.[122] Human beings, he asserted, share responsibility with God in determining the course of human history.[123] The Oberlin theologian Eugene Lyman agreed, suggesting that humans should be viewed as "coworkers with a morally creative God" in efforts to redeem the world.[124] From that perspective progress became contingent not simply on the divine plan but also on the willingness of individuals to undertake the tasks that were necessary to bring that plan to fruition.

This for liberals was the rub. There was simply no assurance that human beings would do the right thing and ample justification for assuming that they would not. Sinfulness, liberal Protestants maintained, was an all too conspicuous and tragic element of the human condition, and it constituted a persistent obstacle to the spiritual progress of individuals and the larger society.

Although historians have not entirely ignored liberal Protestants' views concerning the sinfulness of human nature, they have not given those views either the attention or the emphasis they deserve.[125] This can partly be explained by the fact that compared with traditional Protestant conceptions of human depravity, liberals' ideas of sin and their expositions of the Fatherhood of God could seem quite tepid. It is certainly the case that American liberal Protestants dissented strongly from orthodox formulations of human sinfulness. Committed as they were to the theory of evolution, few liberals could bring themselves to believe that the story of Adam's "Fall" narrated in Genesis was an actual historical event. Some, in fact, militantly opposed that idea. George A. Gordon, for example, asserted that "it is past belief that two human beings created in moral integrity could by one act of disobedience dissolve themselves and their descendants in a universal sea of depravity."[126] As Gordon's statement suggests, liberals also rejected the doctrine of the imputation of guilt from one person to another, although some acknowledged that on many occasions the effects of individuals' sin could be transmitted to their progeny.[127] Finally liberals commonly denounced the doctrine of total depravity as a distorted view of human nature. As creatures who had been created in God's image, they maintained, members of the human species were "made for God and goodness" and possessed the capacity to "think more widely, love more intensely, choose more wisely, and grow into an ever-deepening sense of selfhood."[128] Indeed, they suggested, it was not inappropriate to view sin as "abnormal" in the sense that "impurity, self-will, and ungodliness are unnatural to man, contrary to his true rule of life, fatal to the fulfilling of his end."[129]

If, however, American liberal Protestants believed that "the sin of man is a sin against the law of his own nature" and that partisans of more traditional views had gone to "morbid extremes" in discussing sin, this does not mean that they made light of the reality of sin or its impact on human beings.[130] On the contrary most shared Walter Rauschenbusch's conviction that "any religious tendency or school of theology must be tested by the question whether it does justice to the religious consciousness of sin."[131] Even Henry Ward Beecher, certainly among the more upbeat of liberals in his assessment of human nature, ruefully observed in 1885 that "we need not be afraid of getting rid of original sin, because we can get all the actual transgression that the world needs to take its place."[132] Several decades later the University of Chicago's Shirley Jackson Case echoed Beecher's remarks, declaring that "a study of the social history of the race and an observation of the conduct of humans at the present time disclose pictures of depravity that might well have made Adam blush."[133]

For liberals, neither the reality nor the prevalence of sin was at issue; sin was an all too pervasive blight upon human nature. In fact liberals were commonly hypervigilant in scrutinizing their own message for evidence that they were guilty of either placing undue emphasis on the better elements of human nature, minimizing the "heart-breaking disasters of life," or exaggerating the success that Christians had enjoyed in Christianizing the world.[134] Some liberals even expressed concern that proponents of their worldview or that of others less theologically self-conscious were insufficiently appreciative of the gravity of sin and unduly inclined to emphasize God's equanimity in the face of it.[135] That view prompted Harry Emerson Fosdick to call in 1922 for the inculcation of "a fresh sense of personal and social sin."[136] Self-criticism remained a staple of liberal Protestant rhetoric during the first three decades of the twentieth century. It may well be that another reason historians have not sufficiently appreciated just how seriously Protestant liberals took the issue of human sinfulness is that they have mistaken that rhetoric for an actual description of liberal theological views concerning sin rather than recognizing it as a series of cautionary statements and admonitions.

In describing the nature of sinfulness, which signified "alienation from God," American liberal Protestants commonly began with an explanation of the human condition that seemed to them to be in accord with the facts of natural and redemptive history.[137] The human species, they suggested, represented a unique compound of animalistic impulses that are hereditary remnants of its evolutionary past and more exalted faculties that bear God's image.[138] Sin consisted of a voluntary decision on the part of a human being to submit to his "lower," beastlike qualities rather than "rise to the higher capacities within him."[139] When a human being acted sinfully, William Newton Clarke declared, "the nature that is akin to God yields to the nature that is common to man and beasts."[140] Sin was thus a misuse of human freedom for ignoble ends.[141]

However useful such discourse might be in describing the nature of sin, it did not really address the issue of its cause. Recognizing this, liberals maintained that one must ultimately ascribe sinfulness to the "force of sheer perversity" of the will.[142] This primordial "fact of wickedness, this "self-induced irrationality" that prompted people to renounce their birthright as children of God, George Gordon maintained, should give pause to those harboring exalted expectations of the future.[143] "The pious dreams that see no perverse will in the way of human progress," Gordon declared, "are the worst kind of wildcat currency."[144]

Other liberals likewise ascribed sin to perversity. Lyman Abbott, for example, made a point of emphasizing that "sin is not mere unripeness and immaturity which growth and sunshine will cure."[145] It was something much more malignant, "a deliberate disobedience of the divine law into the knowledge of which the soul has come in its emergence from the animal condition."[146] That disobedience was the product of a selfish inclination on the part of human beings to subordinate the will of God to the gratification of their own desires.[147]

Liberals emphasized that the dogged refusal of human beings to realize their full potential as children of God indicated that sinful tendencies were incredibly tenacious. Abbott, for example, noted that men and women "deliberately, and again and again" resisted the "higher life" for "the self-indulgent appetite, the unregulated passion, the blind and uninspired acquisitiveness."[148] Similarly, Lewis French Stearns declared that "the natural man becomes no holier in the progress of evolution. Sin becomes in many respects worse as the world grows older. The world as a whole is doubtless far better than it was a thousand years ago, but the civilized sinner who has fallen heir to all the benefits of human evolution is worse than the savage sinner."[149] The tenacity of sin seemed equally obvious in the social arena. Shailer Mathews, for example, declared that human sinfulness "is so deeply intrenched in our social life as to be all but ineradicable."[150] Harry Emerson Fosdick illustrated the hold that sin had on people by reminding his readers that "if we let human nature run loose it goes to evil, while he who would be virtuous must struggle to achieve character."[151]

While liberals were acutely aware of the power of sin to thwart humanity's fondest hopes, they were not willing to give up hope altogether. On the contrary, throughout the period between 1870 and 1930 liberals drew comfort from past progress and remained hopeful that they could make positive strides in Christianizing the world.[152] Some of the rhetoric they employed in expressing that hope could appear to be indicative of what Fosdick called (albeit in a different context) a "frothy optimism."[153] Newman Smyth, for example, wrote that "evil is only the incident of creation; it is the passing mote in the sunshine, while the light is abiding."[154] While Smyth did not discount the reality of sin, he identified the Christian hope with the ultimate "triumph of creative and redeeming love."[155] William Adams Brown asserted that Jesus, who represented the clearest and most unequivocal instance of "God in man," was "the type to which all mankind is ultimately destined to conform."[156] The lesson of Christianity, he maintained, was that salvation is "rooted as truly as sin itself in the nature of man."[157]

Even World War I left liberals essentially undaunted in their hopes for future spiritual progress. Walter Rauschenbusch, for example, acknowledged that the war was "a catastrophic stage in the coming of the Kingdom of God," but this simply indicated, he suggested, that "we should estimate the power of sin too lightly if we forecast a smooth road."[158] Similarly, John Wright Buckham, a theologian of liberal persuasion at the Pacific School of Religion, conceded that the "lapse into barbarism" associated with "the Great War and its aftermath" had done much to destroy the "air castles" constructed by some of the more naive proponents of progress in the early years of the century. It not only eloquently confirmed the general lesson of history that sinfulness had significantly retarded realization of the Kingdom of God but also served as a forcible reminder that human progress was not inevitable. Nevertheless, Buckham maintained, despair was inappropriate. Not only could Christians point to the emergence of "some slight semblance of brotherhood" over time, but the *ideal* of progress was "wrought into the very structure of Christianity."[159]

The most sustained discussion of the idea of progress by a partisan of American liberal Protestantism was presented by Harry Emerson Fosdick in the Cole Lectures at Vanderbilt in 1922.[160] In those lectures, published the same year as *Christianity and Progress,* Fosdick carefully dissociated his views from those of exponents of "a universal, mechanical, irresistible movement toward perfection."[161] He suggested that "the first rule for all who believe in a progressive world is not to believe in it too much."[162] "Moral evil," Fosdick declared, "is still the central problem of mankind."[163] Nevertheless, while insisting that "whatever progress is wrought out upon this planet will be sternly fought for and hardly won," he made it clear that he embraced "the hope of making progress."[164] In common with other liberal Protestants, Fosdick believed that while science might well be valuable in disclosing facts and arriving at principles that were able to assist human beings in improving their material fortunes, the only force capable of transforming individuals and fostering the emergence of a righteous and loving society was the "spiritual interpretation of life" conveyed through the life and teachings of Jesus.[165]

The persistence of the liberal Protestant emphasis on the possibility of ongoing spiritual progress for individuals and society stemmed largely from followers' belief in the fatherhood and providence of God, which prompted them to place more weight on the doctrine that humanity is created in God's image than on the doctrine of human depravity. Their belief that "God has organized his grace for absolute victory" was reinforced by their interpretation of the teachings of Jesus, which seemed to place more interest on the intrinsic worth of human nature than on its perversity.[166] However, it was precisely because American liberal Protestants were so clearly aware of the tenacity of sinfulness that they emphasized peoples' need for the Christian Gospel. It seemed as obvious to them, as it did to proponents of the kind of Christian theology they rejected, that only the kind of "overpowering consciousness of God" derived from the life and teachings of Jesus was capable of overcoming the tyranny of selfishness that lay at the heart of humanity's propensity toward evil and of giving human beings the motive and power to repent.[167] Repentance, liberals emphasized, was a precondition for the forgiveness of sins. Like more conservative Christians, liberal Protestants emphasized God's hatred of sin.[168] Hence, they emphasized, "God cannot bless man in his sin."[169] Only "true repentance makes forgiveness possible."[170]

While liberals certainly believed that many human beings would achieve redemption and that society could achieve real progress in Christianizing the social order, their belief in the severity and the persistence of sin prompted most of them to maintain that humanity's ultimate victory over sin would necessarily occur in a realm beyond history. Hence even as William Newton Clarke was asserting that "man does advance as ages pass" and that evils that once were common have become impossible," he was also insisting that "this casts no doubt upon the persistence of evil in the race."[171] Even while maintaining that "sin is but for the day of human history" and that "the human soul is the very temple of God," Newman Smyth felt compelled to "cherish the hope that the process of God's creative work is not ended, its promise and potency not exhausted in the present visible system of things and our mortality, but that death and the resurrection need to be added for its completion."[172] After suggesting that "in the historic process to-day we behold at work forces that slowly eliminate the evil possibilities, and that slowly realize the good possibilities," George A. Gordon acknowledged that "human history on earth must ever remain incomplete. Death must be transcended if optimism is to live; and time must be held to be but the earliest epoch of man's endless career."[173]

In view of their lively sense of the prevalence and the tenacity of sin, it is hardly legitimate to characterize liberal Protestants as exponents of a naive and superficial optimism. If, as it would appear, the total amount of discussion of human sinfulness declined within American culture in the period between 1870 and 1930, that may well have been a function of the conviction on the part of the princes of the pulpit that downplaying of sin was necessary to retain the allegiance of their parishioners; the downward trajectory cannot be laid at the door of liberal Protestant theology. Indeed when Reinhold Niebuhr excoriated liberals in 1927 for being "steeped in a religious optimism which is true to the facts of neither the world of nature nor the world of history," it is not at all clear what he had in mind.[174] Since Niebuhr had not yet dissociated himself decisively from the liberal theological tradition in the late 1920s, perhaps it would be appropriate to place the statement within what by 1927 was a long tradition of tough-minded criticism of their own tradition by liberal Protestants.[175] It is difficult to resist the temptation to ascribe Niebuhr's criticism, along with a number of other comments he made concerning liberalism and a wide range of other topics, to a tendency to substitute caricature and sweeping, tendentious pronouncements for careful analysis.

Fortunately the passage of time and partisan rivalries may afford us the opportunity to view American liberal Protestants' ideas concerning progress from a more balanced perspective. Those ideas now seem to represent a distinct Gospel-centered alternative not only to the stance of more conservative Christians but also to the views of partisans of more secular visions of change. They may have been wrong-headed, but they are worthy of our intellectual respect. Glib or facile they were not.

NOTES

1. I am greatly indebted to Thomas L. Haskell, David Hempton, and Ronald L. Numbers for their insightful comments on an earlier draft of this essay. Thanks too to Donald A. Yerxa for organizing this volume and for thoughtfully editing the final draft. Finally, I should express my appreciation to my wife, Sharon (ILYS), and my son, Jeff, for their ongoing support of my work.

2. Dennis Neal Voskuil, "From Liberalism to Neo-Orthodoxy: The History of a Theological Transition, 1925–1935" (Ph.D. diss., Harvard University, 1974); Sydney E. Ahlstrom, *A Religious History of the American People* (New Haven, Conn.: Yale University Press, 1972), 944–45; William R. Hutchison, *The Modernist Impulse in American Protestantism* (Cambridge, Mass.: Harvard University Press, 1976), 295–98; Mark A. Noll, *A History of Christianity in the United States and Canada* (Grand Rapids, Mich.: Eerdmans, 1992), 433.

3. William R. Hutchison, "Liberal Protestantism and the 'End of Innocence,'" *American Quarterly* 15 (Summer 1963): 136, 138.

4. T. J. Jackson Lears, *No Place of Grace: Antimodernism and the Transformation of American Culture, 1880–1920* (New York: Pantheon, 1981), 23.

5. Ibid., 25.

6. James R. Moore, *The Post-Darwinian Controversies: A Study of the Protestant Struggle to Come to Terms with Darwin in Great Britain and America, 1870–1900* (Cambridge: Cambridge University Press, 1979), 239.

7. Eugene McCarraher, *Christian Critics: Religion and the Impasse in Modern American Social Thought* (Ithaca, N.Y.: Cornell University Press, 2000), 77.

8. Gary Dorrien, *The Making of American Liberal Theology: Imagining Progressive Religion, 1805–1900* (Louisville, Ky.: Westminster John Knox Press, 2001), 403.

9. Ibid., 411. See also H. Shelton Smith, *Changing Conceptions of Original Sin: A Study in American Theology since 1750* (New York: Charles Scribner's Sons, 1955), 197; Sidney E. Mead, *The Lively Experiment: The Shaping of Christianity in America* (New York: Harper & Row, 1963), 142–55; and Winthrop S. Hudson, *The Great Tradition of the American Churches* (1953; repr., Gloucester, Mass.: Peter Smith, 1970), 161.

10. Useful discussions of less gospel-centered, more empirically and naturalistically oriented versions of modernism can be found in Kenneth Cauthen, *The Impact of American Religious Liberalism* (New York: Harper & Row, 1962); Dorrien, *The Making of American Liberal Theology: Imagining Progressive Religion, 1805–1900;* and Gary Dorrien, *The Making of American Liberal Theology: Idealism, Realism, and Modernity, 1900–1950* (Louisville, Ky.: Westminster John Knox Press, 2003).

11. Francis A. Henry, "Reconstruction in Religious Thought," *Princeton Review,* n.s., 14 (1884): 19; Henry Ward Beecher, *Yale Lectures on Preaching,* 1st ser. (1872; repr., New York: Fords, Howard, & Hulbert, 1892), 88.

12. Theodore T. Munger, *The Freedom of Faith* (Boston: Houghton Mifflin, 1883), 11, 6. See also William Adams Brown, "The Old Theology and the New," *Harvard Theological Review* 4 (January 1911): 1, 12–13; Jacob Todd, "Evolution in Religion," *Methodist Review,* 5th ser., 2 (1886): 718; and Lewis F. Stearns, "Reconstruction in Theology," *New Englander,* n.s., 5, no. 41, no. 1 (1882): 82–102.

13. Hutchison, *The Modernist Impulse,* 2.

14. T. Townsend, *The Bible and Other Ancient Literature in the Nineteenth Century* (1884; repr., New York: Chautauqua Press, 1888), 192.

15. Ibid., 192–93. See also John L. Girardeau, "The Discretionary Power of the Church" [1875], in *Sermons,* edited by George A. Blackburn (Columbia, S.C.: The State Company, 1907), 386.

16. Stuart Robinson, "The Pulpit and Skeptical Culture," *Princeton Review,* 4th ser., 3 (1879): 147.

17. H. Johnson, "Theistic Evolution," *Andover Review* 1 (April 1884): 365 [original was in italics]. See also ibid., 372. Additional expressions of this idea can be found in Jon H. Roberts, *Darwinism and the Divine in America: Protestant Intellectuals and Organic Evolution, 1859–1900* (Madison: University of Wisconsin Press, 1988), 137–38.

18. George T. Ladd, "History and the Concept of God," *Bibliotheca Sacra* 37 (October 1880): 599; Alexander V. G. Allen, "The Theological Renaissance of the Nineteenth Century," *Princeton Review,* n.s., 10 (1882): 280–81, quotation on 281. See also George F. Moore, "The Modern Historical Movement and Christian Faith," *Andover Review* 10 (October 1888): 338; and Ladd, "History and the Concept of God," 596.

19. Howard MacQueary, *The Evolution of Man and Christianity* (New York: D. Appleton, 1890), 251.

20. George A. Gordon, *Ultimate Conceptions of Faith* (Boston: Houghton Mifflin, 1903), 134. See also Lewis French Stearns, "The Present Direction of Theological Thought in the Congregational Churches of the United States" (paper read before the International Congregational Council in London, July 15, 1891), in his *Present Day Theology: A Popular Discussion of Leading Doctrines of the Christian Faith* (New York: Charles Scribner's Sons, 1893), 541.

21. Newman Smyth, *Old Faiths in New Light,* 2nd ed. (New York: Charles Scribner's Sons, 1879), 253.

22. William Newton Clarke, *An Outline of Christian Theology* (1898; repr., New York: Charles Scribner's Sons, 1922), 12. See also Egbert Smyth et al., eds., *Progressive Orthodoxy: A Contribution to the Christian Interpretation of Christian Doctrines* (1885; repr., Boston: Houghton Mifflin, 1886), 35; Lyman Abbott, *The Theology of an Evolutionist* (Cambridge, Mass.: Riverside Press, 1897), 70–73; Charles A. Briggs, *Biblical Study,* 2nd ed. (New York: Charles Scribner's Sons, 1885), 364; and Harry Emerson Fosdick, *Christianity and Progress* (New York: Fleming H. Revell Company, 1922), 192–93.

23. Newman Smyth, "Orthodox Rationalism," *Princeton Review,* n.s., 9 (May 1882): 299, 300, 301–2; George P. Fisher, "The Personality of God and Man," *Princeton Review,* n.s., 10 (July 1882): 30–31.

24. Arthur Cushman McGiffert, *The Rise of Modern Religious Ideas* (1915; repr., New York: Macmillan, 1922), 204.

25. Clarke, *An Outline of Christian Theology,* 19. This issue is treated at greater length in Roberts, *Darwinism and the Divine,* 166–69.

26. George T. Ladd, "The New Theology," *New Englander* 35, no. 4 (1876): 666.

27. Myron Adams, *The Continuous Creation: An Application of the Evolutionary Philosophy to the Christian Religion* (Boston: Houghton Mifflin, 1889), 51; Roberts, *Darwinism and the Divine,* 157.

28. Allen, "The Theological Renaissance," 280. See also Henry Ward Beecher, "Progress of Thought in the Church," *North American Review* 135 (August 1882): 106; and Stearns, "Reconstruction in Theology," 87.

29. William Newton Clarke, *Sixty Years with the Bible* (New York: Charles Scribner's Sons, 1912), 149.

30. Brown, "The Old Theology and the New," 16.

31. Henry Churchill King, *Reconstruction in Theology,* 2nd ed. (New York: Macmillan, 1901), 44; Brown, "The Old Theology and the New," 17.

32. Philip S. Moxom, "Symposium on the 'New Theology': What Are Its Essential Features? Is It Better than the Old?," *Homiletic Review* 11 (March 1886): 205; Munger, *Freedom of Faith,* 59.

33. Frank Hugh Foster [Professor, D.D.], "The Authority and Inspiration of the Scriptures," *Bibliotheca Sacra* 52 (January 1895): 69–96, 233. Not all liberals believed that God provided new revelation. Lewis French Stearns, for example, believed that human understanding changed, but he maintained that "God has made no new revelations to our age" (Stearns, "Reconstruction in Theology," 101).

34. Abbott, *Theology of an Evolutionist,* 66. See also Clarke, *Outline of Christian Theology,* 31–32; and McGiffert, *Rise of Modern Religious Ideas,* 177.

35. George Harris, "The Function of the Christian Consciousness," *Andover Review* 2 (October 1884): 348. See also Ladd, "New Theology," 661; and Clarke, *Outline of Christian Theology,* 20.

36. Clarke, *Outline of Christian Theology,* 12. See also Smyth, *Old Faiths,* 253; and Smyth et al., *Progressive Orthodoxy,* 35–36, 40.

37. Briggs, *Biblical Study,* 186.

38. Asher H. Wilcox, "The Ultimate Criteria of Christian Doctrine," *Andover Review* 8 (April 1887): 350–51. See also Moore, "Modern Historical Movement," 339; Smyth et al., *Progressive Orthodoxy,* 231; Henry, "Reconstruction in Religious Thought," 24–25; and William Adams Brown, *Christian Theology in Outline* (New York: Charles Scribner's Sons, 1906), 40.

39. King, *Reconstruction in Theology,* 4.

40. Ibid., 2–4.

41. For a list of commitments retained within Christian tradition, see, for example, Brown, "The Old Theology and the New," 22.

42. Anonymous, "The Peril of Orthodoxy," *Andover Review* 9 (May 1888): 519. See also Stearns, "Reconstruction in Theology," 82.

43. Munger, *Freedom of Faith,* 34. See also King, *Reconstruction in Theology,* 2.

44. Clarke, *Outline of Christian Theology,* 60, 59.

45. Brown, *Christian Theology in Outline,* 40; Moore, "Modern Historical Movement," 337, 339.

46. Ladd, "New Theology," 664, 662.

47. Harris, "The Function of the Christian Consciousness," 334. See also Smyth et al., *Progressive Orthodoxy,* 9; Ladd, "History and the Concept of God," 599; and Dorrien, *Making of American Liberal Theology: Imagining Progressive Religion, 1805–1900,* 292.

48. Newman Smyth, *The Orthodox Theology of To-day* (New York: Charles Scribner's Sons, 1881), 29–31, quotations on 29–30.

49. Ladd, "New Theology," 661–62, 665.

50. Ibid., 665.

51. Smyth et al., *Progressive Orthodoxy,* 9.

52. Moore, "Modern Historical Movement," 334.

53. T. T. Munger, "Evolution and the Faith," *Century,* n.s., 10 (May 1886): 109. See also Newman Smyth, *The Religious Feeling: A Study for Faith* (New York: Scribner, Armstrong & Co., 1877), 155; Ladd, "History and the Concept of God," 598–99; and Lyman Abbott, *Reminiscences* (Boston: Houghton Mifflin, 1915), 460.

54. Munger, "Evolution and the Faith," 109. See also Smyth, *Religious Feeling,* 155.

55. Harris, "Function of the Christian Consciousness," 334.

56. Henry Ward Beecher, *Evolution and Religion* (New York: Fords, Howard, and Hulbert, 1885), 1.

57. Brown, *Christian Theology in Outline,* 39.

58. McGiffert, *Rise of Modern Religious Ideas,* 185–86.

59. King, *Reconstruction in Theology,* 4.

60. Stearns, "Reconstruction in Theology," 82.

61. Munger, *Freedom of Faith,* 32. See also King, *Reconstruction in Theology,* 44.

62. Brown, *Christian Theology in Outline,* 202–3.

63. William Rupp, "The Theory of Evolution and the Christian Faith," *Reformed Quarterly Review* 35 (April 1888): 151. See Washington Gladden, *How Much Is Left of the Old Doctrines? A Book for the People* (Boston: Houghton, Mifflin, 1899), 167; Clarke, *Outline of Christian Theology,* 224–25; Newman Smyth, *Through Science to Faith* (1902; repr., New York: Charles Scribner's Sons, 1904), 117, 119–20; Beecher, *Evolution and Religion,* 46; Smyth et al., *Progressive Orthodoxy,* 35; and Smyth, *Old Faiths,* 266.

64. Smyth, *Through Science,* 170.

65. Rupp, "Theory of Evolution," 151; Shailer Mathews, *The Gospel and the Modern Man* (New York: Macmillan, 1910), 218. See also James T. Bixby, "Morality on a Scientific Basis," *Andover Review* 19 (March 1893): 211–12; Smyth, *Through Science,* 180–81; George A. Gordon, *The New Epoch for Faith* (1901; repr., Hicksville, N.Y.: Regina Press, 1975), 357; Walter Rauschenbusch, *A Theology for the Social Gospel* (1917; repr., New York: Abingdon Press, n.d.), 162.

66. Lewis French Stearns, *The Evidence of Christian Experience* (New York: Charles Scribner's Sons, 1890), 71–72. See also Beecher, *Evolution and Religion,* 152–53; and Gladden, *How Much Is Left,* 167.

67. Joseph LeConte, *Evolution and Its Relation to Religious Thought* (New York: D. Appleton, 1888), 284. See also Beecher, *Yale Lectures on Preaching,* 1st ser., 82–83. This theme, of course, was not limited to partisans of Progressive orthodoxy. See, for example, Samuel Harris, *The Philosophical Basis of Theism* (New York: Charles Scribner's Sons, 1883), 527–28.

68. Munger, *Freedom of Faith,* 13; Harris, *Philosophical Basis of Theism,* 527–28. See also Clarke, *Outline of Christian Theology,* 191–92, 49; and Smyth, *Old Faiths,* 282.

69. Beecher, "Progress of Thought," 108. See also Henry, "Reconstruction in Religious Thought," 26–27.

70. Stearns, *Evidence of Christian Experience,* 72. This view, of course, was not limited to partisans of the New Theology. See, for example, D. D. Wheedon, "Prayer and Science," *Methodist Quarterly Review,* 4th ser., 36 (January 1884): 9.

71. George Harris, *Moral Evolution* (Boston: Houghton, Mifflin, 1896), 233–34. See also Joseph LeConte, "Man's Place in Nature," *Princeton Review,* n.s., 2 (November 1878): 788–89.

72. Edward Thomson, "The Image of God," *Methodist Review,* 5th ser., 4 (September 1888): 725. See also Gladden, *How Much Is Left,* 166–67; Clarke, *Outline of Christian Theology,* 187; and Theodore T. Munger, *The Appeal to Life* (Boston: Houghton, Mifflin, 1887), 295–96.

73. I am certainly not the first to call attention to the salience of the term "personality" in liberal Protestant thought. See, for example, Richard Wightman Fox, "The Culture of Liberal Protestant Progressivism, 1875–1925," *Journal of Interdisciplinary History* 23 (Winter 1993): 646–56. Much of the attention that historians have given to the term has centered on its role in the Social Gospel movement. See McCarraher, *Christian Critics,* 12–13; and William McGuire King, "An Enthusiasm for Humanity: The Social Emphasis in Religion and Its Accommodation in Protestant Theology," in *Religion and Twentieth-Century American Intellectual Life,* edited by Michael J. Lacey (Cambridge: Cambridge University Press, 1989), 53.

74. George A. Gordon, "The Collapse of the New England Theology," *Harvard Theological Review* 1 (April 1908): 161.

75. Clarke, *Outline of Christian Theology,* 68.

76. Brown, *Christian Theology in Outline,* 102. See also ibid., 103, 129.

77. F. H. Johnson, "Coöperative Creation," *Andover Review* 3 (April 1885): 345.

78. Gordon, *Ultimate Conceptions,* 133; Harry F. Ward, *The New Social Order: Principles and Programs* (1919; repr., New York: Macmillan, 1926), 136–37. For the tendency of "scientific" progressives to treat human beings as "objects to be manipulated rather than as possessors of unique individual personalities," see David B. Danbom, *"The World of Hope":*

Progressives and the Struggle for an Ethical Public Life (Philadelphia: Temple University Press, 1987), 120–21.

79. Clarke, *Outline of Christian Theology,* 191; William Newton Clarke, *Can I Believe in God the Father?* (1899; repr., New York: Charles Scribner's Sons, 1912), 79–80.

80. Harry Emerson Fosdick, *Adventurous Religion and Other Essays* (New York: Cornwall Press, 1926), 36–37.

81. Harry Emerson Fosdick, *As I See Religion* (New York: Harper & Brothers, 1932), 44. "The personality of Jesus," Walter Rauschenbusch declared in 1917, "is a call to the emancipation of our own personalities" (Rauschenbusch, *Theology for the Social Gospel,* 162).

82. Fosdick, *As I See Religion,* 44.

83. Shailer Mathews, *The Faith of Modernism* (New York: Macmillan, 1924), 11.

84. King, "Enthusiasm for Humanity," 73; Moore, "Modern Historical Movement," 339. See also Moxom, "Symposium on the 'New Theology,'" 203–4; and Munger, *Freedom of Faith,* 9.

85. Fosdick, *Adventurous Religion,* 204.

86. Clarke, *Outline of Christian Theology,* 397.

87. Smyth et al., *Progressive Orthodoxy,* 124–25; Rauschenbusch, *Theology for the Social Gospel,* 99–103.

88. Mathews, *Gospel and the Modern Man,* 173; Brown, *Christian Theology in Outline,* 39. See also King, "Enthusiasm for Humanity," 72; and Roberts, *Darwinism and the Divine,* 204–5.

89. Walter Rauschenbusch, *Christianity and the Social Crisis* (New York: Macmillan, 1907), 354.

90. William B. Clarke, "The Nature and Working of the Christian Consciousness," *Andover Review* 7 (April 1887): 387.

91. Newman Smyth, *Christian Ethics* (New York: Charles Scribner's Sons, 1892), 241.

92. William Adams Brown, *Modern Theology and the Preaching of the Gospel* (New York: Charles Scribner's Sons, 1914), 117.

93. Fosdick, *Christianity and Progress,* 67; Mathews, *Faith of Modernism,* 182. See also Fosdick, *Christianity and Progress,* 74–77; and Eugene William Lyman, "Can Religious Intuition Give Knowledge of Reality?," in *Religious Realism,* edited by D. C. Macintosh (New York: Macmillan, 1931), 260.

94. Fosdick, *Christianity and Progress,* 54, 78–79, 84–85, quotation on 79; Mathews, *Gospel and the Modern Man,* 86, 273.

95. Munger, *Freedom of Faith,* 33–34, 62.

96. King, *Reconstruction in Theology,* 44.

97. Fosdick, *Christianity and Progress,* 99–101; Ward, *New Social Order,* 137; Smyth, *Through Science,* 173; Munger, *Freedom of Faith,* 22–23; Rauschenbusch, *Christianity and the Social Crisis,* 65–67; King, "Enthusiasm for Humanity," 56; Donald B. Meyer, *The Protestant Search for Political Realism, 1919–1941* (Berkeley and Los Angeles: University of California Press, 1961), 137–38.

98. Fosdick, *Christianity and Progress,* 100.

99. See, for example, Washington Gladden, *Ruling Ideas of the Present Age* (Boston: Houghton, Mifflin, 1895), 289–90; Rauschenbusch, *Christianity and the Social Crisis,* 65–66;

Smyth, *Christian Ethics,* 494; and Rauschenbusch, *Theology for the Social Gospel,* 142–43. William R. Hutchison has estimated that about two thirds of the "most prominent leaders of theological liberalism" between 1875 and 1915 were proponents of the Social Gospel (Hutchison, *Modernist Impulse,* 165).

100. Rauschenbusch, *Christianity and the Social Crisis,* 409, 336.

101. Ibid., 209. See also Rauschenbusch, *Theology for the Social Gospel,* 5.

102. Washington Gladden, *Tools and the Man: Property and Industry under the Christian Law* (Boston: Houghton, Mifflin, 1893), 1. See also Mathews, *Gospel and the Modern Man,* 86; and Brown, *Christian Theology in Outline,* 195. On occasion Walter Rauschenbusch focused more of his emphasis on society than on the individual. See, for example, Rauschenbusch, *Christianity and the Social Crisis,* 65. Rauschenbusch's statements, however, must be viewed with the understanding that he placed a great deal of emphasis on the salience of social interaction for individual personalities.

103. Rauschenbusch, *Theology for the Social Gospel,* 142. In stressing the persistence of the focus on the individual, I am taking a position that is similar to that of King, "Enthusiasm for Humanity," 53–56, but different from, for example, Bruce Kuklick, *Churchmen and Philosophers: From Jonathan Edwards to John Dewey* (New Haven, Conn.: Yale University Press, 1985), 224.

104. Fosdick, *Adventurous Religion,* 35.

105. Ward, *New Social Order,* 142–43. For another statement emphasizing that individuals rather than social structures were the ends of their endeavors, see Mathews, *Gospel and the Modern Man,* 218–19.

106. Fosdick, *Christianity and Progress,* 65.

107. Brown, *Christian Theology in Outline,* 37.

108. Gladden, *Ruling Ideas,* 290.

109. Gordon, *New Epoch,* 18. See also ibid., 361.

110. Ibid., 357. See also ibid., 360.

111. Fosdick, *Christianity and Progress,* 63. See also Anson P. Atterbury, "Five Points in an Evolutionary Confession of Faith," *Christian Thought* 7 (August 1889): 56; Clarke, *Outline of Christian Theology,* 242; and Harris, *Moral Evolution,* 445.

112. Brown, *Christian Theology in Outline,* 203.

113. Clarke, *Outline of Christian Theology,* 397.

114. Moxom, "Symposium on the 'New Theology,'" 206. See also Mathews, *Gospel and the Modern Man,* 82; and Smyth, *Old Faiths,* 67.

115. Brown, *Modern Theology,* 104. William Adams Brown held that God "is an ever-present spirit guiding all that happens to a wise and holy end" (Brown, "The Old Theology and the New," 16). See also Brown, *Christian Theology in Outline,* 98–99; and Clarke, *Can I Believe in God the Father?,* 147–48.

116. Clarke, *Outline of Christian Theology,* 397.

117. Gordon, *Ultimate Conceptions,* 136. See also Smyth et al., *Progressive Orthodoxy,* 36.

118. Brown, *Modern Theology,* 107. See also ibid., 119.

119. Herbert Spencer, *Social Statics: Or, the Conditions Essential to Human Happiness Specified, and the First of Them Developed* (1851; repr., New York: D. Appleton, 1865), 79–80, quotation on 80.

120. Lester F. Ward, *Pure Sociology: A Treatise on the Origin and Spontaneous Development of Society* (New York: Macmillan, 1903), 20.

121. Clarke, *Outline of Christian Theology*, 213. See also William W. Fenn, "War and the Thought of God" [1918], repr. in *American Protestant Thought: The Liberal Era*, edited by William R. Hutchison (New York: Harper & Row, 1968), 157.

122. Smyth, *Through Science*, 200.

123. Ibid., 200, 200–201n1.

124. Eugene W. Lyman, *The Experience of God in Modern Life* (New York: Charles Scribner's Sons, 1918), 145. See also Eugene William Lyman, *The God of the New Age: A Tract for the Times* (Boston: Pilgrim Press, 1918), 18.

125. For discussions of the liberal view of sin, see especially Hutchison, "Liberal Protestantism and the 'End of Innocence,'" 126–39; and Smith, *Changing Conceptions of Original Sin*, 164–97. My own discussion of liberal views owes much to these accounts.

126. Gordon, *New Epoch*, 35. See also Lyman Abbott, *The Evolution of Christianity* (Boston: Houghton, Mifflin, 1892), 122. One exception was Lewis French Stearns; see Stearns, *Evidence of Christian Experience*, 99–100.

127. Gladden, *How Much Is Left*, 121; Clarke, *Outline of Christian Theology*, 242–44; Lewis French Stearns, *Present Day Theology: A Popular Discussion of Leading Doctrines of the Christian Faith* (1893; repr., New York: Charles Scribner's Sons, 1895), 341; Gordon, *New Epoch*, 34–35.

128. Clarke, *Outline of Christian Theology*, 245; Munger, *Appeal to Life*, 296. See also Clarke, *Outline of Christian Theology*, 234; McGiffert, *Rise of Modern Religious Ideas*, 206; and Gordon, *New Epoch*, 34.

129. Clarke, *Outline of Christian Theology*, 234.

130. Abbott, *Evolution of Christianity*, 123; Fosdick, *Christianity and Progress*, 170.

131. Rauschenbusch, *Theology for the Social Gospel*, 32.

132. Beecher, *Evolution and Religion*, 141.

133. Shirley Jackson Case, "Education in Liberalism," in *Contemporary American Theology*, edited by Vergilius Ferm, vol. 1 (New York: Round Table Press, 1932), 120.

134. W. W. Fenn, "Modern Liberalism," *American Journal of Theology* 17 (October 1913): 516–17. See also more generally Hutchison, "Liberal Protestantism and the End of Innocence," 126–39.

135. Fosdick, *Christianity and Progress*, 172–73.

136. Ibid., 175.

137. Harris, *Moral Evolution*, 284.

138. Gordon, *New Epoch*, 35–36.

139. Brown, "The Old Theology and the New," 15. See also Gordon, *New Epoch*, 35–36; and Abbott, *Evolution of Christianity*, 123, 226.

140. Clarke, *Outline of Christian Theology*, 232–33, 240–41, quotation on 232. See also Munger, *Appeal to Life*, 300–301.

141. Stearns, *Present Day Theology*, 341.

142. Gordon, *New Epoch*, 41–42. See also Smyth, *Through Science*, 198.

143. Gordon, *New Epoch*, 41–42.

144. Ibid., 42.

145. Abbott, *Evolution of Christianity,* 227.

146. Ibid.

147. Stearns, *Present Day Theology,* 305; Rauschenbusch, *Theology for the Social Gospel,* 47; Harris, *Moral Evolution,* 280–81; Clarke, *Outline of Christian Theology,* 235–36.

148. Abbott, *Evolution of Christianity,* 226.

149. Stearns, *Present Day Theology,* 308. See also Smyth, *Through Science,* 120.

150. Mathews, *Gospel and the Modern Man,* 172.

151. Fosdick, *Christianity and Progress,* 76.

152. For a contemporary's description of the New Theology as characterized by "a high degree of *hopefulness,*" see Moxom, "Symposium on the 'New Theology,'" 204.

153. Fosdick, *Christianity and Progress,* 176.

154. Smyth, *Old Faiths,* 285.

155. Smyth, *Through Science,* 202–3.

156. Brown, "The Old Theology and the New," 15. See also William Adams Brown, *The Essence of Christianity: A Study in the History of Definition* (New York: Charles Scribner's Sons, 1902), 313.

157. Brown, "The Old Theology and the New," 15. For other expressions of hopefulness in the ultimate triumph over sin, see Gladden, *How Much Is Left,* 130; and Mathews, *Gospel and the Modern Man,* 172.

158. Rauschenbusch, *Theology for the Social Gospel,* 226.

159. John Wright Buckham, "The Christian Platonism of Dean Inge," *Journal of Religion* 4 (January 1924): 82–83.

160. My reading of this work differs significantly from that of William R. Hutchison. See Hutchison, "Liberal Protestantism and the 'End of Innocence,'" 134–35.

161. Fosdick, *Christianity and Progress,* 32, 37–38, quotation on 38.

162. Ibid., 178.

163. Ibid.

164. Ibid., 187, 41.

165. Ibid., 43–85, quotation on 45.

166. Gordon, *Ultimate Conceptions,* 136. See also George A. Gordon, " Collapse of the New England Theology," 150; and Gladden, *Ruling Ideas,* 220.

167. Rauschenbusch, *Theology for the Social Gospel,* 154. See also Clarke, *Outline of Christian Theology,* 245.

168. Clarke, *Can I Believe in God the Father?,* 195–97; Gladden, *How Much Is Left,* 190–91.

169. Smyth et al., *Progressive Orthodoxy,* 48.

170. Brown, *Modern Theology,* 107–8.

171. Clarke, *Outline of Christian Theology,* 242.

172. Smyth, *Old Faiths,* 285, 293.

173. Gordon, *Ultimate Conceptions,* 249. Calling attention to the admonition of Jesus that human beings be perfect, even as their heavenly Father is perfect, Gordon noted that nothing "could be more hopeless or absurd" than that ideal if humans could not assume the existence of a "history beyond this world" (ibid., 250). For other statements affirming the need to look beyond history for the final triumph of God's grace, see Rauschenbusch, *Theology for the Social Gospel,* 227; and Munger, *Freedom of Faith,* 250.

174. Reinhold Niebuhr, *Does Civilization Need Religion? A Study in the Social Resources and Limitations of Religion in Modern Life* (New York: Macmillan, 1927), 9–10. See also Reinhold Niebuhr, "Can Christianity Survive?," *Atlantic Monthly* 135 (January 1925): 88; and Reinhold Niebuhr, *Reflections on the End of an Era* (New York: Charles Scribner's Sons, 1934), 291–92.

175. Richard Wightman Fox, "The Niebuhr Brothers and the Liberal Protestant Heritage," in *Religion and Twentieth-Century American Intellectual Life,* edited by Michael J. Lacey (Cambridge: Cambridge University Press, 1989), 94–115; Richard Wightman Fox, *Reinhold Niebuhr: A Biography* (New York: Pantheon Books, 1985).

Theologically Conservative Christianity and Moral Progress

The Problem of Correlation

GEORGE M. MARSDEN

In the Western world the question of whether more traditional forms of Christianity contribute to the moral progress of society has been sharply contested since the Enlightenment.[1] Skeptics and advocates of liberal Christianity have claimed that theologically conservative Christianity retards moral progress. Theologically more conservative Christians[2]—a designation I am using broadly to include Catholics, Orthodox, evangelicals, and others who hold onto the central traditional theological claims of Christianity[3]—have argued in response that their faiths have contributed to moral progress. They have cited William Wilberforce's work in ending the British slave trade as an example.

Speaking as a confessional Protestant, I want to press some hard questions for more traditional believers such as myself in this debate as to whether more traditional forms of Christian faith have typically contributed to moral progress in the modern world. One could ask the same question about traditional versions of other faiths such as Judaism and Islam, but I am going to confine the discussion to Christianity. I particularly want to confront what is quite honestly a disturbing question from my point of view. One would hope from a theologically conservative perspective that, roughly speaking, the more faithful a theology was to the core affirmations of its tradition, the better would be the record of contributions to moral progress in society. Yet on the face of it, the opposite seems to be the case.

Just as preliminary examples, consider three social-political developments from American history that most people today would regard as contributions to moral progress: the ending of slavery; civil rights for racial minorities; and voting rights for women. In each of these cases there seem to have been more people who were, broadly speaking, theological traditionalists against these reforms, sometimes strongly so, than there were people for them. Moreover, despite some outstanding examples of theologically conservative Christians advocating such causes, there are many more examples of advocates who were either very liberal Christians or secularists (often ex-Christians). If anything it looks as though, despite some exceptions, the rule may be that the weaker the theology, the greater the contribution to moral progress.

I want to present some historically informed reflections on this issue that ought to be of concern to theologically more conservative Christians and of interest to others seeking to understand the cultural impact of such Christianity. I am an American historian, and I am going to speak mostly of American history since that is what I know enough about to discuss with some confidence in such a wide-ranging piece as this. Also, since I am writing this as a reflection on what I see as a genuine problem from a certain point of view, I am also including some more normative reflections on how one might think about the issues involved from that point of view. I want to emphasize at the outset that this essay is a "think piece" that poses a problem, rather than a product of extensive historical research that is supposed to resolve that problem. In other words, these thoughts, based on what are at best informed impressions, are meant as guidelines that may spark some more extensive inquiry, rather than as a presentation of the conclusions of such inquiry.

The most fundamental observation to keep in mind at the outset is that the answer to our question will turn on the prior question of what counts as moral progress. There are relatively few issues such as the ending of the slave trade or the other issues mentioned above on which there is anything approaching universal consensus. We can see the problem immediately if we think of issues such as legalized abortion, gay rights, or more liberal divorce laws. What counts as moral progress on these issues for one large group of people counts as moral regress for another. Moreover on these sorts of contested issues the degree of traditional Christian commitment often helps determine the side of these issues on which one stands.

Other sorts of divisive political issues have less directly to do with specific teachings of theologically conservative churches but still often divide them from more liberal Christians and secularists. For instance in the United States theologically conservative Christians have tended to be on the politically conservative side of big business and small government regarding economic policy and to favor big activist government regarding foreign policy and the military. On such issues political conservatives and political liberals usually disagree not on the professed moral ends that they are pursuing but rather only on the best means for achieving those ends. Both are for economic justice and for keeping the peace, but they hold opposing theories as to what constitutes economic justice or how best to keep the peace. In these cases the partial correlation between theological conservatism and political conservatism seems most often to reflect accidental factors, such as social location and temperament,[4] rather than theological differences. Regardless of the source of these differences,[5] they provide additional examples of issues on which theological conservatives often differ from theological liberals and secularists on what constitutes moral progress.

These preliminary observations leave us with the interpretive problem that all religious advocates of competing social-political views believe that the advancement of their views will constitute moral progress.[6] Although each set of believers, including believers in secular ideologies, can make judgments about moral progress according to its own criteria, there is no way for observers to achieve a fully detached viewpoint by which to judge moral progress according to criteria on which we can expect general agreement. Furthermore, to the extent that a religious group advances its views on such matters among its constituents, that group can point to how its faith has contributed to moral progress, or at least has helped retard moral regress.[7] That is the case concerning all the social issues that are still contested.

These preliminary observations give us a partial answer to the question about conservative theologies and moral progress. Traditionalist theologies do promote moral progress in society if we measure such progress by the standards of those who hold to traditionalist theologies. That is not a trivial observation since the causes advanced are significant. Yet it is also not a satisfying answer since it is true virtually by definition. Furthermore it leaves us with the same problem we started with regarding some major developments that today are almost universally regarded as moral progress but of which most theological conservatives at the time were on the wrong side. So I think we can learn most about the general phenomena involved if, rather than attempting to adjudicate the merits of issues still contested today, we reflect on some issues of moral progress that are no longer contested: the ending of slavery and the advancement of civil rights for African Americans. On these the records of more theologically orthodox religious groups are, on balance, not strong.

Mark Noll has wrestled, for instance, with the issues of American slavery and the Civil War as a theological crisis. In the debate over the Bible and slavery, conclusions were controlled more by regional location and self-interest than by the Bible. Furthermore even in the North few white people were compelled by the point that seems most evident today: that although the Bible condoned slavery, it certainly did not condone race-based slavery of one people by another. The premise that black Africans were inferior and needed to be cared for in some paternalistic system or another blinded most observers from seeing the racial basis of slavery as its most offensive component. Regarding the related issue of the Civil War, theology was hardly a variable, as virtually no religious spokesperson North or South was detached enough to refrain from simply proclaiming God's support for the armies of the region in which he or she happened to live.

If we look at support among white Americans for the civil rights movement of the 1950s and 1960s, theology is slightly more a predictor of political stance, but it seldom outweighs social location. Although some theologically conservative white Christians were strong supporters of civil rights, far more were not. Seldom did religious opponents of civil rights offer substantial theological or biblical arguments for opposing the movement, other than a general claim that the church should stay out of politics, a maxim that theologically conservative white southern Protestants, at least, did not always follow concerning other issues. White Christians supporting the civil rights movement were much more likely to be moderate or liberal theologically. That support often was shaped by theologies that explicitly put ethics above dogma.

Even in the North mainline Protestant support was much more likely to come from the educated leadership than from those in the grassroots constituencies who were more rooted in communities coping with the social changes. The strongest white Christian support for civil rights came from those who were from what would become known as the "knowledge class."

One of the best illustrations of the gap between individual leadership and collective action in the northern United States is a documentary called *A Time for Burning*. It is set in Omaha, Nebraska, in the mid-1960s and concerns a congregation of the Missouri Synod Lutheran Church, a conservative confessional Protestant denomination. The film documents the attempt of a young pastor to get his congregation to deal in a modest way with the challenge of racial integration. He simply proposes that some couples in his congregation volunteer to meet informally with some African American couples from neighboring Lutheran and Presbyterian churches. That is more than the white congregation in a changing neighborhood will stand for, despite considerable individual support of the principle involved. My colleague John McGreevy recounts similar stories for many Catholic parishes—church leaders and some priests pushed for civil rights, but many parishioners would have none of it.[8]

The pattern that emerges is that churches are far too immersed in their social locations to be reliable agents for effecting positive social-political changes. In the case of the old state churches, their dependence on the political order meant that they were most likely to support that order. More democratically oriented churches, such as have long prevailed in the United States, are too dependent on their memberships to be effective agents of prophetic social change. If a church's social-political teachings go against the beliefs of its members, those members can either simply ignore those teachings or find another church. Perhaps the clearest illustrations of social location trumping theology are in matters of warfare in which the vast majority of Christians simply support their nation/region right or wrong, as was the case in the American Civil War and World War I.[9] This rather disheartening conclusion regarding churches and political action is illuminated by turning to Reinhold Niebuhr's classic analysis in *Moral Man and Immoral Society*. Reacting in the 1930s to the social optimism of both liberal religious moralists and scientific secularists such as John Dewey, Niebuhr observed, "What is lacking among these moralists, whether religious or rational, is an understanding of the brutal character of the behavior of all human collectives, and the power of self-interest and collective egoism in all intergroup relations."[10] Niebuhr's observation about collectives applies to churches, which are almost always deeply embedded in a web of social-political interests from which they cannot break free. Apropos to our topic, Niebuhr noted that both the Catholic and Protestant orthodoxies of his day tended to be "defeatist" regarding social change, while the vice of Protestant liberals was their unrealistic "sentimentality."[11]

The cases we have been looking at—antislavery, civil rights, and unquestioning support for nationalistic wars—suggest that the teachings of traditional theology seem to have little to do with conservative Christians' social-political stances. The record becomes even more discouraging if we consider another political accomplishment now almost universally acclaimed, the voting franchise for women. In this case opposition from theological conservatives was related to their theology and moral teaching. In the United States some theologically orthodox Christians in America supported the campaigns for the franchise, but far more did not. Conservative denominations tended to see the vote for women as undermining God-ordained hierarchical values. They often viewed woman suffrage as part of a larger threat to the home and as analogous to questions of women's role in the church regarding which they believed there were clear teachings both in the Bible and in churchly traditions.

The record is no more encouraging in those instances in which theologically conservative religious organizations inspired reforms that opponents considered discriminatory or repressive, such as Sabbath legislation and Prohibition. Both of these reform movements drew from secular arguments of their social benefit, but the base for their success was widespread Protestant belief that the banned activities were inherently sinful, beliefs not shared even by some other significant religious groups. Similar issues have arisen with respect to church-supported reforms such as censorship of books and films, laws concerning birth control, or efforts to ban or counter the teaching of evolution in public schools. Repeatedly the question has been raised whether the standards appropriate for the church should be those for the civil order.[12] Once again the standard for measuring moral progress becomes blurred. Theologically conservative groups doubtless have done some good regarding many of these issues, but like most political action, that good has been mixed with ambiguities.

Given the generally bleak picture that emerges regarding the contributions of theologically conservative groups to moral progress through social-political action, perhaps we should rephrase the question. Our instinct in this very political era is to answer our question by thinking of larger social-political moral causes. Yet as Reinhold Niebuhr reminded us in *Moral Man and Immoral Society,* despite the corruptions or original sin in all of us, it is far more likely that we can cultivate relatively moral individuals than moral societies. Whatever the merits of Niebuhr's exact theory, historically there seems to be a much better case for finding major contributions of theological conservatives to moral progress if we look at the individuals rather than at politics.

At the individual level it is incontrovertible that theologically more conservative groups have had a profound influence in disciplining and often reshaping countless people's lives. The most dramatic cases are seen in religious converts who testify to changes in their lives. Fundamentalist, holiness, and Pentecostal churches, for instance, are filled with people who tell of how prior to their conversions their lives were falling apart due to alcoholism, drugs, sexual promiscuity, abuse, and other forms of dissipation or irresponsibility. Often such people are attracted to churches with strict theologies, personal disciplines, and authoritarian pastors who will help them regulate their lives.[13] Families that were falling apart are put back together. Children who would not have had consistent discipline and moral training receive it. More churchly traditions such as Roman Catholic or confessional Protestant are perhaps even more effective in shaping individuals' lives across generations. Often their teachings and disciplines are systematic and have been reinforced in family devotions and training, in parochial schools, and in extensive church programs for training of children and young people. The history of Sunday schools in the nineteenth and twentieth centuries illustrates how such training was extended outside the immediate church communities to offer at least some basic religious and moral training to children of the unchurched.

In these cases, unlike those we considered regarding collective social-political action, it seems that in general the more strongly conservative the theology, the greater the contribution to moral discipline and hence to social improvement. Such correlations would be difficult to measure or demonstrate, but it is easy to see the reasons why they would obtain. Of course there are extremes in which disciplines might seem anti-social or abusive, and there are cases concerning which social liberals do not like the content of some moral teaching, as on matters of women's roles, abortion, or gay sexual activity. Nonetheless there is a strong case, even from a socially liberal perspective, that the putative ill effects of these latter teachings are at least balanced by many good effects from stable family and church environments that encourage simple virtues such as honesty, self-discipline, personal responsibility, playing by the rules, and law keeping, all of which contribute to healthy functioning of society.[14] Such influences on aggregates of individuals have also had perceptible impact on larger societies. In England there has long been discussion of the effects of Methodism on the working classes of the nineteenth century. Assessments vary, but the impact surely is there.

It is easy to point to the collective impact of religious training in ethno-religious communities in the United States, such as in Catholic parishes, Lutherans in Minnesota, or the one I am most familiar with, the Dutch-Reformed in western Michigan and northwestern Iowa. Such communities are clannish and have other faults. For instance, like the Missouri Synod congregation in Omaha, ethno-religious communities were often racist, especially when directly involved in neighborhoods that were changing. On some issues they might not be as socially progressive as some would like, but all individuals and groups have their faults, so the relevant question is always, compared to whom? Furthermore such churches and communities have founded many charitable organizations, hospitals, and other social service agencies and sometimes have contributed impressively to charities that serve more than their own adherents. More broadly Americans who are active in religious organizations are more likely to give to charities and to engage in volunteer work than are secular Americans, and the religious even surpass secularists in average giving to nonreligious causes.[15] Everything else being equal, the presence of strong religious communities increases the chances of the viability and moral health of a society.

I have been describing here the phenomenon that some refer to as the "moral capital" upon which societies depend. Religious communities are among the principal generators of such capital, and it is in the interest of societies to encourage them to thrive and to preserve their theological and moral distinctivenesses. For instance most laws that would coerce educational institutions of religious groups to abandon their distinctiveness and conform to some state-imposed standards are not in the long-term interest of larger society. Religious groups, of course, are hardly the only sources of moral capital in a society, but they are crucial ones. The moral capital they generate lasts for generations, even if often in altered forms.

The generational aspect of religious training, which depends on families even more than on churches, helps explain another paradox that arises when we talk about more or less orthodox religion and moral progress. Often it seems that individuals who endorse prophetic moral-political reforms are less likely to be religiously conservative and more likely to be either religiously liberal or religious skeptics. My hypothesis regarding this phenomenon is that many people who are brought up with strong religious training find its effects difficult to escape even when they reject the dogmatic tenets of their religious faith. Quite a few of such people who cannot believe the old theology or who lack the requisite spiritual experience nonetheless hold onto some of the moral principles of their upbringing with all the more fervor. In addition they are more likely to look to the government to implement such reforms. In this way theologically more conservative religious groups that tend to be protective of the social status quo become inadvertently among the principal nurseries for more progressive reforms. One can see this phenomenon, for instance, in the leadership of American Protestant liberalism and the Social Gospel, which was drawn largely from people with evangelical upbringing but who lacked the requisite conversion experience and could no longer hold onto traditional theology.[16] Those who remained in the church typically adopted theologies that explicitly elevated moral practice over dogma. Regarding this general phenomenon, there are abundant examples. Many leaders of the reforms of the Progressive movement in American history had strong religious backgrounds, even if most of these had departed from theological orthodoxy. White advocates of the New South in the early twentieth century were more likely than the average to be moderate to liberal in theology. Catholics strict in their upbringing became some of the strongest anti–Vietnam War protesters.

David L. Chappell's *A Stone of Hope: Prophetic Religion and the Death of Jim Crow* provides a striking example of how moral capital built up in a socially conservative setting might be mobilized for a progressive political cause. Chappell argues that a crucial, but sometimes overlooked, element necessary for the success of the American civil rights movements was the prophetic revivalist tradition in the African American religious community. The progressive ideals of the American white liberal political tradition, with their optimism about human nature, were insufficient to bring the civil rights revolution, despite the good intentions of many of the powerful. Martin Luther King Jr. helped bring about a convergence of Niebuhrian political realism and the moral resources of the African American revivalist community that was vital to effective coercion for civil rights.[17] Some of the longest-lasting influences of Christian teachings that almost everyone would associate with moral progress are also the most difficult to measure. We can consider, for instance, the impact of Jesus' teachings on civilization. These indeed seem to act as a leaven whose effects permeate far beyond the bounds of churches that originally propound the teachings. The idea that the poor, the helpless, the stranger, and the oppressed should be especially valued provides a revolutionary ideal for humanity that puts a premium on humility and self-sacrifice on behalf of the weak. Although Jesus was not the only one to teach such ideals, he has been the most influential. The theologian Hendrikus Berkhof has argued that the many implementations of these notions may be seen as harbingers of Christ's kingdom, like "the crocuses in the winter of a fallen world." Berkhof suggested that "an ordinary street scene, such as an ambulance stopping all traffic because one wounded man must be transported, is the result of the coming of the Kingdom."[18] Christians would not accept this theological interpretation, but the example is striking.

In the modern era such ideals are often pursued most vigorously in liberal Christian and secular forms, frequently with mixed results. Charles Taylor argues in *A Secular Age* that by the nineteenth century the outlook that he calls "exclusive humanism" often made altruism the highest virtue and made unbelief or disavowal of any exclusive forms of religion a condition for truly universal altruism.[19] Marxism provides the clearest example of such a universalistic ideal that favors the oppressed. The unsavory consequences of Marxism also best illustrate the theme of irony that keeps recurring in this analysis. In the hope that lofty ideals will have their widest consequence, they are translated into political action. Once they are translated in political action, they are corrupted by power, so that the results are typically a bewildering combination of the beneficial and the oppressive, all in the name of moral progress. Not only can politics corrupt, but so can secular ideologies that carry ideals associated with "moral progress" to extremes. For instance, we might say that on the whole there has been some true moral progress in Euro-American civilization in the past century with regard to valuing those who are different from ourselves—the stranger, the poor, the ill, and the handicapped. Nonetheless the impulse to celebrate diversity that has helped foster these good causes often gets associated with a rampant individualism that abets destructive moral anarchy. In sum theological conservatives have no monopoly on paradoxical moral stances.

With regard to more theologically conservative forms of Christianity on which we are focusing, we are still left with one major question: if these more theologically conservative religious groups have a far better record in promoting moral progress through helping to change individuals rather than through collective political action, what does that say normatively about the stances they should take toward social-political action? Does my account support, for instance, what many old liberals and new conservatives present as a major heresy or, at least, a cop-out? Am I saying that the business of the churches is to save souls and otherwise shape or change individual lives, but they have no social-political task?

That formula is, I think, far too simplistic. I would suggest rather that what turns out to be a Niebuhrian description of the historical record fits best with a more Niebuhrian and Augustinian prescription. Niebuhr drew essentially on Augustine's observation that the "cities of the world" are founded on the principle of protecting their own self-interests. Hence it is unlikely that they will act on the basis of pure Christian moral considerations, which are founded on the principle the opposite of self-interest. Further, to throw a little of Calvin into the mix, those of the City of God—of the redeemed in Christ—though in principle united in his love, are imperfectly sanctified in this life and still suffer from the corruptions of their old selfish natures. So the altruism emanating from the City of God is diluted by a substantial remnant of self-interest. That tendency to put self-interest first is amplified when Christians or church organizations are dealing with the local civil order on which they may depend for their safety or which may be a threat to both their spiritual and mundane interests. Hence Christians acting collectively with respect to the political order are only somewhat more likely to act on moral principle alone than is a government.

This Augustinian-Calvinistic-Niebuhrian starting point regarding the inherent corruptions of human nature that are especially manifested in politics suggests that churches and other groups of Christians will be corrupted if they hitch their wagon to a political cause.[20] That means that Christians, whether collectively or individually, who do engage in politics should regard it as a lowly subordinate allegiance, not to be identified in any way with the essence of the faith.[21] Without entirely renouncing whatever responsibility they may have for doing good by way of the civil order, Christian persons and organizations should characteristically recognize that they see through a glass darkly and are recommending only what seems to them to be the relatively better choices. In practice this means that religious individuals and organizations, while speaking out on political issues of moral concern, should not in effect confessionalize a political stance or in effect link their faith with a government or a political party.

Historically what we see again and again are examples just the opposite of such diffidence with respect to political causes. History is littered with records of Christians, either individually or collectively, who have invoked God's unqualified support for a far from perfect political cause. We also see repeatedly in history that when two such causes clash and each side claims God on its side, the conflicts are all the more intractable and brutal because neither side can imagine that it might be wrong.

The frequency of such cases and the horrors that have been perpetrated in the name of Christianity (and other religions) make it tempting to go beyond arguing for Niebuhrian diffidence when approaching politics to arguing closer to the position of Stanley Hauerwas and others, who argue that the church should simply be the church, witness to what is morally right, but not take any responsibility for the civil order. Advocates of this view point out that one of the three temptations of Christ was the "political temptation" that Satan would give him all the kingdoms of the world. They suggest in strong terms that Christians should think of their allegiance as first of all to another kingdom and themselves as merely "resident aliens" in the kingdoms of the world.[22] I like very much the emphasis in this viewpoint on primary and subordinate allegiances and the metaphor of "resident aliens" as a reminder for Christians not to identify their faith with a political party or order. That is a sensibility that needs to be strongly cultivated, one way or another. However, I think that even resident aliens have some responsibilities to the civil order in which they reside and on which they depend. They have a responsibility not only passively to obey the law but also to do whatever positive good for their neighbor can be done through the powers of the civil order. At the same time they need to recognize that every civil order is severely limited morally and never to be confused in any way with a branch or agency of the City of God. Individual Christians or groups should use political means to promote good causes so long as they recognize that they have only a partial vision of God's will in matters corrupted by politics. They need to recognize that often they will be supporting only the relatively best of the imperfect paths available. Maintaining such distinctions is a hard task, but no one said that the Christian life would be easy.

One reason I want to maintain a place for political action is that civil governments, despite their inevitable corruptions, are among the gifts of God to maintain order and to promote the good. Even though civil governments are unable to act on a purely moral or altruistic basis, they do often choose relatively better moral courses when such courses fit their self-interests. In fact such happy convergences are among the primary reasons that we get some moral progress in political history. We can see that in the matters we have considered, such as ending the slave trade and slavery or providing the vote for women or civil rights for African Americans. In addition we can see it in some of the reforms of the Progressive Era that restrained self-interest in the economic sphere, such as in pure food and drug laws or various ways of regulating commerce or retail, and that relate to the principle that for society as a whole, honesty is the best policy. Since governments and political causes do, despite their limitations, sometimes get things more or less right, it is important to have citizens who advocate what they see as right. Hence while chastening our political concerns with a strong dose of realism and warnings that politics, as the temptation of Jesus suggests, is the devil's playground, we can still find room for and celebrate the William Wilberforces of the world.

NOTES

1. I wish to thank the Colloquium on Religion and History at the University of Notre Dame for their very helpful comments.

2. I recognize, of course, that evangelicals are often theologically innovative in some respects. It is difficult to find either a precise or a concise term for what I mean, and I use "theologically traditionalist" or "theological conservative" or "theologically orthodox" interchangeably, even though I recognize the imprecision.

3. The sorts of Christians I have in mind are those who, despite some wide differences in other respects, agree that the central claims of Christianity have to do with eternal salvation made possible by the redemptive work of Christ through his death on the cross and resurrection from the dead.

4. Self-interest plays a role in every moral choice but is far more dominant in some than in others.

5. The sources of political or economic views are often relevant to our evaluation of the views. For instance some theologically conservative groups in America have had close ties to big business donors who have, at the least, reinforced the conservative economic and political views of the religious groups.

6. A striking example is the statement that Eugene Genovese recorded by a southern slaveholder, the Reverend J. Henry Smith of North Carolina, in December 1861 that "if we fail the progress of civilization will be thrown back a century." See Eugene Genovese, *A Consuming Fire: The Fall of the Confederacy in the Mind of the White Christian South* (Athens: University of Georgia Press, 1998), 102.

7. The idea of "moral progress" is a category arising in the eighteenth-century Enlightenment, and arguably we are not taking theologically traditionalist churches seriously on their own terms if we impose this test on Christians who have other priorities that they see as higher. I am grateful to my colleague Brad Gregory for this observation. Some theologically conservative churches have bought into the idea that promoting moral progress should be a test of the faith. The present exercise does that to some extent, although my question could be rephrased simply in terms of whether a type of religion contributes to what is good for the society, without claiming that "moral progress" is the object or expectation.

8. Barbara Connell and William C. Jersey, directors, *A Time for Burning* (documentary film, 1966); John McGreevy, *Parish Boundaries: The Catholic Encounter with Race in the Twentieth-Century Urban North* (Chicago: University of Chicago Press, 1996).

9. Peace churches take unpopular stands against their national societies, but at the expense of influence in the political sphere.

10. Reinhold Niebuhr, *Moral Man and Immoral Society: A Study in Ethics and Politics* (New York: Charles Scribner's Sons, 1932), xx.

11. Ibid., 78. Today theologically conservative Protestants and Catholics of the religious right often sound more optimistic in proclaiming the possibility of effecting social-political change.

12. Many religious people, mostly moderate to liberal theologically, who see abortion as morally problematic but less than murder argue that this is the crucial question regarding antiabortion legislation.

13. These themes are apparent in Nancy Ammerman's study of a fundamentalist congregation, *Bible Believers: Fundamentalists in the Modern World* (New Brunswick, N.J.: Rutgers

University Press, 1987); and in James Ault's comparable study, *Spirit and Flesh: Life in a Fundamentalist Baptist Church* (New York: Knopf, 2004). See also Ault's documentary film *Born Again: Life in a Fundamentalist Baptist Church* (1987) on the same subject.

14. These observations suggest an agenda for historians of religion and culture. For a long time history has been so dominated by politics that historians often justify their interest in religious history by pointing to its political implications. Recently there has been a lot of talk about studying "lived religion" as an alternative to looking either at politics or at church history and theology dominated by church leaders. Occasionally students of lived religion look at the impact of churches on personal morality, but it seems to me that there might be a lot more room for that, especially for studying the moral teachings of churches on their own terms, as opposed to looking at them simply as examples of quaint conservatism.

15. Arthur C. Brooks, *Who Really Cares* (New York: Basic Books, 2006), presents extensive evidence to this effect. See, for instance, p. 38 for a summary. Brooks tends to overstate his conclusions and their implications, as is pointed out in a review by James Halteman in *Christian Century* 124, no. 12 (June 12, 2007): 32, but the overall findings are nonetheless striking.

16. William R. Hutchison, "Cultural Strain in Protestant Liberalism," *American Historical Review* 76, no. 2 (April 1971): 386–411.

17. David L. Chappell, *A Stone of Hope: Prophetic Religion and the Death of Jim Crow* (Chapel Hill: University of North Carolina Press, 2004). That this moral capital was built up in a context that was both theologically conservative and often socially conservative is suggested by the fact that in 1961 the National Baptist Convention divided over Martin Luther King Jr.'s efforts to involve it more strongly in the civil rights movement.

18. Hendrikus Berkhof, *Christ the Meaning of History*, trans. Lambertus Buursman (Richmond, Va.: John Knox Press, 1966), 181, 188.

19. Charles Taylor, *A Secular Age* (Cambridge, Mass.: Harvard University Press, 2007), 361.

20. Mark Noll points out that the Marxist historian Eric Williams has remarked that "Wilberforce was familiar with all that went on in the hold of a slave ship but ignored what went on at the bottom of a mineshaft." He was, says Williams, on the side of the wealthy of his own class in favoring the Corn Laws and opposing the Reform Bill of 1831. In other words, even the best of us have such blind spots. This is from Mark Noll, *The Rise of Evangelicalism: The Age of Edwards, Whitefield, and the Wesleys* (Downers Grove, Ill.: InterVarsity Press, 2003), 254, citing Eric Williams, *Capitalism and Slavery* (Chapel Hill: University of North Carolina Press, 1944), 182.

21. This sense of modesty will need to be worked out a little differently for liberal Christians who sometimes make ethics the center of the faith. Niebuhr provides a useful model in this respect.

22. See, for example, Stanley Hauerwas, *The Hauerwas Reader* (Durham, N.C.: Duke University Press, 2001). Cf. John Howard Yoder, *The Politics of Jesus* (Grand Rapids, Mich.: Eerdmans, 1972).

Afterword

Cultural Change—The Biggest Question for Historians

Felipe Fernández-Armesto

I want to broach what I contend are the biggest questions for historians: Why do cultural changes happen? Why have they tended to accelerate? The preceding essays suggest, to me, three observations. First, religions sometimes change people for the better, sometimes for the worse, but no overall characterization of their moral impact on societies is possible in the present state of our knowledge. We can perhaps say, at best, that they have a restraining effect on some forms of evil. Second, claims for moral progress in history fail for lack of evidence and lack of a means of measuring moral change. Even the example on which we have focused—the abolition of the slave trade—seems morally equivocal, as in some respects it made the surviving trade worse and unleashed massacres of slave-trading communities who, as far as they were concerned, were engaged in an activity legitimated by tradition.[1] Abolition seems, in any case, to have been an exception in an otherwise static history of moral stagnation. Humans' propensity for good and evil or, to use less loaded terms, altruism and self-ishness has remained the same throughout the history of the species. This raises, of course, the compelling, if more or less familiar, problem of why we make apparent progress in some fields, notably in science and technology, but not in others. Third—and this to me is the most curious conclusion—if moral stasis really has characterized our past, it is a surprising exception to the otherwise apparently universal law of change. It prompts intriguing reflections: that morality is perhaps exempt from evolution, which would be a striking modification of Darwinian expectations; or that it may in a sense be supracultural, which would decisively undermine moral relativism.

Underlying all these conclusions, reflections, and problems lurks a question so fundamental to historians' work that we never even ask it: why does change happen at all? Progress, after all, is only an instance of change, or perhaps a term that attempts an overall characterization of it. But it seems premature to question it before we have satisfied ourselves that we understand the bigger phenomenon of which it is a part or an intended description. Change is a difficult subject to address because everything we say about it is observed from the inside, trapped by a form of uncertainty princi-ple. Change grips us as we try to grasp it. Philosophers who attempted to explain it in antiquity—from the Upanishads to the Eleatics and beyond—commonly fell back on the counterintuitive claim that it is illusory since it seems inexplicable. A changed state of affairs, they reckoned, presupposes a prior state unchanged with respect to it. Alternatively the solution associated with Heraclitus, that change is the essence of nature—that flux, if you like, is the default state of the universe—satisfies observation but, as Plato pointed out in the *Theaetetus,* defies logic.[2] Healing for such disputes is beyond historians' practice. But it may still be worthwhile asking about why change happens in the historian's specific province of culture. Hitherto we have taken this for granted and thought it intractable to or unworthy of enquiry. I believe that we can no longer be so insouciant. Primatology and cultural zoology have given us new standards of comparison, which make the question ineluctable and even urgent.

The novelty of the disclosures of these disciplines is apparent to me when I recall the chimpanzees' tea party, which, like many other Londoners, I attended occasionally as a child. It was a daily event at the zoo in the 1950s but now is banned as politically incorrect and injurious to chimpanzees' dignity. The chimps sat at a table laden with tea-time paraphernalia and foodstuffs, where they entertained the crowd by making as much mess as possible. According to some of the world's leading experts on chimpanzee behavior, they probably deliberately hammed up the performance for the spectators' delectation.[3] We onlookers, however, thought it funny—though the younger of us may not have expressed it thus—because we thought that humans were uniquely cultural animals and that chimps' efforts to imitate our table manners were vitiated by a fundamental inability to understand what manners were. Now the joke is on us, because half a century of research has taught us that we are not alone in possessing culture and that chimpanzees are among a number of nonhuman cultural creatures: practitioners, that is, of behaviors that are socially but not practically functional and are neither instinctive nor advantageous in an evolutionary sense; rather they are transmitted by tradition and acquired by learning.[4] It is now apparent, moreover, that chimpanzees have food-distribution practices of their own—I should not hesitate to call them rites—which may not be as mannered as those of our tea tables but which are nonetheless of broadly the same ilk.

The evidence that some nonhuman animals have culture began to pile up in the early 1950s, when investigators in Japan observed a now-famous macaque monkey instructing her tribe in her newly discovered technique of washing the dirt off sweet potatoes before eating them. Subsequent generations learned how to do it and continue the tradition—with some modifications—to this day. Proof that the practice is a rite rather than a crudely useful function is that the monkeys will always do the washing, even if humans deliver the vegetables ready-cleaned, as if in a supermarket.[5] Since the discovery of macaque culture, innumerable cultural practices have been detected in many species of apes and monkeys and also, according to investigators in the field, in elephants, dolphins, and rats. In some cases there is evidence of cultural divergence among communities of a single species. In some baboon tribes, for instance, males practice monogamy; in others they have harems. Different chimpanzee communities have different technologies; some hunt quite intensively,[6] whereas others do not. In different places orangutans play different games. Yet it remains true to say that cultural divergence—which is an index of the scale and rate of cultural change—is small in nonhuman species, compared with the immense diversity of human cultures. It is remarkable that there are any cultural differences at all between communities of particular species of apes and monkeys, but they oscillate within a narrow band. Dolphin societies and those of rats and elephants exhibit the same or scarcely varying structures, as far as we can tell at present, wherever they are.

Every scientifically testable form of human uniqueness ever alleged has turned out in the light of present knowledge to be invalid. Humans are not uniquely social creatures any more than uniquely tool-making or language-using or self-aware or—probably—morally conscious. All creatures are unique, but human uniqueness is not of a unique kind. We differ from other animals only in degree. However, in this respect the difference of degree is marked: other animals' cultures are more or less static, or at least they exhibit ranges of difference, species by species, much smaller than those observable in human contexts. Human cultures, by contrast, are highly mutable—even volatile. The first big question for the historian therefore is, why do human cultures, alone of those of cultural animals, change so much? Why are we the only culturally volatile species?

To express the problem another way, it would be otiose to attempt to write histories of the societies of any cultural creatures except humans. Even chimpanzees, who are in just about every respect the creatures most closely comparable to humans, hardly have any history. They have politics, which Frans de Waal, the great analyst of chimp political science, has characterized as Machiavellian.[7] But though one alpha male from time to time successfully displaces another, the nature of authority in chimpanzee communities never changes. It would be rash to say that it never could change. One of the most curious episodes observed by Jane Goodall's team of researchers in Tanzania was of a chimp low down the ranking among the males of his tribe who for a time successfully challenged the leaders' dominance by rolling packing cases, appropriated from the primatologists' camp, across his rivals' favored tracks through the forest. At first the incumbents were inclined to defer to him in their puzzlement. But his coup did not last long, and no permanent revolution occurred in the distribution of power or in the way chimpanzee leaders emerge. Nonetheless it is tempting to see in this incident evidence both of how limited the range of chimpanzee political culture is compared to that of humans and of how the distance might be narrowed in the future. Power takeovers do not usually affect the structures among chimpanzees; they merely shift the alpha role, and other typical power relationships, among individuals.[8] We no longer have alpha males running our societies as, presumably, our hominid ancestors once did. We have replaced succession by challenge and combat, which still prevails among chimpanzees, with other means of selecting leaders: by charisma, sacrality, heredity, sagacity, demagogy. Among chimpanzees, however, it is already possible for an individual to attain temporary ascendancy by an innovative strategy. Changes of leadership and even of forms or structures of leadership have also been reported among baboons.[9] Over time new kinds of political change could become systematic in chimpanzee or even baboon societies and those of some other cultural animals, as in our own. I hope to suggest later why this has not yet happened among chimps and how circumstances could favor it in the future.

Meanwhile we can accept that humans are the only species with history. But this form of human distinctiveness has accrued over time. It is not "natural" to humans in the sense of having been a feature of human life since Homo sapiens first emerged. On the contrary, as far as we can tell, for most of our existence our species has been culturally stable—in key respects, as unchanging as other species. The earliest divergences we can attribute to human cultures arose as a result of the migration of Homo sapiens out of our native environment in East Africa about one hundred thousand years ago. Those divergences were consequences of the need to adapt to new and previously unexperienced environments, which produced, for instance, variants in dress and foraging techniques, and of the sheer distances that arose between increasingly sundered communities. I suspect that separation by distance must have stimulated linguistic divergence, which—to judge from the huge differences in language today between contiguous peoples in Australia and New Guinea, who in other respects resemble each other closely in culture—must have been an early form of societies' mutual differentiation. Even so, the differences among widely dispersed peoples in the Paleolithic era were small, by recent standards, and not much greater than those of many other primates. All human communities practiced essentially the same kind of foraging economy. All used similar tool kits and weapons. Most seem to have practiced one or more of a limited range of religions focused on shamanism or on the cult of a deity usually designated as an "earth-mother" figure. If art is the mirror of society, the rate of change in Paleolithic cultures was minimal. The recent discovery of cave paintings at Chauvet that were some ten thousand years older than previously known examples of the genre reveals startling continuity in subjects, techniques, and treatment.[10]

Again the inescapable inference is that social and cultural change is a historical subject susceptible of historical explanation. The peculiar mutability of human society has its origins not in "human nature"—whatever that is—but in the circumstances of the relatively recent past. The increasing pace of change, moreover, is not an inherent property of change but a historical phenomenon. It has occurred—for the most part—within a relatively well-known and relatively well-documented period, which can be said to have coincided roughly with the Holocene and to have quickened spectacularly in the last few centuries.

The need to explain the origins of change and its recent and current accelerations is acute precisely because the pace of change is so fast today: so fast that even within living memory the world seems to have changed unrecognizably, inducing "future shock," fear, bewilderment, and resentment. When people do not understand what is happening to them, they panic. *Grandes peurs* lash society like a flagellant's scourge. Intellectuals take refuge in "postmodern" strategies: indifference, anomie, moral relativism and scientific indeterminacy, the embrace of chaos, *je m'enfoutisme*. In reaction against uncertainty, electorates succumb to noisy little men and glib solutions. Religions transmute into dogmatisms and fundamentalisms. We can best confront or cope with these reactions if we can provide a coherent explanation of the rapidity and reach of change in our world.

Two ways of documenting—or at least of illustrating or evoking—the pace of change in our time appeal to me. We can begin by summoning a series of images, so familiar that they need only be mentioned to be visible to the mind's eye, that capture moments of vividly perceived change, when the world in which people of my generation grew up became unrecognizable. Some of the most potent images that form today's common stock document environmental change. No one attentive to world affairs today can forget images of the Greenland ice melting into the sea, the Amazonian rain forest retreating in flames, new viruses inflicting unpredictable plagues upon the world, desertification stranding rusting hulks in the salt wastes that were once the Aral Sea. These are peculiarly alarming images of our time not so much because of the menace they illustrate for the future, though they certainly do that, as for the way they make vivid the unprecedented nature of change in the recent past. Hitherto we thought of environmental change as typically slow—much slower than cultural change. Now the two realms are so thoroughly interpenetrated that the environment seems as unstable as every other sphere of human impact.

In politics images of the fall of the Berlin Wall recall the surprise of most of those who saw it happen. Although some historians and political scientists anticipated the Soviet collapse,[11] most people overestimated its durability. Almost everyone who witnessed the events of 1989–92 in central and eastern Europe was astounded at the scale and suddenness of the end of the cold war and the dismantling of a system that—for all its menace—conveyed the comfort of familiarity and, according to the consensus of the experts, preserved the peace of the world. Most people, I suspect, would select the 9/11 felling of the World Trade Center in New York as another such moment, which reconfigured world politics along with the skyline of the city. The effects of the event have certainly been far-reaching. They contributed to the onset of a new, aggressive era in United States foreign policy and to the forfeiture or long postponement of the world's opportunity to create a new order, based on international cooperation and global governance, after the end of the cold war. For me, the images of destruction and corruption generated by the Iraq War are far more disturbing because they disclose a world I—with all my skepticism and world-weariness— had never previously detected or foreseen. I had naively believed that one of the great merits of democracies is that it is hard to coax them into war, and that they therefore tended to make the world a better and safer place. The Iraq imbroglio has shown us how easy it is for irresponsible governments to start wars even in democracies.

Images such as these from the political arena are matched by others from the world of economics: images of panic in the bourses and people on the streets whenever the frightening lurches typical of modern economies fell currencies, break banks, bust businesses, and slash stocks. On the whole, however, although these pressures generate far-reaching psychological strains and contribute to the neuroses and psychoses of modern life, I think it is fair to say that economies are surprisingly resilient. Cultural changes, on the other hand, are much harder for society to cope with because when they are deep, rapid, and extensive, they subvert people's identities and challenge their sense of their place in the world. The current scale of global migration, and its effects on countries with net intakes of migrants, is a prime example. I welcome its enriching effects but can understand why many people find it disturbing to see their neighborhoods or even their hometowns changed—the look of buildings and gardens transformed, the shops restocked, the sound of the streets retuned, the places of worship rededicated, the aroma of the food revised. More surprising and more shocking is the fact that cultures can effect self-transmutations as thorough and disturbing, without any outside aid, as the changes migrants make. I call to mind the scenes of grieving that the death of the former Princess of Wales, Diana Spencer, provoked in England. It suddenly became obvious that the England of my youth, to which my father had devoted a book,[12] the England distinguished by reserve and the cult of the stiff upper lip, had vanished, not because foreigners corroded the culture but because the English themselves abandoned it.[13] The stiff upper lip went wobbly, and Di's millions of mourners wallowed in what the teachers of my childhood years would have condemned as exhibitionism and emotional slacking.

This is perhaps an extreme case of a culture unrecognizably self-transformed, but there are many others. I have also followed in my own experience the self-transformation of Spaniards since the Franco era. Here, of course, the political context has changed, but the cultural changes are much more thorough and in some ways independent of those in politics, as Spain has abandoned a vocation to be "different" and has self-consciously remodeled cultural practices to conform to western European models. Spaniards now tolerate pornography, sexual permissiveness, and divorce. They drink and smoke less. They talk their regional languages unselfconsciously. They cross the street when they like. Their manners are more relaxed. In some parts of the country they have changed the horarium of the working day. They dress casually—at least more casually than before.[14] Even in countries that have become exporters of labor, cultural "westernization" has had similar effects. Changes in sexual mores are particularly unsettling because they coincide with generation gaps, challenge family solidarity, and have something of the force of violated taboos. In parts of the West, the rapidity with which homosexual alliances have achieved equality or near-equality of esteem with traditional marriage amounts, in effect, to a new morality. In general the effects of pluralism, which are inestimably beneficial, are also unsettling. I think of the widely reproduced photographs of the pope at prayer in Aya Sophia. Catholics of my generation could hardly behold such images without thinking that the world they now inhabit is very different from the one in which they were catechized. Even a young Rip van Winkle would awake today, after a short nap, to a surprising world and a dislocating experience. The *plus ça change* adage no longer applies: if I can be excused a necessarily paradoxical way of putting it, things can change so much that they are no longer their former selves.

My second way of evoking the pace of contemporary change is to refer to its effect on historians. Historical writing narrates the past but reflects the present. In my time in the profession, the most conspicuous change has been what I call the collapse of the *longue durée*. When I was a student, gradualism was the vogue. My contemporaries and I were taught to see the origins of changes in the grinding structures of competing kinds of determinism. Now it is accepted that great events can arise from small causes[15] and that everything can be explained or is even best explained in its immediate context, or so to say that history as a system resembles the weather, in which the flap of a butterfly's wings can raise a storm. When we seek to explain the decline and fall of the Roman Empire, for instance, we do not return, like Gibbon, to the Antonine age, when the empire was doing rather well, but confine ourselves to the circumstances of the barbarian invasions of the late fourth and fifth centuries. When we want to understand the English civil war, we no longer appeal, as Macaulay did, to "the Whig interpretation" or to supposed long continuities of England's traditions of freedom, stretching back to the Germanic woods, much less to the rise of the bourgeoisie, but concentrate instead on the few years preceding the outbreak of hostilities and on the effects of the Scottish war of 1638. When we explore the causes of the French Revolution, we no longer reach back, as Tocqueville did, to the era of Louis XIV but rather allege a relatively brief crisis that began with the American Revolutionary War. When we discuss the origins of World War I, we no longer do as Alberti did and cite the defects of the nineteenth-century diplomatic system, which actually kept the peace; rather we look at the breakdown of that system in the years preceding the war or even, in an extreme case, at the impetus of the railway timetables of August 1914. And so on; the examples are innumerable. In other words, as the pace of change in our own times has increased, the willingness of historians to believe in long continuities in the past has declined.

As far as I know, no explanation for the increasing pace of change is available, other than the assumption that change is cumulative—which is no explanation but merely an alternative way of describing the phenomenon we have to explain. For an explanation it is tempting to look to the two influences that have proved most reliable in explaining other kinds of change and all behavioral change—including change properly classified as cultural—in nonhuman species: evolution and environment.[16] But neither of these is satisfactory in accounting for the frequency and volatility of short-term cultural change in humans. The critical gap between human and nonhuman cultural species demands a further, peculiarly human explanation. The environment, in any case, is relatively inert compared with human culture, and although there are occasional cases, such as large-scale volcanic eruptions or the sudden evolution of a new and powerful microorganism, when the rhythms of environmental and cultural change coincide, these are too infrequent to account for all the lurches of culture. Evolution too seems generally a too slow-working mechanism to meet the case. Even the syncopations of "punctuated equilibrium" are too slow and too rare. There are cases of rapid evolutionary mutations, but they happen rarely.[17] We can measure the pace of human evolutionary divergence in our DNA, but the results do not stand comparison with the cultural divergence that historians record. Although our species encompasses a relatively wide range of DNA, the variation is infinitesimal, compared with the enormous diversity of our cultures.

The only serious attempt to explain cultural change in evolutionary terms, the theory of memes,[18] is valueless. Not only is there no evidence for the existence of memes (evolved "units" of culture) or of any mechanism by which evolution could select them for transmission to other cultures, but also such evidence as we have supports an incompatible conclusion: the most adaptive cultures are not the fittest for survival but the most prone to catastrophe. Successful survival cannot therefore account for the replication of memes. A system that independently of human choice imposed cultures equipped to survive would select for foraging. Cultures that have stuck to that strategy have survived for scores of millennia, whereas those that have substituted sedentarism, urbanization, agriculture, and all the other adaptations we associate with "civilization" are one with Nineveh and Tyre. Our adaptations bear the fingerprints of free will precisely because, so far, just about all of them have been unsuccessful.[19] Their increasing pace looks like a measure of increasing desperation. To respond by claiming that the test of success for a cultural adaptation is not to contribute to the survival of a host culture but simply to attract imitators—rather as a parasite might succeed by destroying its host organism—is, in effect, to offer no contest, since it leaves human caprice as the only mechanism for explaining how societies choose between cultural traits.

We can at least be confident in asserting that although evolution and the environment create the framework of contingencies within which everything in history happens and that some features of cultures may be explicable in evolutionary and environmental terms, specific cultural changes do happen independently of evolution and environment. Culture as a projection of the human mind and cultural changes originates in the realm of ideas. I do not mean to assert that the mind—or, to focus on exactly what I mean by "mind" in the present context, the capacity for generating ideas—is unaffected by evolution. As far as we can tell, our capacity for thought is itself a product of evolution, and if it is true—as we suppose, on the basis of our present knowledge—that humans have an exceptional capacity for generating ideas, evolution should have played some part in endowing us with it. As a working hypothesis, I propose that ideas are by-products of a well-equipped imagination, which in turn is a product of a well-developed power of anticipation. Evolution selects for anticipation especially in the case of hunting animals, which need to be able to anticipate the behavior both of prey and of rival predators, often in environments that occlude the senses. Homo sapiens need a relatively rich imagination to make up for the feebleness of body, slowness of gait, and weakness of sight and smell that disadvantage us as hunters. This, I suspect, is why humans have so many more ideas than other primates, who resemble us closely in many other respects but who rarely or never eat meat and who typically do not go hunting. Now that chimpanzee communities have taken this step and have embraced the ecology of hunters, I think it is unfanciful to speculate that their trajectory of change could eventually draw closer to ours. As hunting becomes more important in their economies, evolution responds accordingly, and chimps get ever more imaginative.

However that may be, the link between ideas and cultural change is unproblematic. We observe our world. We imagine it differently. We work to realize our imagined world. But this still leaves the increasing pace of cultural change unexplained. If I am right so far, ideas need to multiply in order for cultural change to accelerate. The best attested reason for the multiplication of ideas is the fertilizing effect of exchange. Ideas multiply as the result of dialogue. Cultures change, in part at least, because unfamiliar ideas about how to do things impinge from outside. For example, the work of Jared Diamond has made familiar the notion that Eurasia has been an arena of faster change than other parts of the world because its geography favors intense exchanges of culture between its indigenous civilizations.[20] Isolation retards change; exchange stimulates it. As Diamond points out, New Guinea has a history of farming and sedentary life at least as long-standing as those of other Asian civilizations, and probably longer than those of Africa, Europe, and the Americas. But isolation slowed or checked subsequent development.

This helps us understand why for so much of the human past cultural change was so slow, barely exceeding, as we have seen, the rate of change in other cultural species. The story of our past has been for most of the time one of divergence, as human communities migrated across the globe and in many cases lost touch with one another. Such cultural changes as occurred during the period of divergence are largely explicable in terms of adaptations to the different environments that human migrants encountered. Subsequently, at first gradually or fitfully, as sundered communities reestablished contact, ideas oscillated with increasing frequency across newly established frontiers, generating or contributing to the generation of accelerating change.[21]

Among the changes were projects for extending the reach of exploration and exchange, and technologies to effect them: striking examples of reimaginings of the world, realized in practice. The beginning of a new, and so far relatively short, period of convergence therefore coincided with a quickening of changes of all kinds. The most marked feature of the very recent past—which we call globalization—is, from one point of view, intensified exchange. To put it crudely, change grows out of exchange. The more exchange, the more change. Intercultural contacts do not just reshake the kaleidoscope of the world; they also multiply the crystals it contains.

Is the quickening of the pace of change limitless? Historians properly base their predictions of the future on the experience of the past and tend to be surprised when the normalcy of the world fails to restore itself. If my train of thought is valid so far, we should expect change to slow and even cease. If we ever achieve a truly globalized world, in which we share a common, globalized culture, we shall have reverted to a form of isolation more extreme than any our ancestors experienced. We shall be alone in the universe, with no other cultures—except those of putative beings in other galaxies—with which to communicate. There will be no intercultural exchange to spawn other kinds of innovation. In the meantime, however, we shall continue to live in "interesting times" and suffer the corresponding curse. We have to find ways of living at ease in a disturbingly alchemical world of rapid, total transmutations of culture. In particular we have to be on our guard against the forms of political and religious extremism that thrive in revolutionary circumstances. One strategy is to emphasize that there are still continuities to cling to, and that some features of tradition can endure even hectic change. Jeremy Black has remarked that change is now so pervasive that we should be more surprised that any continuities survive, rather than that the transformations we observe are so sweeping. In part, I suspect, those continuities remain possible as a paradoxical effect of change, for change tends to increase complexity. Indeed change is inseparable from and multiplies the connective elements in the system: the world of today is connected of innumerable links between its dazzlingly varied elements. In some instances complex systems are highly fragile because their parts are interdependent, and failure in one area can cause total arrest. But in general they tend to be surprisingly robust, especially if they are undesigned, with far more links than are strictly necessary, because some links can perish without jeopardizing the continuity of functions. That is the kind of system we live in now. Its lurches are disturbing, but it also conveys a kind of comfort, for its very momentum and its very mutability are becoming its increasingly familiar features. If they were to cease, that change—the last change—would be the most unsettling of all.

NOTES

1. See Curtis A. Keim, "Long-Distance Trade and the Mangbetu," *Journal of African History* 24, no. 1 (1983): 1–22; and Massimo Zaccaria, *Il flagello degli schiavisti* [The Scourge of Slavers]: *Romolo Gessi in Sudan, 1874–1881* (Ravenna: Fernandel, 1999).

2. Modern philosophy seems to have concentrated entirely on how we experience change (Henri Bergson, *The Creative Mind: An Introduction to Metaphysics* [New York: Kensington, 1946]), how we define it or talk about it (Donald Davidson, *Essays in Action and Events* [Oxford: Oxford University Press, 1980], 105–48, 181–203, 293–304), or whether it can be said to constitute process (Alfred North Whitehead, *Process and Reality,* 2nd ed. [New York: Free Press, 1979]).

3. Desmond Morris and Ramona Morris, *Men and Apes* (New York: McGraw-Hill, 1966), 102; Frans de Waal, *The Ape and the Sushi Master: Cultural Reflections of a Primatologist* (New York: Basic Books, 2001), 4; John S. Allen, Julie Park, and Sharon L. Watt, "The Chimpanzee Tea Party: Anthropomorphism, Orientalism, and Colonialism," *Visual Anthropological Review* 10, no. 2 (1994): 45–54.

4. Frans de Waal, ed., *Tree of Origin: What Primate Behavior Can Tell Us about Human Social Evolution* (Cambridge, Mass.: Harvard University Press, 2001); Frans de Waal and Peter L. Tyack, eds., *Animal Social Complexity: Intelligence, Culture, and Individualized Societies* (Cambridge, Mass.: Harvard University Press, 2003); Susan Hurley and Matthew Nudds, eds., *Rational Animals?* (New York: Oxford University Press, 2006). For dolphins, see Karen Pryor and Kenneth S. Norris, eds., *Dolphin Societies: Discoveries and Puzzles* (Berkeley: University of California Press, 1991); and Janet Mann et al., eds., *Cetacean Societies: Field Studies of Dolphins and Whales* (Chicago: University of Chicago Press, 2000). It is worth observing, by way of caution, that in practice many studies remain largely unaffected by the discovery that nonhuman animals have culture. For example, Alexander H. Harcourt and Kelly J. Stewart, *Gorilla Society: Conflict, Compromise, and Cooperation between the Sexes* (Chicago: University of Chicago Press, 2007), sticks to evolutionary and ecological language in relating cultural behavior. Bernard Thierry, Mewa Singh, and Werner Kraumanns, eds., *Macaque Societies: A Model for the Study of Social Organization* (Cambridge: Cambridge University Press, 2004), returns to behaviorist or "socioecological" explanations of conduct generally deemed cultural in the first nonhuman species to have been found to have culture.

5. de Waal, *The Ape and the Sushi Master,* 51.

6. Craig B. Stanford, *Chimpanzee and Red Colobus: The Ecology of Hunter and Prey* (Cambridge, Mass.: Harvard University Press, 1998).

7. Frans de Waal, *Chimpanzee Politics: Power and Sex among Apes* (Baltimore: Johns Hopkins University Press, 1998), 4, 149.

8. Richard Wrangham et al., eds., *Chimpanzee Cultures* (Cambridge, Mass.: Harvard University Press, 1994); Toshisada Nishida, ed., *The Chimpanzees of the Mahale Mountains: Sexual and Life History Strategies* (Tokyo: University of Tokyo Press, 1990); de Waal, *Chimpanzee Politics,* 81–135.

9. Robert M. Sapolsky and Lisa J. Share, "A Pacific Culture among Wild Baboons: Its Emergence and Transmission,"*PLOS Biology* 2, no. 4: e106.doi:10.1371/journal.pbio.00201 06. (accessed September 9, 2011)

10. Jean Clottes, ed., *La Grotte Chauvet: L'art des origines* (Paris: Editions du Seuil, 2001).

11. See Alexander Dallin and Gail W. Lapidus, eds., *The Soviet System: From Crisis to Collapse* (Boulder, Colo.: Westview, 1995).

12. "Augusto Assía," *Los ingleses en su isla* (Barcelona: Ediciones Mercedes, 1946).

13. See, for example, Felipe Fernández-Armesto, ed., *England, 1945–2000,* vol. 12 of *The Folio Society History of England* (London: Folio Society, 2000), 509–47.

14. John Hooper, *The New Spaniards,* 2nd, rev. ed. (London: Penguin, 1995); Giles Tremlett, *Ghosts of Spain: Travels through a Country's Hidden Past* (London: Faber & Faber, 2006).

15. Michael Howard, *The Causes of Wars and Other Essays* (Cambridge, Mass.: Harvard University Press, 1983), 8–9.

16. For a representative array of attempts, see Philip Pomper and David Gary Shaw, eds., *The Return of Science: Evolution, History, and Theory* (Lanham, Md.: Rowman & Littlefield, 2002), especially the general critique by Joseph Fraccia and Richard.C. Lewontin, "Does Culture Evolve?," 233–64.

17. David Sloan Wilson, *Evolution for Everyone: How Darwin's Theory Can Change the Way We Think about Our Lives* (New York: Delacorte Press, 2007).

18. Richard Dawkins, *The Selfish Gene* (New York: Oxford University Press, 1976), 203–15. See also the critique of Daniel L. Smail, *On Deep History and the Brain* (Berkeley: University of California Press, 2008), 90–95.

19. Felipe Fernández-Armesto, *Civilizations* (New York: Free Press, 2001).

20. Jared Diamond, *Guns, Germs and Steel* (New York: W. W. Norton, 1997), esp. 354–75.

21. Felipe Fernández-Armesto, *Pathfinders: A Global History of Exploration* (New York: W. W. Norton, 2006).

Suggestions for Further Readings

Slavery and British Abolitionism

Anstey, Roger. *The Atlantic Slave Trade and British Abolition 1760–1810.* Atlantic Highlands, N.J.: Humanities Press, 1975.

Bailey, Anne C. *African Voices of the Atlantic Slave Trade: Beyond the Silence and the Shame.* Boston: Beacon Press, 2005.

Bender, Thomas, ed. *The Antislavery Debate: Capitalism and Abolitionism as a Problem in Historical Interpretation.* Berkeley: University of California Press, 1992.

Brendlinger, Irv A. *Social Justice through the Eyes of Wesley: John Wesley's Theological Challenge to Slavery.* Ontario, Canada: Joshua Press, 2006.

Brown, Christopher Leslie. *Moral Capital: Foundations of British Abolitionism.* Chapel Hill: University of North Carolina Press, 2006.

Burton, Ann M. "British Evangelicals, Economic Warfare and the Abolition of the Atlantic Slave Trade, 1794–1810." *Anglican and Episcopal History* 65 (1996): 197–225.

Carretta, Vincent. *Equiano the African: Biography of a Self-Made Man.* Athens: University of Georgia Press, 2005.

Carrington, Selwyn H. H. *The Sugar Industry and the Abolition of the Slave Trade, 1775–1810.* Gainesville: University of Florida Press, 2002.

Davis, David Brion. *Inhuman Bondage: The Rise and Fall of Slavery in the New World.* New York: Oxford University Press, 2006.

———. *The Problem of Slavery in Western Culture.* New York: Oxford University Press, 1999.

———. *Slavery and Human Progress.* New York: Oxford University Press, 1984.

Dorsey, Joseph C. *Slave Traffic in the Age of Abolition: Puerto Rico, West Africa, and the Non-Hispanic Caribbean, 1815–1859.* Gainesville: University of Florida Press, 2003.

Drescher, Seymour. *Capitalism and Antislavery: British Mobilization in Comparative Perspective.* New York: Oxford University Press, 1987.

———. *Econocide: British Slavery in the Era of Abolition.* Pittsburgh: University of Pittsburgh Press, 1977.

———. *From Slavery to Freedom: Comparative Studies in the Rise and Fall of Atlantic Slavery.* New York: New York University Press, 1999.

———. *In the Image of God: Religion, Moral Values, and Our Heritage of Slavery.* New Haven, Conn.: Yale University Press, 2001.

———. *The Mighty Experiment: Free Labor versus Slavery in British Emancipation.* New York: Oxford University Press, 2002.

———. "Whose Abolition? Popular Pressure and the Ending of the British Slave Trade." *Past and Present* 143 (May 1994): 136–66.

Eltis, David. *Economic Growth and the Ending of the Transatlantic Slave Trade.* New York: Oxford University Press, 1987.

Engerman, Stanley L. *Slavery, Emancipation, & Freedom: Comparative Perspectives.* Baton Rouge: Louisiana State University Press, 2007.

Hempton, David. *Methodism: Empire of the Spirit.* New Haven, Conn.: Yale University Press, 2005.

Hindmarsh, D. Bruce. *The Evangelical Conversion Narrative: Spiritual Autobiography in Early Modern England.* Oxford: Oxford University Press, 2005.

Hochschild, Adam. *Bury the Chains: Prophets and Rebels in the Fight to Free an Empire's Slaves.* Boston: Houghton Mifflin, 2005.

Hurwitz, Edith F. *Politics and the Public Conscience: Slave Emancipation and the Abolition Movement in Britain.* London: George Allen and Unwin, 1973.

Kielstra, Paul Michael. *The Politics of Slave Trade Suppression in Britain and France, 1814–48: Diplomacy, Morality and Economics.* New York: Palgrave, 2000.

Matthews, Gelien. *Caribbean Slave Revolts and the British Abolitionist Movement.* Baton Rouge: Louisiana State University Press, 2006.

Midgley, Clare. *Women against Slavery: The British Campaigns, 1780–1870.* London: Routledge, 1992.

Oldfield, J. R. *Popular Politics and British Anti-Slavery: The Mobilisation of Public Opinion against the Slave Trade, 1787–1807.* Manchester, U.K.: Manchester University Press, 1995.

Thomas, Hugh. *The Slave Trade: The Story of the Atlantic Slave Trade, 1440–1870.* New York: Simon & Schuster, 1997.

Yerxa, Donald A., ed. *Recent Themes in the History of Africa and the Atlantic World.* Columbia: University of South Carolina Press, 2008.

Progress in History

Dawson, Christopher. *Progress and Religion: An Historical Enquiry.* London: Sheed & Ward, 1929.

Fischer, David Hackett. *Liberty and Freedom: A Visual History of America's Founding Ideas.* New York: Oxford University Press, 2005.

Fogel, Robert W. "Catching Up with the Economy." *American Economic Review* 89 (March 1999): 1–21.

———. *Escape from Hunger and Premature Death, 1700–2100: Europe, America, and the Third World.* New York: Cambridge University Press, 2004.

———. *The Fourth Great Awakening and the Future of Egalitarianism.* Chicago: University of Chicago Press, 2000.

Gray, John. *Heresies: Against Progress and Other Illusions.* London: Granta, 2004.

Kitcher, Philip. *The Advancement of Science: Science without Legend, Objectivity without Illusions.* Oxford: Oxford University Press, 1993.

Kolakowski, Leszek. *Why Is There Something Rather than Nothing?* New York: Basic Books, 2007.

Kuhn, Thomas S. *The Structure of Scientific Revolutions.* Chicago: University of Chicago Press, 1962.

Lasch, Christopher. *The True and Only Heaven: Progress and Its Critics.* New York: W. W. Norton, 1991.

Laudan, Larry. *Progress and Its Problems: Towards a Theory of Scientific Growth.* Berkeley: University of California Press 1977.

Lean, Garth. *God's Politician: William Wilberforce's Struggle.* London: Darton, Longman and Todd, 1980.

Mokyr, Joel. *The Lever of Riches: Technological Creativity and Economic Progress.* New York: Oxford University Press, 1990.

Murray, Charles. *Human Accomplishment: The Pursuit of Excellence in the Arts and Sciences, 800 B.C.–1950.* New York: HarperCollins, 2003.

Nisbet, Robert. *History of the Idea of Progress.* New York: Basic Books, 1980.

Pollard, Sydney. *The Idea of Progress: History and Society.* London: Watts, 1968.

Tuveson, E. L. *Millennium and Utopia: A Study in the Background of the Idea of Progress.* 2nd ed. New York: Russell and Russell, 1964.

Van Doren, Charles. *The Idea of Progress.* New York: Frederick A. Praeger, 1967.

Wright, Robert. *Nonzero: The Logic of Human Destiny.* New York: Pantheon, 2000.

Faith and Historical Practice

Bushman, Richard. *Believing History.* New York: Columbia University Press, 2005.

Butterfield, Herbert. *Christianity and History.* New York: Scribner's, 1950.

Frykenberg, Robert Eric. *History and Belief: The Foundations of Historical Understanding.* Grand Rapids, Mich.: Eerdmans, 1996.

Gregory, Brad S. "No Room for God? History, Science, Metaphysics, and the Study of Religion." *History and Theory* 47 (December 2008): 495–519.

———. "The Other Confessional History: On Secular Bias in the Study of Religion." *History and Theory* 45 (December 2006): 132–49.

Harvey, Van A. *The Historian and the Believer: The Morality of Historical Knowledge and Christian Belief.* New York: Macmillan, 1966.

Keillor, Steven J. *God's Judgments: Interpreting History and the Christian Faith.* Downers Grove, Ill.: InterVarsity Press, 2007.

Kuklick, Bruce. "Believing History." *Books & Culture* (March/April 2005): 6.

———. "Evasive Maneuvers: Can Protestant Historians Play by the Rules of the Secular Academy without Giving the Game Away?" *Books & Culture* (March/April 2004): 21.

Kuklick, Bruce, and Darryl G. Hart, eds. *Religious Advocacy and American History.* Grand Rapids, Mich.: Eerdmans, 1997.

Marsden, George M. "Human Depravity: A Neglected Explanatory Category." In *Figures in the Carpet: Finding the Human Person in the American Past,* edited by Wilfred M. McClay, 15–32. Grand Rapids, Mich.: Eerdmans, 2007.

———. *The Outrageous Idea of Christian Scholarship.* New York: Oxford University Press, 1997.

McIntire, C. T., ed. *God, History, and Historians: Modern Christian View of History.* New York: Oxford University Press, 1977.

———, ed. *Herbert Butterfield: Writings on Christianity and History.* New York: Oxford University Press, 1979.

Niebuhr, Reinhold. *Faith and History: A Comparison of Christian and Modern Views of History.* New York: Charles Scribner's Sons, 1951.

Noll, Mark. "Response to Kuklick." *Books & Culture* (March/April 2005): 6–7.

Salvatore, Nick, ed. *Faith and the Historian: Catholic Perspectives.* Urbana: University of Illinois Press, 2007.

Shannon, Christopher. "Between Outrage and Respectability: Taking Christian History beyond the Logic of Modernization." *Fides et Historia* 34 (Winter/Spring 2002): 4–6.

Tilley, Terrence W. *History, Theology & Faith: Dissolving the Modern Problematic.* Maryknoll, N.Y.: Orbis, 2004.

Wells, Ronald, ed. *History and the Christian Historian.* Grand Rapids, Mich.: Eerdmans, 1998.

Yerxa, Donald A. "That Embarrassing Dream: Big Questions and the Limits of History." *Fides et Historia* 39 (Winter/Spring 2007): 53–65.

Contributors

ERIC ARNESEN is professor of history at George Washington University and past president of the Historical Society. He is the author or editor of seven books, including two award-winning studies, *Brotherhoods of Color: Black Railroad Workers and the Struggle for Equality* (2001) and *Waterfront Workers of New Orleans: Race, Class, and Politics, 1863–1923* (1991). A regular contributor to the *Chicago Tribune,* he received the James Friend Memorial Award for Literary Criticism.

JEREMY BLACK is professor of history at the University of Exeter. One of the world's most prolific academic historians, he is the author of more than one hundred books in addition to over a dozen edited volumes. He is a Fellow of the Royal Society of Arts and a former council member of the Royal Historical Association, and he became a Member of the Order of the British Empire in 2000. He is editor for several book series for Macmillan, Routledge, Arnold, and Reaktion publishers and serves on a number of editorial boards, including those of *History Today, Journal of Military History,* and *Historically Speaking.*

DAVID BRION DAVIS is the Sterling Professor of History Emeritus at Yale University and director emeritus of Yale's Gilder Lehrman Center for the Study of Slavery, Resistance, and Abolition, which he founded in 1998 and directed until 2004. He was president of the Organization of American Historians in 1988–89. He has written or edited eighteen books, including *The Problem of Slavery in Western Culture* (1966), winner of the Pulitzer Prize; *The Problem of Slavery in the Age of Revolution* (1975), winner of the National Book Award for History and Biography, the Albert Beveridge Award, and the Bancroft Prize; *Slavery and Human Progress* (1984); *Revolutions: American Equality and Foreign Liberations* (1990); *In the Image of God: Religion, Moral Values, and Our Heritage of Slavery* (2001); *Challenging the Boundaries of Slavery* (2003); and the magisterial *In Human Bondage: Slavery in the New World* (2006). He received the Society of American Historians' Bruce Catton Prize for Lifetime Achievement (2004) and the American Historical Association's Award for Scholarly Distinction (2007).

FELIPE FERNÁNDEZ-ARMESTO is the William P. Reynolds Professor of History at the University of Notre Dame. He is a member of the editorial board of the University of Chicago Press's *History of Cartography* and the editorial committee of Leiden University's *Studies in Overseas History.* He is the author of nineteen books, including *Columbus* (latest edition, 1996), which was short-listed for the United Kingdom's most valuable literary prize; *Millennium: A History of the Last Thousand Years* (1995); *Truth: A History and a Guide for the Perplexed* (1999); *Civilizations* (2000); *Food: A History [Near a Thousand Tables in the U.S. and Canada]* (2001); *The Americas: A Hemispheric History* (2003); and *Pathfinders: A Global History of Exploration* (2006). He serves on the Council of the Hakluyt Society and was a long-serving chairman of the PEN Literary Foundation. He is a Fellow of the Royal Historical Society, the Royal

Society of Arts, and the Society of Antiquaries and was a Fellow of the Netherlands Institute of Advanced Study in the Humanities and Social Sciences. He was awarded the Caird Medal of the National Maritime Museum (1995), the John Carter Brown Medal (1999), and the International Association of Culinary Professionals Prize (2003).

PETER HARRISON is director of the Centre for the History of European Discourses at the University of Queensland. Prior to holding this position he was the Andreas Idreos Professor of Science and Religion and a Fellow of Harris Manchester College, Oxford University. He has published extensively in the area of cultural and intellectual history, with a particular focus on the philosophical, scientific, and religious thought of the sixteenth to eighteenth centuries. He is the author of *Religion and the Religions in the English Enlightenment* (1990); *The Bible, Protestantism, and the Rise of Natural Science* (1998); and most recently *The Fall of Man and the Foundations of Science* (2007). He is a founding member of the International Society for Science and Religion and is a Fellow of the Australian Academy of the Humanities. In 2003 he was awarded a Centenary Medal for "Service to Australian Society and the Humanities in the study of Philosophy and Religion."

DAVID HEMPTON is Alonzo L. McDonald Family Professor of Evangelical Theological Studies at Harvard Divinity School. He is a Fellow of the Royal Historical Society and former chairman of the Wiles Trust founded in 1951 by Sir Herbert Butterfield to promote innovative thinking on the history of civilization, broadly conceived. Hempton is the author of many books and articles, including *Methodism and Politics in British Society 1750–1850* (1984), winner of the Whitfield Prize of the Royal Historical Society; "Methodism in Irish Society, 1770–1830: Proxime Assessit for the Alexander Prize" of the Royal Historical Society (1986); *Evangelical Protestantism in Ulster Society 1740–1890* (Routledge, 1992); *Religion and Political Culture in Britain and Ireland: From the Glorious Revolution to the Decline of Empire* (1996); *The Religion of the People: Methodism and Popular Religion c. 1750–1900* (Routledge, 1996); *'Faith and Enlightenment' in the New Oxford History of the British Isles* (2002); and *Methodism: Empire of the Spirit* (2005), winner of the Jesse Lee Prize.

BRUCE KUKLICK is Nichols Professor of American History at the University of Pennsylvania. He has written nine books in the fields of American sports; political, diplomatic, and intellectual history, including his history of American thought *Churchmen and Philosophers: Jonathan Edwards to John Dewey* (1985), *The Rise of American Philosophy: Cambridge, Massachusetts, 1860–1930* (1976), and *Philosophy in America, 1720–2000* (2001). The second of these three won the Phi Beta Kappa book award in the humanities, while *Churchmen and Philosophers* has been the subject of a symposium sponsored by the American Academy of Religion. His most popular and successful book is on baseball history, *To Every Thing a Season: Shibe Park and Urban Philadelphia* (1991), which has won the Casey Award and the SABR-Macmillan Baseball Prize. His most recent book is *Blind Oracles: Intellectuals and War from Kennan to Kissinger* (2006). He has been on the editorial boards of a number of publications, including *Journal of the History of Ideas, Journal of the History of Philosophy, Historical Journal, Modern Intellectual History,* and *Historically Speaking.* He served as editor of *American Quarterly* from 1974 to 1983.

GEORGE M. MARSDEN is Francis A. McAnaney Professor of History Emeritus at the University of Notre Dame. His major areas of study have concerned American evangelicalism and the role of Christianity in American higher education. He has written several important books, including *Fundamentalism and American Culture* (1980, 2006), *The Outrageous Idea of Christian Scholarship* (1997), and *The Soul of the American University: From Protestant Establishment to Established Nonbelief* (1994). His *Jonathan Edwards: A Life* (2003) was a finalist for the National Book Critics Circle Award in the biography category for books published in 2003 and won numerous awards, including the Society for Eighteenth-Century Studies' Annibel Jenkins Biography Prize, the Bancroft Prize, the Organization of American Historians' Merle Curti Award in intellectual history, the Historical Society's Eugene Genovese Best Book in American History Prize, and the Philip Schaff Prize sponsored by the American Society of Church History.

WILFRED M. MCCLAY holds the SunTrust Bank Chair of Excellence in Humanities at the University of Tennessee at Chattanooga, where he is also professor of history. He was appointed in 2002 to the National Council on the Humanities, the advisory board for the National Endowment for the Humanities, and was reappointed for a second term in 2006. His book *The Masterless: Self and Society in Modern America* (1994) won the 1995 Merle Curti Award of the Organization of American Historians for the best book in American intellectual history published in the years 1993 and 1994. Among his other books are *The Student's Guide to U.S. History* (2001), *Religion Returns to the Public Square: Faith and Policy in America* (2003), and the edited volume *Figures in the Carpet: Finding the Human Person in the American Past* (2007). He serves on the editorial boards of *First Things, Wilson Quarterly, Society, Touchstone, Historically Speaking,* and *University Bookman.*

BEHAN MCCULLAGH retired recently as Associate Professor and Reader in Philosophy and is now an Honorary Associate in Philosophy at La Trobe University, Melbourne. His principal research interest has been the analysis of historical knowledge and understanding. His books include *Justifying Historical Descriptions* (1984), *The Truth of History* (1998), and *The Logic of History* (2004). He has published extensively in *History and Theory* as well as in other journals, including *Mind, Monist, Social Science Information, Clio, Philosophy of the Social Sciences,* and *Theology.*

ALLAN MEGILL is Professor of History at the University of Virginia. He is the author or editor of a number of books, including *Prophets of Extremity: Nietzsche, Heidegger, Foucault, Derrida* (1985); *Rethinking Objectivity* (1994); *Karl Marx: The Burden of Reason—Why Marx Rejected Politics and the Market* (2002); and most recently *Historical Knowledge, Historical Error: A Contemporary Guide to Practice* (2007). He has served as president of Journal of the History of Ideas, Inc., since 2005 and as a contributing editor of *Historically Speaking* since 2004.

JON H. ROBERTS is Tomorrow Foundation Professor of American Intellectual History at Boston University. His *Darwinism and the Divine in America: Protestant Intellectuals and Organic Evolution, 1859–1900* (1988) won the Frank S. and Elizabeth D. Brewer Prize from the American Society of Church History. He is coauthor (with James Turner) of *The Sacred and the Secular University* (2000).

LAMIN SANNEH is D. Willis James Professor of Missions & World Christianity at Yale University. He also holds a courtesy appointment as Professor of History at Yale College. He is an editor at large of *Christian Century* and serves on the editorial board of several academic journals. He is an Honorary Research Professor at the School of Oriental and African Studies in the University of London and a life member of Clare Hall, Cambridge University. He is the author of *Translating the Message: The Missionary Impact on Culture* (1989), *Encountering the West: Christianity and the Global Cultural Process—The African Dimension* (1993), *The Crown and the Turban: Muslims and West African Pluralism* (1997), *Whose Religion Is Christianity? The Gospel beyond the West* (2003), and *Disciples of All Nations* (2008). For his academic work he was made Commandeur de l'Ordre National du Lion, Senegal's highest national honor.

GARY M. WALTON is Professor Emeritus of Economics at the University of California, Davis. He is coauthor of a number of popular economics textbooks: *History of the American Economy*, 10th ed. (2004); *Understanding Economics Today*, 7th ed. (1999); and *A Prosperous People: The Growth of the American Economy* (1985). He is coauthor of *The Economic Rise of Early America* (1979); *Western River Transportation: The Era of Early Internal Development, 1810–1860* (1975); and *Shipping Maritime Trade, and the Economic Development of Colonial North America* (1972). Since 1990 he has served as president of the Foundation for Teaching Economics.

DONALD A. YERXA is Professor of History Emeritus at Eastern Nazarene College and director of the Historical Society's Religion and Innovation in Human Affairs Grants Program. He is senior editor of *Historically Speaking*, editor of *Fides et Historia*, and contributing editor of *Books & Culture*. He is the author of *Admirals and Empire: The United States Navy and the Caribbean, 1898–1945* (1991) and (with Karl Giberson) *Species of Origins: America's Search for a Creation Story* (2002). He has also edited seven volumes in the University of South Carolina Press's Historians in Conversation series.

Index